D1731922

CITIZENS WITHOUT BORDERS

Yugoslavia and Its Migrant Workers in Western Europe

Among Eastern Europe's postwar socialist states, Yugoslavia was unique in allowing its citizens to seek work abroad in Western Europe's liberal democracies. This book charts the evolution of the relationship between Yugoslavia and its labour migrants who left to work in Western Europe in the 1960s and 1970s. It examines how migrants were perceived by policy-makers and social scientists and how they were portrayed in popular culture, including radio, newspapers, and cinema.

Created to nurture ties with migrants and their children, state cultural, educational, and informational programs were a way of continuing to govern across international borders. These programs relied heavily on the promotion of the idea of homeland. Le Normand examines the many ways in which migrants responded to these efforts and how they perceived their own relationship to the homeland, based on their migration experiences. *Citizens without Borders* shows how, in their efforts to win over migrant workers, the different levels of government – federal, republic, and local – promoted sometimes widely divergent notions of belonging, grounded in different concepts of "home."

BRIGITTE LE NORMAND is an associate professor in the Department of History and Sociology at the University of British Columbia, Okanagan.

Citizens without Borders

*Yugoslavia and Its Migrant
Workers in Western Europe*

BRIGITTE LE NORMAND

UNIVERSITY OF TORONTO PRESS

Toronto Buffalo London

© University of Toronto Press 2021
Toronto Buffalo London
utorontopress.com
Printed in the U.S.A.

ISBN 978-1-4875-0750-3 (cloth)   ISBN 978-1-4875-3638-1 (EPUB)
ISBN 978-1-4875-2515-6 (paper)   ISBN 978-1-4875-3637-4 (PDF)

Library and Archives Canada Cataloguing in Publication

Title: Citizens without borders : Yugoslavia and its migrant workers in
    Western Europe / Brigitte Le Normand.
Names: Le Normand, Brigitte, author.
Description: Includes bibliographical references and index.
Identifiers: Canadiana (print) 20200416626 | Canadiana (ebook) 20200416790 |
    ISBN 9781487525156 (paper) | ISBN 9781487507503 (cloth) | ISBN
    9781487536381 (EPUB) | ISBN 9781487536374 (PDF)
Subjects: LCSH: Yugoslavs – Europe, Western – History – 20th century. |
    LCSH: Foreign workers – Government policy – Yugoslavia – History –
    20th century. | LCSH: Popular culture – Yugoslavia – History –
    20th century. | LCSH: Transnationalism – Political aspects – Yugoslavia –
    History – 20th century.
Classification: LCC D1056.2.Y83 L46 2021 | DDC 331.6/249704–dc23

This book has been published with the help of a grant from the Federation
for the Humanities and Social Sciences, through the Awards to Scholarly
Publications Program, using funds provided by the Social Sciences and
Humanities Research Council of Canada.

University of Toronto Press acknowledges the financial assistance to its
publishing program of the Canada Council for the Arts and the Ontario
Arts Council, an agency of the Government of Ontario.

Canada Council   Conseil des Arts
for the Arts   du Canada

ONTARIO ARTS COUNCIL
CONSEIL DES ARTS DE L'ONTARIO
an Ontario government agency
un organisme du gouvernement de l'Ontario

Funded by the   Financé par le
Government   gouvernement
of Canada   du Canada

Canadä

To Dad, with love

Contents

Illustrations

Acknowledgments

Many people and organizations have helped this book come into being. The initial research for this project was funded by a Max Weber fellowship at the European University Institute and a New Horizons grant from Indiana University. I am grateful for the assistance of staff at the Institute for Migration and Nationality, the Croatian State Archive in Zagreb, and the Yugoslav Archive in Belgrade, which house the bulk of the archival and published materials on which the research is based. A huge thanks also goes out to the staff of the archival section of the Yugoslav Cinematheque, who helped me to identify relevant films and organized private projections. Radio-Television Zagreb kindly provided me with the opportunity to listen to episodes of *To Our Citizens of the World*. I am also deeply indebted to Snježana Tonković from the Imotski Heritage Museum, as well as Suzana Škojo, for their assistance during a challenging research collection trip to Imotksi. They put me in touch with migrants who had returned to the region and helped me to access copies of *Imotska krajina*. They did their best to help me to understand the region's history and politics, and while this led to some difficult conversations, it was critical to shaping my thinking. Tvrtko Jakovina and the University of Zagreb hosted me as a visiting scholar for a summer, allowing me to significantly advance my research. I also benefitted from a research fellowship at the Georg Eckert Institute for International Textbook Research, which provided me with access to rare textbooks. Tatomir Toroman, from the Museum of Yugoslav History in Belgrade, curated a fascinating exhibit on labour migration, using material objects contributed by migrants themselves, entitled *Jugo moja Jugo*; I am grateful for his permission to use some visuals drawn from this exhibit. I also extend my thanks to Slobodan Butir, Jovan Popović, and the Trumbetaš family for allowing to share some of the wonderful art in this volume. Veljko Piljak and Christopher Molnar provided valuable research assistance. Thanks also to Mate Nikola Tokić for his guidance and suggestions as I was first formulating the project, and to the many current and former labour migrants with whom I shared informative and moving conversations. While I was not able to incorporate their life stories into the present volume, I hope to write about them in the future.

Several venues allowed me to showcase my work-in-progress, shaping the development of the project and manuscript. Aside from scholarly conferences, I would like to acknowledge the Centre Canadien d'Études Allemandes et Européenes at the Université de Montréal and the Departments of History at Indiana University, Bloomington, and the University of British Columbia, Vancouver. Short passages of this book have also been published in book chapters in *Socialist Inequalities and Discontent in Yugoslav Socialism* and *East Central European Migrations during the Cold War: A Handbook*.

A number of scholars provided detailed feedback on specific chapters. I express deep thanks to Alix Hui, Karolina Novinscak Kölker, Sanjin Pejković, Francesca Rolandi, and Matthias Thaden. I am particularly thankful for their recommendations of German-language literature; although I was not able to do justice to them given the short timelines and my imperfect language skills, I look forward to engaging with this literature in future research. Karolina also introduced me to Papić's remarkable film *Specijalni vlakovi*. I am also, of course, indebted to the anonymous reviewers who provided invaluable constructive feedback on the entire manuscript, which allowed me to strengthen it and hopefully reach a broader audience. Stephen Shapiro, at the University of Toronto Press, has been an uncommonly responsive, professional, and helpful editor and helped me to think through a number of challenging conceptual questions.

Finally, I would like to acknowledge individuals who supported me in my professional and personal journey while I was working on this project, and in particular, Jean Abshire, Padraic Kenney, Mark Roseman, Patrick Patterson, and all my colleagues in the Department of History and Sociology at the University of British Columbia, Okanagan. No woman is an island, and nowhere is this truer than in the often lonely work of the historian. While I become easily absorbed in my work, I am so very glad for my other world: my wonderful children, Marco, Alice, and Leo, and my partner in all things, Ted. Thanks always also to my parents, who have always encouraged me to pursue my dreams. I am also grateful to the Syilx Okanagan people, on whose unceded territory I live and work, allowing me to write this book.

This is a project I began some twelve years ago, and so it seems inevitable that I will have forgotten some people to whom I owe thanks: I humbly apologize for any such unintentional omissions. Having acknowledged all those who contributed to this book, I also take ownership for any of its flaws – while hoping they might provide the impetus for new and exciting research.

CITIZENS WITHOUT BORDERS

Yugoslavia and Its Migrant Workers in
Western Europe

1 Introduction

They left, first by the hundreds, and then by the thousands, and then by the tens of thousands, until they numbered nearly a million. First on foot through the mountains, and later on buses and trains – even dedicated trains – and automobiles they had purchased with their earnings. Men, women, and children, from remote villages nestled in the Dinaric mountains or deep in the Serbian countryside, and from bustling urban centres. Peasants fleeing a stagnating countryside, young people seeking to establish themselves, and skilled workers and professionals aspiring to a higher standard of living. Far from home, they were exposed to different national, local, political, and workplace cultures, built new relationships with locals and migrants from other countries, and with their fellows, and they were somewhat shielded from the watchful eye of the Yugoslav state.

They left – and yet they did not leave. They returned, once or twice a year and sometimes more frequently, to visit their loved ones, get married, have children, build their homes, give proof of their success, and reinforce their ties to kin, friends, and places. Abroad, many continued to socialize and play competitive sports with their compatriots, read Yugoslav newspapers, listen to Yugoslav radio programs, celebrate Yugoslav holidays, and teach their children the languages and cultures of their homeland.

This book is about Yugoslavia's migrant workers and their families living abroad, and the ties that stretched across international borders, connecting them to several imagined communities: the specific localities where they had lived, their home republics, their ethnic communities, and Yugoslavia. Specifically, it examines the ways in which the Yugoslav state sought to build and maintain a relationship with its citizens living and working abroad, and how these efforts shaped the migrants' understanding of home.

It focuses on the segment of migrants that the Yugoslav state defined as "our citizens / our workers abroad," as distinct from two other groups, *iseljenici*, which were defined as friendly or neutral permanent emigrants of Yugoslav origin, and political émigrés, which were defined as recent emigrants, also permanent, who were hostile to Yugoslavia. Yugoslav authorities had different strategies and programs to engage with each group, although they relied on overlapping infrastructure (such as consular offices and the Matice iseljenika, which can loosely be translated as "emigrants' foundations"). Other migrants did not fit easily into these categories, such as those who left Yugoslavia illegally and claimed asylum in neighbouring Western European states – their motives were both economic and political. The Yugoslav state sought to clarify their status. This book is also about them, insofar as they chose to engage with the programs aimed at "our citizens/workers abroad." Finally, the book also deals with the Yugoslav-born spouses of migrant workers, and their children (whether they were born in Yugoslavia or abroad), insofar as both Yugoslavia and, in many cases, their host states treated them as Yugoslav citizens who were expected to eventually return – regardless of whether or not this actually transpired.

Alone among Eastern Europe's post-war socialist states, Yugoslavia adopted an open border policy in the early 1960s. Joining the ranks of other Southern European states, it allowed, and in some ways even encouraged, its citizens to seek work abroad in northwestern European capitalist economies as a strategy to palliate growing unemployment. Simultaneously located on the east and the south of Europe's post-war divides, Yugoslavia thus represents a unique hybrid of two different approaches to economic development.

Yugoslavia and other states on Europe's southern periphery were responding to the opportunities created by an acute labour shortage in the West European economies, aggravated by population loss in the Great Depression and the Second World War. Western European governments introduced policies and programs to attract foreign workers in large numbers, first from Italy, Spain, Greece, and Portugal, and later from North Africa, Turkey, and Yugoslavia, states considered to be more ideologically or culturally foreign. States such as France, the Federal Republic of Germany (FRG), and Switzerland adopted bilateral labour agreements to facilitate the importation of labour. These "guest worker" agreements presumed that migrants would not claim citizenship rights, but rather, eventually return to their sending state. However, across Europe there was significant diversity in approaches to labour migration, ranging from Switzerland, which insisted on a two-year rotation of labour to prevent workers from setting down roots, to

Sweden, which adopted an explicitly assimilationist position, encouraging workers to apply for citizenship.[1]

The resulting influx of labour from Southern Europe and former imperial possessions helped to realize a period of unprecedented material prosperity in Europe. Hundreds of thousands of Yugoslavs sought their fortune in the Federal Republic of Germany, Austria, France, Switzerland, Sweden, and other states. At the peak of labour migration in 1971, according to official census statistics that actually under-reported real numbers, 860,000 Yugoslav migrant workers were employed in Western Europe, of which 535,000 were in the FDR alone.[2]

As recent work in migration history has emphasized, when people move to new places, their relationships to older places continue to matter. Even more than emigrants who had made a permanent move but maintained familial and cultural ties, labour migrants continued to have a meaningful relationship to Yugoslavia: many left their families behind, sent remittances, and returned home cyclically to visit and work on building a house. Moreover, the Yugoslav state fostered these ties through a variety of mechanisms, enabling migrants to listen to radio and read newspapers from the homeland, watch films, celebrate holidays, and educate their children about Yugoslavia's languages, history, geography, political system, and cultural heritage. These programs were a normal part of government under state socialism: the production and dissemination of culture and information, and the organization of public events, to mobilize the population in service of the state, the nation, and socialism.

At the same time, because migrants were positioned outside of these borders, and therefore simultaneously a part of Yugoslavia and apart from it, they had some control over when, how, and to whom they belonged. In some ways, they were practising a version of what David Fitzgerald has called "citizenship a la carte," whereby "emigrants and the governments of their countries of origin are negotiating citizenship ... based on voluntarism, citizen rights over obligations, and multiple affiliations."[3] In the Yugoslav case, this negotiation was not just a transaction, pivoting on what concessions would secure the migrants' active engagement as citizens – it also hinged on emotional attachments linked to heritage, tradition, myths, symbols, and popular culture, and was stimulated through the mass media, associational life, and educational programs.

Adopting a transnational perspective, this monograph describes the evolution of the relationship between Yugoslavia, a "global" or "emigrant state," and its migrant workers. More specifically, it examines how this state framed and understood migration, and in turn, how this influenced its engagement with migrants. Further, it describes the structures that the state put in place to deliver its policies across international borders, as shaped by Yugoslav federalism, and analyses the ideas that were used to bind migrants emotionally to the state, and in particular, its inconsistencies and variations. Finally, it analyses the ways in which migrants responded to these efforts, as shaped by the migration experience.

Transnationalism, broadly speaking, refers to the emergence and maintenance of "economic, social and political linkages between people, places and institutions crossing nation-state borders and spanning the world."[4] These linkages are a by-product of the intensified migration in the modern era and the proliferation of mechanisms that facilitate relationships across borders, such as communications technology (radio, satellite television, the internet, cellular phones), inexpensive transportation, and international money transfer businesses.

This study is interested in two aspects of transnationalism that relate to what Steven Vertovec has referred to as the reconfiguration of relationships within the triad "identities–borders–orders" – according to which one's identity is tied to specific borders and the social order existing within it.[5] First, communities (or social forms) whose membership spilled over the borders of the nation state are associated with a specific consciousness. Vertovec has described transmigrant consciousness as characterized by "bi-focality" in which "aspects of life 'here' and life 'there' – whether perceived from the migrant's starting or destination point – are constantly monitored and perceived as complementary aspects of a single space of experience."[6] By examining migrants' engagement with the homeland through letters and survey responses, this study seeks to understand the parameters of bi-focality in Yugoslav labour migrant consciousness.

Second, this inquiry is interested in the emergence of a transnational political space, in which nation states engage with, and seek to govern, their citizens living in other states, in an apparent violation of Westphalian sovereignty. And yet, as this study shows, transnational politics didn't necessarily weaken the power of the nation state or render its territorial boundaries irrelevant. Yugoslav citizens were encouraged to continue to see themselves as members of the Yugoslav (multi-)nation state, as defined by precise geographical, linguistic, cultural, and political characteristics. Transnational geographies had particular implications for state-socialism, however – the one-party state could not rely on its usual toolkit to rule its citizens across international borders. It had to find different strategies for governing its citizens abroad, and the ways in which labour migrants thought about and exercised their citizenship changed.[7]

There are striking parallels between Yugoslavia's engagement with its migrant workers and what scholars have referred to as "diaspora engagement." While there is a lack of conceptual clarity around the term "diaspora," as Rogers Brubaker noted, the labour migrants described in this study fit uneasily in this category.[8] The notion of diaspora implies that the group being described has moved away durably or even permanently, losing its ties to the homeland, whereas the Yugoslav state clung to the conceit that its migrant workers had only left temporarily, and it therefore explicitly differentiated labour migrants from other groups defined as diaspora (*emigranti* – political emigrants, and *iseljenika* – neutral or friendly emigrants.) There is, thus, an inherent conceptual tension between "citizen" and "diaspora." As time wore on, however, many of these migrants became more embedded in their new places of residence than in their place of birth, blurring the hard distinction between these two categories.

At the same time, diaspora scholars have drawn our attention to the constructed nature of the very concept of "diaspora," describing how states and other actors bring diasporas into being discursively – what Ragazzi calls the "speech act" – to serve specific purposes, deciding who is "in" and who is "out," according to racial, ethnic, class, political, or other lines.[9] Yet other scholars have noted that the courted group is an active participant in the construction of its diasporic identity, through engagement with and contestation of engagement strategies.[10] This is an important insight for this study, because it suggests that the category "our citizens/workers abroad" was also a construction generated by the state to serve specific ends, one that included some and excluded others. It follows that Yugoslavs who were invited to identify as such also played a role in defining what that identity meant, by embracing certain discourses, pushing back against others, and contributing their own interpretations of the relationship between self and homeland.

The distinction between "citizen" and "diaspora" does matter, in one important way: beyond representing an "imagined community," citizenship is a legal category that came attached with certain codified rights and responsibilities. As Yugoslavia built its engagement strategy for its labour migrants, it was able to draw on these legal obligations to mobilize resources and the administrative apparatus in Yugoslavia. The notion that these workers remained Yugoslav citizens was also central to labour mobility agreements signed with host states that were eager to prevent labour migrants from settling permanently. Yugoslav citizenship thus provided a framework for bilateral cooperation on the delivery of Yugoslav programs to their citizens. Finally, Yugoslav citizens had specific responsibilities as well as rights – they were thus subject to the scrutiny of the Yugoslav security state, which operated covertly on foreign soil and could revoke their passport, and to obligations like military service. While some citizens located outside of Yugoslavia's borders felt secure enough to express critical opinions against Yugoslavia, others expressly kept a low profile.

Recent migration scholarship has problematized binary framings of diasporic relationships, as involving sending states and migrants. While some geographers have emphasized the importance of other actors, including non-state actors (such as political parties, businesses, non-governmental organizations, and cultural organizations), others have sought to deconstruct the very notion of a unitary state, proposing alternative models such as the assemblage.[11] Because Yugoslavia was a socialist state, it is difficult to speak of non-state actors as operating from inside its borders, as all organizations were in some way tied to the state. However, this study demonstrates that the "Yugoslav state," as conceived of as a single, rational actor, was in fact a fiction. While the Yugoslav federation set migration policy, various state offices operating at the federal, republican, and local level were charged with giving it substance and implementing it, and they did not all represent the same rationality. Thus, Yugoslav citizens engaged with different state institutions, promoting different kinds of loyalties, rather than with a single state.

Moreover, when implementing programs that required the cooperation of host states, such as educational initiatives, the Yugoslav state rarely dealt with a single partner in each host state. Rather, it had to negotiate and collaborate with regional and local authorities in addition to national states, and, often, non-state actors. Migrants also engaged with other actors shaping their relationship to Yugoslavia, such as political emigrant organizations hostile to Yugoslavia. Rather than a sending-state-migrant dyad, then, we are confronted with a complex web of relationships – what some geographers have called geometries or topologies of power.[12] For the sake of clarity, this study focuses primarily on relations between migrants and different Yugoslav-state actors, bringing in other actors where relevant to the questions informing this study.

With these conceptual issues in mind, we can ask certain questions: How did the Yugoslav state construct the category "our citizens/workers abroad," and to what end? Who was included, and who was excluded? How did the state engage with this group? And finally, how did Yugoslavs included in this group respond to efforts by the Yugoslav state to engage with them?

Drawing on social scientific research and cinema, I examine how migration and migrants were framed and understood by policymakers, scholars, artists, and the Yugoslav public, and how these ideas in turn shaped cultural, media, and informational policy geared toward migrants. Adopting the position that labour migration was a temporary expedient for dealing with unemployment, Yugoslav authorities assumed that migrants were loyal, motivated exclusively by economic need, and absent only for a short while. They put in place programs to stay in touch with their citizens living abroad, relying in particular on radio broadcasting and newspapers. By the end of the 1960s, however, a widespread concern emerged that Yugoslavs living abroad were becoming corrupted and suffering psychologically as a result of their contact with Western Europe and were losing their attachment to Yugoslavia. More generally, researchers and film-makers began to call labour migration policy into question, pointing to its negative influence on Yugoslav society and asking troubling questions about how it fit into Yugoslav economic policy.

In response, authorities deployed significant resources toward restoring the relationship between the workers and Yugoslavia (the institutions, the idea, and the place). In addition to their existing strategy of reaching out to migrants through radio and print media, they began to support the creation of Yugoslav citizens' associations and organize a large-scale cross-border educational system for migrant youth. For various reasons that are explored in this volume, including longing for home and a desire to participate in the homeland's future, a substantial number of citizens continued to participate actively in Yugoslav social, cultural, and political life through these programs. This was certainly not a universal phenomenon – some migrants explicitly sought to cut ties with the homeland and start a new life, while others simply lost their attachment over time – but it was a significant and representative experience.

Whereas governmental organs emphasized to the migrants that they had not lost and must not lose their ties to their homeland, representations of labour migrants in popular culture suggest a much greater ambivalence, as did the migrants' own views on these questions. Cultural programs shaped their sense of belonging to a certain extent, but migrants participated in them selectively, embracing aspects that lined up with their sense of self and that they found useful, and ignoring or pushing back against the aspects they disagreed with. In some sense, then, migrants negotiated the terms of their relationship with Yugoslavia.

To make matters more complicated, Yugoslav migration and culture policy did not speak with a single voice. Reflecting the decentralized nature of Yugoslav federalism, the different levels of government – federal, republican, and local – promoted sometimes widely divergent notions of belonging, grounded in different concepts of "home," in their efforts to win over migrant workers' hearts and minds. "Homeland" was an inherently vague term – it could refer to different things: to Yugoslavia, to one's home republic, or to one's home town or home region. Even the term "Yugoslavia" had multiple, overlapping meanings – it can refer to a set of institutions, to an idea or political project, and to a physical place. During the nationalist uprising known as the Croatian Spring, these different notions came into open conflict. Some programs aimed at binding migrants more closely to Yugoslavia, such as newspapers, mobilized them into open political contestation.

In some ways, this study is about Yugoslav labour migration as a whole, and yet it focuses in particular on migration from Croatia, because of what this specific case reveals about the tensions inherent to Yugoslavia's engagement with migrants. It is necessary to adopt a Yugoslav-wide framework when analysing migration policy, which was the product of interactions between the federal, republican, and local state and party organs. Some outreach policies were explicitly pan-Yugoslav in nature, such as the Yugoslav workers' clubs, with authorities discouraging the creation of clubs serving only one Yugoslav nationality. In some cases, like the creation of a universal textbook for migrant children, policy was a product of collaboration between the republics. Complicating matters, programs created by one republic for the purposes of engaging its own citizens might attract a Yugoslav-wide audience, such as the radio program *Našim građanima u svijetu* (To our citizens of the world), as well as opinion surveys directed at migrants.

At the same time, in the context of the Croatian Spring, the specific case of migrants from Croatia brings to the fore some of the implications of my argument. First, by highlighting the process of constructing "our citizens/workers abroad," this case reveals how the category could in turn become contested by the political opposition or by actors in the cultural sphere. Second, it demonstrates the consequences of the decentralization of migration policy, and more specifically, cultural, educational, and informational programs articulated around promoting attachment to the homeland. Ultimately, different actors promoted different formulations of the idea of homeland – alternately local, Croatian, and Yugoslav. There were tensions between these formulations, echoing the tensions of the Yugoslav project, and they came into open conflict during the Croatian Spring. This denouement further illustrates the idea of the Yugoslav state as an assemblage of different actors promoting different, competing agendas.[13] Finally, this case highlights the active participation of Croatian migrants in Yugoslav political life, whether by reading newspapers that supported the reformist wing of the League of Communists of Croatia, or by expressing their own views on the topic, filtered through their own experiences of migration. The case of migration from Croatia thus provides a fascinating case study for examining the paradoxes of Yugoslavia's migrant engagement policy.

While this study primarily aims to contribute to our understanding of the specific dynamics of Yugoslavia's migration engagement efforts, the analysis presented here has broader implications for migration scholarship as a field. First, it calls into question a simplistic chronology that underlies work on contemporary migration, which sees diaspora engagement as novel phenomenon starting in the late twentieth century in response to the emergence of the neoliberal world order and the decline of the Westphalian nation state. According to this perspective, in the neoliberal order, states have lost much of their sovereignty and are forced to compete with one another on the global stage to attract financial flows. This is turn has led to a deterritorialization of the exercise of power, as states seek to reclaim subjects beyond their borders.[14] A separate but related argument has also emphasized the importance of the electronic age, and particularly of mobile phones and the internet, as facilitating long-distance communication.[15] As this study shows, however, the distinctiveness of the late twentieth century has been largely exaggerated.[16] Comprehensive efforts by states to maintain ties with their citizens living abroad predate both neoliberalism and electronic media. The Yugoslav case suggests that initiatives like those described in this study provided a model for later efforts.

A Short Historiography of Yugoslav Labour Migration in Europe

This study of the role of cultural policy in shaping Yugoslavia's relationship with migrant workers builds on a larger body of scholarship that deals with labour migration in Europe during the Cold War. Traditionally, scholarly literature on the topic has focused on the place of migrants within their host societies. Older studies, dating from the heyday of guest worker programs, were coloured by the concerns and approaches of their era, defining labour migration as a crisis that needed to be solved. Scholarship informed by a Marxist perspective focused on labour migrants as an exploited underclass, whereas research articulated around questions of identity aimed to identify the obstacles to integration of this population, seen as culturally alien, within the host society.[17]

More recently, researchers have sought to reframe the impact of labour migration. By focusing on representations of migration, and dynamic interactions between migrants and their host society, these studies have highlighted the complexity and fluidity both of migrant understandings of self and of the national identity articulated by the host state.[18] Although I am more interested in the migrants' ties to the sending state, I share these scholars' interest in analysing discourse about and perception of migrants, and in the role of everyday interactions in shaping the migrants' identities.

My study also builds on a rich literature that deals with the significance of labour migration for Yugoslavia. Yugoslav social scientists produced a large volume of research analysing the phenomenon while it was happening. Of particular interest are the publications of the Center for Migration Research at the University of Zagreb, and in particular those of Ivo Baučić, who helped to establish the socio-economic profile of labour migrants.[19] While much of the Yugoslav sociological research was rigorous, it was embedded in the political system that developed migration policy and reflected its preoccupations.

Othmar Haberl, William Zimmerman, and Carl Ulrich Schierup were the first outsiders to subject Yugoslavia's labour migration policy to scrutiny. Haberl provided an in-depth discussion of the genesis and evolution of Yugoslavia's labour migration policy, ending with the economic recession that followed the 1973 oil crisis, which led to a restriction of labour migration in Western Europe.[20] Zimmerman's interest in migration stemmed from his desire as a political scientist to understand the impact of "international-national linkages" on Yugoslav domestic politics. He first advanced a scholarly argument that Yugoslav migrant workers constituted a Seventh Republic, although the term itself likely originated in Yugoslavia, and sketched out the ways in which Yugoslavia governed its migrants living abroad. As such, his study in many ways laid the groundwork for my present inquiry.[21]

Schierup, in contrast, was interested in explaining Yugoslav labour migration as a strategy for economic development, by way of integration into the international division of labour – a futile strategy, in his estimation. He showed that, rather than just a passive response to pull-factors emanating from Western Europe, labour migration was a timely solution to the labour surplus that resulted from Yugoslavia's second wave of economic development from the early 1960s to the early 1970s, which he describes as "capital-intensive industrialization based on the rationalization of technological systems and labour organization, highly capitalized investments and an increase in labour productivity." Schierup's focus on the effects of economic reforms explains why peasants and peasant workers were the largest category of labour migrants. Changes in agricultural policy made it difficult to survive on the land, and they were shut out from jobs in Yugoslavia for their lack of education. While a useful pressure valve, labour migration was not an effective strategy for development, as migrants largely spent their remittances on prestige goods. He also analysed the efforts to implement a return migration policy in Yugoslavia, which were largely a failure, as employers and bureaucrats had no real incentive to employ returnees, and mind-boggling bureaucratic tape impeded any possibility of self-employment.[22]

At the end of his study, Schieup noted the demise of the global economic model that had fostered Yugoslav labour migration, with Western European states choosing to use cheap labour in the developing world, rather than importing labour onto their soil.[23] Ironically, written on the eve of Yugoslavia's self-destruction, Schierup's worries about the prognosis for Yugoslav labour were soon superseded by far greater problems. Yugoslavia's disintegration paused further research on Yugoslav labour migrants, shifting scholarly attention to different kinds of migration – refugees and diaspora.

The twenty-first century has rekindled interest in the topic of Yugoslav guest workers, producing scholarship that has benefitted from the critical distance that comes with hindsight, and the depth of knowledge made possible by access to archival materials. Ulf Brunnbauer and Francesco Ragazzi have put Yugoslav migration in a broader context, emphasizing its deep roots. While Yugoslav labour migration may seem surprising in the context of the Cold War, it was in fact the continuation of a traditional survival strategy for residents in the Balkan peninsula, whether in the form of seasonal migration or longer journeys to the Americas in the nineteenth century, the age of mass migration. The nineteenth century was also the age of the nation state, which heralded a new way of seeing emigration, alternately as a source of national weakening and as a vehicle for social engineering, shaping attempts to regulate migration by the Habsburg monarchy and the Kingdom of Yugoslavia.[24]

Arguably, this view of migration is an attribute of modern states more broadly. State socialism, for instance, sought to close borders as a precondition for the total mobilization of the population into the project of building socialism. Indeed, the threat of mass flight was what led the East German authorities to eventually close the loophole that was West Berlin in 1961 at the risk of causing a confrontation with the United States. The Cold War resulted not only in the hardening of borders; it also loosened them. Yugoslavia's break with the Soviet Union and its subsequent decision to build an independent identity through the adoption of self-management and non-alignment opened the door to liberalizing its Western border in order to encourage exchange with Western Europe.

As Vladimir Ivanović, Christopher Molnar, and Karolina Novinšćak Kölker have demonstrated, the Cold War played a determining role in shaping relations between Yugoslavia and the state to which it sent most of its workers, the Federal Republic of Germany (FRG). Willi Brandt's *Ostpolitik*, characterized by a desire for a rapprochement with Eastern European states, and the FRG's desperate need for labour, enabled the FRG and Yugoslavia to hammer out a bilateral labour agreement. At the same time, powerful forces within West German society remained fiercely anti-communist, successfully manoeuvring for policies that made the lives of Yugoslav migrants precarious.[25]

Much of the scholarship on Yugoslav labour migration has focused on analysing policymaking (both Yugoslav domestic policy and bilateral negotiations with West Germany), building a demographic profile of the migrants, or exploring their everyday life. On the topic of policy, Mark Allan Baskin, Brunnbauer, Ivana Dobrivojević, and Petar Dragišić have charted the emergence of Yugoslavia's approach with close attention to the legal and institutional framework that was set up to manage migration. Stressing the importance of the economic reforms of the 1960s in precipitating mass migration, Slobodan Selinić noted that the Yugoslav state tapped into a significant flow of remittances through its migration policy. Selinić and others have highlighted the role of bilateral agreements in regulating the flow of workers and in safeguarding Yugoslavia's interests and the rights of workers.[26] Baskin, Dobrivojević, and Vladimir Ivanović have provided an overview of the development of migration in response to policy changes, and explored the socioeconomic characteristics of migrants. Whereas this work has examined the development and expansion of migration, Baskin, Ivanović, Jenni Winterhagen, and Sara Bernard have also focused on Yugoslavia's largely ineffectual efforts to reintegrate returnees into the Yugoslav economy, starting in the 1970s. Winterhagen's work is particularly interesting because it contextualizes the implications of federal policy for a specific region – Imotski.[27]

In addition to studies that focus on the political, geopolitical, and economic aspects of the history of labour migration, scholars have examined the lived experience of migration and its impact on communities in both Yugoslavia and abroad. Using an ethnographic approach, Schierup's study of migration in the context of the village of Ljubičevac, in northeastern Serbia, showed how large-scale migration processes interacted with the pre-existing dynamic of the village. By narrowing his inquiry to the scale of the village, he was able to get a clearer picture of the pull factors that drew migrants to work abroad as well as the impact of labour migration on the village. In particular, he documented how poorer migrants could reverse their position in the village's social hierarchy by becoming wealthy, diminishing the prestige of land ownership. Consequently, villagers previously considered wealthy were also pulled into labour migration in a bid to retain their status. Schierup gained this insight by seeing the village as a series of relationships and by giving individual members of the village an opportunity to explain their opinions for themselves.[28]

Other scholars have deepened our understanding of the migrant experience by looking at the intersection of high-level policy and everyday practice, examining how authorities in the host societies and back home interfaced with migrants, and how migrants responded to initiatives directed at them. Molnar's research has highlighted the role played by German policy in enabling émigré groups hostile to Yugoslavia to exploit vulnerable migrant workers. Ivanovič has described the everyday lives of workers in Germany and Austria, characterized by material deprivation and discrimination.

Building on earlier work by Zimmerman and Baskin, Dragišić, Ivanović, and Nikola Baković have further investigated the efforts by the Yugoslav state to mobilize its citizens against the negative influence of the political émigré communities through various strategies, including founding clubs, publishing newspapers, and organizing tours of musical ensembles. In their own way all of these scholars have emphasized the limitations of the state's efforts, both in resources directed to them and the responsiveness of migrants.[29] While invaluable, this pioneering scholarship has left some questions open. It has identified 1968 as a turning point in attitudes toward labour migration, pointing to the role of the Prague Spring in fostering anxieties about national security, and later, to the impact of the Croatian Spring, which politicized migration. It has highlighted the role of mass and specialized media in fostering these anxieties.

However, these studies are missing an important ingredient in the growing panic about migration – perceptions of migrants themselves. How was knowledge about migrants actually produced? In this study, I investigate the construction of the category of "our citizens/workers temporarily employed abroad." While at first this framing obscured the complex nature of migration, eventually, by 1968, authorities became attuned to the discrepancy between the category and reality, provoking a panic and triggering policies to realign reality with the category. I examine two kinds of knowledge-production about migrants that disrupted official quiescence: social scientific knowledge, imbued with claims to scientific objectivity, produced by experts; and cultural knowledge as expressed through film, grounded in storytelling, which drew from scientific accounts, but also from stereotypes, anecdotes, common cultural tropes, anxieties about contemporary social issues, and the creativity of film-makers.

This study explores a broad array of programs intended to bind migrants more closely to the homeland, highlighting the specificity of each mechanism in creating relationships. It provides the first in-depth account of the use of radio broadcasts, local newspapers, and mother-tongue education for migrant children. It also reveals how federal authorities conceived of Yugoslav citizens' clubs, already described in some depth by Baković, Dragišić, Ivanović, and Molnar, as hubs through which a variety of other programs, such as newspapers and mother-tongue education, could be run and disseminated. While earlier accounts of Yugoslav workers' clubs judged them to be largely ineffectual, this study argues that their impact was greater than the sum of migrants who were active members.

While scholars have acknowledged the decentralization of policy-making and implementation in Yugoslavia, they have not examined its implications for the project of building relationships with migrants. The aforementioned scholars have largely approached cultural, educational, and informational programs as attempts by the federation to win over migrants' loyalty. As I show in this book, however, programs were run by federal, republican, and local organizations. While they all appealed to the idea of the homeland with its emotional connotations, they did not promote the same concept of homeland. The involvement of different scales of government also shaped the delivery and effectiveness of programs. While some programs, like the Yugoslav workers' clubs, were supported quite straightforwardly by federal institutions, others, like education for migrant children, were collaborations between different levels of government, requiring complex coordination and negotiation.

Previous historical research has also tended to focus on the FRG, and to a lesser extent on Austria. This reflects the dominance of the FRG as a host state, and likely also represents an understandable strategy to limit the scope of research to a manageable quantity of sources and linguistic competencies. This monograph adopts a different approach, examining the Yugoslav state's cultural, informational, and educational programming across Western Europe. This highlights the fact that Yugoslavia had similar concerns about and investment in the fate of migrants, regardless of their location in Europe, and highlights the remarkable adaptability and ambition of Yugoslav policymakers and diplomats in innovating programs that could be deployed across a variety of contexts and negotiating their implementation. This choice does come at a cost – this study cannot do justice to the distinctions between different host-state contexts and is limited to Yugoslav sources. Because this study primarily concerns Yugoslavia's relationship with its migrant workers, rather than migrant experiences abroad, I would argue that the benefits outweigh the disadvantages, and hope that other historians will do the necessary archival research to fill in our knowledge gaps on the specific experiences of Yugoslav migrant workers in France, Belgium, Sweden, and Switzerland (as well as the United Kingdom, Denmark, the Netherlands, and Luxemburg, where communities were also present, if small).

As the cliché goes, it takes two to make a relationship work, and yet scholarship has not seriously investigated migrant responses to efforts by Yugoslav institutions to reach out to them, beyond remarking on the lack of popularity of certain programs (such as Yugoslav clubs) or the inappropriate behaviour of some migrants in others (such as concerts). This study sheds light on migrants' attitudes to Yugoslavia, and their responses to outreach efforts, by analysing their responses to surveys and their letters to the radio program *To Our Citizens of the World*. This analysis shows that responses depended on a number of factors – in particular, the origin and nature of the outreach, the timing of the responses, and the motivations of the respondents. Migrants' willingness to speak frankly was also shaped by their evaluation of the risks and benefits of doing so, given that their interlocutor was always a state representative. Thus, it makes little sense to provide black-and-white answers to the question of whether migrants responded positively to Yugoslav efforts to secure their loyalty. What is certain, however, is that migrants were responsive. Yugoslav authorities maintained an active, even lively relationship, if a fraught one, with Yugoslav citizens living and working abroad.

Yugoslavia was only one of several Southern European sending states, and it would thus be useful to examine the efforts of other sending states to communicate with its workers. Indeed, the archival record suggests that Yugoslav policymakers considered the programs put in place by Italy, Spain, and Greece for this purpose and were particularly impressed with the Italian efforts. Unfortunately, it is only recently that social scientists have taken a scholarly interest in the policies of sending states, and historians have yet to catch up to this line of inquiry. Much of the political science and sociological literature focusing on the present day has been limited to their efforts to keep control over the terms and flow of migration and to mobilize emigrants, either to attract revenue, or as a lobby for the sending state's national interests.[30]

Labour Migration and the Croatian Spring

The Croatian Spring, likely the most turbulent period in the history of socialist Yugoslavia prior to its final dissolution, is a crucial context to this study. It politicized the issue of labour migration and brought to the fore tensions between different ideas of homeland and hierarchies of loyalty to it. For a time, it also represented a peak of political pluralism within Yugoslavia. This was not political pluralism in the classic sense, as the supremacy of the one-party state was not challenged. Rather, it was a period of bubbling over, when the political elite in Croatia appeared to sanction or at least allow the expression of harsh criticism of Yugoslav institutions, practices, and even values (such as brotherhood and unity, self-management, and socialism more broadly), fostering a mass movement it was ultimately unable to control. Lasting roughly four years between 1967 and 1971, it was characterized by the gradual mobilization of the Croatian population by specific groups within the cultural elite and reformist politicians in the League of Communists of Croatia (Savez komunista Hrvatske – SKH) in favour of greater autonomy for Croatia. While the reformist Croatian Communists tried to shape a movement that promoted liberalization while remaining socialist, and rejected chauvinism, popular attitudes during the Croatian Spring often openly embraced nationalism and expressed anti-Serbian sentiments.

The fall of Aleksandar Ranković in 1966, Tito's chief of police and proponent of a strong federal centre, sent a signal to the Yugoslav republics that the party leadership would accept greater devolution of authority to the republics. It also framed the concept of a strong centre as a remnant of the highly unpopular unitarism of the pre-war Kingdom of Yugoslavia and characterized it as a Serbian project. In its wake, different groups in most of the Yugoslav republics mobilized in favour of greater cultural or political autonomy. In Croatia, this mobilization was spearheaded by the Croatian cultural association Matica Hrvatska (loosely translated as Croatian Foundation) and reformist Communists in the SKH. Whereas Matica Hrvatska was nationalist and anti-socialist in orientation, the reformist Communists attempted to frame their demands as anti-nationalist and consistent with Yugoslav self-management.

The first notable event of the Croatian Spring, under the influence of Matica Hrvatska, was the publishing of the Declaration on the Status and Name of the Croatian Standard Language in March 1967, signed by 130 writers and linguists, which asserted the distinctiveness of the Croatian language. This was significant because it contradicted Yugoslavia's official position on the matter as enshrined in the 1954 Novi Sad declaration, according to which there was a single Serbo-Croatian or Croato-Serbian language with several dialects.

At the same time, a new generation was rising into leadership within the League of Communists of Croatia – most notably Savka Dabčević-Kučar, Miko Tripalo, and Pero Pirker, who would come to be known as the "Triumvirate." At the tenth session of the central committee of the SKH, held from 15 to 17 January 1970, the party leadership unveiled its new line, which was articulated around the double rejection of nationalism and unitarism. According to Dabčević-Kučar, unitarism was the greater threat, and the best way to undermine Croatian nationalism was to address the political and economic grievances that fed it. In particular, the reformist Communists claimed that Croatia was disproportionately burdened by its financial contribution to the federation, and that it should have more control over its own economy and revenue. During the Croatian Spring, political figures and intellectuals criticized labour migration as a drain on Croatia's economy. In particular, they criticized limitations on the foreign currency that individuals and firms were able to keep, which was limited to 7%, with the remainder disadvantageously converted into dinars. Reformists argued that this policy essentially usurped foreign currency from those who earned it and funnelled it into the coffers of the federation, and called for a policy change that would allow Croatia to keep this foreign currency.

While the reformist Communists attempted to keep ethno-nationalist discourse out of discussions of labour migration, accusations of Serb exploitation of Croats were commonly aired. As this study will show, this discourse of Croatian victimization at the hands of Serbs was very powerful for migrant workers from Croatia, who endured significant hardship in order to provide for their families, including long absences from their spouses and children, harsh living conditions, xenophobia, and social isolation. One way that they were mobilized into participating in political debates at this time was through newspapers printed in Croatia that were aimed specifically at engaging with migrants. The level of mobilization was in turn reflected in survey responses collected by the Institute for Migration and Nationality which operated under Matica iseljenika Hrvatske (the Croatian emigrants' foundation charged with maintaining relations with migrants and diaspora, not to be confused with Matica Hrvatska), an important actor in the collection of information and shaping of discourse on migration.

In the long run, efforts by Dabčević-Kučar and other reformist Communists to moderate the ethno-nationalist tendencies of the Croatia Spring were ineffective. While the SKH's strategy was grounded on challenging the status quo without overtly threatening socialism, it did not have full control of the growing popular movement associated with the Croatian Spring – the *masovni pokret* or *Maspok*. Indeed, it shared the stage with Matica Hrvatska, and with student organizations, which increasingly pushed for a more hard-line, nationalist position. Matica Hrvatska, in particular, claimed to support the SKH, but actually promoted much more radical views disingenuously couched in the language of socialism and self-management. It pushed for the recognition of Croatia as the sovereign, national state of Croats, which agreed to associate itself with the Yugoslav federation. It asserted that the Croatian struggle for self-determination had not, in fact, been fulfilled in the national liberation struggle. This nationalist evolution, in turn, alarmed Serbs in Croatia. By the fall of 1971, the SKH had arguably lost control of the mass movement.

Whereas Tito had initially stood back as unrest grew in Croatia, he sent signals to the SKH in July 1971 that he was deeply concerned about polarization along national lines, without outright withdrawing his support for the Triumvirate. Yet, it seems the federal party leadership was already preparing to shut down the mass movement. In the fall of 1971, aware of the precarious situation of the SKH, the student movement organized mass street protests to show their support for the SKH. Nevertheless, Tito put an end to the Croatian Spring at the twenty-first session of the presidency of the LCY in December 1971. The SKH leadership was reproached for not keeping control of nationalist elements within Croatian society, such as Matica Hrvatska and the newspaper *Vjesnik*. Most significantly, Tito made it clear that he no longer supported the Triumvirate. The fallout of the twenty-first session was swift and dramatic: 741 party members were expelled, and leaders of the movement were sent to prison, including Franjo Tuđman, who would later lead Croatia to independence in 1991, and Zvonimir Komarica, the director of the Institute for Migration and Nationality (Zavod za migracije i narodnosti – ZMN). Conservative opponents of the liberal reformists assumed power in the SKH.

The Croatian Spring opened up new possibilities by demonstrating that "the communists' rhetoric could be used effectively against them" by groups like Matica Hrvatska, as Hilde Katrine Haug pointed out. It also made it clear that, at least under Tito, there was little room for further liberalization and meaningful autonomy, and imposed a silence in the public sphere that would last until the 1980s.[31] Discussions of labour migration were affected by this shutting down of debate. Given the significance of migrant worker mobilization in the Croatian Spring, and the way in which migration had been framed not only as a policy failure, but worse, as an intentional federal or Serbian policy of exploitation of Croatia, we can plausibly speculate that this outcome had a highly demoralizing effect on migrant workers from Croatia.

Structure of the Book

This book is divided into two sections – the first part is concerned with how migrants were seen – that is, perceived and constructed as subjects – while the second part examines different ways in which Yugoslav authorities (federal, republican, and local) sought to strengthen the migrants' ties to the homeland, and how migrants responded to these programs.

The second chapter examines the role of policymakers and social scientists in framing and reframing migration. It examines the emergence of a labour migration policy in the early 1960s, which was understood as a by-product of Yugoslavia's economic modernization, and shows how it was tied to certain ideas about migrants – namely, their motivations as economic and their absence as temporary. By the late 1960s, partly in response to studies by experts and consular officials, authorities became concerned that these assumptions might not be correct. They worried that migrants were vulnerable to psychological crisis and manipulation by hostile émigré groups, while others were losing their ties to the homeland. These anxieties triggered an intensified outreach toward migrants. Simultaneously, Croatian intellectuals and politicians within Yugoslavia sought to reframe the terms of the discussion by depicting migration as a means used by Yugoslavia to exploit Croatia. This alternative narrative did not supplant the old one, not only because it was silenced along with the Croatian Spring, but also because of the shifting provenance of migrants, who were increasingly coming from other parts of Yugoslavia.

Whereas policymakers and social scientists saw migrants as aggregate numbers – primarily as statistical data and remittance figures – the Yugoslav public understood migrants and migration through images and narratives. The third chapter examines Yugoslav film production to ask why the migrant worker was such a powerful and ubiquitous figure in popular culture, and what stories were told about migrants. It shows that they had a strong hold on the popular imagination because their life-stories highlighted the tensions inherent to the Yugoslav modernization project, and according to some film-makers, the bankruptcy of that project and its ultimate failure. Migrants were framed as agents of contamination, introducing capitalism's corrosive influence; or in milder form, as clowns, whose delusions were laughable; or alternatively, as victims, coerced into a life of exile, deprivation, and depression or madness. While for some artists the migrant was a convenient object of derision, other artists used representations of migration to criticize and even contest state policy.

This chapter, like the one before it, highlights that migration was understood as a problem – not only by policymakers but also by the public. There was no consensus, however, on what the problem was, and therefore who was responsible and what should be done about it. If the problem was alienation that came with the migration experience, then one solution was programs that reduced that alienation. If the problem was failed economic modernization, the solution was to change economic policy. For a variety of reasons, including the changing European economic conjecture, Yugoslavia did modify its approach to labour migration, by making efforts to repatriate migrant workers, as chronicled by scholars like Schierup and Bernard. It continued, nonetheless, to rely heavily on labour migration. The second half of this volume describes and analyses programs to reduce migrant alienation and build closer ties with workers living abroad.

The second part of the book, which is roughly organized chronologically, examines efforts within Yugoslavia to build a relationship with migrants and strengthen their attachment and loyalty to the homeland. One of the earliest mechanisms used was mass media, in the form of radio and newspapers, which were designed and produced in Yugoslavia and then disseminated across international borders. Chapter 4 explores the development and runaway success of the Radio Program *To Our Citizens in the World* broadcast by Radio-Television Zagreb (RTZ). The radio program, which focused on playing popular music requests, transmitting greetings to relatives, and sharing useful information with migrants, cultivated listeners by forming an emotional bond with migrants. Their letters show that they came to see the program as a trusted friend and ally, including in their dealings with the state bureaucracy, even though the radio program was in fact a state-run project. The program eschewed contentious discussions on ethnic identity and politics, emphasizing migrants' shared culture and circumstances.

In contrast, the newspaper *Imotska krajina*, funded by a district branch of the Socialist Alliance of Working People of Yugolavia (Socialistički savez radnog naroda jugoslavije – SAWPY/SSRNJ) mass organization, built a relationship with migrants on an intensely local identity rooted in the Croatian Dalmatian hinterland. Chapter 5 shows how, in *Imotska krajina*, "homeland" was not an empty signifier whose contents varied from reader to reader, but a precise place tied to a specific dialect, landscape, and way of life. During the Croatian Spring, the newspaper increasingly highlighted the region's belonging to the larger Croatian homeland as well. Its discussions of the impact of labour migration on the region were increasingly politicized in the service of the movement for greater Croatian autonomy within Yugoslavia, until the Communist party leadership crushed the Croatian Spring and the newspaper was disciplined. *To Our Citizens* and *Imotska krajina* show that state institutions adopted different approaches to connecting with migrants and advanced different understandings of the idea of "homeland."

As authorities grew increasingly anxious about the vulnerability of migrant workers in the late 1960s and sought to intensify their outreach efforts, they paid increasing attention to the burgeoning of Yugoslav associational life. As the sixth chapter explains, they sought to co-opt and develop a European-wide network of Yugoslav workers' clubs, which might be used as hubs through which, in tandem with diplomatic missions, Yugoslavia could effectively govern its workers across national borders. Yugoslav workers' associations varied enormously in their size and activity, but the most successful ones offered a gamut of programs including a library, sports leagues, cultural and technical clubs, language classes, professional training, and activities for children. Because they organized popular cultural and social events and commemorations on the occasion of Yugoslav national holidays, they reached a far larger audience than just their membership, creating a feeling of community among Yugoslavs living abroad. Unlike the mass media, which Yugoslav authorities ultimately controlled, Yugoslav workers' associations were a unique collaboration between the state and its citizens.

Having examined these efforts to shape migrants' relationship to the homeland, chapter 7 takes a closer look at the opinions of the subjects on policies regarding their migration experience and Yugoslavia, as recorded by a survey conducted in 1970 by the Institute for Migration and Nationality to inquire about migrants' attitudes to the possibility of returning home. Although it was in some ways simply another attempt to better understand migrants in order to govern them more effectively, the open-ended format of the survey provided an opening for migrants to express themselves in their own words, and many seized it. This chapter examines how migrants appropriated the survey and narrated their life stories. While migrants were susceptible to efforts by different political actors (such as the Yugoslav state, Croatian reformists, and émigré organizations hostile to Yugoslavia) to shape their opinions, they articulated narratives about their specific migration story, reflecting their interactions with the host society and with the homeland. Their experiences abroad shaped their perceptions of Yugoslavia and emboldened them to think about how things might be done differently back home.

Chapters 8 and 9 examine the Yugoslav state's efforts in the 1970s and 1980s, not to maintain a relationship with its migrant workers, but to initiate one with their offspring, by setting up a transnational educational system. Chapter 8 looks at the emergence of this program and its evolution from an institutional perspective. The Federal Office for International Scientific, Educational-Cultural and Technical Collaboration (YUZAMS) took on the arduous task of bilateral negotiations with states that had significant numbers of migrant children to implement a feasible system that would include cost-sharing. At the same time, because education was a republican jurisdiction in Yugoslavia, it coordinated efforts between the republics to provide education. The result was an ambitious and remarkably flexible program through which Yugoslavia sent materials and even teachers abroad to deliver instruction to migrant children in their parents' languages and in Yugoslavia's history, geography, culture, and socio-political system.

Chapter 9 takes a closer look at the delivery of the educational program, starting with the role of the teacher, who was framed not only as an educator, but as an organizer and role model within Yugoslav communities abroad. It also examines the content of the pan-Yugoslav textbooks, finally published in the 1980s after much delay, to ease the difficulties of teaching children from different republics. These textbooks aimed to transmit to children an understanding of the homeland grounded in intuition and experience as well as learning about Yugoslavia's heritage and history, with special focus on the symbols of the partisan struggle and Tito. Scholars and practitioners expressed serious concerns in the 1980s that these efforts to keep the second-generation Yugoslav had failed. Ultimately, their work echoed the assumptions of the Yugoslav authorities that migrants could belong to only one place. And yet the children's own sense of self was more complex, testifying both to a transnational life experience and a continued curiosity about, and even desire for, Yugoslavia.

Sources and Scope of the Book

The research for this book was based primarily on archival research at the Yugoslav archive in Belgrade and the Croatian State Archive in Zagreb, and published materials in scholarly publications and newspapers from the 1960s and 1970s. Additionally, it draws on film collections kept by the archive of the Yugoslav Kinoteka and Zagreb film, as well as Dragutin Trumbetaš's body of work.

The first part of the book, which focuses on how migrants were "seen," is based on analysis and publications and archival materials related to policymaking. Because federal and republican policymakers were constantly gathering information on labour migrants, I also look at social-scientific research materials and publications that played an important role in fine-tuning and redefining the concept of our citizens abroad. Popular understandings of labour migration also participated in reframing discourse and found expression in documentary and fictional film production. In the second part of this study, which focuses on "building ties," my analysis is based on published and archival materials that attest to the development and deployment of different cultural, educational, and informational programs aimed at engaging with migrant workers – more specifically, news and radio media, Yugoslav clubs, and education programs for migrants' children. Finally, it explores migrant perspectives through archival materials produced by migrants themselves – letters sent to radio programs and newspapers, as well as individual responses sent to a survey run by the Institute for Migration and Nationality that operated under the auspices of Matica iseljenika Hrvatske.

Because my knowledge of the languages of Yugoslavia is limited to Bosnian-Croatian-Serbian, I chose to focus on Yugoslavia's relationship with those migrants who spoke this language. Because the majority of migrants came from Croatia, and later, Serbia, it could be argued that this limitation is minor. However, we should not assume that Slovenes, Macedonians, and members of the national minorities had the same understanding of or relationship with Yugoslavia. Much of the English-language historiography of Yugoslavia has excluded their stories. While this study will regrettably not rectify this limitation, I hope that better-qualified scholars will fill in these lacuna.

Every historian must make choices about what to include in and exclude from analysis. Because I am interested in understanding Yugoslavia's relationship with its migrant workers, and particularly how state actors evoked the idea of homeland, and nurtured the idea of connection to the homeland, I have limited my analysis to activities that fit into the category of communication – that is, mass media, education, and propaganda. Yugoslavia engaged with its workers across international borders in other ways – it sent the Association of Yugoslav Trade Unions (Savez sindikata Jugoslavije) to advocate for workers' rights and social workers to support workers in adapting to life abroad – which I have had to set aside in the interest of staying focused on the specific project of communication. For the same reasons, I analyse only those programs directed specifically at labour migrants, excluding those who were considered by Yugoslavia to have left permanently.

Because my focus is on the relationship between migrants and their sending state, as noted earlier, I have opted to include migrants working across Western Europe, rather than focusing on only one or two host states, which would force me to exclude a great deal of interesting and revealing archival material. I have also opted not to describe the varying host-state policies that affected labour migrants and popular attitudes in different European states. There is no doubt that migrants' attitudes toward their sending-state were shaped by their experiences in their host state. This is in fact a point that I make when analysing migrants' letters to radio programs and newspapers, and in survey responses. However, while fascinating, comparing how different contexts shaped opinions toward the homeland is beyond the scope of this monograph.

My research for this book was bound by rules governing the use of archival records, which limited my access to more recent records. This is why I delve primarily into the 1980s in my chapters on film and on education, where I could draw on sources other than archival records. Although in some ways arbitrary, there are good reasons to stay focused on the 1960s and 1970s, as circumstances changed significantly in the following decade. When Tito died in 1980, Yugoslavia lost its fiercest advocate and most powerful symbol. The dynamic between federal political actors changed fundamentally, initiating the gradual unravelling of the country. By 1987, Slobodan Milošević was at the head of the Serbian League of Communists and unabashedly advocating for renegotiating the terms of the federation to strengthen Serbia's power, whereas Croatian and Slovenian politicians pushed for greater decentralization and liberalization. Moreover, Yugoslavia's economy plunged ever deeper into economic crisis in the 1980s, including high unemployment and runaway inflation. Thus, the Yugoslavia that the migrants were now relating to was a place, set of ideas, and institutions that were very different from those in earlier decades. It was not only Yugoslavia that had changed – the migrants' themselves had in many cases left two decades ago or more, and their legal status and rights had also evolved. Thus, more than a new chapter, the 1980s call for a study of their own.

PART I

Seeing Migrants

2 Seeing Migration Like a State

In his influential book *Seeing like a State*, James Scott argued that modern states simplify complex realities, to make societies legible in order to control and reshape them. Using the analogy of the map, he explained, "They do not successfully represent the actual activity of the society they depicted, nor were they intended to: they represented only that slice of it that interested the official observer. They were, moreover, not just maps. Rather, they were maps that, when allied with state power, would enable much of the reality they depicted to be remade."[1]

Scott's insight is a fitting starting point for this exploration of Yugoslavia's migrant workers and their relationship to the Yugoslav state, for much of what we know about the migrant workers we derive from information collected by Yugoslav authorities and experts or by host-state bureaucracies. As these states produced knowledge about migrants, they were not merely recording an objective reality – they were also constructing it, first epistemologically, and then in the material world.

We should be clear here: post-war labour migration was not a Titoist invention. Historians – the author included – have tended to emphasize the unique quality of Yugoslav's open border policy and its encouragement of cross-border labour migration in the context of state socialism. Yet, this labour migration can also be seen as a continuation of an established pattern predating the Cold War that had existed for hundreds of years. Indeed, cross-border migration also continued, in a trickle, following the descent of the Iron Curtain. To a significant degree, as this chapter will show, Yugoslavia's open border policy was a response to pressures from below, driven by the aspirations and choices of individuals who sought to cross the border with or without official sanction – many of whom were likely deploying a survival strategy that had been used by their forefathers and, to a lesser extent, foremothers.

At the same time, the category of "our workers temporarily employed abroad" was fundamentally an invention, in the same sense that the category of "diaspora" is an invention, as numerous migration scholars have noted. Just as states brought diasporas into being to serve specific purposes, deciding who is included and who is excluded from this category, the Yugoslav state's creation of the category of "our citizens/workers abroad" attempted to distinguish between labour migrants and economic emigrants (or classic diaspora), and political emigrants hostile to the Yugoslav state. As Francesco Ragazzi has argued, "The new category of 'workers temporarily abroad' formed a new, separate group, which was dealt with by a different rationality, and different bureaucratic entities and practices. It was also the object of a differentiated kind of bureaucratic knowledge."[2]

Thus, while labour migration was an objective phenomenon, "our workers temporarily employed abroad" was a construct developed by the Yugoslav state to provide a framework for its efforts to govern its population across national borders. The category itself was based on several questionable assumptions whose self-evident quality obscured tensions and contradictions. Namely, these workers were held to be surplus labour, driven exclusively by economic motivations, who would return shortly, once Yugoslavia's economy caught up. This category, interestingly, did not include household members, because it was assumed that migrants would leave them behind during their short absence. Obscuring this fact, "our workers" was used interchangeably with "our citizens" in policy documents. This conflation also highlighted the degree to which citizenship was defined through labour in state socialism. These assumptions shaped policy, providing a framework for Yugoslavia's continued efforts to govern its migrants across state borders. As a socialist state, Yugoslavia expected to intervene in many facets of the social, economic, and political life of its citizens, even if they were living abroad. It also sought to maintain an active relationship with migrants through radio broadcasts and newspapers produced in Yugoslavia – efforts explored in greater detail in chapters 4 and 5. Assumptions about migrants and their aspirations also shaped the collection and production of knowledge about migrants, influencing the design, implementation, and interpretation of research on migrant issues.

Many Yugoslavs living and working abroad embraced the formulation "our workers abroad" with all its attendant associations, lending it legitimacy. They gave this label substance through their interactions with the state, and fleshed it out by expressing what it meant to them, and how it reflected their own experience. They used it to make claims on the state – for their rights as citizens and for extra resources to remain connected. Entitled to certain rights and benefits, many migrants played the part expected of them, sometimes disingenuously, but usually in good faith. These interactions helped to bring the category of "our workers temporarily employed abroad" into existence. Yugoslavs also took on this identity to attack the state for its failure to live up to its commitments. Yet others rejected this label, embracing other ways of belonging. This did not pose a problem for Yugoslav authorities until they perceived contestation to be a widespread phenomenon in the late 1960s.

A climate of crisis beginning in 1968 destabilized convictions about labour migration and migrants. This moral panic was triggered by growing concerns that the understanding of the phenomenon was out of sync with the reality. Observations made by diplomatic missions, coupled with scientific studies, suggested that a significant number of migrants were not in fact surplus unskilled labour, but rather semi-skilled and skilled workers attracted by better opportunities in Western Europe. Moreover, the notion that political and economic migrants were distinct categories was becoming harder to support, and migrants appeared to be postponing their return indefinitely. This was particularly worrisome in the aftermath of the invasion of Czechoslovakia in 1968 by Warsaw Pact countries, prompting Tito to worry that "three armies" were missing as a result of labour migration.[3] Popular discourse also portrayed migrants as disloyal materialists lured by Western consumer goods. In the face of these concerning signs, federal authorities intensified their efforts to "remake reality" in the image of the "map," through programs intended to reinforce migrants' attachment to socialist Yugoslavia.

In the context of the Croatian national awakening, however, actors like Zvonimir Komarica, who headed the Institute for Migration and Nationality created by Matica iseljenika Hrvatske, sought to reframe migration by portraying it not as an inevitable phase on Yugoslavia's path to economic prosperity, but rather as the product of discriminatory and flawed economic policies that victimized Croatia. This discourse, like the one it aimed to replace, was an oversimplification, or, as James Scott put it, "that slice that interested the official observer" in the interest of advancing a pre-existing agenda. In this case, it was less about "reshaping" migrants than it was about reshaping relations between Croatia and Yugoslavia. The plight of the labour migrant became a rallying cry in the Croatian Spring. The new narrative ultimately distracted from significant shifts in the character of labour migration starting in the early 1970s – most significantly, the decreasing proportion of workers from Croatia choosing to work abroad, in tandem with the increasing numbers from Bosnia-Herzegovina and Serbia and its provinces.

From Marginal Phenomenon to State Policy

Although social scientists like Baskin and Schierup have explained Yugoslavia's labour migration strategy primarily as a result of the economic reforms of the 1960s, the archival record suggests that it was also a response to bottom-up pressures – the unsanctioned departure of Yugoslav citizens seeking employment abroad, even prior to the reforms. The start of the Western European economic boom in the 1960s stimulated the demand for foreign labour, and Yugoslavs responded enthusiastically. By Zimmerman's estimate, the number of Yugoslav workers in Europe increased from 3,000 in 1954 to 28,000 in 1961.[4] The Committee for Foreign Economic Relations estimated in 1962 that some 86,940 Yugoslavs were living in Europe, who had left for the express purpose of working abroad (31,800 who were authorized, and 55,140 who were not).[5]

Many of these had left surreptitiously. As Francesca Rolandi has chronicled, between 1945 and 1968, an average of 4,500 Yugoslavs crossed into Italy yearly, with border and coastal populations being most prone to this action. While some crossed the border illegally, increasing numbers were leaving with a passport and choosing not to return. The archival record suggests that motivations for border-crossing varied, including a desire to avoid military service, aspirations to higher income, and for some, unemployment. Those who crossed the Italian border were likely to claim refugee status, which presumed that the claimant was persecuted in Yugoslavia, but Italian and Yugoslav authorities both suspected that their true motivations were economic. German authorities were of the same opinion, particularly after Tito's turn away from Stalinism. Arguably, motivations for migration, as today, were complex, combining frustration with Communist authorities, post-war hardship, personal circumstances, and promise of a better life elsewhere.[6]

The unauthorized and unregulated flood of migrants created problems for Yugoslavia. The state had no control over the type of worker that was leaving and was deeply concerned about the risk of a brain drain. Moreover, these citizens were at risk outside the borders of their homeland, lacking social insurance coverage and other protections, and easy prey for hostile émigré communities. The Yugoslav economic reforms of the mid-1960s merely created an additional motivation to allow labour migration by increasing unemployment.[7]

Rather than a clear policy shift, Yugoslavia's adoption of a labour migration strategy was incremental. Starting in 1957, the Yugoslav state cautiously opened the door to labour migration. Requests by Yugoslavs judged to be poor and unemployed, and who wished to look abroad for work, were approved. The figures testify to a growing interest in this possibility: in Bosnia-Herzegovina, 179 passports were issued in 1957 and almost the same exact number the second year, with an unexplained dip in 1959 to 90 passports. Then, in 1960, 366 passports were approved, followed by 1,776 in 1961, and 5,003 in 1962.[8] Residents of Croatia were particularly eager to seize this opportunity: in 1961, 1,850 requests were made to take employment abroad, radically increasing to 14,933 the following year and 25,121 in 1963. While the Croatian authorities initially approved the majority of the requests (61% in 1961, and 75% in 1962), it restricted the number of approvals in 1963, likely in response to the introduction of formal guidelines, approving fewer than 40%.[9]

According to Brunnbauer, Yugoslavia's adoption of an open-border policy was based on multi-year process of learning and debate starting in 1960. Policymakers gained their knowledge about the behaviour of migrants, and the potential threats and opportunities that came with open borders, by observing and interacting with emigrants. In particular, he stresses the role of the Matice iseljenika, cultural foundations operating at the level of the republics whose purpose was to maintain ties with emigrants. Policymakers were also impressed by the important sums of foreign currency that came from migrant transfers and repatriated savings, which at the time even dwarfed profits from tourism. They debated the benefits and risks of opening the border over the course of 1962–3. Recognizing that illegal cross-border flows were significant, and that the cost of enforcing the border or ignoring its violation were too high, they opted to provide legal channels that they could hopefully steer and supervise.[10]

In addition to popular pressure to work abroad, the liberalization of the border regime was driven by Yugoslavia's wish to participate in the global tourism boom, as Igor Tchoukarine has demonstrated.[11] These motivations overcame the Communists' deep reservations about labour migration, based on misgivings about the strategy to address economic underdevelopment by sending workers abroad to toil in the capitalist economy, and concerns that workers would be subject to anti-Yugoslav propaganda. Concerns about the negative influence of foreigners on Yugoslav tourists were similarly set aside.[12]

Prior to opening the floodgates to labour migration, Yugoslav authorities sought to create order in the ranks of individuals with ties to Yugoslavia already living abroad, which included ethnic Croats and

Slovenes living in Austria, descendants of earlier waves of migration, and postwar emigrants who had fled Communist rule or left in search of better employment. Yugoslavia's strict border policy meant that a large number of Yugoslavs who had left during or after the war were in violation of Yugoslav law, and consequently, at odds with the state. Federal authorities were cognizant that their citizens who were crossing the border illegally in search of a better life were swelling the ranks of hostile emigrant organizations. They thus attempted to improve relations with emigrants through passage of an amnesty law in 1962, which indemnified Yugoslavs who had crossed the border illegally, as well as by rescinding the "law on the removal of citizenship from officers and non-commissioned officers of the former Yugoslav army, which will not return to the homeland, as well as members of military formations which served the occupier and fled abroad, as well as persons who fled after the liberation."[13]

Yugoslav authorities were convinced that, aside from hard-core anti-Yugoslav emigrants who were exempt from the amnesty, a majority of these emigrants would welcome the opportunity to resume a normal relationship with Yugoslavia, transitioning from political to economic migrants. This would in turn promote a greater flow of foreign currency back to Yugoslavia. A 1963 memo of the Socialist Alliance of Working People of Yugoslavia, the primary organization for mass mobilization, credited these two laws for changing the attitudes of the emigrant community.[14] Fifty thousand migrants were able to obtain a passport through the amnesty. While some officials believed it had undercut hostile emigrant organizations, others were less satisfied – and indeed, these organizations would not only survive but grow in the coming decade.[15] In the minds of its designers, however, the amnesty law allowed Yugoslavia to distinguish easily between hostile political émigrés, which could be actively fought and undermined, and economic migrants, ostensibly friendly to Yugoslavia, with whom close relations could be cultivated.

Having separated the proverbial sheep from the goats, federal authorities then proceeded to liberalize the border and create mechanisms to regulate the flow of workers to other countries. To that end, in 1963, the Federal Labour Secretariat founded a federal commission for workers' employment abroad, and shortly thereafter, SAWPY issued "instructions on procedures for employment of workers abroad," which first established the designation "worker temporarily employed abroad." The main thrust of Yugoslavia's policy was to facilitate the export of low-skilled labour while taking measures to prevent the departure of skilled labour. Keeping tabs on migrants in this way would allow Yugoslavia to coax migrants to send their earnings back to Yugoslavia, injecting valuable foreign currencies into the Yugoslav economy. Starting in 1964, workers could seek employment through official channels, as republican employment bureaus were empowered to strike agreements with foreign employers. The Yugoslav state also signed several bilateral labour agreements, with France in 1965, with Austria and Sweden in 1966, and finally, with the FRG in 1968. In 1965, the Law on Travel Permits of Yugoslav Citizens made it possible to easily apply for ten-year passports and obtain exit visas, effectively liberalizing the border regime. The following year, a Law on the Amendments of the Law on the Organization and Finance of Employment eliminated most restrictions on working abroad.[16]

Having gradually arrived at a somewhat cogent labour migration policy, Yugoslav authorities then formulated an official justification for it. One justification was ethical, on the basis Yugoslav citizens had "the right to seek and find better working and living conditions." This reflected a new orientation toward the rights of the individual that accompanied the political liberalization following Aleksandar Ranković's fall. Policymakers also argued that labour migration was an inevitable outcome of economic globalization, in which developed economies drew on labour from less-developed states. Moreover, it was a necessary step in Yugoslavia's economic development, following economic reforms that aimed to increase industrial productivity, and in so doing, produced an increase in unemployment.[17] The "temporary" quality of migration was essential, both in offsetting critiques of the labour migration policy as contrary to socialist values, and in justifying Yugoslavia's continued oversight over the migrants.

Yugoslav migration policy was premised on the existence of a distinct migrant type, which it described as "our worker temporarily employed abroad." This worker was defined as surplus labour – primarily former peasants from rural areas with limited education who had been made redundant in Yugoslavia's developing economy. It was assumed that the motivation for leaving was economic, and most of all, not political. Migrants were also expected to be abroad only temporarily, returning to Yugoslavia once its economy had caught up to that of Western developed economies.

Governing and Administering "Citizens Temporarily Employed Abroad"

Yugoslavia's relationship with its migrant workers was based on this premise. As far as Yugoslav governments and state institutions were concerned, migrants were treated as citizens who were away temporarily and were expected to return before long, and who continued mean-while to participate fully in Yugoslav political, economic, and social life, primarily through their ties with kin and home. They were expected to send remittances home to their families and visit during the holidays. Authorities also wanted them to open up Yugoslav bank accounts, pur-chase Yugoslav goods, celebrate national holidays, read Yugoslav news-papers, tune in to Yugoslav radio, and not only stay abreast of reforms and other important political topics in Yugoslavia, but even have their say in debates on proposed constitutional amendments.

In accordance with Yugoslavia's federal structure, and the idea that labour migrants should be treated like all other Yugoslav citizens, they were considered to be full members of their republic of primary resi-dence. Thus, a migrant who had most recently lived in Croatia would be subject to governance and administration by the Republic of Croa-tia. This would create significant challenges in formulating and imple-menting policy on labour migration. While the federation might initi-ate a particular policy direction, if it fell under republican jurisdiction, such as culture or education, federal institutions would need to bring the republics on board and coordinate between them. Those policies then needed to be implemented across state borders, which required the cooperation of federal, republican, and sometimes even local actors. More often than not, not everyone fulfilled their responsibilities or came forward with resources with the same diligence, hampering effective services to migrants.

The conceit that it was possible and desirable to continue govern-ing labour migrants as if they had never left was contested. Others, including the press and migrants themselves, articulated an alternative concept of the place of labour migrants within Yugoslav society, argu-ing that they constituted a Seventh Republic. This was not based only on how numerous they were, but also on the fact that they faced unique challenges and shared experiences that distinguished them from other Yugoslavs. The origins of this term are not known, but it was used as early as 1954 by a politician, Ljubo Leontić, to refer to emigration more broadly.[18] An open letter from 1970 signed by five Yugoslav citizens' clubs from the FRG and Switzerland explicitly deployed this term to demand separate political representation for labour migrants within the Federal Assembly.[19]

Interestingly, in spite of Zimmerman's assertion that Yugoslavia sought to govern the Seventh Republic, authorities were actually quite averse to this formulation. In response to the above-mentioned open letter, the Committee for Cross-Border Migration reasserted the legiti-macy of the official position on labour migration: "In this regard, we are of the opinion that our citizens are only temporarily employed abroad, that they are an integral, inalienable part or our socialist community with all the rights and responsibilities of all other Yugoslav citizens, and not by any means members of some kind of 'seventh republic' as is stated in the 'open letter.'"

With regard to the specific question of political representation, the committee merely countered that "if many of our citizens living abroad have not been able to vote, this is merely the result of technical problems, which we have unfortunately not been able to resolve to date."[20] It entirely side-stepped the issue of whether or not the migrants could adequately be represented by delegates speaking on behalf of their home communities, rather than by fellow labour migrants dedicated to addressing their specific needs and problems. Normally eager to report on problems associated with labour migration, the press was unusually critical of the "open letter," most likely at the instigation of the committee, characterizing it as the effort of "a few" Yugoslav clubs, whose views were unrepresentative of the majority of migrant opinion.[21]

Governing and administering the Seventh Republic, consequently, was a complex and multifaceted affair. A bewildering array of bodies preoccupied themselves with monitoring labour migration. The very multiplicity of actors continued to prevent coordination and implementation of policies. Without attempting to draw up an exhaustive inventory, it is useful to provide an overview of the most significant such bodies. Legislative and executive bodies at every level of government formed specialized institutions and organizations to examine questions and formulate policies on labour migration.

At the federal level, the most prominent were the Council for Emigration Questions, founded in 1958 (Savet za pitanje iseljenika, later renamed Savezna komisija za pitanje iseljenika) and the Committee for Cross-Border Migration, which took over the labour migration portfolio in 1969 (Komitet za pitanja spoljnih migracija), both of which answered to the Federal Executive Council. The Council for Emigration Questions coordinated the efforts of all other federal institutions on emigrants and migrants, collected information about trends, organized the distribution of propaganda and the organization of programming for emigrants and migrants, liaised with other organizations to provide access to commercial services such as banking and tourism, and distributed funding and materials to emigrant and migrant organizations. It worked in collaboration with the State Secretary for Foreign Affairs (Državni sekretarijat za inostrane poslove – DSIP).[22] In addition to its Consular Affairs Administration, which regularly dealt with labour migration, DSIP also had a dedicated Labour Migrant Administration (Uprava za radnike na radu u inostranstvu).

Some republican governments, including the Croatian and Slovenian, had their own committees focused on migration and immigration. The Croatian Sabor founded a Council for international relations (Savjet za odnose s inozemstvom) in 1967, and the Executive Council of the Republic of Croatia similarly had a Commission on Cross-Border Migration (Komisija za vanjske migracije, changing its name in 1977 to Republički komitet za odnose s inozemstvom).

Beyond state institutions, social and political organizations were responsible for outreach with labour migrants, and, as such, accumulated knowledge about the migrants that was relayed back and fed into policymaking processes. The Socialist Alliance of Working People of Yugoslavia (Socijalistički savez radnog naroda – SRNJ / SAWPY), Yugoslavia's primary mass organization, had specialized committees focused on labour migration. A Commission for International Cooperation and Relations (Komisija za međunarodnu saradnju i veze) operated under its executive committee, and a Coordinating Committee for Labour Migrant Affairs (Koordinacioni odbor SK SSRNJ za pitanja radnika u inostranstvu) operated at the level of the SAWPY federal conference. At the republican level, SAWPY had additional committees, such as the Commission for International and Emigration Questions, in the Croatian context. Having initially left labour migration in the hands of SAWPY, in 1971 the League of Communists of Yugoslavia (Savez komunista Jugoslavije – LCY) formed its own specialized body, called the Delegation for the Activities of the LCY in Connection to the Departure and Temporary Work of Our Workers Abroad. This body was concerned primarily with organizing Communists who had left to work abroad.

Aside from SAWPY and the LCY, the Matice iseljenika also played a significant role. Not to be confused with Matica Hrvatska and Matica Srpska, which were distinct cultural foundations focused on the promotion of the Croatian and Serbian national cultures within Yugoslavia, the Matice iseljenika were founded in the 1950s for the maintaining relations with emigrants, primarily through promotion of cultural traditions. As labour migration emerged and grew, it played an important role in disseminating information and providing cultural activities for migrants. Matica iseljenika Hrvatske, founded in 1951, was arguably the most influential of these organizations. It organized tours of Yugoslav cultural and artistic groups abroad, and assisted with providing supplies to citizens' associations. In 1965, it was finally able to follow through with a project first formulated in 1958, to create a scholarly institute to study Croatian emigration and labour migration.

This institute, the Institute for Migration and Nationality (Zavod za migracije I narodnosti – ZMN) also played a critical role in producing knowledge about labour migration.[23]

In addition to these specialized state bodies and mass organizations, a number of federal bodies concerned themselves with labour migration as part of a broader portfolio. Some of these institutions dealt with the labour and social security aspects of labour migration: in 1971, they included the Federal Employment Council (Savezni savet za rad), the Federal Employment Office (Savezni biro za poslove zapošljavanja), and the Federal Social Security Office (savezni zavod za socijalno osiguranje). The Council of Yugoslav Trade Unions (Savez sindikata Jugoslavije – SSJ) advocated in the interests of migrants in discussions with foreign trade unions and political parties. At the republican level, employment offices (Zavod za zapošljavanje) processed the workers' requests to work abroad and connected them with employers.

Other federal bodies preoccupied with communication and cultural outreach are more central to this study. They included the Coordinating Council for Matice iseljenika (Koordinacioni odbor matica iseljenika Jugoslavije) and the Federal Council for Education and Culture (Savezni savet za obrazovanje i kulture). The Federal Secretariat for Information (Savezni sekretarijat za informacije – SSINF) concerned itself with migrants' access to reliable information and collaborated with the State Secretary for Foreign Affairs in running the Cultural-Information Centres, described in chapter 3 in greater detail.[24] As Nikola Baković has pointed out, SSINF's activities implied "that Yugoslav institutions extended their jurisdiction across their borders and outside regular diplomatic channels in a transterritorial manner" – an observation that can arguably be applied to several of these federal bodies.[25]

Measuring Migration

The rapid growth in migration quickly alarmed Yugoslav authorities at all levels of government. Reasonably reliable figures on the numbers of migrants were not available until the 1971 survey. Nevertheless, a 1966 report by the Federal Employment Office estimated that at least 184,000 Yugoslavs were working abroad, doubling in comparison to the 87,000 estimated in 1962.[26]

Because residents of Croatia featured so prominently among migrants, Croatian authorities were particularly eager to gain a clearer picture of migration and the profile of migrants. In 1966, the Institute for Migration and Nationality undertook the first comprehensive sociological study on "Yugoslavia in European labour migration" (*SFRJ u evropskim migracijama rada*), led by Zvonimir Komarica, Mladen Zvonarević, and Ivo Vinski. It was an ambitious project carried out with the financial support of the republican employment office, the Privredna banka Zagreb bank, the Federal Council for Emigration Questions, the Vjesnik publishing house, and Radio-Television Zagreb (RTZ).[27]

Aside from collecting basic demographic and socio-economic data, the study sought to understand more subjective issues, such as migrants' motivations, plans, changes in their opinions, the influence of Yugoslav media, and their willingness to send remittances back home. They also asked questions to discover the impact of labour migration on migrants' families back home, and the expectations of individuals who were about to leave to work abroad.

To collect these data, researchers targeted three different demographics: migrants, individuals in Yugoslavia planning to become migrants, and families of migrants in Yugoslavia. Working from a lengthy standard questionnaire containing forty questions (not including questions on socio-economic status), they sent several researchers abroad to interview workers where they lived. They also sent questionnaires to 3,000 Yugoslavs who had sent correspondence to RTZ, which ran a popular weekly radio show aimed at labour migrants, *Našim Građanima u Svijetu*. The radio station also provided addresses of families of migrants, to which they sent a separate questionnaire. Finally, they also conducted oral surveys with people who applied for work abroad through the republican employment office. In all, they collected 1,280 oral surveys and 1,140 surveys by mail from migrants, as well as 278 responses from would-be migrants (from the 300 contacted) and 172 from family members.[28]

The researchers who were sent to Germany, Austria, France, Sweden, and the Netherlands to conduct interviews in person with workers left fascinating reports that shed light on the difficulty of collecting reliable information on migrant workers, and demonstrate how the researchers' preconceptions of migrants could shape the research results. Interestingly, their concerns were not expressed in the final report of the study.

To begin with, most interviewers reported that respondents were fearful and did not trust them, as was "evident both from their verbal reactions and their behaviour, as well as from their reluctance to answer delicate questions. I only found complete honesty in one respondent," according to one report. Ivan Čizmić, who later became a migration historian, noted that, in Austria, "our workers have learned from experience to be cautious when speaking to strangers. They want to be sure they are not dealing with provocateurs." Another interviewer in Sweden explained that migrants didn't trust that the study was indeed anonymous, didn't believe the outcome of the study would help them in any way, and were terrorized by hostile émigré organizations. In order to gain migrants' trust of the migrants, interviewers resorted to tactics that included making small talk. Čizmić and another interviewer had some success pretending to be a reporter for *Našim Građanima u Svijetu*. Not only does this practice raise questions about the ethics of using deception in research, but it may have influenced survey responses.[29]

The respondents transgressed the rules of the study in other ways. Because most of them had roommates, interviewers found it was not possible to conduct the interviews individually. This could skew the answers – Čizmić observed that, in a group, respondents tended to report lower incomes and claim they had no savings. The respondents demanded to have copies of the questionnaire, which was supposed to be kept confidential. They also gave partial answers or circled parts of the question instead of writing down answers. Interviewers in the Netherlands attributed the latter behaviour to their respondents' backwardness. One report suggested that "some of the respondents are evaluated by the interviewers to be limited people (*ograničeni*), and it would be worthwhile to instruct interviewers to write down their general impression of the intellectual level of the respondents." Another report from the Netherlands explained the failure to answer questions as due to "semi-literacy and the very low cultural level of the respondents, as well as indifference to the subject."[30] This tendency to view the respondents as primitive and unintelligent, and to explain their unwillingness to respond as a function of backwardness illustrates how the dominant stereotype of migrants as uneducated peasants may have prejudiced the interpretation of data.

Other preconceived ideas about migrant workers as being loyal to Yugoslavia similarly shaped the outcome of the study. Karlo Budar, reporting from France, indicated that he left out 10 or so responses from the 214 that he received, on the basis that they were in an aggressive or arrogant tone and therefore must have been submitted by hostile émigrés posing as workers.[31]

While these reports primarily shed light on the ways in which the interviewers could influence the outcome of the study, there are also hints that migrants themselves were not just passive actors, but in fact saw the study as an instrument for reaching their own ends, which may also have influenced their answers. "I would in particular warn that not one worker plans to remain in the Netherlands, and that their greatest concern is finding work upon their return in the homeland. ... Workers see the purpose of the survey as being

Table 1. Respondents by Republic of Origin, 1967 Survey

Republic	Oral survey (%)	Postal survey (%)
Bosnia-Herzegovina	9.3	28.0
Croatia	53.2	59.0
Serbia, Vojvodina, and Kosovo	25.9	11.0
Montenegro		0.1
Macedonia	11.6	1.0
Slovenia		0.9

to resolve this problem. Every other objective is for them superfluous."[32] Thus they might have distorted their answers in the hope of obtaining assistance.

There are also problems with the surveys that were mailed in, although the final report, which was only circulated internally and never published, was somewhat more candid about these issues. These respondents were not representative of the Yugoslav migrant population as a whole, as they were listeners to a Serbo-Croatian language program who had chosen to write to the program. Not only were they already self-selected as having a greater attachment to the homeland, but they were also far more likely to be Serbo-Croatian speakers and potentially Croats. This did not prevent the study from claiming that the proportion of each nationality in the sample was "close to reality," although elsewhere it acknowledged that non-Serbo-Croatian speakers were likely underrepresented. Of the respondents, 62.7% were of Croatian nationality, 23.7% Serbian, and 4.8% Slovenian. All other groups (including Bosnian Muslims) made up less than 2% of responses. Residents of Croatia made up 53% of all participants in the oral survey, and 59% of those in the written survey (see table 1.) Subsequent studies confirm that residents of Croatia and people of Croatian nationality were significantly over-represented, and the statistics offered here under the guise of scientific research should therefore be taken with a grain of salt.[33]

The interpretation of the survey results was also flawed in places in ways that seemed strategic rather than accidental. For example, they used stratified quota sampling, to reflect certain basic assumptions about the population. Specific proportions of respondents were sought out on the basis of their country of employment, gender, age, and qualifications. It is thus not particularly surprising that, having specifically sought out a large number of workers between the age of twenty and forty (85% of the sample), 82% of their respondents fitted that description. Yet the study offered the following reflection, as if it was based on an original finding: "We see that almost 82% [of the sample] represent the most productive age group. ... If we take into consideration that we are to a significant degree talking about the dynamic part of society, which is not afraid of difficulties, then we cannot be satisfied."[34]

Elsewhere, the study again offered a tendentious interpretation of the data. Asked about their motivations for leaving, respondents were given the possibility of providing three choices. The survey grouped responses into three categories: survival, quality of life, and a third category vaguely consisting of environmental factors and "an atmosphere of exodus." Although 63% of respondents replied "low earnings at home," 23% "unemployment," and 9% "I have too little land," it is not possible to claim, as did the report, that 95% of respondents were motivated by survival, given that any given respondent might have chosen all three answers.[35]

Such sloppy readings of the data were used by the authors to build a damning case against the impact of labour migration on Croatian society. In the context of a 200-page report, these errors or misrepresentations may seem minor, but they are worth noting because of the use that Komarica would later make of the findings at the height of the Croatian Spring.

Keeping these flaws and biases in mind, a sceptical reading of the study yields valuable insights into the profile of the average migrant, and the motivations. The report focused on the results of the oral survey, bringing in the postal survey results when there was a significant discrepancy. The majority of respondents were male (82%). While most migrants were uneducated, a significant proportion had achieved a higher level of education. Fifty-six per cent had completed eight or fewer years of elementary school, while 43.3% had completed specialized schooling, trades, high school, and university education. Migrants were evenly split between those who claimed to have fought in the national liberation struggle and those who did not.[36]

The study confirmed that the strongest motivations for leaving were economic, keeping in mind that respondents were obliged to choose answers from a prepared list (a maximum of three choices). The two most popular answers were "weak earnings in the country" (63.2%) and "I wished to earn income towards a home or an apartment" (45.8%). Twenty-three per cent left as a result of unemployment. While the study insisted, as noted above, that survival was the migrants' dominant motivation, many aspired to a higher standard of living than was available in Yugoslavia – most of all, they wished to become home-owners.

It also raises the question of where the line between survival and aspiration should be drawn – and indeed, what the point would be of drawing such a line.[37]

The answers also highlighted the extent to which migrants depended on informal mechanisms, kinship, and friendship networks – and more worryingly, emigrant organizations – both to leave Yugoslavia and to get their bearings once they had arrived, rather than on Yugoslav state institutions. The majority of respondents (63.8%) had found work abroad through friends, acquaintances, or relatives, whereas only 21.6% had done so through the employment bureaus. These results confirmed estimates that only a third of migrants had used official channels to obtain employment. Once they had arrived abroad, over half of workers had depended on friends from Yugoslavia to get adjusted. Twenty-one per cent had received help from Yugoslavs they had met while abroad, and 31.9%, from an emigrant organization – it was not specified of what type. Only 2.6% claimed to have received help from Yugoslav diplomatic missions. Sixty-three per cent claimed that they borrowed money from friends to support their quest to establish themselves abroad.[38]

The study also provided interesting data on the length of stay, revealing that most migrants were recent arrivals and that most still intended to return home shortly. Just under half of respondents had been there for less than a year, while 33.9% had been abroad for one to three years, and another 15.7% had already spent over three years abroad. Most migrants intended to stay for only a short time beyond the time they had already spent – only 16.3% of respondents anticipated remaining for more than another three years, although another 26.9% said that they did not know when they would return.[39]

The study also confirmed that most workers were unskilled workers from rural areas, although skilled workers represented a significant fraction. The majority of respondents were unskilled labour (57.4%), while 35.5% were skilled workers, and another 4.2% were highly qualified workers. Roughly half of the unskilled workers had in fact previously been from rural areas and did not have industrial experience. Given the methodology of the oral survey, which was to recruit respondents "where they lived," that is, in workers' settlements, and then through snowball sampling, it is not surprising that professionals were not represented in the results. The single most significant challenge they faced was lack of language skills (78%), although 23.6% also complained about difficult working conditions due to cold, heat, noise, and the physically demanding nature of the work.[40]

Responses on income suggest that workers were able to earn enough to save and send a substantial portion of their salary home. Although potentially under-reporting their true salaries, respondents reported incomes concentrated in the range of 101,000–200,000 and 201,000–300,000 dinars per month (29.4% and 38.5%, respectively). A significant portion of their income was spent on housing and food: 21.2% spent less than 50,000, while 37.9% spent 50,000–100,000 dinars, and 21.9% spent 101,000–150,000 dinars. Still, nearly half reported sending at least 100,000 dinars home per month, and another 7.8% sent home up to 200,000 dinars. We can only speculate why 23.3% sent nothing home: Did they not have dependents back in Yugoslavia? Or perhaps were they part of a migrant underclass that earned too little to send home? Respondents told researchers they would return to Yugoslavia for salaries that were on average lower than their salaries abroad, hinting at the pull of home. Thus, 58% said they would return if they were assured a salary of 76,000–100,000 dinars.[41]

While migrants were adept at saving, much to the dismay of Yugoslav authorities, it seems that few chose to deposit their earnings in Yugoslav banks. In this study, only 18.1% did so, with others naming a variety of reasons, ranging from unfavourable interest rates to lack of trust in Yugoslav banks and overly complicated withdrawal procedures. Additionally, 35% claimed to have no savings – but we must keep in mind researchers' suspicions that migrants may not have been honest about earnings and savings.[42]

Other data help us to form a picture of the workers' lifestyle, which was a modest one focused on scrimping and saving. The majority of workers lived alone (22.3%) or with one or more friends (55.5) – indeed, almost a quarter had three or more room-mates. Yet, already in 1966, when Yugoslavia's temporary labour migration policy was fairly new, 18.5% of migrants lived with their families, while 41.9% of respondents were housed by their employer in barracks, rooming houses, and similar bachelor housing. Of the remaining, 27.1% rented a room, 17.2% rented an apartment, and 11.4% lived in a hotel. Many respondents depended on the company cafeteria for their meals – almost half ate their lunches there, and roughly a quarter relied on the cafeteria for breakfast, and the same percentage for dinner. Other migrants ate in restaurants: 7.3% for breakfast, 11.3% for lunch, and 17.3% for dinner – like the cafeteria, these options would have been appealing to men living far from the attentions of wives and mothers. Still, perhaps motivated by a desire to save, 62.2% prepared their own breakfast, 37.1% their lunch, and 54.5% their dinner.[43]

Not only was this a meagre existence, but it could also be a lonely and isolated one. Sixty-five per cent of migrants participating in the survey listed separation from their families as among the most significant disadvantages of living abroad, 48% cited loneliness, and 18% indicated they had no friends.[44] The most frequent answer to the question of how respondents spent their free time was "Most often I am in my apartment alone – I rarely go out" (45.1%). Nearly as many respondents replied that "they have fun with their friends, in their apartment" (42.9%). Insofar as they did go out, it was either to take a walk (36.4%) or to see a film (32.5%). Only 7.9% admitted to going to church, but even fewer said that they frequented a Yugoslav citizens' association (2.1%).[45]

When asked about the advantages, migrants overwhelmingly focused on the ways in which it enabled a higher standard of living. Eighty-three per cent pointed to higher earnings, and 42% said that there was a larger choice of consumer goods. Interestingly, only 10% said that there was "more freedom," and 17% answered that "life abroad has no special advantages," suggesting that a minority of migrants were either disappointed about the choice they had made, or that they would have stayed home had they been given the choice.[46]

The vast majority of migrants aspired to return home to Yugoslavia (86.9%), with just under 10% admitting their intention to remain abroad. Nearly half aspired to return to work in the social sector (48%), while 17.1% hoped to open a small business, and 15.8% hoped to return to agriculture, preferably with more or better land (7.7%).[47]

Beyond the snapshot that the survey provides of migrants in 1966, it also offers a fascinating glimpse into its authors' growing unease about the implications of labour migration. More specifically, the opinion questions they asked and the analysis they produced expressed deep anxiety that migrants were becoming alienated from Yugoslavia and its values.

For example, questions in the survey concerned migrants' opinions of diplomatic missions, political émigrés, the Yugoslav media, and Yugoslav citizens' associations. Migrants were asked about unpleasant experiences they might have had when returning to Yugoslavia, and about the impact of labour migration on their familial relationships. They were also asked about their attitude toward striking, as a proxy for measuring class-consciousness. These questions were to gauge the influence of living abroad on their opinions and behaviour, and the strength of their attachment to Yugoslavia.

The respondents' answers raised serious concerns, suggesting that the longer migrants stayed abroad, the less they felt an attachment to Yugoslavia and its values. Migrants who had lived abroad for three years or more had a less negative view of political émigrés than did more recent arrivals, and were nearly twice as likely to read the émigré press than new arrivals (48% and 25% respectively). These longer-term migrants were also more than twice as likely to recommend that their children go abroad, leading to the conclusion that "their emotional ties to their own country have become loose and indeterminate."[48] The longer respondents had lived abroad, the more likely they were to leave permanently, which the report described as a "process of denationalization." Similarly, a longer stay translated into decreased interest in joining a Yugoslav citizens' association.[49]

Their answers to a question about their preference for owning a small business abroad, or of having a well-paid job in the social sector in Yugoslavia were also alarming. Whereas over 93% of migrants living abroad a year or less preferred a well-paid job in Yugoslavia, this was true of only 73% of migrants who had left Yugoslavia three or more years ago. "No other question speaks more clearly of the creation of a 'capitalist mentality' among our people than this one," warned the report. It also noted that migrants who had been abroad longer were less willing to strike, indicating a loss of class consciousness.[50]

Even seemingly positive responses about family relationships were interpreted as signs of "denationalization" or alienation. Whereas roughly 23% of respondents who had been abroad up to three years reported having problems with family relationships, this was true of only 16% of those who had been there longer. "One of the reasons for this," the report speculated, "can be the fact that years of absence have weakened the relationships between those people and their families back home, that earlier problems have ceased to matter. The other reason can be that those living abroad have brought their families to live with them, also eliminating the earlier problems."[51]

As the report summed up its bleak prognosis, "After three years of living abroad, our person has conquered the most challenging difficulties and adapted to a foreign world, and above all, has mastered a foreign language. Other than that, family and other more emotional relations with the homeland have become weaker, and we have before us a person who is ready to definitively leave the country."[52]

Migration Reframed

The study by the Institute for Migration and Nationality caught the attention of policymakers and was widely cited in reports calling for greater attention to be paid to the consequences of labour migration.[53] The report's circulation coincided with a growing and generalized anxiety among policymakers at all levels of government about the realities of labour migration. These fears were stoked by reports from observers in the field who warned that migrants were staying abroad indefinitely.

Some were even bringing their families, while others suffered from isolation, becoming easy prey for émigré organizations. These reports raised questions about the very premise of Yugoslav labour migration policy – that the temporary nature of the absence would not threaten the workers' sense of belonging to Yugoslavia, and that economic migrants could be kept separate from political emigrants. At the federal or republican level, policymakers issued urgent calls to increase cultural outreach toward workers, to stave off alienation and undermine the corrosive influence of political émigrés. Awareness of the impact of migration also provoked a backlash against labour migration, particularly in Croatia, where it became a significant issue in the Croatian national revival.

Several reports described how political emigrants preyed on vulnerable workers from the moment they stepped foot in their host state. Hostile emigrants offered to assist workers with problems they encountered upon their arrival. Migrants unfamiliar with the local language and with administrative procedures, laws, and regulations depended on their assistance, particularly in the FRG, prior to the establishment of diplomatic relations between that country and Yugoslavia. Others came to them for material support. Croatian political emigrants offered to act as go-betweens for migrants who arrived on a tourist visa and did not have a job waiting for them, and in this manner built relationships with them, sometimes recruiting them into extremist organizations.[54]

Afterward, emigrants aggressively tried to recruit workers into their organizations, showing up at their place of residence, or accosting them in places where they spent their free time, such as parks, train stations, and emigrant-run cafés and restaurants. In particular, they distributed publications that were designed to manipulate migrants. These publications attacked Yugoslavia relentlessly, reprinting critical articles from Yugoslav newspapers, to which they added their own even more critical commentary. They also offered practical advice on navigating life abroad. At first they advised workers to apply for political asylum, but they no longer insisted on this once Yugoslavia normalized relations with Western European states. The emigrants also had at least one radio program, hosted by Radio Cologne. Hostile emigrants bullied migrants into attending religious services based on their nationality, where they were exposed to more anti-Yugoslav propaganda. Authorities considered both the Catholic and Serbian Orthodox church to be allies of the political emigration.[55]

In the authorities' estimation, most migrants remained loyal to Yugoslavia or, at worst, adopted a neutral attitude out of fear of émigré reprisals. According to the embassy in Bonn, emigrant gangs, which it described as belonging to both the "Ustaša" and "Četniks," subjected migrants they believed to be loyal to Yugoslavia to incessant harassment and repeated assaults. Among the numerous cases listed in its report was that of Vladimir Veljković, who had been beaten after entering a restaurant merely for calling out "Good day, comrades" to the other Yugoslav patrons. Another victim, Živadin Zdravković, was attacked after buying the Belgrade-based newspaper *Politika*. In another case, twenty-nine workers resigned from their jobs at Tiefbau and returned to Yugoslavia after an emigrant group threatened to kill all Serbs working for the firm. Extremist groups sent armed thugs to workers' settlements and barracks to beat them up, resulting in about ten deaths.[56]

Particularly alarming to the authorities was the fact that emigrant organizations recruited workers, particularly amongst the young and impressionable. The embassy in Bonn had received several reports from loyal citizens of their countrymen joining hostile organizations in Neuss (across from Düsseldorf), Wuppertal, and elsewhere. Some of these recruits became involved in criminal and even terrorist activities. A group of emigrants, including holders of the "red passport," had led an armed assault on a bar in Cologne, leading to a shoot-out in which the barman and one of the attackers was injured. Commenting on this episode, the consular official added, "The scene playing out was unbelievable and reminded one of Ustaša or Četnik wartime rampage."[57] The Serbian government's commission for foreign affairs claimed that several migrants had been sent on missions to Yugoslavia to carry out terrorist acts.[58]

Other observers testified to the emotional frailty of workers, which was as much a product of social isolation as of prolonged exile from the homeland. For the SSJ, the solution was to intensify cultural outreach to migrants:

> At the end of the working week (Saturday and Sunday are by law free) our workers abroad begin to experience a psychological crisis. Most often, not knowing the language of the country in which they work, they are not able to use the available cultural goods. Puzzled as to how to use their free time, they often fall into a state of apathy or take refuge in gambling and drunkenness, because they are not offered any sort of more suitable entertainment. These psychological problems ... would be much attenuated if they were to regularly have access to Yugoslav press, books, journals, vinyl records, tapes, and national and popular music, etc.[59]

While some migrants were victims of social isolation, opening them up to manipulation by political emigrants, others were being assimilated into their host societies; both were "lost" to Yugoslavia. The Council for Emigrant Affairs of the Croatian republican government noted that workers were increasingly bringing their families to live with them in their host country, that mixed marriages were more frequent, and that some of these host countries – namely, Belgium, Sweden, and France – had adopted an assimilationist policy, while others were following suit. It added that those who were returning from abroad were once again leaving, as a result of their inability to find work in Yugoslavia.[60]

While ostensibly revealing and describing a major demographic, social, and economic crisis, the Institute for Migration and Nationality's 1966 study on labour migration was also shaped by the broader political crisis of the Croatian Spring. Zvonimir Komarica, an author of the study and also director of the Institute for Migration and Nationality, used the study to promote an alternative, nationalistic interpretation of labour migration that emphasized the predominantly Croatian identity of migrants, and their victimization by the Yugoslav federation – a discourse that also had proponents, in stronger terms, among émigré organizations. While Croatian reformist Communists such as Savka Dabčević-Kučar and Miko Tripalo intentionally avoided discourse that could be seen as antagonistic to the Yugoslav project, Komarica's framing echoed their arguments that the remittances of Croatian migrants should feed back into the Croatian economy.

One of many issues raised by the SKH as part of its larger effort to renegotiate Croatia's autonomy within the federation was its frustration with the current policy on foreign currency. Individuals and enterprises were allowed to keep only 7% of their foreign currency earnings and needed to exchange the remainder for convertible dinars, benefitting the large banks based in Belgrade. This frustrated not only Croatia's large and growing tourism industry and export sector, but also migrant workers and local governments in economically underdeveloped regions where labour migration was widespread. The SKH had been unable to convince the other republics to support Croatia in its bid to change this policy. Dabčević-Kučar argued in favour of the redefinition of Yugoslavism based on the real and meaningful equality between nations and nationalities. She also called for the withdrawal of the federation from the internal affairs of the republics, as the logical implication of self-management. Thus, the tenth session called for the renegotiation of relations between republics, and between Croatia and the federation.[61]

It was in this context that Zvonimir Komarica made interventions in the public sphere on the topic of labour migration. In November 1968 he published two articles in the insert for labour migrants in the popular Yugoslav weekly *Vjesnik u Srijedu*, in which he highlighted the over-representation of residents of Croatia and of ethnic Croats among labour migrants, which he argued was not compatible with socialism. This was followed in 1970 by a polemical work on labour migration entitled *Yugoslavia in Contemporary European Migrations*, largely based on the findings of the 1966 study, supplemented by data from two other sources – a study by the Federal Employment Office from the same period, and statistics from the diverse employment offices – to which he added his own estimates and conjecture. In this publication, Komarica advanced tendentious claims to build an argument that the misman-agement of Croatia's economy was responsible for Croatia's dispropor-tionate participation in labour migration.[62]

Komarica pointed out that, whereas it would be logical for the major-ity of migrants to come from underdeveloped territories, the contrary was true: the majority of workers came from Croatia, which with Slovenia had Yugoslavia's most developed economy. He argued that Croatia had suffered a serious shortfall in investment following the 1965 economic reforms, leading to high unemployment. This in turn had forced workers to seek work abroad, resulting in Croatia losing its most dynamic citizens and leading to a decrease in natural popula-tion growth. Worse still, labour migration had not been harnessed to stimulate the Croatian economy, creating jobs for returning migrants and stanching the bleed.[63] While Komarica was careful not to point the finger at those responsible, he essentially advanced an argument about Croatia's victimization within the federation. He then made this argu-ment more explicitly in a speech at Matica Hrvatska at the beginning of 1971, which was reprinted verbatim in the newspaper *Imotska krajina*, as discussed in chapter 5.

In his book, Komarica manipulated and interpreted data to support his argument. Thus, he suggested that 90% of Croatian labour migrants were in fact from urban areas, and distorted data to minimize the fact that a significant number of migrants were driven not by necessity but by the desire to improve their standard of living, a motivation that Komarica characterized as greed. It was hardly necessary to engage in such sophistry to make a case that labour migration was driven by eco-nomic stagnation, but Komarica was determined to portray Croatia and Croatian workers as victims.[64]

Under the guise of science, the data crunching was really meant to justify his policy recommendations for economic reforms, detailed in the last section of the book. In his words, "The reasons for migration being, as we have shown, economic, they can only be resolved by eco-nomic means and methods. And in our society, they are primarily in the sphere of the distribution of the national product and a selective investment policy."[65] Komarica ended with twenty-three recommendations on economic and migration policy. His third recommendation seemed to address most directly the predicament that he had depicted so vividly in his study – that far from benefitting from labour migration, Croatia continued to stagnate economically, leading to continuing waves of labour migration. Komarica urged policymakers to "take measures to ensure that the Croatian Republican Fund for Underdeveloped Territories and Croatian business banks dispose of foreign currency earnings that arrive in the Republic of Croatia."[66]

Komarica's book, speeches, and editorials are examples of a broader wave of recriminations focused on labour migration that gained traction in the Croatian national revival. At the third conference of the SKH, held on 5 and 6 October 1970, Savka Dabčević-Kučar acknowledged the salience of the issue of labour migration in discussions amongst delegates, while cautioning against ethno-nationalist interpretations that were circulating. Dabčević-Kučar noted that labour migration was indeed a critical problem, depriving Croatia of 12.8% of its active population, most of which did not return.

She did not argue in favour of eliminating opportunities to work abroad, seeing labour migration as an opportunity from an economic, scientific, cultural, and personal growth perspective – indeed, such a position would have gone against the SKH's liberalizing platform as well the aspirations of a significant number of Croatians. Rather, she proposed to increase possibilities for employment back in Yugoslavia, implement measures to retain skilled and highly skilled workers, manage employment abroad more effectively, and foster the maintenance of ties between workers and the homeland, "narrow" (Croatia) and "broad" (Yugoslavia). To increase employment opportunities, she advocated making it easier for migrants to invest their remittances in business banks, which then would invest in new jobs. She also tied the return of migrant workers to the SKH's broader program for economic reforms, meant to increase Croatia's competitiveness by decreasing regulation and redistribution. At the same time, she warned Croatian Communists that well-intentioned individuals had been seduced by the discourse promoted by enemies of Yugoslavia, according to which "socialist self-management has worsened Croatia's economic position, and a policy of biological extermination is being conducted against Croatia." Indeed, she argued that addressing the imbalances of labour migration would also benefit Yugoslavia as a whole.[67]

Contemporaneous research into migration also reflected this unsettling of ideas and call to rethink labour migration. Their previous survey having concluded that migrants were becoming alienated from the homeland, researchers at the Institute for Migration and Nationality conducted another large-scale survey-based study in 1970–1 to inquire into "conditions of return of our workers from temporary work abroad." The study was characterized by a greater curiosity about migrant motivations and opinions, eschewing earlier convictions about "our citizens abroad." No longer was it assumed that migrants would return of their own volition – the objective of the survey was to "obtain a concrete picture of the attitude of the respondents toward the socio-economic system in the country and abroad and of the phenomenon of migration, [identify] pull factors and necessary elements for return, and contribute to the proper formulation of a migration policy that is an integral part of the economic and development policy in our country."[68]

The research reflected a new awareness that people were changed by the experience of migration. Their hypothesis was that "motives of return are quantitatively and qualitatively different from motives of departure because of the changed socio-economic status of the respondents." Labour migrants would not be swayed to return merely with a job or higher pay, they speculated – they would "desire more." Using the abstruse language of self-management, they argued that migrants would want to "affirm themselves as social beings in their entirety, as subjects with a specific political consciousness," whose aspirations might be satisfied through the creation of opportunities in the social plan.[69] In other words, having climbed up Maslow's pyramid by satisfying their material needs, migrants would now aspire to self-realization.

This new understanding of, and respect for, migrants was in turn reflected in the design of the survey. The 1966 study had also collected data on the opinions and habits of migrants, but questions were either in multiple-choice format, or asked focused questions, such as "What would you rather read about in the newspaper?" or "What should be improved in the functioning of the Yugoslav consulate?" Moreover, as previously noted, the research subjects of the 1966 study were often treated with scorn as backward peasants incapable of intelligent answers. In contrast, the new study invited respondents to respond on their own terms through an open-ended question: "Under what circumstances would you return to the homeland?" The results of the survey are discussed at length in chapter 7 – what is important to note here is the evolution in thinking about migration by 1970. Previously defined as uneducated workers – surplus labour – driven exclusively by economic motivations and inevitably returning home, they were now understood to be complex individuals with complex motivations and attitudes who needed to be actively courted.

The Changing Face of Migration

At the height of Croatian nationalist agitation that sought (and ulti-mately failed) to reframe the way in which labour migration was under-stood, Yugoslavia carried out a census that revealed the changing face of labour migration. For the first time in history, Yugoslavia's adminis-tration decided to include workers temporarily employed abroad in the 1971 census, and to tabulate statistics on migrant workers separately. The 1971 census, while troubled by some of its own methodological challenges, provided a more rigorous snapshot of labour migration, five years after the Institute for Migration and Nationality collected its own data.

While this census was the first attempt to systematically collect data on migrant workers, and while it provided the first comprehensive pic-ture of the phenomenon of temporary labour migration, it presented significant flaws, which Ivo Baučić, who became a leading scholar on Yugoslav migrant workers, inventoried. Some problems, such as those related to collecting data about a population that is by definition absent, can be described as methodological problems. Census takers were obliged to rely on family members and neighbours, who did not necessarily have the most accurate information on hand. In Baučić's estimation, "Family members or neighbours who give information frequently do not know in what line of work or in what sector of the economy these workers were, let alone what they are doing and where they are living abroad." Another surprising blunder was the absence of a mechanism to collect data on family members who joined migrants in living abroad.[70]

Other shortcomings, however, were a direct consequence of the way in which labour migrants were officially defined as temporary. While this issue might appear technical at first glance, it had much to do with the narrative that the state told about labour migration. The term "temporary" was difficult to define, because it was too vague to fit the complex reality of the migration experience. What was the maximal length of temporary migration – was it still temporary if one had been away for more than five years? Given that we know that migrants con-stantly re-evaluated their return date, and that many never did return permanently, was "temporary" merely defined by intention? Did it apply to people who kept their Yugoslav citizenship, even if they never returned? Did it apply to those who were planning to return only after they retired? Could workers in overseas countries be "temporary" even if they were usually excluded from the category of "our workers tem-porarily abroad"? Would the poor economic conjecture in Yugoslavia in 1971 and associated lack of prospects for return have influenced responses?[71]

The instructions on this matter – which were never transmitted in written form to those carrying out the survey – indicated that the census-takers should rely on the opinion of the person giving the information about the migrant. On the surface this seems to have been quite liberal, in the sense that the state was inviting citizens to define themselves, or at very least, asking this of members of their household, instead of imposing a label on them. However, this flexibility was problematic in the context of a census, whose very utility is based on assigning fixed categories. Moreover, as Ivo Baučić noted in bold letters, "The people who give the data on workers abroad regularly are not in a position to evaluate the 'temporary' nature of their stay outside the country." A survey of the manner in which census-takers in the different Croatian municipalities (općine) interpreted temporary migration also disclosed that they relied on different interpretations of the concept. Baučić estimated that, as a consequence of these problems, the numbers of migrant workers were significantly underestimated in the census. This view was supported by the fact that the census figures were inferior to those reported by foreign countries in which migrants were employed. Thus, while the census counted some 671,908 Yugoslavs working abroad (in Europe and beyond), the official records of those states at the same time added up to 790,500. While the Yugoslav Federal Statistical Office might be reproached for sloppy methodology, the criteria for "temporariness" were nearly impossible to define. Baučić himself was only able to propose combining approximate indicators such as length of time abroad and family situation, which once again forced someone – the census-taker in this case – to make a subjective judgment.[72]

The census also glossed over the "messy" nature of migrant life in other ways. For example, the instructions indicated that, given that individuals might migrate for work on separate occasions, returning home in between, the date of their last departure should be given. Visits home didn't count. What was not clear, however, was whether, if a stint at home was sufficiently long, it counted as an interruption of work abroad. Baučić noted, "It is particularly unclear how census-takers dealt with seasonal work abroad, where they spend a part of the year in their place of residence in Yugoslavia. This is particularly characteristic of workers who work abroad in the construction industry, as many stop working a few months during the winter, and come home." Consequently, he warned, statistics regarding the year of departure for work abroad were not reliable.[73]

Given these limitations of the resulting data, some of which were due to the inherent problems in quantifying a population and the messiness of human existence, and some of which were a consequence of how the category "our citizens/workers abroad" was framed, how should the historian respond? As Francine Hirsch and others have shown, censuses are an opportunity to reflect on the categories that were employed, and the reasons for these categories. They were political projects – not only reflecting the preconceptions and assumptions held by political and scholarly elites, but also used to justify particular policies. Censuses are thus inherently interesting as instruments of what Scott has called "high Modernism."[74]

Yet the data themselves are also worth presenting, if we understand them as imperfect images of a real phenomenon, refracted through the unconsciously and intentionally warped lens of the state. In the different post-war censuses in Yugoslavia, for instance, citizens were offered different configurations of choices to denote ethnicity, language, and religion, in line with the evolution of Yugoslav nationality policy. Whereas Muslim was considered a religion and not an ethnicity in 1948, by 1961 it had been included in the category of ethnicity.[75] The state's invention in 1971 of the census category "worker temporarily employed abroad" is thus best understood as a political project and ideological category that glossed over a vexing temporality and fraught questions of motivations and loyalty.

Having accepted that the categories were themselves problematic, and that the numbers that carried with them the authority of state authority and scientific rigour were at best approximations, we can turn to the findings themselves. Baučić's study, based on the 1971 census, provides a fascinating array of tables analysing the census results. Beyond a few tables that focused on specific host states, it didn't differentiate between migrants to Europe and overseas, but it is still interesting to compare with the 1966 study, which allow commonalities and differences to come to the fore. This issue is also mitigated by the fact that over 80% of migrants were located in Europe.[76]

According to the census, the number of Yugoslavs working in Europe had reached 596,869, at a time when the total Yugoslav population numbered only slightly more than twenty million inhabitants. (Using figures provided by the host states, Baučić instead suggested the figure 647,000.) This meant that roughly 3% of the Yugoslav population was working abroad. Residents of Croatia were still disproportionately represented: 4.5% of the total population of Croatia was working in Europe, and they accounted for 31% of all migrants, a large proportion, although significantly less than the 53.2% claimed by the 1966 study.[77]

While these discrepancies might be attributable partly to the bias in that earlier study, it also reflected the changing face of labour migration.

A number of results were consistent with the findings of the 1967 survey, suggesting that, overall, the profile of the labour migrant had remained the same. The average age of workers had not changed significantly. Indeed, the census showed that an astonishing percentage of Yugoslav youth – somewhere between 9% and 12% of citizens between the ages of twenty and thirty-four – were working abroad.[78] The majority of migrants continued to have a low level of education. Ten per cent had not finished the first four years of elementary school (compared to 24.3% of the Yugoslav population over ten years of age), and 66% had completed only four to eight years of elementary school (compared to 57% of the Yugoslav population). However, it seems that a significant number of migrants with lower levels of education had received skills training: 61.1% of labour migrants had either been working as skilled or highly skilled workers, or had professional qualifications, prior to leaving Yugoslavia. This showed that Yugoslavia had not prevented skilled workers from leaving for greener pastures; the threat of a brain drain continued to loom. Over half had formerly worked in agriculture, similar to the results of the 1967 survey, while a further 31.5% had worked in industry or mining.[79]

Beyond the continuities, there were new trends. The proportion of women among labour migrants had increased since the 1960s, totalling 31.4%, which was nearly in line with the percentage of women among those employed in Yugoslavia (31.8%). In Sweden and Switzerland, they accounted for nearly 40% of all Yugoslav labour migrants.[80]

The census revealed that the proportion of migrants from the different Yugoslav republics varied widely from European state to state. Thus, while residents of Croatia dominated strongly in the FRG and Switzerland, residents of Serbia dominated in France, Austria, Sweden, and the Benelux countries. Residents of Croatia overwhelmingly chose to work in the FRG (67.7%). Residents of Bosnia Herzgovina, Slovenia, Vojvodina, and Kosovo also tended to go the FRG in much greater numbers than to any other European state. In Serbia, in contrast, only 35.5% of residents opted to go there, with 21.8% picking Austria, and 17.3% choosing France.[81]

Keeping in mind the previously mentioned problems in establishing the date of departure of migrants, the census also suggested an interesting trend in the relative proportion of migrants from each republic over time. Whereas residents of Croatia had made up more than half of all migrants who had left in 1963 or earlier, their proportion decreased for subsequent years. They made up only 24% of all migrants hired in

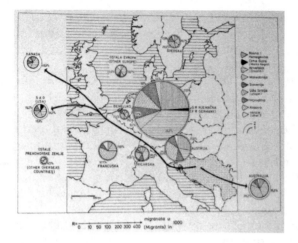

Figure 1. Share of the individual republics and autonomous provinces in the total number of Yugoslav workers in individual countries of employment (Baučić, *Radnici u inozemstvu*, 42–4)

1971, surpassed by migrants from Bosnia (28.3%) and Serbia and its provinces (33.5%, with Serbia proper accounting for 19.9%).[82]

Republics differed in the type of migrants they contributed to the overall pool. Seventy per cent of migrants from Bosnia-Herzegovina had previously practised agriculture, compared to half of all Yugoslav migrants. In contrast, Croatia and Serbia disproportionately contributed skilled professions such as chemists, physicists, and experts in transportation, technology, natural sciences, and health sciences. For example, Croatia contributed 37.3% of technology experts and 37.2% of health science experts (the figures were 31.2% and 30.3% for Serbia proper). In all likelihood, this partly reflected disparities in the occupational structures of these republics.[83]

Looking at ethnicity rather than residence, ethnic Croats constituted 39% of all labour migrants, followed by ethnic Serbs, who represented 28.5% of all migrants. Macedonians, Muslims, Slovenes, and Albanians each made up 5–7% each. Added together, Serbo-Croatian speakers made up nearly 75% of labour migrants. As Croats were 22% of the population of Yugoslavia, they were significantly over-presented. This over-representation applied to Croats both in Croatia and in Bosnia-Herzegovina. Indeed, Croats accounted for 42.3% of Bosnia's migrants, although it made up only 20.6% of its population.[84]

Table 2. Percentage of Migrants Abroad in Relation to Total Population, 1971 Census

	Municipality	Migrants abroad (%)	Republic or autonomous province
1	Imotski	18.6	Croatia
2	Ozalj	17.7	Croatia
3	Duvno	17.2	Bosnia-Herzegovina
4	Resen	16.0	Macedonia
5	Livno	15.4	Bosnia-Herzegovina
6	Čitluk	13.9	Bosnia-Herzegovina
7	Grude	12.9	Bosnia-Herzegovina
8	Lištica	12.4	Bosnia-Herzegovina
9	Lastovo	12.1	Croatia
10	Bitola	11.9	Macedonia

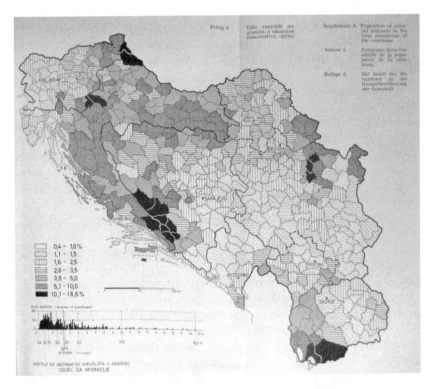

Figure 2. Proportion of external migrants in the total population of the commune (Baučić, *Radnici u inozemstvu*, appendix 6)

The census data also provided some much finer-grained data, show-ing how different *općine* or *opštine* (an administrative designation refer-ring to municipalities or to boroughs, depending on the location) had been disproportionately affected by labour migration. The largest num-bers of migrants had come from Zagreb, Croatia (25,831), then Bitola, Macedonia (13,415), and Čakovec, Croatia (11,856). Other municipali-ties, however, stood out in the percentage of migrants abroad in relation to total district population. Six of the top ten contributing municipalities were at the intersection of the Zagorje region of Croatia, the Trpopolje region in Bosnia, and northwestern Herzegovina.

In contrast, Slovenia dominated the rankings for municipalities in which persons with higher education, and skilled and very skilled labour dominated the pool of migrants. Thus, half of the top ten districts in this category were Slovene - in four districts from Ljubljana as well as Vrhnika, more than 64% of migrants fitted this description. Urban and regional centres such as Zagreb, Herceg Novi, Kotor, Rijeka, Niš, and several districts from Belgrade and Sarajevo also figured in the list of districts in which more than half the migrants were skilled and highly educated. There were also some surprising cases, such as the northern Adriatic island of Rab, where 4.5% of the population was employed abroad, of which 57% were skilled, very skilled, or highly educated.[85]

The 1971 survey confirmed assumptions about the character of labour migration – in particular, the over-representation of Croatia and of ethnic Croats, as well as the dominance of young, uneducated males from rural areas. But while it validated repeated generalizations about Yugoslav labour migration, it also revealed that migration was not homogeneous. Migrants from different Yugoslav republics were drawn to different West European states. Within each republic, different municipalities were affected to different degrees by migration. More-over, the census suggested that migration was changing in interesting ways, with women increasingly taking part, and Bosnia-Herzegovina and Serbia and its autonomous provinces representing a greater pro-portion of migrants than ever before. Educated migrants and skilled labour also represented a worrisome fraction of all migrants.

A later study by Baučić suggested that concerns that migrants were anchoring themselves more durably in Western Europe were well founded. By 1979, out of 1,080,000 Yugoslav citizens living in Europe, 390,000 were dependents. In some countries, the proportion of depen-dents was even larger – in France, for example, 42% of Yugoslavs liv-ing abroad were dependents, and in Sweden 49%. While this did not preclude migrants from returning to Yugoslavia with their families, it made it less likely, particularly since increasing numbers of children were growing up abroad without learning their parents' mother tongue. At the same time, starting in 1974, the numbers of migrants returning to Yugoslavia began to exceed the number leaving, leading Baučić to call it a "turning point." Whereas 150,000 Yugoslavs went to work abroad between 1974 and 1978, 315,000 returned. Thus, two parallel events were taking place: while significant numbers of migrants were returning home, others were bringing their families to live with them abroad, likely in response to the restriction of foreign labour visas that several Western European states adopted in the wake of the 1973 oil crisis and ensuing recession.[86]

As for Croatia's over-representation, it too was disappearing. According to the federal statistics office, Croatia's share in Yugoslavia's overall population living abroad (in Europe and overseas) had declined from 33.4% in 1971 to 24.3% in 1981. Serbia had not only caught up with Croatia, but even surpassed it, making up 24.5% of all migrants. Croatians living abroad had in fact decreased, from 224,722 in 1971, to 151,619 in 1981.[87]

Conclusion

Before the emergence of a labour migration policy, Yugoslav citizens sought to leave, legally or otherwise, to take advantage of the opportunities in Western Europe. Within Yugoslavia, authorities struggled to make sense of this migratory flow: Who were these people? And what were their motivations? In order to regain control over its population and govern it more effectively, Yugoslav authorities created the category "our workers temporarily employed abroad," defined as economic migrants who were expected to return within a few years. This category enabled authorities to legalize labour migration and harness it, primarily by mobilizing remittances in foreign currency. Labour migrants in Europe were to be treated as distinct from Yugoslav emigrants living abroad, in particular emigrants hostile to Yugoslavia.

As Ragazzi has pointed out, bureaucracy – or, more accurately, particularly in the Yugoslav context, bureaucracies – were important in giving form to the category "our workers temporarily employed abroad." The category itself was informed by a bureaucratic rationality: extraterritorial citizens who continued to interact with the state as loyal subjects. Bureaucracies collected information on migrants through employment offices, consular channels, and censuses, and on the basis of this knowledge, prescribed ways for migrants to interact with the authorities, and mediated those interactions. Beyond bureaucracies, other actors also produced knowledge about migrants – such as the Institute for

Migration and Nationality, which was a research institute, albeit one with the explicit mission to serve state interests.

The rigidity and inconsistencies of the category "our workers abroad" in some ways impeded and distorted the collection of information on migrants – leading, for example, to the discarding of information that was not consistent with assumptions, or the exclusion of subjects that did not correspond neatly. In spite of this "noise," by the late 1960s it was becoming apparent that the assumptions underpinning the category "our workers abroad" were flawed or incorrect, and that the category was an oversimplification that did not reflect the realities of migrants' lives. By 1968, experts warned that migrants were staying longer than anticipated, losing their ties to the homeland, and mingling with political emigrants. Knowledge production on migration redefined labour migration, no longer as an opportunity, but as a problem that needed to be addressed. This led to an intensification of programs that built relationships with migrant workers and created new ones, through appeals to workers' emotional ties to the homeland. Efforts included fostering the growth of Yugoslav workers' associations, promoting the dissemination of information through print media, radio-broadcasting, and new channels like the Cultural-Information Centres, and instituting a cross-border educational system – programs that are described in the second part of this volume.

Simultaneously, Croatian experts and political elites attempted to reinterpret labour migration as both a cause and symptom of Croatia's underdevelopment and exploitation by the federation. This alternative framing of labour migration as a problem also shaped migrant engagement programs. Ironically, because of Yugoslavia's federal nature, outreach to labour migrants was carried out to a large extent at the republican level, and to a lesser extent, at the local level. Consequently, the very strategies that had been used to foster ties with the Yugoslav federation could be subverted to mobilize migrants in support of alternative political projects, as happened during the Croatian Spring with the newspaper *Imotska krajina* (see chapter 5). Yet the results of the 1971 census, which were reinforced by later studies, highlight that this counter-narrative was itself an oversimplifcation of the complex reality of labour migration.

Governments and bureaucracies and their rivals rely on the collection of quantifiable data and its aggregation into statistics to make reality intelligible for the purpose of tailoring policies. The resulting knowledge, however, was dry and tended to rob the migrants that it purported to describe of their agency and humanity. Other stories were told about the experience of migration. As the next chapter will show, artists and film-makers produced poetic narratives about individuals and communities. These too relied partially on oversimplification and stereotyping, and tended to portray migrants as powerless. As chapters 4, 5, and 7 show, migrants themselves shared their own stories through letters and survey responses. While these sometimes reinforced these official and popular narratives, they also highlighted their personal agency and challenged binary ways of thinking about belonging.

3 Picturing Migrants: The *Gastarbajter* in Yugoslav Film

Governments, policymakers, and administrators saw migrants through the prism of statistics and graphs. They were abstractions: numbers, categories, desirable or undesirable characteristics, always considered in aggregate form. But this was only one way of seeing the *gastarbajteri*, as they were colloquially known – a Serbo-Croaticization of the German term *gastarbeiter*, or guest worker. Artists, film-makers, and Yugoslav public opinion saw migration very differently – they pictured individuals, families, and stories that spanned the European continent. Through their creations they simultaneously represented the migrant experience and interpreted its significance, often using it as a vehicle to critique social trends and policies. Film, in particular, provides a marvellous insight into how labour migrants were perceived by Yugoslav society. As the Yugoslav authorities recognized, it was the most accessible of all art forms, accessing a wide audience. As such, film both reflected common perceptions of labour migration and influenced them. Additionally, the audiovisual nature of the medium provides precision about how migrants were thought to look, behave, and sound, beyond that provided merely by the written word.

While some attention has been paid to media depictions of migration, the question of how migrants were seen and represented in Yugoslav artistic production has been limited to discussions of film plots by Ivanović and Bernard, and Nicholas Miller's exploration of Miodrad (Mića) Popović's paintings dealing with labour migration.[1] Before discussing film production, it is worth examining how migration was portrayed through a different medium. Interestingly, like several of the film-makers discussed in this chapter, Popović was also associated with the avant-garde New Film (*Novi Film*) movement, but it is through the plastic arts that he chose to deal with migration, producing paintings depicting scenes in the lives of labour migrants.

For Miller, Popović's work illustrates the trajectory of a larger circle of intellectuals whose optimism after the Second World War about the promise of communism was gradually replaced with disillusionment. His Gvozden cycle, inaugurated in 1971 and evolving through the 1970s, staged a series of snapshots from the life of the labour migrant Gvozden, whose name and likeness evoked a character from one of Popović's films – a young partisan in the film *Delije*. The paintings started out as part of the *Scenes* series, which was intended, according to Miller, to "unmask the myth that social equality had been achieved in a self-managed Yugoslavia."[2]

Popović's work echoes several themes that dominated representations of migrants in film, as discussed in the remainder of this study – in particular, social isolation, degradation, and alienation. His paintings, in dark and muted shades of black, blue, and brown, had a cinematic quality to them, as if they were stills from a film on Gvozden's wanderings. At the same time, they were more open-ended than the films discussed in this chapter, inviting the viewer to fill in the narrative. These scenes depict Gvozden as lonely and robbed of his dignity, showing him blowing his nose, sitting on the toilet, and peering through a window at prostitutes. His eerie paintings of Gvozden spending the night at the train station, walking along a train wagon with his suitcase, eating a sandwich while crossing the road, and sleeping barefoot on a park bench conveyed a sense of being adrift. He is perpetually in transit, "unsettled" – none of Popović's paintings show Gvozden at work or at home. According to Miller, only one of these paintings was overtly political, juxtaposing the tragic fate of Gvozden with a poster celebrating the workers' first of May holiday. Over time, Popović began to identify Gvozden and other migrants in his work as Serbs, lending an ethno-nationalist flavour to his social critique that was in line with the political evolution of dissent in Serbia at the time.[3]

Filmic representations of labour migration echo one aspect of Miller's argument, that portraying migration was a way to comment on the failures of state socialism. Labour migration was a ubiquitous theme in film, because it seemed to capture key tensions at the heart of the Yugoslav project: socialism and capitalism (and consumerist hedonism, in particular), modernization and backwardness, modernity and tradition, cosmopolitanism and rootedness. Migration stories featured in a wide range of film, ranging from state propaganda, documentary shorts, and fictional shorts to full-length features. This last category included commercial productions intended for wide release and arthouse *films d'auteur*, comedies, and dramas. This chapter is based on the analysis of

Figure 3. Mića Popović.
Čekaonica 2. razred

thirty films produced between 1968 and 1984. This is not an exhaustive list – I am aware of several more that are no longer available for viewing, and a few have inevitably escaped my attention. These films told the migrants' individual stories – sometimes hopeful, sometimes comical, but almost always tinged with tragedy. As a whole, they presented a highly critical vision of the impact of labour migration and a deeply moving lament on the intertwined fates of labour migrants and their families and villages.

As Radina Vučetić has argued, and Aleksandar Petrović has illustrated in a two-volume memoir that is somewhat closer to a scrapbook, the relationship between the Yugoslav state and party on the one hand, and the artistic community on the other hand, was complicated and evolving. Whereas in the 1960s, the party tolerated a high degree of pluralism and experimentation, the 1968 student protests and worries about the rise of Croatian and Serbian nationalism resulted in intensified censorship, starting in the early 1970s. As a result, many innovative and provocative film-makers were prevented from working in the republics in which they were based, or forced to leave Yugoslavia altogether.[4]

What are we to make, then, of the enormous production of representations of labour migrants, often highly critical of the impact of Yugoslavia's labour migration policy? On the one hand, the ubiquity of labour migration as a theme suggests that it was an accepted topic, no matter how caustically films portrayed labour migration policy. This in turn raises the following question: if the state and party did not perceive these films as undermining its legitimacy, why should we? Indeed, for Vučetić, what most damaged the party's legitimacy was its recourse to censorship. If that is the case, then the party's willingness to allow debate over labour migration surely was to its credit.

At the same time, the persistent attention to this theme paid by prominent film-makers associated with New Film should give pause. Rather than a cohesive group with a coherent agenda, Yugoslav New Film can be described as a broader change in orientation amongst young film-makers, who saw film as a vehicle to promote democratization and engage with the social and ethical problems facing Yugoslav society, which emerged in the mid-1960s, in the same moment of political relaxation that produced Yugoslavia's open border policy. New Film – also known as Black Wave Cinema (*Crni talas*) – has traditionally been understood as the first truly critical and autonomous Yugoslav film movement, contrasting both with patriotic films celebrating the exploits of the partisans during the Second World War, and more commercial fare, which had no real ideological content but aimed primarily to entertain. In reality, New Film-makers were a heterogeneous bunch with varied approaches and objectives. In a discussion on New Film at the 1967 edition of the Pula film festival – Yugoslavia's most prestigious film event, theatre critic Lado Kralj argued that film needed to "show reality as it really is," while film theorist Dušan Stojanović thought it should "replace one mythology with a multitude of mythologies." As Pavle Levi has shown, New Film's tendency to experiment with form was intrinsically linked to the project of democratizing society by disrupting entrenched practices of didactic and dogmatic storytelling.[5]

The directors with a background in New Film who made films dealing with labour migration – Živojin (Žika) Pavlović, Želimir Žilnik, and Dušan Makavejev – did so after New Film waned in 1972. One exception is Krsto Papić, whose first films on migration date from 1968 and 1972, but these were documentary films, which film scholars do not usually consider as part of New Film. Nonetheless, their depictions of migrants and migration were meant to be provocative, whether we are talking about Papić's scathing critique of Yugoslav migration policy, Pavlović's rumination on the tragic consequences of migration on rural households, or Žilnik's explorations of the migrant as a misfit on the margins of society in Yugoslavia and abroad. Later film-makers with a similar affinity for provocation shared this interest in migration as a topos for social and political critique, such as Karolj Viček.

Film-makers who were less experimental and provocative and more commercially oriented, such as Nikola Babić, Aleksandar Đorđević, Goran Paskaljević, Dragoslav Lazić, Aleksandar Petković, and Bogdan

Žižić, were equally drawn to the figure of the migrant. For some, the migrant was a convenient stereotype that helped move the plot along, like the criminal in *Košava* or the gigolo in *Avanture Borivoja Šurdilovića*. However, a number of commercially successful films also tackled the topic of labour migration head on. These films can also be understood not just as compelling storytelling but as social critique and commentary, and they were understood as such by film reviewers.[6] Obviously, these films lacked overt political messages. Insofar as someone was responsible for the "problem" of labour migration, it was the migrants themselves. At the same time, these films were screened in a society where labour migration had already been politicized, as in the case of the Croatian Spring.

This chapter begins by examining a subset of film-makers who repeatedly returned to the theme of labour migration, with a focus on two Novi Film directors, Krsto Papić and Želimir Žilnik, and one mainstream director, Bogdan Žižić. Here the focus is on discerning what labour migration meant to them. Although they wrestled with the subject for different reasons, they all saw the labour migrant as a site or topos for examining the contradictions at the heart of socialist Yugoslavia. The second part of the chapter considers the corpus of films that deal with labour migration as a whole, drawing out some recurring themes. While some films caricatured labour migrants as fools and agents of corruption, ridiculous or threatening to Yugoslav society, more commonly films called into question the promises of socialist modernization, highlighting the state's failure to bring prosperity to the countryside, condemning migrants to a lifetime of exile and misery, with often tragic consequences.[7]

Bernard has argued that, while early productions featured sympathetic portrayals, later films depicted *gastarbajteri* as "perpetrators of injustice and crime," an evolution that she attributes to the intensification of return migration and to the "rupture of the fragile equilibrium between Yugoslav supranational and ethno-national identity promoted by the federation since the 1960s."[8] While acknowledging a trend towards more negative representations of migrants, this chapter notes that many critical portrayals were also, paradoxically, empathetic. While some films expressed anxiety about the *gastarbajteri* and relied on facile stereotypes, others commented on the failures of the socialist modernization project.

Wrestling with Migration: Papić, Žižić, and Žilnik

Like Mića Popović, a number of significant Yugoslav film-makers returned to the topic of labour migration more than once, including

Krsto Papić, Rudolf Sremec, and Bogdan Žižić, based in Croatia, and Goran Paskaljević and Želimir Žilnik, based in Serbia. Fascinatingly, all of these film-makers arrived at the topic of labour migration through documentary film, with the exception of Žižić, who eventually turned to documentary film. Nikola Babić, who made only one film on the topic, *Ludi Dani* (1977), also developed his inspiration for the film while making documentaries on the Dalmatian Zagora region, which was heavily affected by migration. The documentarian's gaze, then, was critical in shaping representations of labour migration. The resulting films sought to document and dramatize stories that actually happened, in the places where they happened, in the words and personas of those who experienced them. This sensibility subsequently carried over into these film-makers' fictional films.

The personal circumstances and visions of individual film-makers also shaped their treatment of migration. Most film-makers, with Krsto Papić and Bogdan Žižić as two prominent examples, were interested in migrants from a Yugoslav (or even narrowly Croatian) perspective, often portraying them as victims and migration as a problem to address. Želimir Žilnik, in contrast, had a more open-ended, ambivalent relationship with migrants, potentially seeing his own fate as a film-maker in exile reflected in theirs.

Krsto Papić was one of the first to broach the topic of labour migration, with his artful short film *Halo München* (1968). Ostensibly a documentary, it featured a schoolhouse scene that was almost certainly staged, revealing Papić's predilection for conveying authenticity through naturalistic cinéma verité cinematography. Shot in black-and-white, the film eschewed voice-overs for a series of panoramas and close-ups that highlighted the contrast between the old and the new: the peasant trying to use the telephone at the post office; traditional dress juxtaposed with fedoras and tweed jackets from Germany; donkeys next to automobiles; the marketplace where cattle are sold next to vinyl records; the Virgin Mary and the Yugoslav flag. The contrasts were striking rather than jarring or distressing. *Halo München* framed labour migration as a continuation of an age-old practice of bringing income to a barren region.

By 1972, Papić's gaze had changed, likely influenced by his own experiences and the demoralization that followed the Croatian Spring. Papić was increasingly attracting the negative attentions of authorities threatened by what they perceived to be a critical and nihilistic "black wave" in Yugoslav cinema. His film *Lisice* (1969) had won the golden Arena at the Pula film festival, but Yugoslav authorities prevented it from being shown at Cannes, where it had been put on the official program. Although it shared many attributes of his earlier film on the topic, including cinéma verité techniques, the use of black-and-white, an affection for close-ups, and focus on contrasts, his documentary short *Specijalni Vlakovi* (1972) cast a much more critical light on labour migration.

Specijalni Vlakovi focused on the journey of migrants who had signed up for work abroad at the employment offices, through their arrival in Munich. The contrast here was not between tradition and modernity, but between the powerlessness of the migrants and the power of the officials, both Yugoslav and German, who controlled their fate. German power manifested in ways reminiscent of the Nazis, as illustrated in a humiliating scene where a German doctor issues verbal orders to a worker clad only in his underwear, to establish his fitness for employment. The Holocaust was also evoked in the use of the term "special train" – ominously echoing the Holocaust – and the way in which the migrant workers are herded into a dark, unwelcoming bunker upon their arrival in Munich, and addressed as numbers, rather than names, over the sound system. If Germany's quest for world hegemony had officially been quashed in 1945, it clearly persisted, Papić suggested, through its domination of the European economy in the boom years.

Yugoslav complicity was illustrated by the conspicuous consumption of civil servants involved in administering the labour migration program – in particular, an employee charged by the employment office with accompanying the special train to Munich. As the character drones on about his role, Papić's unsparing camera zooms in on his sunglasses, the ring on his finger, and the pipe on which he is puffing, all ostentatious symbols of his material success. The smug civil servant clashed eloquently with emotional scenes in the train compartments, in which individual migrants tearfully explain their desperate job situations and the decision they have been forced to make to leave their loved ones. Without abandoning the conceit of being a "fly on the wall," *Specijalni Vlakovi* engaged in editorializing, suggesting that, not only was the Yugoslav state conspiring with Germany to send its own citizens into slavery, it was also profiting from them.

Perhaps because he was the cinematic poet of the Dalmatian Zagora, which was strongly affected by labour migration, Papić returned several times to the topic. He made two other documentaries, *O strancima u Francuskoj* (1970), which predated *Specijalni Vlakovi* and focused on Turkish migrant workers in France, and *Charter Let Broj* (1975), which followed four women who left Croatia to marry economic emigrants in Australia. The figure of the labour migrant also appeared in his feature films *Priča iz Hrvatske* (1991) and *Kad mrtvi zapjevaju* (1998).

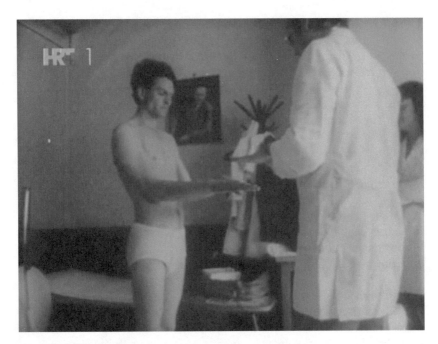

Figure 4. The labour migrant undergoes a humiliating physical examination in German, in his underwear (Papić, *Specijalni Vlakovi*)

Figure 5. Papić highlighted the ostentation of the Yugoslav civil servant accompanying the "special trains" (Papić, *Specijalni Vlakovi*)

The latter two films engaged with migrant return and the breakdown of Yugoslavia. In *Priča iz Hrvatske*, a father and son must leave Croatia in the wake of the Croatian Spring as a result of political repression and job loss. Their return coincides with Tito's death and a renewal of repression and political conflict. The protagonists in *Kad mrtvi zapjevaju* are returning labour migrants who stumble into the attack by the Yugoslav People's Army on Croatia following its declaration of independence.

On the surface, Bogdan Žižić's films had a good deal in common with Krsto Papić's *Specijalni Vlakovi*, in that they focused on the high cost of labour migration. Unlike Papić, however, Žižić focused on the negative impact of living abroad, rather than on the policies that enabled and even promoted labour migration. His films were accessible, even melodramatic, without formulating an explicit critique of the Yugoslav authorities. This approach contributed to his films' wide distribution and popular success, and allowed him to avoid problems with the authorities.

Like *Specijalni Vlakovi*, his first film on the topic, *Nož* (1974), a taut short film that straddled the line between comedy and drama, took place on a train between the FRG and Yugoslavia. It featured a crazed *gastarbajter* – whether he was insane to begin with, or driven mad by life abroad and drink is unclear. Dressed in characteristic flashy labour migrant apparel, he loudly brags about his adventures in Germany and intimidates and harasses his fellow passengers. Having pulled out an enormous knife to show off, he suddenly begins to terrorize the other passengers with it. Ultimately, a train policeman arrives and attempts to wrestle the knife from his hand. The film ends with the deranged migrant smashing the train window, jumping through it, and running away, only to be shot dead. Rather than an explicit effort to reflect on labour migration, this film used the figure of a migrant as a plot device, playing up popular stereotypes of migrants as morally questionable adventurers obsessed with conspicuous consumption.

Žižić showed a more meaningful engagement with labour migration in the feature-length film *Ne naginji se van* (1977), which was inspired by his conversations with migrant and artist Dragutin (Drago) Trumbetaš, himself the subject of Žižić's documentary short *Gastarbajter Trumbetaš* (1977). The documentary explored the daily life and tribulations of the labour migrant through close pans of Trumbetaš's drawings, onto which he superimposed audio recordings of the places and activities that were depicted, interspersed with similar live action scenes from West Germany.

Figure 6. The flamboyant and deranged migrant threatening his fellow passengers (Bogdan Žižić, *Nož*)

The drawings featured in the documentary film are representative of his overall oeuvre. Though often categorized as "naive art," his style was in fact characterized by biting, satirical humour. One drawing featured in the film depicts an endless column of migrants with suitcases, all walking in the same direction, while another shows them crowded into the hallway of a German administrative building. Yet another shows migrants at work on a construction site, surrounded by graffiti insulting them, and signs for businesses that profit from them. One particularly tragic drawing depicts a migrant killed in a car accident, with the bitter title "One fewer." Trumbetaš and Žižić pull no punches in highlighting the xenophobia of West German society.

The majority of his drawings depict migrants in their free time, at home in barracks shared with room-mates from other countries, in their rented rooms, in apartment building hallways, in public spaces during their free time. They play on the contrast between the flashy prosperity

Figure 7. Drago Trumbetaš depicted migrants in their modest living quarters. Dragutin Trumbetaš, *Gastarbeiter Gedichte 1969–1980* (Velika Gorice: Turopolja, 1995), 13.

of West German public space and the modesty of the migrant's every-day life. Like Popović's paintings, his art does not shy away from vulgarity, depicting migrants having sex with prostitutes, passed out drunk, and urinating. While it can be shocking, his work is also deeply empathetic, the work of someone who knew labour migration first-hand and depicted migrants as profoundly human and vulnerable. Through his film, Žižić sought less to tell his own story than to give a platform to Trumbetaš. His deliberate camerawork invites the viewer

Figure 8. An entrepreneur selling *burek*, the typical Yugoslav meat or cheese pastry, finds customers on the worksite in Germany in one of Trumbetaš's lively scenes. Trumbetaš, *Gastarbeiter Gedichte*, 71.

to dwell on colourful details and to spend a moment in the shoes of a migrant worker.

In contrast, *Ne Naginji se Van* (Don't lean out the window, 1977), which won the Golden Arena at the Pula Film Festival, was in Žizić's characteristic voice. A quintessential quest narrative, the film follows a young man from the Zagora region, Filip, as he strikes out on a journey to West Germany to make his fortune, in the footsteps of an older fellow villager, Mate, who has seduced him by flaunting his material prosperity during a visit home. Ultimately, Filip comes to realize that Mate was lying and that this prosperity was illusory. The young man is exploited by a ring of Yugoslav human traffickers, who confiscate his passport in exchange for dangerous work and miserable living conditions. Having witnessed the despair of other migrants, even to the point of suicide, he sinks into depression himself. Filip eventually realizes that he has no future in Germany and that the greatest threat is in fact the loss of his tie to the ancestral lands. He accompanies Mate's casket back to their home village. The customs list reveals that Mate left his wife very little. *Ne naginji se van* was a heavy-handed moral tale illustrating the perils of materialism. In this story, migrants were either frauds and thugs or naive young people seduced by Western consumerism.

Žižić returned to the topic again with *Rani Snijeg u Münchenu*. In an interview, he explained that the box office success of *Ne naginji se van* had motivated Jadran film to make another film on the same topic.[9] Although this film offered a less simplistic depiction of migrants' motivations, it was ultimately still a tale about the destructive impact of labour migration on the family and loss of identity. In particular, he was interested in exploring the generational conflict between a father who sacrificed his life to build a house and automotive garage back home for his son Ivica, and Ivica who feels more German than Yugoslav, in spite of the fact that the Germans do not consider him as one of their own. Ultimately, Ivica's choice to break ties with his father and Yugoslavia results in tragedy, with his father committing suicide. While this film was mainly a commentary on the idea of alienation from the homeland, it acknowledged the different circumstances of the second generation, who never had an attachment to Yugoslavia. The central protagonist, Ivica, stood up to his father and married the girl of his dreams, a German. In the final scene, however, he stands in his parents' apartment wearing his father's overcoat, having just discovered his body, and peers through the window at his wife and friend frolicking in the snow, evoking the impossibility of ever fully belonging to their world.

Like Krsto Papić, Želimir Žilnik had attracted the ire of Yugoslav authorities and identified with the "Black Wave" because of his provocative films dealing with unemployment, poverty, and homelessness, and politically charged issues like the Prague invasion and the 1968 student uprising in Belgrade. Finding it increasingly difficult to make films in Yugoslavia, he moved to Germany in the mid-1970s, where he continued to make films. As Ewa Mazierska has noted, although in some ways a political exile in Germany, he now trained his critical eye on German society.[10] Always drawn to those living on the margins of society, he became intensely interested in labour migration and realized a number of films on the topic. His films suggest that Žilnik in some ways identified with the figure of the labour migrant, being forced by circumstances in Yugoslavia to pursue his work abroad.

Žilnik's later films on migration reflect this sensibility: he found migrants interesting as individuals, rather than as Yugoslavs or members of some other group. He was attracted to exploring the subjectivity of the migrant, instead of using them to make a point about Yugoslav society. For example, in *Inventur – Metzstrasse 11* (1975), Žilnik had the inhabitants of one German apartment building file down the stairs and say a few words about themselves. The diversity of the inhabitants is striking, featuring migrants from Italy, Greece, Turkey, and Yugoslavia, as well as a German woman. The film was unscripted, which not only allowed the participants to have some agency in how they portray themselves, but also eschewed an overarching narrative. At the same time, the migrants struggle to express themselves in German, highlighting the limitations of their agency within German society. Žilnik made a number of other documentary shorts exploring migrants' lives on the margins of German society, including *Request* (1974), *Protected Heritage* (1975), *House Orders* (1975), and *Farewell* (1976).

Like Žižić, Žilnik also directed a feature-length fictional film on the second generation, *Druga Generacija* (1984), based on material from his documentary film *Prvo tromesečje Pavla Hromiša* (1983.) In contrast to Žižić's film, however, this was less didactic and more open-ended – closer in this sense to Popović's Gvozden cycle. The narrative focuses on fifteen-year-old Pavle, who decides to leave Stuttgart, where he has spent most of his life but where he feels he has no future. He goes to live with his grandmother in rural Vojvodina and registers at the local school. Confronted with a very different schooling system and way of life, he feels out of place and decides to return to Stuttgart. Once there, however, his mother informs him that he must return to Yugoslavia. This is a real crisis moment for Pavle – "I fit neither here nor there," he complains.

Upon his return, he attends a boarding school with other young migrant offspring. Finally, Pavle seems to have found a group of people, misfits like him, with whom he can relate. Together, they compare the values and cultures of their various host societies and Yugoslavia. But Pavle is at heart a reckless adventurer, and he gets into trouble after helping a friend steal and wreck a glider from his friend's parents. Pavle says that he's sick of crossing borders and decides to stay in Yugoslavia, enrolling in a military high school without telling his parents. Žilnik seems to imply that what Pavle really craves is structure and discipline, or perhaps even the opportunity to give up his identity as an individual by becoming a soldier.

Unlike Ivica in *Rani Snijeg u Münchenu* and the characters in other films, Pavle has a complex personality and relationship both to Yugoslavia and his host country. He does not have a stable identity – not only does he not clearly identify as German or Yugoslav, but his grandmother belongs to the Rusyn minority. His efforts to tell simple stories to himself – that he will be happy in Yugoslavia or that he can sever ties with Yugoslavia – end in disappointment. Ultimately, Pavle is forced to accept that he belongs to both worlds, and at the same time to neither. He is forced to grapple with the value systems of both societies, without having the luxury of idealizing one or the other. Moreover, Žilnik leaves us with no question that Pavle is an actor with agency – he makes his own choices, and has to pay the consequences. He cannot blame either Yugoslavia or Germany for his adolescent mistakes.

The Documentarist Gaze

As noted above, Yugoslav cinema first came to the theme of the labour migration by way of the documentary film. A remarkable number of short documentaries were produced on labour migration, particularly between 1971 and 1975, and several are recorded as having inspired fictional films. These shorts explored a variety of topics, including the living and working conditions of the migrant workers abroad, journeys to and from their home village, and the impact of their absence on the home village. The image of the labour migrant that they constructed was largely of a young, male, uneducated villager who worked in an industrial setting in Germany. The focus on the "archetypal migrant" tended to obscure the real diversity of migrant experiences, leaving out women, those who worked in the service sector, and those who were highly educated and from urban settings.

The documentary impulse manifested itself in a desire to authentically portray migrants, and in some cases to give a voice not only to the migrants but also to their families. Aside from *Specijalni Vlakovi*, Miroslav Mikuljan's *Za poslom* (1971) sought to provide insight into the migrants' character and motivations by intercepting them prior to their departures at the Zagreb train station to ask them questions about their lives and ambitions. In *Za poslom*, migrants expressed their aspirations for a better standard of living, as well as their preference for staying in

Yugoslavia, if only there was work, a theme that would be reiterated in most other documentary films.

As we have seen with Žižić and Žilnik, documentarists were equally curious about the migrants' lives once they arrived at their destination. In *Stranac* (1974), Rudolf Sremec focused attention on the estrangement of the migrants' offspring from their homeland. He trained his camera on the mother tongue courses that the Yugoslav state financed in collaboration with the German state, which were supposed to maintain the connection with Yugoslavia. The children, many of whom had been born and grew up abroad, did not learn the language well and preferred to learn other languages. Like Žilnik's later films on Pavle Hromiš, this film raised the spectre of a generation of Yugoslav citizens who were alienated from their culture and national identity.

Several documentaries focused on the migrants' return home during holidays, often in the Dalmatian Zagora region. Representations of holiday celebrations in such films as *Halo München, Jugo moja* (Milutin Kosovac, 1973), and *Dernek* (Zoran Tadić, 1975) focused on the stark contrast between the men with their Western hairstyles, accoutrements, and automobiles, and rural landscapes, villages without paved roads, and their female and elderly populations dressed in peasant clothing. Even the men themselves seemed to embody this contradiction, participating in archaic traditions like the *ganga* (improvisational folkloric singing), *šijanje* (a game of chance) and rock-throwing contests. This was a fleeting encounter between two very different worlds, West and East; the world of work, which took place outside of Yugoslavia, and the world of family, which migrants left behind. Even if the men brought the trappings of modernity with them to the village for an enchanted week or month, they would soon disappear.

It is on this absence that other films, including *Cijeli život* (Rudolf Sremec, 1975), *Zemljo primi me* (Rudolf Sremec, 1972), *Teret* (Goran Paskaljević, 1974), and *Na objedu* (Vafik Hadžismaljović, 1972), chose to focus. *Teret* featured interviews with children who have been forced to take over running the family homestead in the absence of their parents, as well as an elderly couple who had to take the responsibility of raising their daughter's infant. *Cijeli život* and *Na objedu* (Vafik Hadžismaljović, 1972) similarly focused on the weighty absence of the migrants. While both films captured the deep emotional suffering of the migrants' children and parents, *Na objedu* also took up the matter of *gastarbajters* who had died abroad, presumably on the worksite. For the widows and children of these men, both the absence and the grief that accompanied it had become permanent. While all these films conveyed the economic underdevelopment that fuelled labour migration, *Zemljo primi me* addressed it explicitly, highlighting the absence of electricity and the impossibility of hiring migrant workers in the Drniš municipality, a situation bleakly qualified as "inescapable."

A very few documentary films presented an explicitly positive picture of labour migration. *Jugo Moja* was financed by the Employment Office of Bosnia-Herzegovina, the Republican Union of Retirement and Disability Pensions, and Privredna bank, suggesting that its goal was explicitly to promote state policy. This documentary short by Milutin Kosovac portrayed the migrants' return during the winter holidays, a festive occasion for spending their earnings, distributing consumer goods procured abroad, socializing, getting married, and procreating. While the film highlighted the workers' reluctance to leave and their families' sadness, the film overall painted a joyful picture. Božidar Rančić's films are similarly optimistic. His first documentary short, *Radnik Evrope* (1974), showed a cross-section of workers in the FRG at work, at home, and exercising their rights as workers. The film framed Yugoslavia's migrant workers as part of a broader European phenomenon, and emphasized their working-class identities and the solidarity between workers in the FRG. His second film on the topic, *Mirko i Manfred* (1975), developed these themes through the stories of two families. Mirko was a labour migrant who had saved enough to return home to Cista Velika, in the Zagora region, where he had built a motel incongruously shaped like a boat. Manfred, in contrast, was a German plumber who married a Yugoslav from the same region (a woman much like Mirko's own daughters) and opted to move his family to his wife's home town.

In these films, labour migration not only helped migrants to achieve their goals, it also allowed Yugoslavs to strengthen international workers' solidarity. *Jugo moja* and *Radnik Evrope* both end on the optimistic note that the creation of workplaces in Yugoslavia will allow workers to return once and for all. *Radnik Evrope* also emphasizes the temporariness of the absence by evoking the proximity of realizing the goal of building one's home, and commenting, against the backdrop of teary-eyed reunions at a train station: "Perhaps they'll stay at home this time, as it's hard to leave." But, as *Cijeli život* poignantly emphasized, this was not a real choice for most migrants: in this film, a child listens to a message recorded for him by his parents. They hope to return, they say, perhaps in three years' time. That moment when it was time to return seemed remarkably elusive. In the majority of documentary films, rather than a passing phase or opportunity, migration was a strategy for survival, an obligation that carried a very heavy toll.

Labour Migration in Fictional Film

Whereas the documentary genre's claims to authenticity allowed it to tell powerful stories about migrants, narrative film allowed film-makers to fully develop themes first identified in documentary film, such as home-sickness, disappointed aspirations, dislocation, and loss. Many brought to their films the documentarist's sensibility and methods. Some, like Nikola Babić, grounded their characters in the experiences of migrants, drawing from interviews, anecdotes, and observation, even consulting scientific work on the subject.[11] This raw material was then shaped by popular beliefs about migrants and the film-makers' own imagination.

Labour migrants were compelling characters, simultaneously insiders and outsiders. They embodied a kind of modernity through their contact with Western European society, but social critics wondered if this was the kind of modernity to which Yugoslavia should aspire. While they might earn respect for their material success, that success was also suspect, as it seemed to conflict with key elements of the socialist ideology that permeated Yugoslav society, such as egalitarianism, a suspicion of conspicuous consumption, a commitment to building socialism, and patriotism. That prosperity was also suspect because it seemed to make no meaningful difference to the pervasive poverty at the root of migration. Was the migrant a success story or a victim?

Some films presented migrants as stereotypes, whereas others sought to engage with them as complex individuals. In their storytelling, they fleshed out the dramatic personas of migrants, exploring their psychological universe, as well as their relationships with their families, compatriots, and members of the host society. Ultimately, representations of migrants can be distilled to a few stereotypes that spoke to the migrants' fraught relationship with the Yugoslav body politic, and more specifically their status as outsiders: the migrant as social disease, as laughingstock, and as victim. These figures were used to tell a particular story, about the failure of the socialist modernization project.

Interestingly, while documentaries had tended to cast labour migrants in a sympathetic light, the first film-makers to include *gastarbajters* as central characters in their films tended portray them either as dangers to Yugoslav society or as manifestations of a crisis of Yugoslav society. This is the case with Bogdan Žižić's films *Nož* (1974) and *Ne Naginji se van*, Vuk Babić's feature-length film *Breme* (1972), and Žika Pavlović's *Let mrtve ptice* (1973). The archetype of the *gastarbajter* as a social disease reached its most exaggerated form in a later film, Karolj Viček's critically panned *Zalazak sunca* (1982).

While in *Nož Žižić* took the figure of the mentally troubled migrant and turned him into a sociopathic threat to Yugoslav society, in *Naginji se van* he used the figure of the flashy migrant, embodied by the character Mate, and the leitmotif of the return to the village. Abandoning comedy for tragedy, he portrayed the migrant as having a nefarious influence on his fellow countryfolk. Vuk Babić, Pavlović, and Viček created similar migrant characters – greedy, hedonistic show-offs who shatter the fragile balance in their villages and hometowns, promoting corruption or driving locals to desperate measures. To a certain extent, these films exuded an implicit critique of the Yugoslav modernization project by highlighting the failure of the promise of socialist modernization, but the subversive potential of that critique was diminished by the pathologizing of the migrant, portrayed as an agent of corruption.

In *Breme*, or "the burden," the labour migrant acts as a catalyst for the tragedy waiting to unfold. His reappearance triggers a psychological crisis in the main protagonist, a shiftless young man who does not seem to belong anywhere. He feels as if his colleagues make fun of him at work, and he fights with his brother because he does not want to take care of the small family farm, but does not want to relinquish his right to it. In love with a young woman in the village, he cannot act on his affections because he cannot promise her a good life. The entire village seems frozen in time, the inhabitants tending the land as they have for centuries. Suddenly a former friend returns from a two-year stint in Europe and shows off the fruits of his labour: a fancy car and a variety of consumer goods. He explains that he has returned to amuse himself. The impressionable young man joins him in drunken revelry. When his love interest explains that she is leaving for Australia to try her fortune as well, he decides to end it all and hangs himself with a cattle whip.

Breme combined the story of the labour migrant with a broader commentary on Yugoslavia's inability to bring prosperity to its countryside. The central character of the story and his village already had no future, left behind in the dust of Yugoslavia's supposed modernization. The migrant's arrival merely shines a harsh light on the ugly reality and hopeless future of life in the village. While some take their cue and tearfully leave their homeland, others are driven deeper into despair.

Steva or "Beli Konj" (White Horse), Viček's migrant in *Zalazak sunca*, based on Nandor Gion's novel *My Brother Job*, has much in common with the unsavoury character from *Breme*. He too makes a dramatic entrance in a Mercedes-Benz, gleaming against the brown tones of the Vojvodina winter. He has come home from Germany not only to amuse himself, but more importantly to show off his success to his admiring former classmates. Konj's old stomping ground is the town of Kerubin, which bears a striking resemblance to Novi Sad. Yet, even in an urban setting, Konj's arrival sends shockwaves through the community.

While Babić used the figure of the migrant to highlight the stagnation of the village, Viček uses him to explore the webs of corruption in late socialist Yugoslavia. We learn that Konj has been spreading corruption in Kerubin even while living abroad, taking advantage of the venality of local politicians and businessmen. One film critic's summary of the plot illustrates how the migrants' status as go-betweens had acquired powerfully negative connotations: "He has brought the first whisky to his home town, smuggled the first Mercedes, regularly provided foreign currency to local officials, put money in foreign banks. White Horse has come back for a final settling of accounts. For his earlier services he wants everything: power, women, recognition, prestige."[12] Konj convinces the town president to allow him to open a café and gentleman's club in the city hall building by promising to invest foreign currency. In turn, the president expects him to help him buy new machinery from Germany to revive the ailing local economy. As the plot unfolds, a local factory is burned down, a local tavern trashed, a historic landmark defiled, and scarce resources embezzled. If the scheme ultimately fails, it is not because it is discovered, but because Konj's arrogance upsets the local hierarchies of power. Like the protagonist of *Nož*, Konj dies, a victim of his own hubris, a victim of a car bomb.

Konj is, in some ways, a symptom of the general decay of socialist Yugoslavia, of its obsession with conspicuous consumption and the illusion of prosperity and of its addiction to foreign currency. Like the *gastarbajter* in *Breme*, he is a mediocrity who has been empowered by his sojourn in the West. He returns, pockets full, to be admired by and take advantage of his townspeople. Instead of contributing to the improvement and growth of the town, he participates in its exploitation and degradation. Toward the end of the film, watching the wedding procession of his former friend Tamaš, he reveals his true feelings of contempt towards Yugoslavia. "Provincials! I have always said that the Balkans were a piece of Asia in Europe."

Dragoslav Lažić scripted a similar "bad guy" in his action-film *Košava* (1974), which takes place in Belgrade. The film actually centres upon a confrontation between two migrants, Beli, a violent, egotistical character who was involved in organized crime, and the other, Adam, a gentle, generous, and romantic fellow, both of whom vie for the attentions of a young woman. Although skilled at operating cranes, Adam is unable to find work upon his return to Yugoslavia, as a result of the economic crisis, and is obliged to bribe the crime boss in order to get a job in his trade. As in all good action films, the hero prevails: Adam prevents Beli from kidnapping his girl, the thug is killed, and the rest of the crime syndicate is arrested. Audience members could rest easy at night. In *Let mrtve ptice*, Pavlović also deployed the figure of the migrant as an agent of corruption – I will return to this particular film at the end of the chapter, when I explore the representation of gender roles in films dealing with migration.

Aside from the figure of the migrant as sociopath, the migrant as laughingstock appeared in at least three films: Nikola Babić's occasionally brilliant *Ludi Dani* (1977), Aleksandar Đorđević's slapstick comedy *Avanture Borivoja Šurdilovića* (1980), and Ratko Orozović's short film *Čizme broj 46* (1984). Rather than portraying migrants as a real threat, they made light of the migrant's obsession with accumulating material wealth. At the same time, through humour, gentle or acerbic, such films discouraged behaviours judged to be laughable and, to a certain extent, pathologized migration by depicting migrants as ridiculous or foolish.

In *Ludi Dani* the migrant workers have returned to their village in Croatia for the holidays. Jure, who wears a plaid jacket and two large rings, drives a Mercedes and gambles with German marks at the local tavern, and gets in a confrontation with another labour migrant, Šimon "Klempo" Losinj. The shabbily dressed Klempo bets that he is wealthier than Jure, who accepts the wager. The village goes to Jure's brand-new house and makes an inventory of his wealth. It then goes to Klempo's ramshackle home. To the shock of the entire village, Klempo picks up his mother from her bed and opens up the mattress, revealing an astounding fortune in German marks. Jure's arrogance has gotten the best of him. Though the nouveau-riche Jure is the primary focus of ridicule, the shabby Klempo is himself a comical figure: a migrant who toils abroad only to continue living in poverty at home, stuffing his earnings into a mattress.

While this would seem a sufficient exposition of the foolishness of labour migrants, the story does not end there. Instead of collecting on his bet, Klempo orders Jure to undress, completing his humiliation. At this point, however, the tone of the film changes. Jure takes refuge in the tavern, gets senselessly drunk, sexually assaults the waitress, and gets into an altercation with a friend. "*Gastarbajters* ... when they go crazy, you can't recognize them," comments an observer. Emphasizing this notion that migrants were in some kind of altered state, Babić himself described migrants visiting home as being like "war returnees" or "bearded children" possessed by a "lunatic joy."[13] The story ends predictably with Jure's friend fatally shooting him. The comedy has turned into a tragedy.

Figure 9. The archetypal migrant showing off his flashy clothes and Mercedes (Nikola Babić, *Ludi Dani*)

The figure of the nouveau-riche migrant who returns home to enjoy the fruits of his labour, only to be humiliated, is also taken up in a short film, *Čizme broj 46*. Here, a migrant arrives unexpectedly in his village near Livno, in Bosnia-Herzegovina. He pauses in front of his home, admiring all the improvements that his earnings have financed, when suddenly he notices a large pair of rubber boots on his front stoop. He immediately suspects his wife of cheating on him with his friend Juriša. In a rage, he leaves a suitcase behind and leaves town. As it turns out, however, the boots belong to his son. Again, the joke is tinged with tragedy – the migrant has been away for so long that he has not seen his child grow up.

Aleksandar Đorđević's comic *gastarbajter* is based on an altogether different premise: he is an impostor. On a visit to Belgrade, he behaves like a very important person, dining in the finest restaurants and turning his nose up at the local *kafana*. Borivoje Šurdilović, a hapless and somewhat lazy innocent, is taken in by his act and decides to follow him to Germany. There, he discovers that his acquaintance is really just a kept man who takes advantage of wealthy women. Moreover, he has just been turfed out by his latest conquest and must find another prey He advises Borivoje on how to find work, leading to a series of comic

Figure 10. The migrant home for a visit contemplates the fruit of his labour – but leaves without visiting with his family as the result of a comical misunderstanding (Ratko Orozović, *Čizme broj 46*)

misadventures, in which Borivoje refuses a job washing poodles for a pet groomer named Bobo and gets fired after trying out a stint as a massage-therapist.

The third common image of the migrant was that of victim. Whereas the migrant as agent of corruption was framed as an outsider, a morally compromised individual who should be excluded, or at least punished, and the migrant as buffoon was to be laughed at, the migrant as victim was framed as an insider (*naš čovjek*) with whom the audience was invited to empathize and pity. The identification of a victim raised the troubling question of who was responsible for their pain and suffering. Often film-makers seemed to point the finger at other migrants, as in *Ne naginji se van* or *Košava*, or at the protagonists themselves, who had fallen for the allure of materialism and suffered the consequences, like characters in a Greek tragedy. However, in other films migrants were portrayed not as choosing to go abroad out of greed, but as compelled to do so out of necessity. These stories suggested that the Yugoslav state was in some way responsible through its inaction and broken promises.

Ne naginji se van is a good example of a film that deflected the responsibility of bad choices onto bad influences – the character of Mate – as well as a character flaw of the "victim migrant"– in this case, Filip's naivety. *Ne naginji se van* was structured as a coming-of-age narrative, in which the chastened hero emerges wiser from his experiences. Aleksandar Petković's *Aller Retour* (or *Tamo i Natrag*, 1978) presented a similar narrative but one that ends unambiguously in tragedy. The protagonist, Žika Jovanović, arrives at the train station in Paris with his wife and teenage son. Like Filip, he did not come on a work visa and finds he has to resort to working and living in very difficult circumstances. The host country in this film is not just a hostile environment, as Frankfurt was in *Ne naginji se van*; it also actively persecutes the migrants. Žika and his neighbours are under constant siege by authorities who want to tear down their home. The stresses of life as a labour migrant lead him into further trouble with the law. He gets into a fight with a neighbour and injures him. Once out of jail, Žika learns he will be deported back to Yugoslavia. However, on the insistence of his son Marko, who has gotten used to life in France, he and his family flee to a remote town in the French countryside. Here too, happiness eludes them, and Žika takes to drinking heavily. He beats his wife, who, in desperation, sends for the police. Žika avoids deportation, however; he dies moments later, presumably of despair. The film ends with a shot of a train pulling into the Belgrade train station.

Like Žižić, Petković highlights how Yugoslavs exploited one another – in this case, not just criminals and emigrants, but also fellow migrants trying to survive. Even more than Žižić, Petković communicated that, far from the land of plenty, Western Europe was a jungle in which only the fittest survived. The French authorities persecute the migrants, and Yugoslav consular officials are unable or unwilling to help them. At first glance, Comrade Mitrović, the dapper, cigar-puffing consular official, seems to be speaking common sense when he tells the migrants to comply with the French authorities. At the same time, speaking from his position of privilege and wealth, barely containing his contempt as he listens to the migrants explain that they are there because they can't find work, and aspire to build a home, he stands in for the callousness and disingenuity of the Yugoslav authorities. Whereas the Mercedes conveyed commodity fetishism, building a home was associated with providing for one's family. And unlike the adventure-seeking Filip, Žika is a married man with two children, simply seeking to earn a living. Žika's descent into madness and death parallels that of Ivica's father in *Rani*

Snijeg u Münchenu, whose dreams of building a home and workshop for his son back home were dashed when his son refuses to return.

The drama of the migrant forced to leave home is also at the heart of *Suton* (Goran Paskaljević, 1982). As was the case with *Ne naginji se van* and *Druga Generacija*, Goran Paskaljević was directly inspired by the documentary film he had made earlier, *Teret* (1974). In *Suton* we encounter the migrants themselves, a married couple, only through the letters they send home to the southern Serbian village of Lukovo. Again the drama centres upon the inability of families to sustain themselves on the land. However, the real victims of the story are not the migrants themselves but their children, who are forced to run the household and farm the family land during their prolonged absence.

This task falls mainly on their son Ivan, a boy of perhaps ten or twelve years old, who struggles with this responsibility, which some-times involves hiring workers two or three times his age. He lives with his younger sister Ana and his grandfather Marko, who had himself been a labour migrant to the United States in his youth. Ivan and Ana's parents have not visited in two years. Their father finally sends a letter explaining that he has separated from their mother, has taken up with a German woman, and does not intend to return. Marko withholds this information from his grandchildren as long as possible, preferring to let them live in blissful ignorance, but Ivan eventually learns the truth after his grandfather dies. He puts on a brave face, acting the way he supposes adults should, but collapses in sobbing as soon as he is alone. The next day, however, he has gone back to toiling on the land with his sister – Ivan and Ana do not have the luxury of grieving. *Suton*'s real drama concerns children robbed both of their parents and of their childhood.

Masculinity as a Prism for Social Critique

Films on labour migrants reflected on the persistence of patriarchy in the countryside as part of a broader critique of socialist modernity char-acterized by uneven material progress, which broke down traditional social structures without replacing them with a viable socialist alterna-tive. In this narrative, rural dwellers were doubly penalized: left out of modernization and yet torn apart by its side effects. Representations of the harm of labour migration in both documentary and fictional film were heavily gendered. Film-makers portrayed labour migration as problematic because it broke down the family unit, exposed migrants to seduction and other sexual immorality, and troubled traditional gender roles, a message to which their publics were receptive.

As a socialist state, Yugoslavia espoused gender equality, which was even constitutionally enshrined. In practice, however, the experiences of women varied drastically between urban and rural areas. The early years of Tito's Yugoslavia were characterized by support for women's liberation, carried out largely by the Women's Anti-Fascist Front, which focused on dismantling patriarchal traditions in the countryside. Their version of women's emancipation was consistent with aspirations across the Eastern Bloc, of liberation from superstition, violence, and enslavement to reproduction, and full participation in society as political actors and workers. By 1953, however, the front was disbanded, its demise driven by activists' convictions that efforts to emancipate women should be more systematic and, more cynically, by authorities' desire to contain and control women's radical action. The widespread conviction that gender oppression was a symptom of capitalism limited efforts to effectively promote women's rights until the 1970s, when a new wave of feminists began to draw attention to the marginalization of women in Yugoslav society.[14]

With minor exceptions (like Verica in *Ne naginji se van*), migrant workers were depicted as male, in spite of the fact that women accounted for almost a third of all migrants by 1971. While this is a curious omission, Bernard has noted that this silence in about women labour migrants extends to academic research. She adds that it is a reflection of their invisibility both at home and in their host societies.[15] Women are also present in these films, usually in supporting roles, often marginal – foils for the male protagonists. They were represented primarily as grandmothers and wives left behind in villages, or alternatively, as women set adrift by modernity abroad – lonely shopgirls, prostitutes, or distraught migrants. For these film-makers, women were not interesting subjects in their own right. Indeed, several films display an interesting ambivalence towards the old patriarchal ways, as if to respond to the deceptions of modernization with nostalgia for tradition.

Three films illustrate this crisis of masculinity: the short documentary film *Teret* by Goran Paskaljević (1974), the full-length *Ne naginji se van* (Žižić, 1977), and the full-length *Let mrtve ptice*, by Živojin Pavlović (1973).

Teret is made up of a series of short interviews with family members of migrant workers in Pomoravlje, western Serbia, in 1973, with snippets of scenes of village life. A little girl, elderly parents, and a young boy are interviewed. The overarching theme of the interviews is the absence of one or both parents, which compels other family members to step into roles for which they are ill-suited. The elderly parents, for example, are forced by their daughter's choice to work abroad to care for her infant child, a task for which they complain they are too weary and frail.

The longest and most striking interview, however, is with the young boy. This man-child clearly captured Paskaljević's imagination, as he seems to have provided the material for *Suton*. Wearing his best Sunday suit and tie, he walks through his muddy property, giving a guided tour to the cameraman, providing a poignant image of a child forced to behave like a full-grown man. As he explains how his life has changed since his father's departure to work abroad, tears begin to well in his eyes and his voice cracks, signs of emotion that he does his best to conceal. His life is one of hard work and social isolation. In particular, he describes the difficulty of hiring labour to help with the seasonal work, given his young age. He adds, however, that it is even worse when his father comes home to help, because he and his siblings are overwhelmed with sadness when he leaves. He also remarks that he has no one to play with and spends his scarce free time alone at the movies. The film ends with the boy walking away from the camera, surreptitiously wiping tears from his eyes. Through his interview questions and his camerawork, Paskaljević provides us with a portrait not only of a child who suffers from the absence of his father, but even more shockingly, of a child forced to take on his father's role.

In *Suton*, Paskaljević changed minor but significant elements, which dramatized the theme of the broken family even more. Here the boy's father is not only absent but delinquent, leaving his mother and refusing to ever return. Young Ivan finds comfort and guidance instead in his grandfather, but even this surrogate father cannot redeem the broken family, as he dies of old age toward the end of the film, leaving the boy and his sister alone to work the property. It is worth pointing out that while the father figure's absence in both films signals a breakdown of the social order, the boy's stepping into his father's shoes reasserts the traditional patriarchal family structure, if in weakened form.

The opening scenes of *Ne naginji se van*, in which labour migrant Mate returns home to the Zagora from Germany to impress his fellow villagers and visit his family, also evokes the alienation of the labour migrant from his family, although in this instance it seems primarily to affect his wife. While the children are thrilled to see their father, go for a spin in his Mercedes, and receive his gifts, his wife cannot relate to her husband, in spite of her joy in seeing him again. Mate asserts his traditional role as the patriarch, ordering his wife to send away the children so that he can make love to her. Faced with the impossibility of instant intimacy, however, he falls back on the only thing of value in his life – his material possessions, in this instance, a waterproof digital watch that

Figure 11. A boy in his best Sunday suit gives a tearful interview while standing in front of his family's land (Goran Paskaljević, *Teret*)

lights up in the dark. The choice of a digital watch was not arbitrary – these electronics had first been introduced on the market in 1972 and were expensive luxury goods.

It is not merely the distance that alienates Mate from his wife – it is also his exposure to the sexual depredations of Germany, which is depicted in the film as a sort of Gomorrah. Indeed, the young protagonist of the film, Filip, is persuaded to try his luck in Germany in part by Mate's lascivious talk of seducing German women. The second person whom Filip meets in Germany is, in fact, a Yugoslav prostitute. Faced with the hardship and solitude of the migrant's life, Filip turns to pornography and the comfort of prostitutes, only to be saved by the sounds of folk music from his native region. German consumer society is presented as a corrupting influence, a peddler of illusions of prosperity and sensual pleasure. The irony, in Žižić's account, is that the Yugoslav migrants themselves peddle the illusions, prostitute themselves, and exploit one another.

Žižić expands the notion of the broken family by using it as a metaphor for the alienation of modern life and of life abroad. The entire film is framed by Filip's quest for his "brother" Mate. In a sense, Filip is in a constant quest to reconstitute family. Kinship becomes defined by co-nationality. Taken aback by a German woman's hostility upon his arrival in the city, he addresses her as "sister." The prostitute who comforts him after this scene says to him, "She isn't your sister. I could be your sister … or your mother." Indeed, she takes him under her wing and provides him with shelter, but this surrogate family is fleeting. Anđela, the dowdy bathroom attendant whose gentle folk-singing pulls him out of desperation, similarly evokes the memory of motherhood. Aside from these moments of meaningful contact, Filip is cast adrift in a violent male migrant society. Ultimately, Filip's redemption is portrayed as a kind of return of the prodigal son. Having recognized the futility of his quest for material success, he finally finds his "brother" Mate, who confirms on his deathbed that his boasting was a lie. He then accompanies Mate's casket back to the village, bears witness to Mate's actual poverty, and presumably returns to his real family.

Interestingly, Žižić dangles before his audience the possibility of making a new family abroad, only to quash that idea as yet another illusion. Filip falls in love with a Yugoslav shop-clerk, whose domestic virtues are illustrated by her tidy, cheerful, and demure demeanour, her cooking skills and spotless apartment – which provide Filip with a sense of home – and her unwillingness to return to her apartment with Filip at the end of an evening of dancing, testifying to her moral rectitude. In spite of their tender feelings for one another, however, Filip and Verica cannot remain together. Filip asks her to return home with him, but she refuses because she has made a life for herself in Germany. On her part, she insists that Filip remain with her, promising to support him financially after she finishes school and gets a job, and to buy him the records he loves so much. It is painfully obvious to the viewer that this is an offer that Filip cannot accept – one that would effectively castrate him symbolically. When Filip replies to her, "Verica, I am alienated. You are alienated" (otuđen), he is not just referring to their distance from the homeland, but also to the fact that she is proposing a model of gender relations that is alien to him. His return home is also a return to patriarchal gender relations, as illustrated by the parade of women in mourning at Mate's homecoming and funeral.

While Ne naginji se van takes place primarily abroad – a novelty that added to some of its popular appeal – Let mrtve ptice further develops the theme of the migrant worker as a contaminating agent, importing corruption and sexual immorality into the pure and vulnerable Yugoslav countryside. As in many other films in the same vein, we are presented with a countryside in decline. The landscape is beautiful, in contrast to its depiction in other films, such as Teret, Breme, or Zalazak *sunca*, which depict the countryside as a bleak, muddy wasteland. But it is also stagnant, starved of labour by migration, and dependent on migrant remittances for investment, however modest. This is a vulnerable milieu, prone to exploitation by the unscrupulous migrant.

The main protagonist of *Let mrtve ptice* is Ferenc, a wealthy migrant who can impress the locals with his sophisticated ways and his Mercedes. While his brother Tjaš struggles to eke out a living on the land, Ferenc is looking to make easy money by turning a local mill into a restaurant. Ferenc is also a sexual deviant, an adulterer, and a home-wrecker. Not only does he rape his own wife, Roza, but he also seduces his sister-in-law, Tjaš's wife, Anika. His sexual escapades provoke Roza into attempting suicide –which she chooses to do with broken tiles from the bathroom renovation that Ferenc is financing. Ferenc's egotism sends the household into a spiral of tragedy and violence. Roza's suicide attempt leads to Ferenc and Tjaš's father suffering a fatal heart attack. Ferenc suggests to Tjaš that his wife has been engaging in further indiscretions with another man, leading him to murder Anika in a jealous rage.

The degree to which the critique of migration and its impact on Yugoslavia was articulated through the prism of troubled masculinities – delinquent sons, failed fathers, and rapists – is striking. Even more remarkable is how some films seemed to reassert the value of traditional family structure, all while proclaiming the moribund nature of the Yugoslav countryside. While Pavlović's family in *Let mrtve ptice* is characteristically doomed to implosion, Paskaljević's Ivan is depicted as a martyr, continuing a valiant (if perhaps futile) struggle, and Žižić's Filip returns to his village, wise to the ways of the world, and committed to the humble and patriarchal but morally righteous ways of the Zagora. Embedded in this critique of uneven Yugoslav modernization, then, was a yearning for the past, or at very least a suggestion that it was the lesser of two evils.

Conclusion

Whereas the previous chapter focused on examining the role of Yugoslav state actors in creating the diasporic category "our citizen/worker living abroad," the impact of the framing of this category, and its contestation by other state actors, this chapter has examined the role of film-makers and their audiences in framing and reframing labour migration – not through statistics and sociological argumentation, but through storytelling. The portrayal of labour migrants in Yugoslav film had clear parallels with their representation in official discourse and scholarly studies. They were represented as men from economically backwards regions, primarily unskilled workers, who left Yugoslavia with the intention to return and who remained fundamentally Yugoslav subjects.

Film also reflected the growing anxiety in the late 1960s about the true nature of migration and its negative impact on Yugoslav society. More often than not, labour migration was portrayed as a problem, a false answer to the dilemma of Yugoslav underdevelopment. Film-makers were particularly interested in two interrelated themes: the motivations of migrants, and the impact of their absence – or their return – on their communities. They portrayed migrants as driven by material necessity and an appetite for conspicuous consumption, echoing political discussions about migration. Beyond the focus on rural economic stagnation that dominated public debates about migration, most films painted a damning portrait of its influence on Yugoslav communities, spreading illusions, immorality, corruption, and even social discord, disrupting gender roles, and splitting families apart.

A number of negative stereotypes coalesced: the migrant as social ill, laughingstock, and victim. Whereas the first two stereotypes held the migrants themselves responsible for the deleterious consequences of their choices, film-makers portraying migrants as victims opened the question of responsibility of the state in enabling labour migration and in failing to address the conditions that gave rise to it. Such films echoed criticisms of migration that were aired during the Croatian Spring, without necessarily infusing them with ethno-nationalist meanings. Films that dealt with labour migration captured the ambivalence of film-makers and their audiences toward the evolution of Yugoslav society in the 1960s. On the one hand, Yugoslavia had made great strides toward industrialization, urbanization, and increasing the standard of living, changes most visible in urban centres. In opening the borders, Yugoslavia had provided access to Western consumer goods and given its citizens a freedom of movement unheard of in the Eastern Bloc. At the same time, economic modernization had been highly uneven, leaving entire regions behind while taunting them with visions of Western consumerism. The stagnant countryside was depicted as both bad and good – bad because it could not provide for its people, and yet essential as a source of identity, without which Yugoslavs withered inside and died.

While depictions in film of victims called on viewers to empathize with labour migrants, they also had a tendency to rob them of agency by portraying them as being at the mercy of forces much greater than them. Few films in this mode, including documentaries, represented migrants as making choices and successfully coping with and even overcoming their challenges. As the remainder of the book will show, programs aimed specifically at migrants promoted a very different discourse, describing migrants not as lost sheep but as cherished contributing members of Yugoslav society. Migrants responded to these diverse portrayals in different ways, embracing certain aspects as authentic and rejecting others. Just as state actors used storytelling to mobilize migrants in service of their agendas, so migrants themselves had recourse to storytelling to represent themselves and advance their own objectives.

PART II

Building Ties

4 A Listening Ear: Cultivating Citizens through Radio Broadcasting

One of the most powerful ways that Yugoslavia cultivated a relationship with its migrant workers was through the use of mass media – print media like newspapers and magazines, as well as radio and television programming. Many labour migrants were desperately homesick and isolated from their host societies. For these migrants, the press and radio and television shows were a lifeline connecting them to their loved ones and local communities, informing them about goings-on in Yugoslavia, providing advice on navigating work and life abroad, and bringing to them their beloved pop ballads and traditional melodies. Yugoslavia used these vehicles to promote a sense of attachment to Yugoslavia, to inform and organize workers abroad, and to communicate its perspective on domestic and global affairs, with the hope to counteract the corrupting influence of hostile émigré associations.

As socialist states and liberal democracies had long recognized, broadcasting (and radio in particular) was a privileged medium for reaching the masses. As Stephen Lovell has noted, in early Soviet Russia, radio was seen as a civilizing force that transcended distance and penetrated the most backwards rural areas. Above all, Soviet society understood the power of radio to strengthen collective identity: radio "was a metaphor for the power of technology to remake human society – to make it more 'rational' and modern, but also to bring about the kind of collective society that could be firmly counterposed to the individualistic 'bourgeois' world."[1] Lenin quickly mobilized radio broadcasting in the 1920s to transmit agitprop across the Soviet Union, and radio was later used to increase the cultural level of the Soviet population.[2]

Broadcasting had the advantage of reaching a broader audience than newspapers, including those who were illiterate or semi-literate. Unlike print media, for which a physical distribution network needed to be organized across international borders, the emission of radio waves could be entirely organized on Yugoslav soil, and signals crossed large distances almost instantaneously, reaching Yugoslavs abroad in their homes. Because listeners gathered synchronously, radio-broadcasting created an opportunity for creating and strengthening imagined communities transcending international borders to an even greater extent than newspapers, the medium on which Benedict Anderson focused.[3] Radio did indeed become the preferred way for Yugoslavs to stay informed about the homeland. According to a 1977 study, 76.2% of migrants living in West Berlin obtained their knowledge of events in Yugoslavia via radio, compared to 53.7% from Yugoslav newspapers and 43.3% from television programming.[4]

Indeed, as scholars have shown, these characteristics turned radio into a powerful weapon. By the 1960s, there was a well-established tradition of transnational radio-broadcasting, from the resistance-promoting broadcasts emitted from London during the Second World War, and the anti-colonial, revolutionary broadcasts of Voice of Fighting Algeria, to the anti-communist programming of Voice of America and Radio Free Europe transmitted to the Eastern Bloc during the Cold War.[5] *To Our Citizens in the World* (*Našim građanima u svijetu*) fulfilled the same role as wartime anti-occupation radio and anti-colonial broadcasts in tightly linking national identity to the act of listening to the radio. At the same time, it distinguished itself from these other initiatives in that, far from being seen as subversive, it was largely perceived either as harmless or as beneficial by the foreign states in which it was received – a means for labour migrants to remain connected to their homeland and, therefore, stave off pretensions of permanent immigration.

Certain states, such as the FRG, established their own radio-programming aimed at migrant workers. Yugoslavia was initially wary of such initiatives out of concern that they were under the sway of anti-Yugoslav emigrants, particularly with programming produced by Radio Cologne. While Yugoslavia's own radio-programming was designed to compete with such programs, by the 1970s, improving relations between Germany and Yugoslavia led to possibilities for collaboration.[6]

The popular radio program *To Our Citizens in the World*, produced by Radio Zagreb starting in 1964 and directed by Cino Handl, was one of the first programs created to build relationships between Yugoslavia and its citizens living abroad. In creating such programming, Radio Zagreb followed in the footsteps of Radiotelevisione Italiana (RAI), which was already broadcasting programming for Italians working abroad.[7] *To Our Citizens* quickly grew an enormous audience by creating a specific culture of listenership, in which the audience went back and forth between attentive listening and responding to the program by sending letters containing musical requests and queries for information and support. Unlike Soviet radio, which remained resistant to the broadcasting of popular culture, *To Our Citizens* created a community of listeners united by their love of popular Yugoslav music.[8] The resulting expectations that listeners developed vis-à-vis the radio program forged strong transnational ties, both in the sense of actual transactions with the institution of the radio station and imagined community with the homeland.

Migrants' dealings with the radio program had a strong affective component, centred on love, nostalgia, longing, joy, and, when expectations were betrayed, disappointment and anger. These emotions were often tied to embodied experiences, which included feeling cold or warm, crying, and trembling. Migration scholars have recently recognized the significance of emotions in understanding the experience of migration. In particular, they have highlighted the role of emotions like familial love and hope in motivating migration, and in persevering through the hardships of living and working in a foreign land. Emotional states can be understood as part of engagement in the construction of the self and of the social – that is, in negotiating relations with others. Focusing on emotional life thus allows us to recognize the agency of migrants in making life choices and making sense of their lives.[9]

Christou's definition of emotions as "the central medium through which embodied, mnemonic and representational experiences intersect" highlights the complexity of a phenomenon that simultaneously encompasses neural and physiological responses, and social construction.[10] Listening to their favourite radio program and writing responses to it provided listeners with the opportunity to reflect on their embodied experiences, with reference to their memories of home. This in turn fed into the construction and performance of the self. The act of listening to radio, then, provided migrants with an opportunity to process their current circumstances, review and revise their identities, and recommit themselves to their friends and family back home and to the homeland, however they defined it. It should be noted that this was only one aspect of their emotional lives, that did not necessarily preclude positive emotions toward, and relationship-building with, the host society.

The People's Radio: *To Our Citizens in the World*

To Our Citizens in the World was launched on 15 February 1964 to further strengthen ties with workers living abroad. More specifically, it was designed to meet their cultural, educational, and informational needs, help connect migrants to their country and family, and counteract the influence of the reactionary emigrant mass media. Initially a half-hour long, it expanded to an hour-long format and was broadcast Saturday in the evening, a time of day when radio waves travelled farthest. For a time, RTZ combined with Radio Beograd and Radio Sarajevo to offer a combined forty-five-minute program, but the two other radio stations pulled out, leaving RTZ to run the program alone. RTZ's emitter was strong enough that migrants in the FRG had no trouble receiving it, and it was listened to as far away as Sweden, Belgium, Holland, Denmark, and Norway. Bavarian radio, Radio Köln and Radio Prague also carried this program on their airwaves.

Other shows broadcast to labour migrants included Radio Beograd's *Dobro jutro zemljaci* and *Večeras zajedno*, Radio Ljubljana's *Našim građanima u svijetu*, and Radio Sarajevo's *Petkom s vama*, but none was as popular as Handl's program. Indeed, within seven months of broadcasting, Handl's show celebrated receiving its ten thousandth letter from a listener, and by the end of September 1965 the number of letters had exceeded twenty-five thousand.[11] According to Letić and Baučić, in 1977 it was still the most popular radio program for migrants from the Republic of Croatia after the news: 21.6% of listeners indicated that they listened to this program most frequently, of all the programming on Yugoslav radio stations.[12]

To Our Citizens was conceived as a plain-spoken, down-to-earth radio program with a human touch, which would attract listeners who would perhaps not pick up a newspaper. It also distinguished itself from newspapers explicitly targeted to labour migrants, like *YU Novosti*, in that it was listened to both at home and abroad; indeed, over half of listeners lived within Yugoslavia's borders. The radio program became a sort of central node connecting labour migrants, their friends and family, and Yugoslav (primarily Croatian republican) state institutions. It was an instrument of governance, allowing the state to surveil and cultivate its citizens living abroad; but migrants also used it as a vehicle to connect with their loved ones and liaise with the state to resolve their personal problems while living abroad.

As Michelle Hilmes and others have noted, radio is uniquely suited to bringing into existence Benedict Anderson's "imagined community" by enabling listeners to tune in simultaneously and be aware that thousands of other invisible listeners were doing the same. Radio, Hilmes continues, "promised simultaneity of experience without direct contact, exposure to the public in the privacy of one's home." It gave broadcasters the ability to shape and control the public sphere and to reach groups and individuals who were otherwise isolated from the body politic. It also transformed migrants' private sphere – their barracks and apartments – into temporary public spaces belonging, crucially, not to their place of residence, but to their homelands.[13] It is likely this feature of radio programming – its ability to transform participation in the public sphere into an activity taking place in the home – that made it more palatable to foreign authorities than extracurricular activities for school-aged children, which encroached on the most sacred of public institutions and spaces, the school.

The program, much like the Yugoslav society that it mediated, was very much a hybrid between a socialist vision of radio-broadcasting, focused on mobilizing, organizing, and educating the population, and a Western-style consumer-driven model privileging popular music.[14] It was geared toward the ideal type of "our citizen/worker living abroad" – an economic migrant who maintained close ties to family and expected to return home within a few years. Two-thirds of the program was dedicated to playing music, more specifically, requests that were sent in by mail by listeners along with greetings to be sent to their families. The average show in 1964 reportedly included five songs and an impressive seventy-two greetings. Listeners also sent in questions and requested advice on practical matters pertaining to migration, accounting for roughly 20% of the correspondence.[15]

The editorial board established early on that it did not want to be seen as a spokesperson for the regime – it did not want to speak on behalf of banks, customs, or social security, for example. It wanted to be the people's radio.[16] This image was carefully curated and somewhat disingenuous; in reality, the radio very much served the interests of the state institutions that paid its bills. The question of "propaganda" was often discussed in meetings involving the radio show, Matica iseljenika Hrvatske and other guests. The term "propaganda" did not have the negative connotations we associate with it in contemporary parlance, but rather, referred to the act of persuasive communication – what we (in our own capitalist-inflected jargon) might call marketing – it focused on shaping migrants' perception of Yugoslavia and their behaviour. Sometimes this "marketing" was really just that – persuading migrants to buy things. The program joined forces with Jugoton to promote Yugoslav music to migrant workers through *Sounds from the Homeland* (*Zvuci iz domovine*) magazine. The monthly publication came with seven vinyl records containing poetry, folkloric and popular music, interviews, and beginner German lessons. The show's editorial board also met with representatives of Croatian business, namely Radio Industrija Zagreb and Rijeka-based Brodokomerc import-export, to discuss how to market Croatian products to labour migrants, and beat competing firms from Belgrade. They even considered whether labour migrants could be used to market their products abroad.[17]

Host and director Handl and others saw labour migrants as sophisticated, difficult consumers of information and puzzled over how best to reach them – in both medium and message. Handl in particular believed labour migrants were a more challenging audience than the older generations of emigrants, even though they were easier to stay in touch with. Handl believed they were sophisticated, potentially because they had a much closer knowledge of contemporary Yugoslav affairs and were thus more discriminating. Their ability to compare Yugoslavia and Western consumer societies may also have been on his mind. He argued that media produced for these modern migrants could not be heavy-handed, but rather needed to be exceptionally "witty, intelligent, fresh, new, interesting, actual, [and even] eccentric."[18]

In the early stages of the program, its editorial board had a lively discussion about their target audience with government officials concerned with labour migration. Whereas Cino Handl argued that the program should be directed at Croats, especially since they were the largest group of Yugoslavs abroad, a colleague from Radio Televizija Zagreb suggested that such identifications lost their salience for migrants living abroad. He responded, "Croatia exists in Yugoslavia, but it doesn't mean anything beyond our borders. Our citizens are citizens of our country. We are talking about workers living in modern conditions. No sentimentality! They should think of themselves as socialists rather than Croats. The principle is hard to put in practice, but it's necessary. ... After all, people left for pragmatic reasons." In other words, the program should appeal to a modern, pragmatic world view, rather than to retrograde identity politics – a suggestion that was very much in line with the framing of "our workers living abroad" by authorities.[19]

While no decision was recorded on this matter, the program settled on a format that proved phenomenally popular with audiences: it shied away from politics and put popular culture and human connections at the heart of its programming. As a result, it was perpetually inundated by letters sent from everywhere that labour migrants worked. From February to December 1964, 40% of letters were sent from the FRG and 10% from the remainder of European states. According to Handl, they received so much correspondence – hundreds of items every week – that they were simply unable to keep pace. Although they were unable to satisfy the hundreds of requests for songs and greetings, at least they attempted to answer as many questions as possible about the practicalities of living and working abroad. Migrants most frequently inquired about social security, banking, customs, the police, and relationships with Yugoslav employers. Handl and his team farmed the requests out to volunteer advisors with relevant expertise, who were able to answer some of the questions.[20]

Handl's other comments on the letters, however, highlight how the show's creators perceived its core mission as knowing migrants in order to cultivate a closer relationship with them and shape their perceptions and opinions, very much in line with the objectives of state institutions, as described in chapter 2. Handl argued that, while currently unfeasible, it was important to reply to every single letter, and advocated that a special section be created at the radio station for this purpose. In the meanwhile, the radio program kept an archive of all letters received – not only as letters awaiting replies, but also as a repository of contact information critical to communicating with migrants, and more broadly, a source of knowledge about them. As if addressing himself to the historian reading his words a half-century later, Handl mused, "I believe that, in a year or so, we will pack this up, give it to our sociologists, give it to a government office to have a look at these things, and it will become a knowledge base for worker mobility."[21]

A subset of these letters from 1964 to 1966 has been preserved, providing a glimpse into the social and personal world of labour migrants. As material objects they are themselves remarkable, connecting us to the listeners as individuals. Written on quality letter-paper or on scraps of paper, in a self-assured or clumsy hand, they testify to the universality of the urge to remain connected, cutting across class lines. In many of the letters punctuation was absent and spelling mistakes were common, hinting at incomplete literacy.

The letters also tell us about listening practices, highlighting how radio could be an active and social activity rather than a passive and individual one. Several letters describe how Yugoslavs gathered around the radio every Saturday to listen to the program and reminisce about the homeland.[22] Writing letters – like listening to the radio – was also sometimes a social affair: several letters, most likely composed after listening to the program, were signed by groups of listeners. However, this was not a universal experience; others described not knowing any Yugoslavs where they lived. For these other listeners, the social aspect of radio was an act of the imagination: it consisted in the knowledge that tens of thousands of others were simultaneously sharing the same listening experience.[23]

Figure 12. Listening to the radio could be a social activity (*Jugo moja Jugo* exhibit, Museum of Yugoslav History)

The archived letters suggest that the program had achieved a Yugoslav-wide profile. Insofar as they self-identified, most of the letter-writers were Croatian, but this is unsurprising, given the over-representation of Croatian migrants at this time. Citizens of other republics also figured among the correspondents. While Croatians often requested Croatian popular and traditional music, these melodies were not identified as nationally exclusive, but as part of a pan-Yugoslav culture. Radio listeners were also likely to be newspaper readers, as a number of listeners asked for clarification on something they had read in *Vjesnik u srijedu*.

The letters confirm that sending greetings and requesting music was the most common purpose for writing. Listeners requested popular hits with a strong preference for songs, often in the melancholy *sevdah* style, that spoke to the struggles of living far away from one's loved ones. Popular requests included "Poleti golube moj" (Fly away, my dove), likely the version performed by Gvozden Radičević; "Tebi majko misli lete" (Mother, my thoughts fly to you), which Nedeljko Bilkić had recorded in 1963; "Pozdravi je sunce milo" (Give her my greetings, dear sun); "S one strane Plive" (From this side of the Pliva); and the mariachi-inflected "Pjesma majci" (A song, or poem, for mother) performed by Slavko Perović i trio Tenori. All followed a similar pattern to "Fly away, my dove": obliged to live in a foreign land, the singer pines after his mother or beloved, and for his homeland:

Poleti, golube moj	Fly away, my dove
odnesi pozdrav mojoj ljubljenoj	carry a greeting to my beloved
Kaži joj da je moj život tužan bez nje	Tell her that my life is sad without her
kao što je tebi bez jata tvoga....	As it is sad for you without your flock....
Daleko usamljen sada	Far away, alone now
uvek mislim na svoj rodni kraj	I always think of the place I come from
tužno provodim dane i duge noći	I spend the days and nights in sadness
i na dragu mislim, kada ću joj doći	and think of my beloved, when I will return to her
Kaži joj, golube moj	Tell her, my dove
da moja ljubav pripada samo njoj	that my love belongs to only her.

The radio program also received a few angry letters from disappointed listeners who had made a request that had never been aired. These letters suggest that listeners believed they had a personal and reciprocal relationship with the radio program, which entailed certain responsibilities.[24]

Faced with the weekly deluge of requests, the show's production team developed a variety of strategies. For example, Ivo Belamarić, who produced the music portion of the program, grouped requests according to the type of greeting they wished to send, or the region of origin of the listeners. He followed greetings from a group of Bosnian listeners with a Bosnian melody. Such practices reinforced ethnic or regional identities amongst labour migrants. Belamarić also explained that it would be inadvisable to follow through with every request, because the program would become an endless sequence of sad songs and *sevdahs*, which would make the mothers of migrant workers cry. Belamarić added that he was particularly moved by requests from children for their parents. He saw his role as mediating messages and emotions through music, a task he found arduous.[25]

Some listeners put into words how the program helped them to feel connected to Yugoslavia. For example, they expressed thanks to the program for helping them to stay informed about recent events in Yugoslavia. Others greeted their fellow Yugoslavs, providing a neat illustration of the concept of imagined community. Some sent their greetings to Tito or expressed joy at hearing a speech by him.[26] For many, the program filled a deeply felt need. Živko Lazić, a frequent correspondent, described the program as "our only recreation."[27]

Like a sorcerer, the airwaves conjured home and community from thin air in a way that printed text could not and provoked a strong emotional reaction. Anica, from Riederich in the FRG, shared, "When I hear the voices of our dear speakers, it seems to me that I am not as lonely, and even that I am amongst you and in our dear Zagreb." Petar and Ivan, in Oberkochen-Wurth, wrote, "We are ecstatic not to have been forgotten, and to be once again pulled into the embrace of the homeland." Ana sent a postcard birthday greeting on which she had written, "When I heard your program my heart danced with joy." For Franka, in Blumberg, the experience was bittersweet: "I always listen with tears in my eyes, when I hear our station, our songs, and our language."[28] Hearing the voices of other Yugoslavs, as mediated by the radio announcers, was a critical part of the listening experience that instilled in listeners a sense of belonging. "Listening to the wishes that our people feel for the homeland so touches me to the heart, it sends through me a tremor of joy that would be hard to describe to you."[29] Descriptions of crying, shaking bodies, and hearts dancing with joy are reminders that listening to the radio was not just an intellectual experience – it was an emotional and even physiological one. Women mentioned tears more frequently than men, but men too described being overwhelmed by emotion.

The letters reveal how the experience of migration shaped migrant identities, in their own words. Several migrants described the place in which they lived as lacking warmth, again evoking embodied experience. According to one woman living in the FRG, "Here you don't feel warmth, sunshine, or the scent of flowers. They bloom, but they have no scent. The sun shines, but it gives off no heat. The tears just keep coming."[30] A number of listeners affirmed that the experience of living abroad had increased their love for and sense of belonging to "the homeland" (*domovina, zavičaj*) – an ambiguous turn of phrase, rarely more concisely defined, which could refer to their place of origin, their republic, or to Yugoslavia.[31] Others experienced culture shock that sharpened their sense of otherness, without necessarily experiencing it as trauma. In the words of one migrant, everything was different, from language, to food and customs, to the work ethic:

> We felt from the first that this isn't Yugoslavia. They received us well on our arrival. They say, "guten Morgen," and we ask what they want. They say it's their greeting. They give us a breakfast and snack that is so thin we can see right through it. We open our suitcases and pull out the bacon. Early in the morning a car is waiting to take us to work. ... When we arrive at the construction site they greet us with "gluck auf." We ask what they want from us now, and they say that this is their miner's greeting. And then they tell us, "langsam" (work slowly now), because Germans (*Švaba*) say you need to work your whole life at the same tempo.[32]

Can we conclude from these letters that all migrants felt an intense attachment to Yugoslavia, and that their feelings became even stronger as a result of culture shock? We can speculate that some migrants were eager to dissolve into Western European society, with all its trappings of modern consumer society and high culture, and distance themselves from their Yugoslav roots. This option would have been available to better-educated migrants. These listeners might not have bothered tuning into the program. Other migrants may have listened to it and even written, but also have felt at home in their host societies. What we can say with certainty is that the radio program was designed to intensify the sense of attachment to the homeland, and a review of letters sent in by listeners suggests that it was successful.

Along with emotionally charged letters speaking to isolation, homesickness, and belonging were much more pragmatic letters requesting advice and assistance. While these inquiries did not speak directly to belonging, they did testify to migrants' continued investment in Yugoslavia and reliance on Yugoslav institutions for knowledge and assistance. The radio program took on some of the roles traditionally associated with consular and diplomatic services. Whereas migrants thought of consulates as inaccessible, too busy to help, and even potentially hostile, it was much easier to write and post a letter, and they believed that the radio station cared about their problems. Migrants put pen to paper not only to ask for information and assistance, but also to voice their opinions, offer advice, warn others of perils, and tell their story. The radio program was both confidant and two-way information clearing house.

A number of inquiries were about migrants' legal status and rights, speaking to the complexities of negotiating life in two states. Many sought clarification about regulations on job contracts, as well as social security, which could get complicated. Others used the shaki radio program as a soapbox to express their frustration with particular policies. For example, workers chafed at the paperwork they needed to submit in order to receive social security in Yugoslavia, which their German employers frequently refused to fill out. In some cases, workers had changed jobs many times, making it particularly time-consuming to fill out the forms.[33]

Transnational mobility often made for a complicated family life. One woman asked about the possibility of collecting child support from her husband who was working abroad and had ceased sending money home. Conversely, a young man had gotten a German girl pregnant and wanted to know whether he could pay child support from Yugoslavia. Questions about passports and visas were also common. One woman who had lost her passport wanted to return home for a vacation; the consulate being too far away, she asked if the program could help her. Other letters were from frustrated listeners who wanted to know why their spouses and children were not being issued passports, preventing them from visiting abroad or joining their spouse in Western Europe. In a few cases, Yugoslav citizens also had difficulty obtaining entry visas to return home. One family was in a veritable Catch-22, because he had taken out Swedish citizenship. He wished to return home on vacation, but was afraid he wouldn't be let in to Yugoslavia, and that his wife would not be let back in to Sweden. Yugoslavia's border was somewhat more open in theory than in reality.[34]

A significant number of letters concerned the transportation of consumer goods to Yugoslavia. Countless migrants inquired about customs. Many asked how much duty they would be charged on a used tractor or car, moped, television, transistor radio, vacuum cleaner, or medicine. Others wrote to complain about customs charges they deemed completely unreasonable.[35] Nikola V., from Hamburg, was outraged that he had been charged 46,541 dinars in duties on a fourteen-kilogram package of textiles, women's clothing, and a pair of shoes.[36] This was more than twice the monthly salary of a foundry worker in Belgrade in 1965 (22,000 dinars).[37]

They also asked how to purchase goods from Yugoslavia, for enjoyment abroad (such as records) or for use back home (such as prefabricated homes, construction materials, and appliances).[38] Once they had purchased them, they wrote to complain about delays in receiving their goods and, sometimes, to request that the radio program intervene on their behalf. One migrant had ordered a car from Zastava, paying with foreign currency, and had not yet received his goods.[39] Others complained about the Belgrade-based import firms, which took three months to a year to deliver.[40]

Cino Handl and his team worked diligently to answer all questions they received, although it is not clear whether they were able to do so on-air, or resorted to written responses. According to Handl, the task of looking for answers was normal "journalist's work" involving knocking on the doors of institutions, such as the employment office, Matica iseljenika, and the Commission for Emigrant Questions. He noted that the questions that were resolved most quickly were about passports and visas, and those that took the most time concerned social security. Answers about customs, he added, were often unsatisfactory and did not reflect the interests of society.[41]

Migrants also wrote on behalf of themselves or others in difficult situations. One asked for help following the death of a Yugoslav man in Donzdorf, because no one knew whether he had family in Yugoslavia or where he had come from. It is noteworthy that he contacted the radio station rather than the nearest consulate.[42] Occasionally, listeners asked for assistance in re-establishing contact with people with whom they had lost touch, asking the radio announcers to broadcast their contact information. One woman appealed to the radio station to read her letter about a fifty-year-old woman she regarded as her mother, with whom she'd lost touch after this woman was hospitalized. She hoped that relatives who read the letter might get in contact and let her know how the woman was doing.[43]

The radio program also responded to a request to visit a hospitalized woman and child to reassure a worried husband in Germany.[44] One of Handl's proudest memories was intervening on behalf of a young man who associated with a Croatian nationalist organization, who wished to visit his father's grave. On air, Handl invited him to visit Yugoslavia and asked the consulate in Bonn to assist him – an approach that apparently bore fruit.[45] Handl's story presents To Our Citizens as a program that reached out to all Yugoslavs – not just loyal citizens – to heal national wounds and welcome stray sheep back into the fold.

Occasionally letters warned about scams and threats. Josip Mileta recounted a conversation with three compatriots who had been taken advantage of by a Yugoslav con artist. He had told them their passports were invalid, and took 700 DM from them to resolve the issue.[46] Another listener thought it important to warn his fellow citizens, on the basis of his experience working in Germany and visiting Sweden, that while Germans valued Yugoslav workers and treated them well, Swedes treated them very poorly, insulting them and putting them in housing unfit for humans.[47]

Some listeners contributed suggestions that ranged from how to improve services to migrants, to how labour migrants could contribute back to Yugoslav society. For example, Živko Lazić proposed that migrants be charged a tax to help support the radio program, while another listener offered this would be a good way to pay for a more powerful transmission tower that sent a stronger signal. Lazić also suggested that migrants be required to make a monthly deposit with the national bank that could be used to support migrants upon their return, or pay child support when a parent became delinquent.[48] Stjepan Gajski proposed that migrants be able to purchase bonds to found new factories, in exchange for the promise of work – an idea that would in fact later be put into practice.[49]

The Zagreb flood in the fall of 1964 illustrated the extent to which migrants trusted the radio program in a crisis. The riverbanks burst in late October, engulfing 30% of Zagreb, in the southern parts of the city, home to 180,000 people. The flooding killed ten people and forced the evacuation of 45,000 inhabitants.[50] Ten thousand homes were destroyed, and a further 30,000 were rendered uninhabitable. Listeners were particularly anxious about their homes and loved ones, wondering about the fate of their immediate families and relatives and hoping that the program might inquire on their behalf. For Franjo and Slavica H. in Mannheim, the program was their "only hope" to find their loved ones.[51] Drago R. sent an urgent plea from Luxembourg:

> I am turning to you with a big request, since Zagreb has been in a big flood and is in great danger – this is especially true of my parents, who are near the Sava in Gredevo 137. My dad's name is Djuro R., and I beg you to visit them to see if they are still alive. I sent a telegram and until now haven't heard back. How are they doing? They are alone. There is no one to help them, and so I beg you to bring them my greetings and let me know whether they are still alive.[52]

Remarkably, the radio program appears to have taken these requests to heart, as at least one listener sent his thanks for informing him that his wife and children were safe.[53]

Mayor Većeslav Holjevec sent a letter to the radio program appealing to the Croatian diaspora and Yugoslav migrant workers. On the threshold of winter, inhabitants were without basic necessities; they needed home articles, furniture and linen, winter food stocks, heating fuel, as well as electrical appliances, televisions, radios, shavers, and other machines. He urged Yugoslav citizens living abroad to send appliances, clothing, food, and money. Listeners responded. Many wrote to express their desire to make a contribution, while others sent funds directly to the station. Tomo, writing from Ober Roden, sent fifty German marks, while Nikola in Neukirchen contributed sixty marks and solicited contributions from other Yugoslavs he knew. He wrote, "If we all contributed something, we could build a factory in our homeland," and asked the newspaper to share his fundraising story on the air to motivate others. Other listeners inquired whether customs regulations would be suspended to allow them to bring aid back home.[54]

Roughly half of the letters sent to the show were actually mailed from Yugoslavia, revealing that it was also very popular domestically.[55] In other words, listeners from across Yugoslavia were tuning in to a program that was meant for migrants. Were they primarily friends or family of migrants anticipating an on-air greeting from a loved one? Or did they also have other reasons to listen, if only because they enjoyed the music, or perhaps were considering a stint abroad? The letters provide some clues: at least two were from listeners in rural areas struggling to make ends meet, inquiring about the possibility of finding work abroad. Whatever the reasons for listening, the program not only helped migrants feel as if they belonged to Yugoslavia, it also conveyed to its domestic audience all kinds of knowledge and beliefs about migrants and migration. First and foremost, it sent an unequivocal message to Yugoslavs that migrants remained loyal citizens of Yugoslavia. But it also provided them with a glimpse, however limited, of life abroad.

Conclusion

Radio broadcasting was one of the first programs to help mediate a relationship between the state and its citizens abroad. Radio waves easily carried music and information into the homes of migrants scattered across Western Europe and used emotion to create a powerful sense of community with the homeland that transcended distance and borders. Thanks to the immediacy of the medium, listeners could, for an hour or half-hour at a time, feel as if they were spending time together with other migrants and with their loved ones in Yugoslavia.

The enormous success of *To Our Citizens* played a part in Yugoslavia's decision to broaden its broadcasting activities beyond programs on the four main radio stations (RTZ, Radio Belgrade, Radio Ljubljana, and Radio Sarajevo). RTZ was central in the expansion of those activities. In 1970, it founded a correspondents liason office that distributed audiovisual materials, in collaboration with radio stations from other republics and provinces, to radio stations in the FRG, Switzerland, France, Sweden, and Benelux countries. These stations then broadcast programming that combined information and entertainment for Yugoslav audiences, ranging from fifteen-minute weekly programs on Radio Luxemburg, to daily forty-minute programs on Radio Köln. RTZ also sent television materials to ZDF Mainz, WDR, and Television Stockholm. These local broadcasts subjected programming to the oversight of foreign states, but they also attracted a wider audience by resolving the problem of broadcast ranges, which had limited reception.[56]

To Our Citizens illustrates how early attempts to communicate with migrants were influenced by the construct "our workers living abroad." The program perceived Yugoslavia's relationship to labour migrants as unproblematic, close, and positive, even as a business opportunity. It focused on connecting migrants to their families back home through a mixture of popular music, greeting exchanges, and practical information. While the purpose of the radio program was "building ties," the nature of the medium and the design of the program also allowed Yugoslavs back home to "see migrants." While driven by migrant voices, and therefore in some ways more authentic than film representations, the portrayal of the migrant experience was massaged by the program production team, as they strove to balance entertainment and assistance, angst and uplift.

The program demonstrates that many migrants responded positively to the state's programs to engage with them, because it fulfilled their emotional and practical needs. Through their engagement with the program through letter-writing, they consented to the role that was given to them as loyal citizens of the homeland, and in return they expected assistance – primarily in keeping in touch with their loved ones, addressing practical problems at home and abroad, and carrying out missions in the homeland in their absence. These interactions helped to bring the construct "our workers living abroad" to life.

As a final note, the program also demonstrates how the transnational framework of migration challenged Yugoslavia's decentralized internal political model. Funded by the republic of Croatia, *To Our Citizens* was intended to mediate between the republic of Croatia and its inhabitants, but in practice, its audience was pan-Yugoslav. The program's conscious choice to ignore identity politics made this possible, and it arguably profited from its broad appeal. Thus, the idea of "homeland" that it promoted was intentionally vague, an empty container into which all listeners could pour their personal memories and imaginations. In this respect, *To Our Citizens* stands apart from other programs, such as the newspaper *Imotska krajina*, discussed in the next chapter, which offered a much more specific idea of "homeland." It also stands apart from the educational program discussed in chapters 7 and 8, which were not able to side-step the issue of jurisdiction, and thus had to grapple with the meaning of homeland in the context of the ideology of "brotherhood and unity."

5 A Nation Talking to Itself: Yugoslav Newspapers for Migrants

Yugoslav migrants could also stay in touch with the homeland by reading the print media. Migrants living in major urban centres had access to a variety of newspapers and magazines from across Yugoslavia, including *Vjesnik, Vjesnik u srijedu, Večernji List, Arena,* and *Sportske novosti* (from Croatia), *Ilustrovana politika* (from Belgrade), *Oslobođenje* (from Sarajevo), and *Večer* (from Maribor). While *Večer, Večernji List, Vjesnik,* and *Oslobođenje* were daily newspapers, *Vjesnik u srijedu* was a weekly newsmagazine, *Sportske novosti* was a daily sports newspaper, and *Arena* and *Ilustrovana politika* were weekly full-colour magazines (the first focusing on film and television, and the last on current affairs).

Editions and entire publications aimed specifically at migrants were launched, such as the federally funded *Novosti iz Jugoslavije* in 1966, which changed its name in 1970 to *YU novosti. Vjesnik u srijedu* also came out with a four-page insert targeted at migrant workers, and *Oslobođenje* started a specialized publication in 1973. Five to ten thousand copies of the edition for Germany of the newspaper *Vjesnik* were published daily. Aside from these publications, there were smaller, more local initiatives, such as *Imotska krajina* – a newspaper from a rural area heavily dependent on labour migration, published in order to maintain ties with its workers abroad. It was certainly unusual, and possibly unique.[1]

While radio programming had the advantage that it reached a broad spectrum of listeners, from the educated to the illiterate – those seeking an emotional connection as well as detailed information – it was the most ephemeral of all media. In contrast, print could transmit much more content and did not depend on migrants having access to a radio or being available at the time of transmission. A single newspaper could be shared by one person with another, and lent out by clubs and libraries. Unlike radio, it was also not weakened by distance or competing radio frequencies. As with all other cultural programs aimed at migrant workers, newspapers were complementary to radio programming, and indeed, letters from listeners and readers regularly referenced other media. According to a 1977 study, the proportion of Yugoslavs living abroad who regularly read Yugoslav newspapers was nearly as high as that of Yugoslav residents – 33.7% as compared to 39.8%. In 1969, Yugoslav periodicals sold 534,527 copies abroad, with *Vjesnik u srijedu* and *Sportske novosti* topping the charts, selling 125,000 and 107,200 copies respectively. These figures significantly underestimate the number of readers, as each copy would be passed from one reader to the next, and thus consumed multiple times.[2]

This chapter explores how newspapers kept readers connected to Yugoslavia by examining what they would have encountered in newspapers like *Vjesnik u srijedu*, the periodical boasting the highest circulation, and *YU novosti*, and how they responded. It then takes a close look at how newspapers could nurture workers' loyalties to their homeland, by focusing on a local newspaper, *Imotska krajina*. In contrast to the RTZ radio program *To Our Citizens of the World*, which crafted a sense of belonging to Yugoslavia rooted in the experience of listening with other migrants and citizens back home, as well as in pan-Yugoslav popular music, *Imotska krajina* cultivated a particularistic identity rooted in the sounds, landscapes, and traditions of the region of Imotski, in the Dalmatian Zagora. The idea of homeland it articulated was ambivalent: its content paid lip service to the idea of Yugoslavia, but its primary reference points were the Zagora region and Croatian-ness, both in the sense of a national identity and an identification with the Republic of Croatia. The Croatian Spring provided an opportunity for the tensions around these different concepts of homeland to crystalize and become visible.

Vjesnik u Srijedu and Novosti iz Jugoslavije

Vjesnik u srijedu (*VUS*) was launched on the first of March 1964, shortly after *To Our Citizens of the World*. The foreign edition available to labour migrants included a four-page insert with content tailored to citizens living abroad, entitled "To Our Citizens in the World." While the news-weekly was initially pitched to long-term emigrants as well as labour migrants, it very quickly focused on the latter. In its inaugural issue, it declared that it would inform readers on the events in Yugoslavia in the past week and local news from the entire country. Following in the footsteps of *To Our Citizens*, it also pledged to answer every single letter it received, whether in print or by mail.[3]

VUS made good on its promises. Every issue of the newspaper carried at least a half-page spread with news from across Croatia, and sometimes the rest of Yugoslavia: production figures for factories, planned improvements to local roads, and prices in the marketplace. It also dedicated at least half a page to answering questions from migrant workers, similar to those sent to *To Our Citizens*. Eventually the newspaper received so many questions that it limited the column to listing the name of the writer and the answer to the question, omitting the question itself. This unusual strategy turned the column into a variation on the personals page in the newspaper, where only the intended reader might make sense of a message.

A separate column was dedicated to providing medical advice. Offering clear, scientific explanations in plain language, it highlights the difficulties for migrant workers in satisfying their need for medical help while working abroad. Although they were often eligible for medical care in their host countries, they had difficulty communicating with health-care providers or did not receive adequate answers to their questions. One woman, for example, asked for advice for bile duct problems, while another inquired about varicose veins, and yet another was concerned that he was becoming deaf, and a father wondered what to do about his son's crooked teeth. Questions about women's health, such as infertility and prolapse of reproductive organs, appeared regularly, suggesting that the column provided a useful service to women who may have felt uncomfortable confiding in a foreign doctor.[4]

More broadly, there was a real focus on printing migrant voices. Interviews with migrants on their experiences and opinions were regularly featured. *VUS* also printed longer articles and editorials that were of interest specifically to migrants. For example, they included a speech by Tito on labour migrants, or explanations about social security regulations and agreements in Yugoslavia and abroad.[5] Finally, each issue included local news items from the Republic of Croatia under the rubric "Brief News from the Homeland," a smattering of domestic and international news items, human interest stories, and articles on historical, cultural, or geographic topics.

The format of *VUS* format was adopted by other publications, tailored to their specific audiences. *Novosti iz Jugoslavije*, published by the Federal Employment Office, provided similar content, but addressed to a Yugoslav-wide audience. In this bimonthly newspaper, readers found copious information on how to navigate rules and regulations that applied to labour migrants, as well as news from across the country. Whereas *VUS* projected an image of wanting to help workers with the complexities of living and working abroad, *Novosti iz Jugoslavije* was a reference guide for domestic and foreign policies, with articles like "Married Men Pay Less Tax," "Foreign Currency Bank Accounts in Yugoslavia," and "Belgium: Without Authorization You Cannot Obtain an Entry Visa."[6] Perhaps because it sounded like the mouthpiece of the Federal Employment Office, *Novosti iz Jugoslavije* never achieved the same popularity as *VUS*. While *VUS* had a distribution of 125,000 in 1970, *Novosti iz Jugoslavije* never exceeded 25,000 issues.[7]

Newspapers like *VUS* and *Novosti iz Jugoslavije* filled acted as two-way communication channels, helping readers to keep abreast of events in Yugoslavia and providing a means through which migrants could express their opinions and ask questions. By allowing migrants to read their own voices, interspersed with news stories on Yugoslavia, they represented migrants as an integral part of Yugoslav society. Although *VUS* had a Croatian focus, it included content from the federation in each issue – whether on Tito, federal policies, or happenings in other republics. It thus represented the homeland as both Croatian and Yugoslav. During the Croatian Spring, however, *VUS* gained a reputation for stoking Croatian nationalism, demonstrating that its format could easily be adapted to different political projects.

A Letter from Home: *Imotska krajina*

To examine alternative constructions of homeland in the migrant-oriented press, this chapter focuses on yet another newspaper, *Imotska krajina*, which was published in the Imotski region after which it was named. As noted in chapter 2, the region boasted one of the highest labour migration rates in all of Yugoslavia. It was also notable for its reputation as a Croatian ethno-nationalist stronghold, and more specifically, as a hotbed of support for the fascist Ustaša movement and for the Independent State of Croatia (Nezavisne države Hrvatske, NDH) during and after the Second World War. After the war, this history allegedly predisposed migrants in the postwar period to be hostile to the Yugoslav project.

It is unclear whether these stereotypes are well founded, as scholars have yet to investigate the history of the region through the Second World War and its aftermath in any detail. Nonetheless, there are hints of the region's Ustaša and, more broadly, anti-communist past. Notable Ustaša figures, such as Ivan Rojnica, were born in Imotski. Frane Sulić, a bureaucrat in the NDH, also born in the region in the town of Zagvozdu, sent a report in 1941 to NDH ideologue Mile Budak stating that the founding of the Ustaša state had been welcomed with much rejoicing by the peasants of the Imotski region.[8] Hardly an impartial observer, his testimony should be taken with a grain of salt.

Beyond such circumstantial evidence, much of what we do know comes from historians making a case for the Partisans as ruthless war criminals. It is perhaps not surprising, then, that they insist on the widespread nature of continued anti-communist opposition in the aftermath of the war. *Imotska krajina* was purportedly home to a branch of the Croatian Liberation Movement (Hrvatski oslobodilački pokret – HOP).[9] Ivica Lučić similarly documents the existence of Križari activity – guerrillas who continued fighting the Partisan regime after the war ended – as well as mass executions of Križari in the Imotski region. His discussion reminds us that anti-communist opposition in Imotski cannot be separated from that in neighbouring Herzegovina. In spite of different administrative geographies that placed them in different republics, in practice they constituted an integrated territory.[10]

At the same time, Nedeljko Kujundžić's study, published during the socialist era, argued that the Ustaša did not gain broad popular support in the region, and that over four thousand Imoćani joined the Partisan-led people's liberation struggle.[11] Nonetheless, although not conclusive, the fragmentary history of anti-communist activities in the region suggests that the region was susceptible to alternative ways of identifying to those promoted by the federal authorities.

If *VUS* constructed an idea of homeland that combined Croatia and Yugoslavia, *Imotska krajina* anchored it at the scale of the village and region. Whereas *VUS* had a Croatia-wide audience and was run by a major publishing house, *Imotska krajina* was a remarkably ambitious project by local actors in the Dalmatian hinterland to produce and distribute a bimonthly newspaper to connect with its large population living abroad. Like the radio show *To Our Citizens*, *Imotska krajina* not only connected migrants to each other, and to the state; it also connected migrants to their homelands, putting itself forward as a kind of enabler for a transnational national public sphere.

The newspaper was initiated by the local branch of SAWPY, which was the largest mass organization in Yugoslavia, whose purpose was to include as much of the population as possible in carrying out the agenda of the League of Communists of Yugoslavia. In explaining the motivation behind the newspaper, the editor-in-chief Milivoj Rebić indicated that there had been need for better information on the goings-on in the region for decades. Even so, the intention was clearly to respond to the challenges posed by labour migration and create an imagined community of people from the region, one that transcended national borders.[12] For locals, the newspaper would be "an initiator of actions and a never-boring record of events. And for our workers temporarily employed abroad and numerous diaspora around the world, it will be a letter from home."[13] This entailed not only producing local content, but also building a network of "foreign" correspondents who could write stories about issues that mattered to migrant workers in their host states. It also required selling enough subscriptions to remain solvent to residents of the Imotski region living abroad – Imoćani – and answering their letters.

While the contents of a newspaper of such local interest might seem arcane at first glance, they reveal that the construction of belonging and the definition of homeland could be intensely local. The imagined community, or homeland, projected by *Imotska krajina* was grounded in regional landscapes, dialects, folklore, and rhythms. At the same time, during the Croatian Spring, *Imotska krajina* embraced a broader understanding of the homeland, rooted in Croatian national identity and tied to the fate of the Republic of Croatia within Yugoslavia. Thus, the newspaper illustrates the connections in how the local, the national, and the transnational might be mobilized in the construction of homeland.

Imotska krajina contained a variety of news stories and features. As promised, it endeavoured to be a "letter from home," printing numerous stories of local interest, such as reports on public works, economic development, or the harvest. Stories written in dialect related colourful conversations between locals. Every issue also contained cartoons and humorous anecdotes, and occasionally poems and other creations by local schoolchildren. It also informed readers about political events such as municipal council meetings, local party and state meetings, visits by republican and federal party and state officials, party plenums, and Tito's foreign policy, and contained opinion pieces on political topics. These items were clearly intended to shape popular opinion according to the party consensus, which was one of the important roles of SAWPY – the paper's founder and sponsor.

As in *VUS*, certain sections were aimed specifically at migrants, under the headings "From Our Migrants" and "For Our Migrants." These sections included stories about migrants living abroad, travelling home, or visiting home, as well as informative articles on subjects such as how to avoid problems with foreign or Yugoslav bureaucracy, and resources for workers living abroad. It also included several interactive features – the highly popular "Greetings and Good Wishes" section, an advice column, and letters to the editor, which included responses from the editor to each letter. These sections focused on engaging migrants by celebrating them and serving their needs. Finally, we should not forget about advertising. Although not intentionally targeted only at migrants, in practice the only advertisers who seem to have been interested in the newspaper were banks seeking to attract remittances.

Anecdotes in Dialect

Most issues of *Imotska krajina* included stories written in dialect, often relating a conversation between locals, but sometimes describing a scene or landscape, which I will refer to as anecdotes. These texts illustrate how local identity was rooted in tradition and the absence of migrants. The dialect in use in the Imotski region is quite specific – highly distinctive and hard for outsiders to understand, and geographically very contained, although spilling over the border between Croatia and Bosnia-Herzegovina. The authors' choice to write in dialect anchored the characters, events, landscapes, and conversations firmly in the local, but it did more than just that. The use of dialect has to be contextualized in broader debates over the Serbo-Croatian language in the 1960s and 1970s. As part of its efforts to defuse tensions between Croats and Serbs that had exploded into open conflict during the Second World War, the Yugoslav socialist regime had endorsed a single, shared, standard language, Serbo-Croatian, as formally ratified in the 1954 Novi Sad agreement. While it allowed for two variants that were spoken and spelled slightly differently, *ijekavski* and *ekavski*, it worked towards a single vocabulary derived from both the Croatian and Serbian traditions. Croatian intellectuals criticized this project as a covert attempt to impose the Serbian variant, and in 1967 three linguists issued a rival Croatian dictionary, which was quickly condemned as a nationalist deviation. The use of dialect in the place of Serbo-Croatian can thus be seen as subtle resistance to the modernizing and homogenizing project of Serbo-Croatian, albeit one that avoided the charge of nationalism by taking refuge in a specifically local dialect.

The use of dialect to relate folkloric knowledge can also be contextualized in the even longer history of the south Slavic literature. In the nineteenth century there was a European-wide movement of collecting folk literature in the vernacular, inspired by the Grimm brothers. In the south Slavic lands Jernej Kopitar, Vuk Stefanović Karadžić, and Luka Marjanović were some of the best-known collectors. The compendia of folk songs and stories that they assembled was a buttress for claims to a modern national identity and the basis for a standardized vernacular language. Thus, inherent to the project was a tension between recording and promoting authentic dialects, and creating a unified national language.[14] In choosing to write in dialect, then, the authors were echoing the identity-building work of earlier generations, proposing an alternative foundational folklore for its citizens. This is particularly significant, given that this dialect was also spoken in neighbouring villages across the nearby border in Bosnia-Herzegovina. These anecdotes can be understood as promoting a particular local understanding of the self – one that suggested an alternative geography of belonging, one that erased or even challenged the internal political boundaries in Yugoslavia.

The main characters of the anecdotes in *Imotska krajina* were frequently elders, whose conversations read like ruminations over time and the persistence or loss of tradition. In "Swelter," two older men share a conversation as they rest from working in the fields, making new pickets for the fences. They talk about the how quickly the time has gone, the hardships they have experienced along the way, the wine they are drinking, and the disappearance of the old ways. A stark contrast emerges from the conversation between the old and modern ways of life. The men reminisce about hard labour in the mines as labour migrants in Belgium and the United States, and the struggle to work the land in an unforgiving environment. They are disappointed that, after a life of hardship, their own children have left for foreign lands, leaving them to continue working in the fields. Interestingly, the old men continue caring for the land, even though there is no longer any need for it. Not only do they extract very little from it, but it is also much easier to go to the grocery store. There is a real ambivalence in their reflections on modernization – on the one hand, it is no longer necessary to break one's back tilling the land, but on the other, they have lost the ability to communicate with their grandchildren. "I have a hundred problems when I try to explain to my grandchildren what are ingles, rocks, ingle chains, plough, wooden hoops for livestock, bullock carts. ... They don't understand that ... and they will never know what our life was like. ... Now, that is what hurts me, here in my chest, and it doesn't let me sleep at night – the ignorance young people have about us elderly people and how it once was."[15] In this way of understanding, it was the land, however harsh and unyielding, that connected the generations.

The idea of the older generation as guardians and preservers of the "old ways" surfaces also in "Vintage."[16] Like "Swelter," with its evocation of the intoxicating summer heat, "Vintage" reminds readers of the close ties of village life to the seasons. Here it is two women speaking; instead of standing in the fields, they are sitting in church. Their ages are not disclosed, but we can assume they are at least middle-aged, as their children are old enough to drink wine. Echoing the men, they talk about the hard work of caring for the land and transforming its bounty into traditional products.

This conversation conveys two ideas – that the women have become the carriers of tradition, and that this role is a heavy burden for them. Their focus is on the wine, as it is harvest time, and the grapes need to be picked and processed. Mara, the more talkative of the two, describes all the tasks she has done and that remain to be done – tasks that were traditionally performed by the entire household but that now fall exclusively to the women and children. Her remaining task is to make wine for her family and to sell at the annual wine fair. She complains that the hard labour consumes her and wears her down. Her companion echoes this idea: "There, when you do everything you need with the field, tobacco, grapes, clover, and animals, winter arrives. All things considered, you've been nowhere, and you did nothing." She also alludes to traditional activities that used to accompany the harvest and that are no longer attended to – making barrels, weaving baskets, buying new vines and trimming the old ones. Thus, the reader is presented with an image of a region in decline, toiled over by women and children, devoid of new investment, reduced to subsistence agriculture.[17]

Aside from old men and women, the other main character in these anecdotes is the landscape – a thoroughly rural landscape, sparsely populated, wild, parched, and hostile to life, but also beloved. Listen to this ode to this rural landscape, wilted by a summer heat wave:

> I remember … before you couldn't wait for barley to seed or mulberry to blossom. During those tough years of famine, with the indigence and food scarcity, the year would seem to last twice as long. And those tough heat waves and swelters. The swelter kills, and the heat burns everything. When you look over to the fields or at sinkholes, you can see a sort of blueish fog created by the heat, rising into the air like the flames from the hearth. You would feel a tingling in your head and body, and see flashes before your eyes. … And the birds. The cuckoos would start to sing, and the frogs in the field sing together with the moles underground, singing one song after another. First the cuckoos would start during the day, the frogs would continue in the afternoon, and the moles would finish in the night-time. Luckily, the birds aren't the same as they were before. They are gone, or I don't know what we would do. You see, you cannot even hear the cuckoo anymore. You only know that the heat burned everything because of the crickets. In the night, the nightingale sings in my cherry tree; it rouses my soul after the swelter has tired it during the day. Everything alive hides in the shade until two o'clock.[18]

This is not a landscape of abundance, but rather one of scarcity, hardship, and drought. And yet Jure's words exude affection, because this is also an enchanted landscape. The heat destroys the harvest and leads to famine, but it also intoxicates and mesmerizes. The narrator's senses are overwhelmed – tingling sensations, flashes, and the constant roar of animal calls, until the nightingale finally awakens not only his aware-ness, but his very soul, in the freshness of the evening.

In both texts the Imotska krajina is both a place out of (modern) time, and a place structured by (cyclical) time. The outside world subtly intervenes in these texts – thus, Mara tells her friend that her husband still accomplishes his traditional role of distilling the brandy or *rakija* in the winter months when he returns from working abroad. She adds that he has brought innovations into his distilling methods from abroad. The women also sit on new benches inside the church – presumably financed from migrant remittances – and browse through prayer books "from around the world." In the main, however, these are descriptions of places rooted in tradition, local landscapes, and the seasons. Aside from references to grocery stores and threshing machines, the modern world is as conspicuously absent as are the able-bodied men.

These anecdotes can be interpreted as having several interlacing intentions. The first was to act as a "letter from home," reminding migrant workers of the goings-on in their home town or village. These texts also reminded workers of the implications of their absence and expressed a deep anticipation of their return. Through the evocation of traditions that were lost and those that persisted, they also transmitted folkloric knowledge. This might seem like a futile endeavour – after all, what use could these migrant workers have for such knowledge – the anecdotes themselves expressed a strong sense that this way of life was disappearing. Sharing this knowledge was important not because it was useful, but because, like the wine that the women dutifully made, and other traditional practices like distilling *rakija* or singing *ganga*, it con-nected them to the landscape and to older generations. In other words, it was a way for them to preserve their "true" ancestral identity as they laboured in exile in the capitalist West.

A Letter from Abroad: Letters to the Editor

Imotska krajina was not only a letter from home, it also provided migrants with opportunities to write back. There were two main venues for migrant voices. The first was the "Wishes and Greetings" column, in which migrants could send a loving word to friends and kin. The other was the Letter to the Editor column entitled "Your Letters." Remark-ably, the editor made a point of publishing a reply to every single letter published, regardless of whether the writer had asked for a response. These two columns appear to have been enormously popular, if we are to believe the claims of the editor, who regularly apologized for not being able to publish all the requests and having to shorten letters. Mail arrived from around the world, but the provenance, mainly from Germany, seemed to reflect the demographic profile of the average migrant worker from Croatia.

Most letters chosen for publication fell into common themes and followed certain formulas. As with listeners writing to RTZ, homesickness was a predominant theme – migrants writing about their deep longing for home. Indeed, few if any writers were happy working abroad – much more common were highly emotional letters stressing despair. A significant proportion of letters related to the newspaper itself – expressing a sincere appreciation for its existence or inquiring about subscriptions. One letter echoed the very words of the newspaper in its inaugural edition: "I really like your newspaper. When I receive it, it's like getting a letter from home."[19] Some letters testify to the way in which a single copy of the newspaper circulated from hand to hand: one writer said that he would bring his newspaper to the construction site where he worked, and that a crowd would form around him.[20] This was a reminder that, while newspapers were a more individualistic medium than radio programs, which became opportunities for migrants to gather and listen together, newspapers were also sometimes consumed socially. It also suggests that the newspaper reached a broader audience than just Imoćani. Migrants also wrote in to ask the newspaper to cover the goings-on in their villages and to ask for updates on public works projects. While it is natural that the newspaper should toot its own horn, it seems migrants perceived the newspaper as a valuable source of information and connection to home.

A number of writers used "Your Letters" as a forum to express frustration and anger. Some migrants wrote about the way in which the region was being slandered. One writer, for example, expressed pride in coming from this "poor" region and deplored the fact that some people looked down on the Imoćani, portraying them as "passive."[21] Letters also expressed frustration with government policy. These letters all hinged on the conviction that the region had been left behind by Yugoslavia – and even worse, that the remittances that might be used to develop the region were being funnelled elsewhere. Some letters expressed frustration with the slow pace of improvements to their community, such as electrification or construction of schools. One angry letter called the local political leadership "useless" and added, "All they do at meetings is beat dead horses." This reader opined that the migrants were in a position to help – they only needed to find local partners.[22]

Mediating the Croatian Spring

Although these letters likely faithfully represented the discontent of *Imotska krajina* readers, the newspaper should be understood not just as a billboard, but as a shaper of migrant opinion. The press transferred information to labour migrants about political developments in Yugoslavia during the Croatian national revival and helped to shape their political positions. The Vjesnik publishing house, which published the daily *Vjesnik* and the weekly *Vjesnik u srijedu,* gained a reputation for promoting the views of the reformist Communists. According to Batović, the Vjesnik publishing house was among several news organizations in Croatia that promoted liberalization (along with RTZ, which produced *To Our Citizens*). Starting in 1967, *VUS* focused attention on several problems, including the precarious situation of labour migrants and the questionable fortunes made by export companies such as Belgrade-based Genex, and by 1969, it turned its attention to the national question. The influence of VUS was such that the Belgrade satirical magazine referred to it as "Vustaša," a nickname that associated the newspaper with the notorious fascist regime from the Second World War.[23]

While scholars have noted the role of the Vjesnik publishing house in mobilizing Croatians behind the SKH, it was not the only media outlet to do so. The much smaller *Imotska krajina*, which came into existence at the peak of the Croatian Spring, in 1970, also agitated on behalf of the reformists, while adopting a highly emotive nationalist discourse. At first publishing occasional articles and letters to the editor that criticized the foreign currency policy in a relatively measured tone, by March 1971 the newspaper regularly published inflammatory denunciations of federal policies and warnings about the erosion of the Croatian nation. It drew explicit connections between the tragic fate of migrant workers and the supposed victimization of Croatia within the federation, infusing Croatian nationalism with localized meanings. It was thus instrumental in mobilizing labour migrants behind the SKH and against the federation.

During the Croatian Spring, the newspaper linked the small, isolated region to broader geographical scales, weaving the local, the national, the transnational, and the federal into a complex tapestry. It related the everyday life, struggles, and achievements of migrants living abroad, and the families they had left behind, to Croatian nationhood and Yugoslav political life. By shifting from everyday life and folklore to politics, the newspaper expanded the idea of "homeland" to encompass all of

Croatia. Simultaneously, it evoked a relationship to Yugoslavia that was ambiguous, even unstable. Echoing the very tensions of the Croatian Spring, texts in the newspaper vacillated between condemning the federation's exploitation of the region and of the Republic, and pledging loyalty to Tito and self-managed socialism.

Readers of *Imotska krajina* were drawn into the Croatian Spring primarily by the contentious issue of remittances. Without drawing an untenable distinction between an "authentic" consciousness and media discourse that somehow manipulates and shapes it, readers appeared to be responsive to the newspaper's focus on this issue because it addressed their own preoccupations – the policy on foreign currency effectively forced them to exchange their earnings for much less desirable Yugoslav dinars.

The editorial "Foreign Currency" by regular contributor Ivo Gudelj is typical of opinion pieces published in 1970 on the topic. He pointed out that workers were unable to spend their remittances on anything of real value and decried their exploitation at the hands of retailers and banks. "Someone is making a fortune on the backs of our migrants," and according to Gudelj, that someone was Yugoslavia. This situation would not improve until the official exchange rate of the dinar was brought in line with its actual exchange rate – until then, "our worker will continue to feel like someone is taking that which belongs to him." Furthermore, he pointed out the unfair treatment of local municipalities, which were handicapped in their ability to make profitable use of migrant remittances. While migrants received a discount for paying for goods in foreign currency, local administrations did not benefit from any such discount when they paid for public works using migrant contributions, in spite of the enormous challenges they faced.[24]

Starting in 1971, opinion pieces began to appear regularly linking the Imotski region's woes, not only to Croatia's current status within Yugoslavia, but more conspiratorially to a history of oppression of the Croatian nation. Like *VUS*, *Imotska krajina* reproduced a lecture given by Zvonimir Komarica on this theme, which he delivered at Matica Hrvatska, an organization heavily involved in the radicalization of the Croatian Spring. Komarica, who headed the Institute for Migration and Nationality, situated the current wave of labour migration in a longer historical continuum, focusing on three earlier waves: the Turkish invasion of the sixteenth century, the period of Hungarian rule in the nineteenth century, and the interwar dictatorship. His main argument was that none of these waves of migration was natural, the result of underdevelopment or population surplus. Rather, they were the outcome of politics and policy. Komarica then linked the issue of migration to the current reform movement.[25]

A special insert on 15 March 1971, which printed speeches made at the local conference of the League of Communists, showcased the local impact of the Croatian Spring. The focus of the conference was the way in which other newspapers – particularly those based in Serbia, including those of federation-wide circulation – had misrepresented the events at a voters' assembly in the village of Aržano, at which a speech by Croatian Spring leader Marko Veselica had been debated, smearing the local political leadership and characterizing the region as nationalist. Both the voters' assembly and the conference of the League of Communists demonstrate that there was substantial local excitement around the activities of the Croatian Spring. Local political actors felt as if they were active participants in it – indeed, as the president of the local conference of the Youth League declared with characteristic youthful impetuosity, "It is obvious from all this that what we are doing in Imotski is not to the liking of our tutors. Nor have they liked our work after the life-changing tenth session of the Central Committee of the Croatian Communist Party, which was in line with the conclusions of that session. The underdevelopment of the Croatian nation suits them." He added in a conspiratorial tone, "It's in someone's interest to attack Imotski, the people, and Matica Hrvatska in our Republic." Other contributors took a different line of defence – Branko Škare, principal of the local high school (*gimnazija*), for example, defended Imotski's supposedly impeccable anti-fascist record during the Second World War, thus aligning it with Yugoslavia.[26]

But it is not just that Imotski was seen as an integral part of Croatia; it is also that the Croatian Spring was understood in specifically local terms – particularly, through the prism of migration. Thus, Andjelko Šućur, who sat on the Health and Social Security Council, raised the problems facing labour migrants and their families back home, which he framed as a Croatian (rather than specifically local) problem.[27] Mirko Dragović, president of the inter-district conference of the Communist Party of Dalmatia, brought the discussion to a close by tackling the issue of foreign currency: "We must clearly and openly say that dinar and foreign currency income belong to the one who earns them. Those who earn the currency can unfortunately not be here to discuss it with us, because they are busy freezing and earning foreign currency. We owe it to them to fight for their and our right to dispose of foreign currency, just like any other income. We also have to say that even if our man or our republic has a surplus of foreign currency, it should be available for them to sell on the market, rather than according to some invented exchange rate." In other words, the Croatian Spring was presented to readers of *Imotska krajina* as a response to specifically local problems.[28]

Miko Tripalo's visit on 15 April 1971 displayed the tension inherent to this localized conflation of the local and the national. A member of the Presidency of the League of Communists of Yugoslavia, Tripalo was a high-profile leader in the Croatian Spring. Upon his arrival, he visited Imotski town as well as a number of local villages. He also listened to the president of the municipal assembly discuss the economic challenges of the area. Tripalo's own speech stands in stark contrast to the speeches of the local conference of the League of Communists of Imotski – it was a generic speech, targeted to a general audience, that would have made as much sense in Zagreb or Rijeka as in Imotski. Aside from a few sentences devoted to the issue of foreign currency, little in the speech was tailored to local problems. But it is telling that he was presented with a traditional woven purse with five German marks inside it – a reminder of the plight of the migrant workers – which he is pictured as wearing around his neck on the cover page of the newspaper. For the people of Imotski, if not for Tripalo, the Croatian Spring was first and foremost an aspiration to free themselves from the bondage of labour migration.[29]

While it is obviously impossible to treat the "Your Letters" column as an objective record of reader responses to this coverage, they suggest not only that migrants continued to be deeply involved in local and national politics, but also that they agreed with the newspaper's characterization of their predicament. Letters to the editor acted as a forum for migrants to participate in the political life of Imotski and Croatia. Their letters echoed many of the concerns and perspectives that found expression in the political articles discussed in the following section. Citing a report that he had heard on *To Our Citizens*, one reader complained that the banks that received the remittances didn't care about the region and proposed that the Imoćani should found a bank of their own, to ensure that locals paid fair rates.[30] By printing such letters, the newspaper legitimated a discourse of outrage.

In its responses, the editorial board validated and, indeed, amplified the migrants' sense of grievance and imbued it with meaning in the context of the SKH's reformist agenda. In response to one reader who lamented the fate of migrant workers, the editor emphasized the irony that "migrants sweat to earn remittances so that others might profit from it," continuing the cycle of poverty. In response to another letter in the same issue, the editor agreed that the Imotski region had indeed been forgotten (*zaboravljena*), but that change was on its way: new laws

Figures 13 and 14. The cartoons in *Imotksa krajina* often focused on the frustrations of labour migrants. *Left:* "You know, mate [*kume*], yesterday it's been a full ten years since we left for Germany on *temporary* work!" (*Imotska krajina*, 1 April 1970) *Right:* The father, in traditional attire, explains to his son about the expenses involved in cultivating the land. Son, in labour migrant attire: "And then, what is left?" Father: "What God gives you and what your children send you from abroad" (*Imotska krajina*, 1 October 1970)

on foreign exchange transactions were about to be implemented, and these were passed by "the people that we elected."[31]

Cartoons provide another glimpse into the newspaper's escalating politicization. Cartoons in *Imotska krajina* had always been a vehicle to highlight the absurdity of the labour migrants' predicament, focusing in particular on their elusive aspirations for a better life. They made light of the fallacy that migration was "temporary" (figure 13). They also drew attention to the limited impact of remittances on the local economy, either as a survival strategy for households stuck in out-dated subsistence farming (figure 14) or as a source of financing for an overabundance of restaurants, which did not represent meaningful economic development (figure 15). By 1971, such cartoons – which took gentle jabs at the migrants themselves and their foolish ambitions – were increasingly supplemented by cartoons that pointed the finger at Yugoslav authorities for bad policymaking, incompetence, and, most of all, corruption (figures 16 and 17).

Figure 15. "And be sure, son, to earn money in Germany so that we can open a restaurant like everyone else in our village!" (*Imotska krajina*, 1 September 1971)

Figures 16 and 17. In 1971, cartoons in *Imotska krajina* increasingly attacked Yugoslav authorities and institutions as parasitical and incompetent. *Left top*: "They say that you bought three cars. I see only one." "One I had to leave at customs, and the other I gave for the federal provision." *Left middle*: after devaluation of the dinar, people are more interested in lining up for passports than for jobs in Yugoslavia. *Left bottom*: "Give me an example of what you, in the district administration, have done for our workers temporarily employed abroad in Germany, so that they may stay here." "What are you talking about? We held 127 meetings with them!" (*Imotska krajina*, 15 March 1971) *Right*: "He surely works in Germany?" "No, he works for a bank." (*Imotska krajina*, 1 June 1971)

The municipal library in the town of Imotski, which to my knowledge is the only public repository of this newspaper, does not carry the 1972 issues of *Imotska krajina*, but an editorial entitled "Amongst You Again" in the 1 January 1973 issue reveals that the newspaper had not been published for more than ten months. Its absence is consistent with the timing of the crackdown against individuals and organizations deemed to be nationalist following the twenty-first session of the LCY in December 1971. The unsigned editorial claimed that the newspaper had in fact stopped operations as the result of a dispute with the printer, Zadružna Štampa in Zagreb, relating to unpaid debt. While the coincidence seems curious, this is a plausible account, as indeed the newspaper had previously shared with workers its precarious financial situation, in a bid to stimulate subscriptions, and had increased the cost of subscriptions upon its relaunching. Moreover, it seems that Milivoj Rebić, the editor-in-chief in 1970–1, and Ivo Gudelj, who had written some of the most inflammatory articles, continued writing for the newspaper, so they were clearly not punished for the newspaper's political position. Nonetheless, as the editorial acknowledged, the timing of the newspaper's hiatus had occasioned substantial gossip amongst migrant workers, and it should raise our eyebrows too.[32]

Unsurprisingly, from 1973 onward, the newspaper abandoned its belligerent tone. It now returned to sharing "human interest" stories and discussing the local life in the region. Local concerns about underdevelopment and employment, previously linked to national politics, were now decoupled from them. While continuing to focus on the human cost of labour migration, it distanced itself from the tone of outrage it had adopted during the Croatian Spring. A speech by Božidar Peša, a local delegate to the seventh congress of the SKH, printed in the newspaper, admitted that "Imotski had occupied one of the most important places in the nationalist strategy. Counting on the underdevelopment of the Imotski region and in particular on the large number of those employed abroad, nationalist leaders tried to spread their 'avant-garde' ideas in our area. In that effort they had some success, leaning on similarly minded people in the district leadership." However, Peša continued, following the reprimand of the reformist wing of the SKH, Communists in Imotski energetically purged the nationalists from their ranks.[33] Whether or not Peša's characterization of the nature of political mobilization in the region was accurate, the message was clear: *Imotska krajina* would no longer disseminate nationalist discourse.

The newspaper now promoted a different narrative on the fate of labour migrants, which was no longer a product of historical injustice and exploitation by the federation, but instead, of Croatia's greater integration into the global economy.[34] Indeed, much ink was spilled over the global economic downturn that following the 1973 oil crisis, and more specifically, the threat posed to migrants' jobs abroad.[35] While the migrants' anxiety was palpable, the newspaper adopted a tone of measured optimism, describing how policymakers were seeking to bring migrants home by stabilizing Yugoslavia's economy and creating new jobs.[36] It highlighted efforts by the government and League of Communists to facilitate worker return by investing in creating jobs, particularly by allowing migrants to invest their remittances to local enterprises, such as in Pionirka, a textile factory.[37]

One article celebrating achievements in this area, entitled "Production Begins in Cista," is typical of many others. It recounted how, less than two years prior, representatives of the Pionirka enterprise and of the Zagreb credit bank had met with labour migrants on vacation to pitch their project of opening new factories in the area. They appealed to migrants to invest their remittances, which a number of attendees supposedly immediately did, "and that is how construction began on factories in Cista Provo and Cista Velika." The plan ran into minor difficulties, delaying the start of production – "Where aren't there problems?" it asked, rhetorically – but the factory finally opened with about a hundred female employees. The journalist interviewed a few employees, who beamed about what this meant to them. Iva Mustapić, for example, said, "When my husband heard about the foreign currency term deposit, he immediately told me to invest 6,000 marks, for my happiness. And I'm happy. See, now I'm working. He knew what a foreign land means, because he has been wandering in Germany for ten years, and he wished for me to remain here with the children and my mother-in-law." Other women expressed their desire to reinvest their own earnings in creating jobs for their husbands. Leaving aside the question of whether Pionirka and other such foreign-currency investment schemes were truly as successful as the newspaper proclaimed, this was a discourse of success, in which labour migration finally financed local development.[38]

Imotska krajina also sent a clear message that migrants were respected and valued members of Yugoslav society.[39] Letters to the editor reflected this new orientation – readers no longer encountered expressions of outrage by their peers. This did not mean that labour migrants had ceased sending such letters, or indeed changed their minds, but the newspaper sent a clear signal that dissent articulated in terms of national belonging was no longer tolerated.

Conclusion

Authorities and media professionals operating at different levels of government in Yugoslavia used newspapers like *Novosti iz Jugoslavije*, *VUS*, and *Imotska krajina* to open channels of communication with migrants working internationally, characterized by reciprocity of exchange. While there was greater emphasis in the print media on disseminating news and practical information than on the radio, where musical entertainment was the main vehicle for wooing migrants, newspapers also engaged the migrants' emotions. *Imotska krajina* expressly sought to elicit nostalgia as a means of strengthening bonds between migrants and their homeland, and encouraged anger, even outrage, during the Croatian Spring, and letters to the newspaper suggest that migrants were responsive to these efforts.

Whereas radio programs like RTZ's *To Our Citizens of the World* had constructed a largely apolitical pan-Yugoslav concept of homeland that was charged with positive feelings, *Imotska krajina* proposed an alternative notion of homeland, defined by the sounds and sights of the Dalmatian hinterland. This notion of homeland was mobilized in service of the Croatian national revival, illustrating the interplay of the local, national, and transnational in the construction of homeland. While scholars have speculated on the role of political émigré communities in Western Europe in souring migrants against Yugoslavia, the case of *Imotska krajina* reminds us that actors within Yugoslavia also played a key part in this process. It also decentres the history of the Croatian Spring by shifting focus away from Zagreb, which all traditional accounts have emphasized, to a part of Croatia that was marginal, not just geographically, but also in its relationship to the centre of power.

In exploring the interconnections between local, national, and transnational identities, the case of *Imotska krajina* helps to clarify the relationship between lines of inquiry in Yugoslav historiography that have either not been linked or have been framed as contradictory. Explanations of Yugoslavia's demise, for example, have either emphasized its roots in ethno-nationalism, or privileged the role of economic dislocation or political decentralization. Without presuming to explain Yugoslavia's ultimate fate, this chapter highlights the linkages between these different phenomena. It does so by focusing on the scale of the local and its connections to other scales (republican, federal, and transnational).

The lives of their migrants and the fate of their local communities were affected by the global exchange of labour and federal migration and remittance policies. In discussing the impact of labour migration on the region, writers for *Imotska krajina* echoed many of the themes depicted in films about labour migrants: the absence of loved ones, their periodic visits, and what they brought home, which included remittances, goods, fashions, ideas, and behaviours. They tended to depict labour migration as economically, socially, and culturally impoverishing to an already backward region. It is worth noting that, from their perspective, the economic, social, and cultural were intrinsically interconnected.

Media provided a vehicle for local actors, including party members and journalists, to mobilize migrants by harnessing their localized grievances and tying them into broader political movements in the republic. In turn, republican actors, whether politicians like Tripalo or more obscure figures like Komarica, were eager to capitalize on this support. In this manner, newspapers enabled debates about the migration policy to transition from the pages of official memos and research reports into the conversations of migrants and their friends and families.

6 Weaving a Web of Transnational Governance: Yugoslav Workers' Associations

In December 2016, the Museum of Yugoslav History in Belgrade – formerly the Museum of the 25 May – inaugurated an exhibition on the Yugoslav migrant workers, entitled *Jugo moja Jugo*. In addition to the museum's own artefacts, the exhibit featured an impressive array of items collected by migrant workers over the years. Particularly striking were the carefully preserved memorabilia from citizens' associations: photo albums, scrapbooks, framed pictures of sports teams and tournaments, and membership cards testifying to a vibrant associational life.

In conversations with migrant workers from Croatia, however, my interlocutors rejected the idea that the citizens' clubs were genuine popular associations. Rather, they told me that they were tools of the Yugoslav state to control and spy on workers, which they shunned. The case of the Yugoslav citizens' clubs illustrates the ambiguous nature of these associations, as policy instruments that the Yugoslav state used to govern its citizens, and simultaneously as communities that filled their members' lives with meaning.

Socialist Yugoslavia turned to associational life as a strategy to address ideological contradictions posed by its labour migration policy. State socialism was premised on the notion that the only way to end the exploitation of workers under capitalism was to for the state to own the means of production – and yet Yugoslavia tolerated the fact that a significant proportion of its workforce toiled in capitalist states. At least until the Prague Spring, socialist states also sought to "build socialism" by saturating society with party-led organizations whose function was to mobilize citizens and to provide a clear ideological framework for their activities – and yet Yugoslavia allowed its workers to be immersed in societies that were permeated with the values of capitalism and isolated and marginalized its citizens. Worse still, émigré organizations hostile to Yugoslavia then sought to mobilize and proselytize to these vulnerable workers.

Deeply concerned that workers were becoming alienated, Yugoslav authorities responded by trying to recreate, on the other side of its borders, a socialist, Yugoslav framework that would attract and capture workers, and in so doing reconnect them to Yugoslavia and its ideological pillars of brotherhood and unity, and workers' self-management. This required development of what we might call an organizational infrastructure: after devising an approach to engage with workers, authorities then needed to establish a network of institutions with specific mandates to put this approach into action.

While other scholars working on Yugoslav workers' associations have framed them as top-down tools of the state and downplayed their authenticity as popular associations, an examination of their genesis calls this view into question. This chapter reveals how significant aspects of migration policy were shaped on the geographic and hierarchical margins of the federal state. Yugoslav citizens themselves founded popular associations – mainly social clubs, sports leagues, and folklore groups. They caught the attention of consular officials, who understood the potential of popular associations as vehicles to reconnect citizens to the body politic, a message that they relayed back to the centres of power – federal and republican state and party organs.[1]

Policymakers, in turn, directed diplomatic missions to invest in these associations, coax them into line with official Yugoslav ideology, and foster the founding of new clubs. Thus the popular associations became the primary vehicles for a kind of "soft power" policy that Yugoslavia directed at its own citizens. The clubs gathered migrant workers together as citizens, to spread and gather information, provide education, consume culture, promote a Yugoslav identity, and deliver a variety of other services. The clubs were the key nodes in a network that stretched across Europe, used by Yugoslav state and party institutions to reach its citizens living abroad. Their survival was not assured but depended on the vibrancy of their membership.

Yugoslav citizens' clubs have attracted the attention of a few scholars – notably Nikola Baković, Petar Dragišić, and Vladimir Ivanović. While Dragišić's and Ivanović's valuable scholarship has focused on documenting state policy toward the clubs in the former case, and their place in the lives of workers in the latter case, Baković has persuasively argued that the clubs were part of a broader transnational strategy to preserve the loyalty of its workers and include them in Yugoslav cultural, political, and economic life. He has also made a compelling case for the periodization I use here. This chapter relates some of his insights to my argument that associations should be understood as nodes in a transnational web of governance. Recognizing the decentralized nature of the project, I also touch on the variations in associational life across Europe. Moreover, beyond seeing citizens' clubs merely as a tool of the state, I argue that they had purchase because they also served the needs of their members.

The Emergence of a Strategy

Initially, diplomatic missions were the main face-to-face points of contact for labour migrants – outposts of Yugoslav sovereignty that had a continuous presence. Other state institutions preoccupied themselves with advocating for workers abroad, most notably the League of Trade Unions of Yugoslavia (SSJ) and the Socialist Alliance of Working People of Yugoslavia (SAWPY/SSRNJ), but their presence was irregular, confined to occasional tours by delegations. Municipalities and rural districts also organized annual meetings with workers during the winter holidays, which they used to share updates about local developments, disseminate information on policies and programs relevant to migrants, and address their questions and concerns. During the rest of the year, however, migrants needing to resolve issues related to their lives back home had only the diplomatic missions to turn to. As early as 1966, diplomatic missions were advised that they should hire employees with the necessary expertise in labour and welfare law in Yugoslavia, and the legal system of the host state, in order to provide adequate service to workers living abroad.[2]

Even before the formal start of the open-border policy, Yugoslavia's diplomatic missions had a two-fold portfolio. Their first mandate was carrying out consular tasks of an administrative or legal character, which included activities under its direct jurisdiction, such as citizenship and visas, and liaising on behalf of workers with Yugoslav public institutions, such as the federal social insurance office or the Yugoslav customs service. It also involved a variety of other tasks, including certifying official documents, intervening on behalf of workers when their rights were being violated, and providing practical information about Yugoslav policies.[3] While such activities were common to most state's diplomatic missions, their second mandate was more unusual: to carry out what the consular service referred to as "propaganda-political work" among emigrant and labour migrant communities. In relation to migrant workers, this included providing access to Yugoslav media and organizing cultural events and film screenings.[4]

From the start, the diplomatic missions felt that they were poorly equipped to tackle the challenges posed by labour migration. For one, they did not have a dedicated section or staff to serve labour migrants

as a particular category of citizens, or protocols or even training providing guidance on how to effectively deal with common concerns.
Moreover, as they would raise time and time again, they were woefully
understaffed to deal with the growing flood of workers. Additionally,
migrants who didn't live in the immediate vicinity of consulates rarely
had the time or resources to visit them – which was a real problem
for these workers when they encountered problems requiring consular
assistance.[5]

Yet another problem was the fact that the police and employers in host
states looked askance at frequent contact between diplomatic missions
and migrants. In a 1962 report, the consular service reported that "there
have been several cases in which employers have fired our workers,
because they noticed that they occasionally visit our missions, or have
contact with embassy employees. In those instances, the employers
openly admitted that they were obliged to let the workers go, because
they do not wish to have trouble with the police."[6] Some migrants also
avoided visiting diplomatic missions because they might be attacked
by émigré organizations.

Clubs offered an alternative mechanism for labour migrants to connect with one another. The archival record suggests that, by the mid-
1960s, a variety of popular associations founded by Yugoslav citizens
were coming to the attention of state and party organs. These were distinct from the diaspora organizations that served emigrants who had
settled abroad permanently. The Federal Council of Migration Questions (*Savezni savet za iseljenička pitanja*) contained enthusiastic reports
by the Yugoslav ambassador to Denmark about the opening of new
clubs in Helsingborg and Ronneby in 1967, towns in southern Sweden.
It also contained materials from the same year about the activities of
the Yugoslav club in Zurich, which by 1967 had already been operating
for four years, therefore predating Yugoslavia's full-scale adoption of a
labour migration policy. It had two thousand members and organized
a variety of social activities, including a trip to Paris.[7]

Diplomatic missions initially expressed guarded support for the
spread of Yugoslav popular associations. They supported clubs that
had a strong popular base, as in Helsingborg and Zurich. Where associations did not already exist, support depended on the particular circumstances and the judgment of the local staff. In discussions with a
delegation from the Livno-Duvno region sent to visit the FRG by local
branches of SAWPY and Matica iseljenika Bosnije-Hercegovine, the
general consul in Munich advocated opening clubs in two or three
major urban centres, such as Munich, Frankfurt, and Cologne. He
asked for funding for this purpose, emphasizing that the success of this

endeavour would hang on substantial financial support.[8] In contrast, the consulate in Hamburg advised that "as it stands, the conditions for opening Yugoslav workers' or citizens' clubs are not in place," mainly because there was an insufficient concentration of workers. The consulate added that any efforts in this direction would be a waste of time and resources. Instead, it proposed to invest in enhancing its weekly gatherings at the consulate, "to create a tradition and habit among workers of regularly getting together in a place that is not an ordinary pub, around a program of a certain quality that has a specified content."[9]

Those necessary conditions were quickly met, as the number of labour migrants rose from an estimated 380,000 in 1966 to 531,000 in 1970, making sustaining a club a more feasible proposition.[10] Indeed, prior to Yugoslavia's adoption of an explicit policy to support workers' clubs, workers had founded clubs in at least twenty-three cities across Western Europe, attesting to the enterprising spirit of migrant workers. Clubs had opened in Germany (Berlin, Munich, Schwenningen, Stuttgart, Cologne, Lindau, and other cities); Austria (Baden, Wels, Grödig, Vienna), Switzerland (Bern, Geneva, Zurich), Sweden (Stockholm, Södertälje, and, as previously mentioned, Helsingborg and Ronneby), Belgium (Seraing, Brussels), England (London), and France (Paris and Marseille). The Union of Cultural and Educational Organizations of Yugoslavia estimated that tens of thousands of migrant workers were involved in such organizations.[11]

Aside from these clubs, which had the endorsement of local consular officials, there were other associations, over which Yugoslavia had no control. A number of these clubs had a national character, but most allowed citizens of other nationalities to join. Many were dominated by actors hostile to – or at the very least critical of – Yugoslavia. In fact, as Molnar has documented in the case of Munich, émigré organizations and the Catholic and Orthodox churches and Islamic organizations were quick to recognize the vulnerability and loneliness of migrant workers, responding by organizing associations that provided support and entertainment.[12] For example, as one report from 1973 complained, in Klagenfurt, the Catholic organization Caritas organized social activities that served only Slovenes; in Vorarlberg, one football team was called "Croatia" and was run by a cleric; and in Salzburg, where there was no workers' club, the Catholic church served as a gathering place for Yugoslav citizens, under the auspices of a priest who had made "hostile comments" against Yugoslavia.[13] In some ways, then, Yugoslavia was drawn into the business of club patronage partly by the need to compete for its workers' loyalty, a point made also by Baković.[14]

Yugoslav citizens' clubs had several advantages as vehicles for governing the Seventh Republic, in tandem with the diplomatic missions. For one, they did not attract the same level of suspicion as diplomatic missions from local employers and authorities. Moreover, they were much better suited to organizing cultural life, which was a powerful attractant for migrants and a key instrument for nurturing a Yugoslav identity and preventing assimilation into host societies. Supporting citizens' organizations was a way for overworked consular staff to outsource some of their work, with much better results.

Just as significantly, Yugoslav workers' clubs were ideologically sound: they were an expression of worker "self-organization," the very principle at the heart of self-management. In other words, not only could citizens' clubs – under the watchful eye of diplomatic missions – be used to foster an ideologically sound Yugoslav identity, rooted in brotherhood and unity; they would also reinforce the ideas and practices of Yugoslav socialism. Given the diplomatic missions' role in gently and inconspicuously supervising and steering these associations in approved directions, self-management of citizens' clubs functioned in ways that are reminiscent of bodies on Yugoslav territory: in appearance, democratic, but in practice, guided by state and party interests.

By 1970, in the midst of growing concerns about the alienation of labour migrants from Yugoslavia, Yugoslav state institutions were already envisioning clubs as key components of a trans-border network for governing Yugoslav citizens. The Labour Migrant Administration operating under DSIP issued a report in that year calling for coordinated support for the development of a network of citizens' clubs, recognizing them as the most effective and widespread vehicle to connect with migrants. According to the report, the Yugoslav citizens' clubs "have as a goal to gather all Yugoslavs, regardless of language, or national or religious belonging."

A description of the clubs' mandate highlights the extent to which Yugoslav authorities saw the clubs as instruments of governance: "Their main objective would be to watch over the rights and responsibilities of our workers, which are important for their continued presence on the relevant territory; the organization and promotion of informational, cultural, leisure, and athletic life in line with the workers' best interests; and the development of friendly relations with the representatives of foreign governments, trade unions, and organizations of a similar nature. Clubs and their branches are the best suited for the all-encompassing organization of citizens, because they can develop a variety of different activities, including those of a political nature, which are increasingly topical."[15] The report further called on the republics as well as a number of organizations whose jurisdiction included migrants, such as the SSJ, the Matice iseljenika, the veterans' organizations, and women's, youth, and professional associations, to intensify their engagement with labour migrants and their clubs.[16]

The LCY also committed itself to supporting associational life abroad. In 1971, the LCY instituted an office named the Delegation for the Activities of the LCY in Connection to the Departure and Temporary Work of Our Workers Abroad (Opunomoćstvo za delatnost Saveza komunista u vezi sa odlaskom i privremenim radom naših radnika u inostranstvo), to monitor labour migration and consider and respond to its challenges and implications. Initially, it mandated the creation of LCY bodies in foreign states to activate its members living abroad, of which there were an estimated fifty thousand. This was a remarkable initiative, considering the Cold War and, in particular, the open hostility of most host states to Communism.[17]

The delegation had a mandate "to engage in preparing workers politically and ideologically prior to their departure, keeping them informed during their stay abroad, and guiding their ideological and political life abroad." It specifically instructed its members living abroad to participate actively in associational life. Following its first meeting, the Command produced a document summarizing its positions on labour migration. Endorsing associations as the most effective way to fight against the negative influences of living abroad, and to protect workers' rights, it noted that only 5–15% of workers were members of clubs. Thus, LCY members should engage themselves in strengthening these associations.[18]

Nikola Baković has provided a concise account of this singular effort to expand a Communist party across state borders with a focus on the FRG. It created local branches operating under the supervision of commissions (povereništva) and sent professional party operatives abroad to organize workers, recruit new members, engage in propaganda, and maintain relations with Western communist and social democratic parties. These party operatives were also instructed to become active in citizens' associations. It also drew up an inventory of all LCY party members working abroad.[19]

Unsurprisingly, in the FRG this policy elicited alarm and resistance from local authorities and organizations concerned with the spread of communism and the "Yugoslavization" of public space. Baković argues that the LCY did not change its policies until a backlash arose against its propaganda activities in 1973. Yet the archival record shows that it recognized its approach as being unrealistic even earlier. By May 1972, the Delegation had opted to stop sending operatives abroad, with the exception of workers in Yugoslav firms operating abroad. Instead, it directed its members to "develop their activities" in the context of already existing Yugoslav workers' organizations.[20] Nevertheless, Baković's research suggests that the LCY continued to engage in controversial activities, even after its policy shift in 1972, and some of these activities may merely have been pushed underground. What is certain is that the LCY continued to monitor and shape the activities of the Yugoslav citizens' clubs.

Together, SAWPY and the LCY attempted to produce an overarching concept that would apply to all Yugoslav citizens' clubs. In a document entitled "Theses on Self-Organization," they determined the respective responsibilities of the LCY and of SAWPY toward the clubs. The document also established several principles: clubs should have a statute; citizens should have the right to choose the club to which they belonged; clubs do not engage in (their own) commercial activities; clubs should treat all languages equally; and clubs should not collaborate in any way with emigrant associations hostile to Yugoslavia. It is not clear how strictly these rules were enforced, or indeed, enforceable.[21]

State and party organs were trying to impose order on a rather messy reality. A substantial number of associations did not fit the neat categories they had in mind. The ideal was a Yugoslav citizens' club that housed several sections – cultural (dance, music performance), sports (football, chess, table tennis, etc.), and perhaps even technical (radio, photography, modelling, etc.) Aside from this model, there were also sports leagues and folklore groups that operated independently from any club, as well as clubs that identified themselves by one nationality, and clubs that were run out of restaurants. Baković shows how SAWPY's Coordinating Committee was itself riven with conflicts on how to deal with mono-national clubs, eventually opting to allow them, providing that they had responsible leadership and did not exclude members of other nationalities if they tried to join. Ultimately, the extraterritorial location of these associations protected them from Yugoslavia's aspirations to discipline them, although it could choose which associations to support and which to exclude.[22]

Theorizing the Yugoslav Citizens' Clubs

A generous literature is focused on migrant associations in the social sciences, mostly analysing their activities in the present. This scholarship has examined the associations' role in representing and intervening on behalf of migrants in the host society, and in building and sustaining relationships with the sending state. They have also highlighted the crucial role of these associations in providing migrants a "home away from home," particularly for migrant groups that are particularly marginalized, such as Ecuadorians in Italy or Cameroonians in South Africa. Scholars focusing on interactions between the sending state and migrant associations have highlighted how associations have channelled migrant earnings into relief efforts during national disasters, as well as investments in infrastructure and business ventures. Examining Ecuadorian and Argentinian associations in Spain and Italy, Margheretis concluded that "states have been relatively effective in tapping into migrants' symbolic and emotional attachments to the homeland, but they have obtained meager results in terms of grounding such attachment in strong organizations, persistent transnational political engagement, and political links."[23]

Yugoslav clubs were, however, distinguished from these other associations, by two important characteristics. First, they were addressed not to long-term migrants or diaspora, but to citizens who by definition were supposed to stay abroad for only a short time. Consequently, the focus of their activities was different, and in particular less focused on facilitating integration into the host society. The second follows from the first: while migrant associations are often courted by and under the influence of the sending state, Yugoslavia took on the role of official patron of the associations. As can be expected from a one-party state, it sought to control and limit the influence of any competing institution, whether the Catholic church or diasporic cultural groups.

Consequently, there was a tension inherent in these associations – on the one hand, they were clearly driven by migrant needs and concerns and depended heavily on the time and efforts of their members. On the other, they were perceived by the Yugoslav state as a vehicle to communicate with, supervise, and provide services to its citizens living abroad. This presents scholars with a conundrum – were they an example of civil society, of members of a given society organizing around particular interests into "special-purpose associations," to use the term employed by Tilly and Woods?[24] Or should they be seen as an instrument of the socialist state, popular only in name, used to mobilize citizens around the twin national and socialist projects, like labour brigades, Pioneer troops, and women's organizations?[25] The Yugoslav citizens' clubs did not comfortably fit either definition.

The literature on associations that is framed in terms of civil society assumes the autonomy of the public sphere. Yet, while some dissent was tolerated in Yugoslav society, in alternation with periods of ideological repression, it is difficult to speak of an autonomous public sphere, as socialist states, Yugoslavia included, rejected the very premise of autonomous associational life. All officially organized organizations in Yugoslavia came under the umbrella of state or party. The case of Yugoslav citizens' associations was somewhat unusual as a result of their situation *extra muros*, which allowed them, de facto, a significant degree of autonomy. Indeed, until the federation decided to support them, they were left largely to fend for themselves, depending on the degree of interest of the closest diplomatic mission. Even after this time, the state's control over the clubs was limited – diplomatic missions did not have the resources to run the clubs themselves and thus had to place their trust in the loyalty of the club leadership. Moreover, as they operated beyond Yugoslav state borders, consular officials had no legal authority over the associations and so were in no position to dictate anything to them. The best they could do was to threaten or intimidate, cut off the modest flow of funding, and report misbehaving individuals and groups to the Federal Secretariat of Foreign Affairs, raising the possibility of sanctions when they returned to Yugoslavia.

This relative autonomy, however, did not make "civil society" of Yugoslav citizens' clubs. The abundant literature on the function of associations in the development of the modern state and of liberal democracy has emphasized their role in driving change and in sustaining democracy. German historians have focused on the role of associations in the birth of the modern German state, as vehicles for transferring bourgeois values. For Putnam, Leonardi, and Nanetti, a vibrant ecology of associations underpins the good functioning of postwar local government in Italy. In all these accounts, associations play a critical role in shaping political life and in advancing the interests and claims of different social actors. The members of Yugoslav citizens' clubs did make claims on the state – they demanded the recognition of labour migrants as full citizens, and material support to sustain their activities as a community. These were limited claims, however – they did not seek to change or influence the state or hold it accountable. In some ways they were more like clients of the state, loyal to it and dependent on it for their continued survival.[26]

While the clubs highlight some problems inherent to the "state-civil society" dyad, at least in the case of state socialism, the scholarship that sees associations as mediators between the private sphere and the state, and as "schools for democracy," has some relevance for the case of Yugoslav citizens' clubs. Indeed, as mentioned above, federal authorities explicitly saw clubs as useful "schools for self-management," and, as will be discussed in chapter 9, they also came to see them as essential mediators between the migrant-family-in-crisis and the Yugoslav state.

Migrant associations had a relationship to the Yugoslav state that was different from that of other mass organizations because they were located beyond its borders. At the same time, they differed from the more traditional immigrant associations, which were also located outside the sending state's borders. While the latter also presumed a continuing relationship with the homeland, it was a weaker one. They were far more interested in facilitating successful establishment in the host society than were the Yugoslav citizens' clubs, while sharing with them a desire to foster a sense of community and a commitment to preserving language and culture. Because immigrant associations saw their field of action primarily as being the state of settlement, their activities included lobbying for the interests of the immigrants and providing opportunities for newcomers to network with earlier immigrants who had adjusted to their new home, and possibly turn this social capital into economic capital. This was not the case with the Yugoslav citizens' clubs.

What the citizens' clubs did exceedingly well, in a context in which migrants were "temporarily abroad" (or, put otherwise, permanently unsettled), was to act as a "home away from home," in some ways much more familiar, cosy, and welcoming than the actual residences that many migrants occupied, such as dormitories or rented rooms. Clubs that could afford to rent premises often had a recreation room, where workers could socialize, and at least a modest library. They thus functioned as domestic spaces, providing an interesting twist on the argument made by Amy Milne-Smith about British high society, who sought out clubs to as a substitute for home, as their posh residences were not really domestic spaces either. As Baković has pointed out, most clubs also had a bar, much to the chagrin of the Yugoslav authorities, who perceived this as not conducive to promoting socialist morality. Patrons enjoyed socializing over drinks, and club leaders appreciated the income generated from selling alcohol. This is one example of workers resisting the subjugation of their space to the imperatives of the state.[27]

Unlike the German *Vereine* or British gentlemen's clubs, Yugoslav citizens' clubs were open to both men and women, but in practice, women seem to have confined their visits to special occasions, socials, and weekend hours while their children attended Yugoslav language and culture classes or Pioneer meetings. Thus, during "ordinary" hours, clubs were spaces of masculine sociability, and on special occasions and weekends, a broader spectrum of migrant society would gather there. They were a place to speak and hear one's mother tongue and to meet and visit with others sharing similar life experiences, values, and aspirations. There is anecdotal evidence that they were also primarily working-class spaces, which well-educated Yugoslavs did not visit regularly.

Tilly's insights on social movements, including what he calls "special-purpose associations," are also useful here. He notes that such associations should not be understood as groups of people sharing a common identity, but rather as vehicles for creating new identities by gathering disparate individuals in the service of a common purpose. Clubs and other associations (such as sports teams and dance groups) did not merely bring together individuals already sharing a common identity – they attracted migrants who had come from across Yugoslavia, speaking different languages and dialects, bringing different traditions grounded

Figure 18. Club members created memorabilia to celebrate their associations' accomplishments, like this carefully preserved collage from a series of fifteen, 1970–85 (*Jugo moja Jugo*, Museum of Yugoslav History)

in different histories and landscapes, but sharing a common predicament and similar aspirations, and channelled their efforts. In a sense, then, the clubs helped to bring a Yugoslav identity into being for these migrants, by gathering them regularly to share common experiences.

It is important to highlight that a club's impact radiated beyond its membership roster and spatial confines. It was not necessary to be a club member to participate in the club's activities. While only a small percentage – ranging from 10 to 15% of Yugoslavs living abroad – were dues-paying members, much larger numbers of Yugoslavs living abroad took part in the socials, watched film screenings, and attended concerts, football games, and national holiday ceremonies organized and promoted by the clubs. Some events, like the concerts organized to celebrate national holidays, attracted an audience of thousands – one such concert in Vienna drew 12,500, while another in Stuttgart was attended by 4,000 Yugoslavs.[28] Even if only for a moment, these events recreated an experience of community.

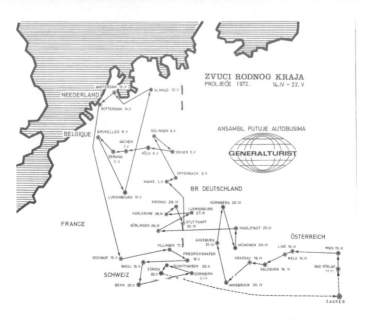

Figures 19 and 20. Associations helped to facilitate tours like this one, by the RTZ touring ensemble Zvuci rodnog kraja in 1972, by providing logistical support and drawing their membership as audiences

Figure 21. Social evenings were amongst the most popular events organized by Yugoslav workers' clubs; although Trumbetaš did not attend such clubs' events, his drawing of labour migrants enjoying an evening of dancing could just as well have represented such a social (Trumbetaš, *Gastarbeiter Gedichte 1969–1980*)

Some events were more scripted than others. Football games and socials were largely local apolitical affairs and clearly played an important role in fostering a sense of community. Others were heavily ideological, bore SAWPY's imprimatur, and were aimed at infusing this sense of community with a very specific socialist and multinational content. Touring musical ensembles were organized by the Yugoslav state and by the touring groups themselves, with the assistance of citizens' associations, which publicized them locally. Baković has shown that touring shows were very rigidly scripted to inspire patriotism in their audience. Because they relied heavily on traditional folk music, the shows were also carefully programmed to respect Yugoslav nationality policy. For example, in the very large productions put on by Yugoslavia's major radio stations, the first half of the program was devoted to folk music. Singers from each republic appeared onstage in national costume and performed two songs each in turn, with a focus on patriotic songs from the Second World War.[29]

Ever vigilant, diplomatic officials attended these performances and reported on their reception. Baković has noted a few occasions where the audience was rowdy, cheering only performers from one ethnicity, or booing classical music performers. These incidents remind us that merely attending a concert did not ensure acceptance of its ideological content. Several other reports, however, describe a very enthusiastic reception. One observer told of the patriotic fervour that swept over a reception that followed a performance by the Radio Belgrade Večeras Zajedno ensemble in Gothenburg, Sweden. The attendees broke out into a spontaneous *kolo* dance (*kozaračko kolo*) and began to chant "Tito and the party!" and "If needed, we will all be the army!"[30] Later, in response to the significant cost of these touring productions, SAWPY diversified its approach to cultural programming, relying more on smaller touring ensembles, including the citizens' clubs' own folklore troops, who were already performing at national holiday celebrations. Yugoslavs living abroad were thus not only consumers of culture pre-packaged for them, but also producers and re-producers.[31]

The federal state also used citizens' clubs to communicate with workers on important political matters. During the constitutional reforms of 1973, SAWPY sent envoys to present the proposed changes to workers. They held information sessions in diplomatic missions and at the premises of Yugoslav and foreign employers. In several European cities, including Vienna, Zurich, Winterthur, Berlin, Frankfurt, Paris, and London, they also met with Yugoslav citizens' clubs and other associations. These meetings were often well attended – the meeting in Berlin attracted an audience of four hundred; and the one hosted by the Debating club in Frankfurt drew five hundred Yugoslavs.

While Baković has characterized these meetings as propaganda, they went beyond unidirectional political agitation. A key part of each lecture was the question period that followed, and it appears that audience members came with many questions and comments, which envoys assiduously collected in their reports back to SAWPY. While the purpose of these reports was in part to monitor migrant opinion and loyalty, they also took their suggestions seriously and passed them along. As a product of state socialism, the constitution was a document that encompassed broader swaths of the federation's life than a liberal-democratic constitution would, such as labour and the mechanisms regulating the economy. Thus, insofar as they intended to return one day, migrants felt that it was of keen relevance to their lives.[32]

Questions and suggestions fell into two categories: migrants wanted to understand how the constitutional changes would affect them, so they inquired about implications of the reforms for customs duties, their right to social insurance, and their ability to own land and build on it. They also displayed keen interest in the implications of proposed reforms for Yugoslavia. They sought to understand the concept of associated labour – the proposed reorganization of production and self-management that was at the heart of the constitutional reform – as well as the new balance of power between the federation, the republics, and localities, and argued for a tightening of the maximum salary differential in Yugoslavia. Other contributions concerned both their status as migrants and changes in Yugoslavia: did the right to work imply the right to employment, which would allow migrants to return to Yugoslavia? The suggestion by some migrant workers that they should be able to send delegates to representative bodies highlights how these meetings were an opportunity for migrants to reaffirm their integral belonging to the Yugoslav body politic, and indeed, call for a deeper exercise of citizenship.

The Mosaic of Yugoslav Citizens' Clubs

Unsurprisingly, in spite of Yugoslavia's efforts to impose a standard model on associational life, the landscape of Yugoslav citizens' clubs was diverse, reflecting the fact that they were founded by different individuals in different contexts, without initial coordination. This evolution also has implications for the historian hoping to study them – as autonomous organizations, the records they produced ended up in the archival record only occasionally and by accident. Most of the material on clubs was written by consular officials, envoys, and Yugoslav policymakers who received this information second hand. The documentation they produced was spotty, usually superficial, and sometimes unreliable, providing divergent accounts of the number of clubs and their vitality. The numbers of clubs sometimes overstated their significance, as some had fallen on hard times and existed in name only. Insofar as they were accurate, they provided only a snapshot of a moment in time. The associational landscape was always changing, with clubs constantly emerging and growing as others faded away.

With these vagaries in mind, we can sketch out a series of impressions of Yugoslav associational life across Western Europe. Associational life varied widely from state to state, region to region, and city to city, depending on the concentration of workers; the attitude and financial support of the local diplomatic mission, and of local political groups and organizations; the composition of the workforce; and the initiative of local individuals. The strength of local émigré groups, and the pre-existence of church initiatives directed at migrant workers also likely played a role, but it is unclear whether it undermined associational life or inadvertently promoted it by drawing more attention and resources from Yugoslavia. The success or failure of Yugoslav citizens' clubs was not predictable, with associational life establishing itself more quickly in Switzerland than in Germany, in spite of there being far fewer Yugoslavs there, and floundering in France, in spite of its significant number of workers.

Although the majority of Yugoslav workers clustered in the FRG, associational life seems to have developed and established itself most quickly in Switzerland. By 1972 there were clubs in Zurich, Bern, Geneva, Basel, Winterthur, Uzwil, and Thun. Eighty per cent of Yugoslavs in Switzerland, which totalled forty thousand in 1972, were concentrated in the Zurich region. This created the ideal conditions for the club in Zurich to emerge and grow into a one of the largest and most sophisticated associations in Europe. The club was divided into eighteen sections, which met in different locations. It included three folkloric dance ensembles, five chess teams, and five football teams. In the first eight months of 1970, club members prepared thirty different performances and hosted fifteen performances from Yugoslav touring ensembles, fifteen movie nights, and fifteen parties. In 1972, fifty evening events were held, attracting an estimated total of fifteen thousand attendees. In addition, the club held ten lectures and sixty-two meetings and organized several exhibitions as well as sports competitions.

In addition to promoting a vibrant Yugoslav cultural and social life, some of its activities aimed to make life easier for workers in Switzerland. The club organized ten German-language courses and driving exams in Serbo-Croatian, translated approximately ten thousand documents, and intervened, supposedly on average seven times a day, on behalf of workers in matters concerning employment, the judicial system, etc. It also began to offer elementary school, adult education, and trades educa tion in partnership with the Workers' University of New Belgrade. The club acted as an affiliate of other Yugoslav enterprises, opening bank accounts with Jugobanka and the Beobanka, and signing up members for subscriptions of Yugoslav newspapers and periodicals. Its commercial activities also included distributing advertising, chartering coaches and flights to Yugoslavia, and selling accident and life insurance.[33]

In spite of its remarkable size and dynamism, the Zurich club was plagued by organizational and funding problems. The central administration controlled the purse strings and spent most of the club's income, which came from membership fees, on paying full-time administrative staff. Sections were forced to apply to the administration for funding to cover their activities and were often turned down, leading to deep frustration. The club leadership was also accused of having unprofessional interpersonal relationships. Such mismanagement had led to a general demoralization, and the club's membership plummeted from 2,451 in 1971 to 1,360 a year later.[34]

In response to this crisis, the club leadership agreed to cut its full-time staff and decentralize decision-making to the sections, transforming itself into an association of autonomous clubs. Following the decentralization of associational life in Zurich, seventeen clubs remained, as well as eighteen football teams, with an additional four clubs located in the Bern region, and two other football clubs.[35]

The centralized structure of the Zurich club prior to 1973 was unusual. Elsewhere, clubs emerged as individual institutions, although they often collaborated with other associations in the same area. These clubs were usually smaller than the club in Zurich, but some of them were equally dynamic. While some clubs had under a hundred members, many had two hundred of more. By 1975, one report estimated that there were over two hundred associations across Western Europe: a hundred clubs in the FRG, forty-two in Sweden, twenty in Switzerland, fifteen in Austria, seven in Denmark, ten in Benelux, and seven in other states. Most associations were multinational, but over twenty represented a particular ethnicity – primarily Slovenes and Macedonians, as well as a few Albanian associations. The Croatian republican authorities had decided not to endorse Croatian-specific associations, although it was interested in finding ways to integrate existing clubs that were not explicitly hostile toward Yugoslavia into the network of Yugoslav associations. Another undated report, likely from the same era, estimated that thirty thousand Yugoslavs were members of clubs.[36]

In the FRG, clubs often benefitted from the support of local German organizations and political parties, which dampened some of the financial precarity that seemed to plague the associations across Europe. In Frankfurt, which was home to some seventeen thousand Yugoslavs (about sixty thousand in the greater Frankfurt region), the Workers' University (Akademie der Arbeit) agreed to provide space for a centre dedicated to cultural and leisure activities for Yugoslav workers, run by the workers themselves. This centre organized a cultural and sports program that was as lively as Zurich's and boasted a library of 4,500 books in all languages of the Yugoslav nationalities and minorities, of which nearly one thousand were signed out at any given time, as well as newspapers and periodicals from all the republics and provinces.[37]

The German state of Baden-Württemberg, which featured a concentration of Yugoslav workers, counted nine clubs in 1973. The largest were the Slovenian-dominated Triglav club, which had three hundred members, and the Klub Jugoslovena, which had over two hundred members. Two of the other clubs were also Slovenian, and one was Macedonian. Four of the clubs, on the smaller side, did not have physical premises, which limited their ability to act as "homes away from home." Remarkably, Stuttgart also boasted forty-two Yugoslav football clubs, attracting an audience of 89,000 supporters in the fall of 1973.[38]

The other state in which large numbers of Yugoslavs were concentrated was Bavaria. In 1969 a Yugoslav citizens' club was founded in Munich, featuring drama, music, folkloric, and football sections, and a reading room. It also offered subscriptions to Yugoslav newspapers and magazines, including local publications from Medjumurje and Varaždin, bank credit through the Kreditna Banka in Zagreb, and organized bus transportation back to Slovenia, Croatia, and Serbia for the holidays, as well as the possibility of chartering buses for groups of fifty or more. It experienced a trajectory of decline similar to that of the club in Zurich – by 1973 it was in crisis and had effectively ceased operations, ostensibly for lack of a suitable meeting space. Smaller clubs operated in Rosenheim and Lindau, as well as the Triglav club in Munich, which was open only to Slovenes. Clubs were also occasionally organized inside factories, such as Autounion, which employed substantial numbers of Yugoslavs.[39]

In contrast, in other parts of the FRG, Yugoslav citizens' associations were still embryonic in 1973, such as in Mainz and northern Germany. Over time, as the numbers of Yugoslav workers increased, clubs in other parts of Germany gained momentum. Thus, by 1979 there were 22,000 Yugoslavs in Bielefeld, Nordrhein Westphalen, and eighteen clubs. The club in Hannover was judged by one visitor in 1973 to be "one of the best in Germany." It apparently kept detailed index cards on four to five thousand Yugoslav citizens and aspired to do so for all those on its territory. This particular example points to the potential of clubs as tools of surveillance and governance.[40]

As of December 1972, Austria, home to 166,156 Yugoslav citizens, hosted twenty Yugoslav clubs and another fifty sections that engaged in the same kinds of activities as their counterparts in Sweden and Germany. By 1974 this activity had expanded to twenty-seven Yugoslav clubs, two joint Yugoslav-Austrian clubs, and over one hundred soccer clubs. It was estimated, however, that only 10% of citizens took part in club activities. Clubs in Austria seemed particularly crippled by insolvency, which stood in the way of expanding their activities. One official visiting during the constitutional reform consultations commented that, as a general rule, they were in sub-par locations, with poor ventilation and poor sanitary installations. Whereas associations in the FRG received financial support from German institutions, those in Austria did not. Consequently, club leadership explored different kinds of ways of generating income, including running bars and providing translation services, which had enabled certain individuals to use the clubs to enrich themselves. While unscrupulous individuals might prosper, the clubs were in dire need of greater material support.[41]

In Sweden, home to 41,000 Yugoslavs in 1975, the growth of Yugoslav associational life was actively promoted by consular officials, working through the Union of Yugoslav Associations (Savez jugoslovenskih udruženja). As a result, the number of associations increased from five in 1971 to approximately fifty in four years, with seven to eight thousand members. This success was attributed partly to the opening up of club administrations to Croats, which had not previously been well represented. As in other countries, all-Yugoslav associations co-existed with other ones focused on specific nationalities, but open to all Yugoslavs and loyal to Yugoslavia. One observer noted that "both types of clubs continue to present some negative tendencies – unitarism for the first, and national isolationism with the second," but he estimated that, "with patient work, they can be overcome."[42]

Although France hosted a significant number of workers – an estimated 70,000 in 1970 – clubs had a much harder time taking root there.[43] By 1972, when clubs were already beginning to flourish in the rest of Europe, one report noted that there were no citizens' clubs in France. This absence of organized club life was echoed by a delegation sent to France in October 1973 in the context of the constitutional reform. The Yugoslav ambassador had previously been holding gatherings in his residence but had ceased doing so. In Paris there was an architects' association, the Brotherhood and Unity Cultural-Artistic Society, and a few football clubs, but no real Yugoslav citizens' club that addressed workers' more general need to socialize. Yugoslav emigrants in Paris operated restaurants and cafés claiming to be "clubs," but they didn't

Figure 22. Membership cards for the Vojvodina football club, Vienna

organize events for workers, nor did "clubs" in factory barracks like those belonging to Peugeot and Michelin, which were just spaces where Yugoslavs socialized in their free time, equipped with televisions and record-players. Yugoslav authorities commented cynically that factory management had instituted these spaces as a means to shorten the amount of time designated to rest, and they kept the keys to these rooms. These comments focusing on what clubs were not illuminate what did define true associational life in the eyes of the Yugoslav authorities: regular, self-organized, structured social life open to all Yugoslav citizens.

In its report the 1973 delegation announced optimistically that a committee of intellectuals and workers had formed to initiate a new club in Paris and to investigate the possibility of opening clubs in other French cities. However, a report the following year revealed that there had been little progress. In Paris, the Cultural-Information Centre (Kulturni

Informativni Centar – KIC) filled the void, providing cultural programming for workers. One observer attributed this failure to the lack of
material support from French institutions such as trade unions, echoing
the struggles of the clubs in Austria. Even so, when officials from Yugoslavia visited in 1973 to talk with workers about constitutional reforms,
150 activists from clubs and other associations attended, suggesting
that associational life actually had managed to take root.[44]

In the Netherlands the number of migrant workers was modest –
officially 12,830 in 1972 – both in relation to the total of foreign workers
employed on its territory (300,000) and to the total number of Yugoslav
migrant workers in Europe. More than a quarter of these were employed
by Yugoslav firms working in the Netherlands. Nearly half of these workers were concentrated in Rotterdam, which had the only Yugoslav citizens'
club. None of the other cities has sufficient workers to support an autonomous association of this nature, but the Dutch Office for Assistance to Foreign Workers had also set up social clubs in a number of urban centres.
As in France, some employers also had dedicated spaces in their workers'
settlement equipped with televisions, radios, record-players, records and
newspapers from Yugoslavia, chess games, and in some cases, table tennis.

Compared to France, where there were far more Yugoslavs, associational life in the Netherlands was surprisingly lively. This was partly due
to the presence of Yugoslav firms in the Netherlands – Industromontaža,
Jugomontaža, Tehnomonta – which organized sports teams to play
against one another, and against other Yugoslav teams in northwestern
Europe. The Yugoslav centre in Rotterdam, located right next to the main
train station, and the social clubs regularly organized socials. The Yugoslav centre also offered more comprehensive programming, including a
library, language lessons in Dutch, German, and English, a folklore section, and adult education. The Yugoslav authorities noted with disap-
proval that a number of fights had broken out at a private bar run on the
club premises, and as a result, the Dutch Office for the Assistance to Foreign Workers was investigating the possibility of taking over this locale.[45]

Although associational life in England in 1973 was limited to London, the Yugoslav club there appears to have been quite active. Unlike
clubs in other states, it was located on the premises of the Yugoslav
embassy. In addition to the usual sports section, it also boasted a wom-
en's section, a youth section, and a propaganda-informational section
(reflecting its partnership with the embassy). It also offered language
and culture classes to ninety students. Although it did not pay rent and
benefitted from sponsorships from the embassy and Yugoslav firms
working in Great Britain, it too struggled with solvency and sought
financial support as well as materials from Yugoslavia.[46]

Support and Partnerships

The variety of Yugoslav associations – first and foremost, the Yugoslav citizens' clubs, but also to a certain extent the cultural groups and
sports leagues – acted as magnets around which Yugoslav communities
coalesced, and then as bridges connecting citizens back to the imagined
Yugoslav community and the Yugoslav state. But they did not do this
spontaneously or without assistance. As part of its strategy for binding
its citizens closer to Yugoslavia through the associations, the federal
administration offered a variety of supports.

The diplomatic missions were the first to build a relationship with the
Yugoslav citizens' clubs. Their role was to provide them with materials,
such as newspapers, books, brochures, films, and musical recordings, as
well as audiovisual equipment such as film projectors and tape record-
ers. They were also expected to facilitate the organization of cultural
events by liaising with performing groups in Yugoslavia. Additionally,
they provided some financial support on an ad hoc basis and collaborated with the clubs on events such as ceremonies on national holidays.
They also kept an eye on the club leadership and were expected to intervene if political or financial improprieties were detected.

Several cases of interpersonal conflict and allegations of abuse of
power in club administrations appear in the archival record. Most often,
money was involved in one way or another. In some cases, the difficulties of securing funding for the club were seen as leading to questionable
decisions. This was the case with the aforementioned mismanagement
of the club in Zurich. Schemes to get funding for associations by running bars or providing translation services were also seen as shady and
promoting immoral behaviour.

In other cases, however, unscrupulous individuals appear to have
exploited the clubs to amass personal wealth. In Stockholm, for example, a
group of "dissatisfied workers from the Stockholm area" wrote to SAWPY
to complain about the club in that city, accusing a certain "Comrade Aca"
of running the association as his private business or even fiefdom. According to the letter-writers, the club was not open to everyone: they had only
ever seen members of one of the nationalities – unspecified – gathered
there, all unemployed. The dissatisfied workers had tried to find out the
club's opening hours in order to organize activities but were not able to
obtain contact information for the administration. They added:

> The Slovenes wanted to open a section, but they were told that this is not
> allowed by the embassy, at least according to Comrade Aca..., They say –
> and maybe it's not true, you'll know better than us – that you sent ten

million crowns to the clubs, which Aca took for himself, with the approval of the club administration. Then someone from the embassy, some friend of his [*kum njemu*] helped him to buy a car for his wife, with a serious discount. They say Aca has your strong support, if that is possible. ... [T]here must be 500 days in his year, he claims so many daily expense allowances, over twenty million a year.[47]

While the case of the Stockholm club and Comrade Aca seems particularly egregious, it was not unique. Vjekoslava U., a tireless activist in the Yugoslav community of Versmold, close to Bielefeld, reported similar concerns to the local consulate about the "Jedinstvo" club in 1978. In this case too the president was accused of mismanagement of the club for personal enrichment. He collected all the earnings from the social evenings and the billiards table, without keeping any sort of record. He also ran a side-business selling hard liquor to club members on club premises and at football games. Vjekoslava estimated that he had embezzled some 15,500 DM in this manner. She also complained about other kinds of bad behaviour, such as fostering resentment between Yugoslav households, behaving vindictively toward other clubs, and failing to pass on important information to club members. A former member of the administration of the "Jedinstvo" club in Vienna complained to SAWPY in 1973 about a similar combination of mismanagement and corruption. Clearly these were not isolated incidents. The autonomy of the clubs was a double-edged sword, creating a space for initiative and meaningful community, but also for corruption and abuse.[48]

Diplomatic missions and authorities in Yugoslavia would get concerned when they were alerted to such problems because they knew that they endangered the success of associations and demoralized club members. At those moments, associations no longer performed their assigned role of binding citizens to the homeland. Diplomatic missions might step in discretely and put pressure on clubs to rid themselves of offending parties, although in other instances they seem not to have taken action, particularly in distant communities.

A more durable solution was to work from the inside – or, put more cynically, infiltrate the associations. As part of its larger push to activate communists living abroad, the LCY proposed to do just that. A 1972 document, stated, "We need to train and insert moral and politically suitable people wherever possible, from the janitors and superintendents of buildings where our workers live, to clubs and other organizations that gather our workers. We can do this in particular through our choice of educators, social workers, and trade union workers and trustees. Different forms of organizations (clubs, sports organizations, various associations, etc.) need to be linked up with relevant organizations at home. That is, we need to use all legal means available to secure a stronger influence."[49] Indeed, in the same period, Yugoslavia was establishing a transnational education program for the children of migrant workers that would grow to sizeable proportions, a fascinating story that unfolds in chapters 8 and 9. Educators were expected to take on a role of responsibility in citizens' associations.

Beyond ensuring that clubs had adequate leadership, the federation also sought to ensure that associations were properly supplied with information and cultural products. Recognizing the inadequacy of current mechanisms for communicating with workers and alarmed at the growing numbers of migrants, the federal executive council authorized the creation of Cultural-Information Centres in 1972. The KICs, which operated under the DSIP, were charged with disseminating information and promoting Yugoslav culture to migrant workers and citizens of the FRG, France, Austria, Switzerland, and Sweden. In essence, they were a combination of help desk, cultural centre, media centre, and multimedia library. They also assisted workers with questions about their legal rights and entitlements, which involved liaising with the Yugoslav republics to obtain relevant materials. The first KIC was founded in Stuttgart in November 1972, followed by others in Cologne, Paris, and Vienna. Others were planned for Stockholm and Zurich.[50]

While the KIC in Stuttgart initially downplayed its significance in communicating with workers, highlighting instead the importance of radio, television, and press media, it developed extensive resources and programming directed at migrant workers, much of which were delivered through the clubs. In the first half of 1980, for example, it sent copies of songs and poems to 550 club sections to help them prepare the national First of May and Day of Youth celebrations. Having noticed that workers had trouble understanding explanations of state regulations and policies over the radio, it printed and sent out a brochure entitled "Answers from Radio Zagreb" with answers to questions sent by radio listeners. It also passed along materials from the Association of Technical Cultural Organizations (Savez organizacije za tehničku kulturu), which provided guidance on forming and running amateur groups focused on photography and film, radio, automobiles, modelling, and invention and innovation. The KIC also sought to increase the reach of Yugoslav media among their citizens by launching a campaign to increase Yugoslav newspaper subscriptions and producing a news bulletin called "News from Home."[51]

In collaboration with the clubs, in 1980 the KIC in Stuttgart organized several exhibits: aquarelles by Stjepan Rajković, a photo exhibit on Tito's funeral, as well as thematic exhibits on Tito's life, musical production in Yugoslavia, the batons used in the Relay of Youth, which celebrated Tito's birthday, and another one of the Day of Youth itself. In addition, the KIC organized lectures on current events, held film screenings for adults and children, and organized cultural performances across the FRG. Shows included an amateur theatre group from Kikinda, folklore ensembles from across Yugoslavia, and the RTV Sarajevo orchestra featuring, among others, the famed *sevdah* performer Safet Isović. This last event having taken place shortly after Tito's death, the performers sang revolutionary songs with a focus on Tito and were "exceptionally acclaimed." The KIC also assisted in the organization of the "Seventh Meeting of the Slovenes of Western Europe," held that year in Tübingen. Children's theatre troops were also brought in, and the "Vesela sveska" caravan – which was a literary festival featuring well-known children's authors – also toured Germany. Many more cultural events that year were in fact cancelled in response to Tito's deteriorating health and death.[52]

The KICs took on a particularly active role in the wake of Tito's death, shaping the way in which the German media covered this event and assisting the clubs in organizing commemorations. Clubs received from them a sizeable package of materials on Tito's life and death, including photos, eulogies, and commemorative posters with memorable quotes. The Stuttgart KIC even recorded Lenin's funeral march onto fifty cassette tapes and sent them to clubs, advising them to make further copies as required and to play the march as background music wherever Tito's condolence book was displayed. At the end of April it prepared a photo exhibit on Tito's life, which they copied and sent to thirty clubs for display. In this manner, the KICs sought to shape the ways in which Tito was mourned and remembered.[53]

They also used his passing as an opportunity to connect migrants to citizens back home. Drawing on its connections, the KIC in Stuttgart organized for local television reporters to cover commemorations organized by clubs. It then collected the news stories on videotape, which it sent to the correspondents' centre in Zagreb. "In this manner, we provided a practical way for the public in Yugoslavia to become aware of the strong morale of our people in the FRG" and of their feelings toward Tito. Claiming that their employees worked "day and night" during the mourning period, the KIC boasted that many clubs had contacted them to express their satisfaction with the "timely, substantive, and valuable information" they had received.[54]

Arguably, the Stuttgart KIC's moment of glory was the Day of Youth celebration organized after Tito's death. This event was highly symbolically charged, providing the opportunity for citizens to not only celebrate Tito's birthday once more, but also to recommit to the Yugoslav project in spite of the disappearance of its fiercest advocate. The KIC convinced event organizers to add a football match between Hajduk Split and Partizan Belgrade at Stuttgart's Neckar Stadium to the usual program. They also arranged participation of RTV Sarajevo along with several high-profile soloists, organized the decoration of the stadium, and printed 180,000 programs. Celebrations also featured a parade celebrating the achievements of Yugoslav popular associations in the FRG: club representatives, sports teams, folklore ensembles, youth who would participate in next summer's labour action in Yugoslavia (*radna akcija*), and schoolchildren who were learning to speak their parents' languages.[55]

The celebrations were attended by an astonishing forty thousand Yugoslavs, in addition to the 6,500 participants. Attendees displayed banners with the names of their associations and sports teams. The match was televised by RTV Sarajevo, and the entire event was covered extensively in the Yugoslav press. Borba's headline neatly encapsulated the feeling of the moment: "When Stuttgart Was Yugoslavia." News articles and photographs described a sort of patriotic euphoria. Most likely there were those in the stands who had come to cheer for Hajduk, and who had no love for Tito or the Yugoslav project, but their mere presence lent legitimacy to the message of Yugoslav pride and unity. In many ways the Day of Youth in 1980 was the apotheosis of Yugoslav associational life abroad. But though one of the banners captured in a news photograph proclaimed "Tito's way is the only way," his demise marked the beginning of a slow disintegration that would plunge the Yugoslav citizens' associations into a deep identity crisis from which it was difficult to recover. While some would emerge with new nationalized monikers, the heyday of the citizens' clubs was over.[56]

Conclusion

Born on the margins of the Yugoslav state through the initiative of citizens living abroad and consular officials, Yugoslav workers' clubs were simultaneously instruments for the Yugoslav state to monitor, govern, and control its citizens living abroad, and for popular organizations relying on the initiative and enthusiasm of its membership to survive. However, in response to growing concern about the vulnerability and loyalty of migrants, starting in the 1970s the Yugoslav state increasingly sought to be involved in the running of the clubs. As tools of the state, they acted as a pan-European network allowing the Yugoslav state to run programs and distribute information, propaganda, and cultural products. As popular associations, they provided a place for Yugoslav migrants to socialize, access support, and stay connected to the homeland.

These two roles sometimes pulled in opposite directions, leaving migrants suspicious that associations were mere instruments of state propaganda, and Yugoslav officials frustrated and powerless in the face of uncooperative or ineffective club leadership. Even in states where clubs were numerous and well-subscribed, they were never able to mobilize a significant proportion of Yugoslavs living and working abroad. Nonetheless, their impact should not be underestimated. For a relatively small percentage of migrants who were members, the associations played an important role in their lives, providing a means through which they could continue participating in Yugoslav social, cultural, and political life. They organized celebrations for national holidays, provided access to Yugoslav literature and film, hosted Yugoslav performance troops, and facilitated discussions on constitutional reforms. They acted as access points for other initiatives to cultivate relationships with migrants, such as newspapers and educational programs. The clubs' impact, however, was not limited to their membership. Through the cultural activities and celebrations they organized, they reached a much broader audience.

Whereas radio and newspaper created imagined community, workers' clubs provided an opportunity to build real, embodied communities, creating physical spaces that belonged, in some sense, to Yugoslavia, and enabling relationships. They also gave a privileged role to migrants themselves in shaping that community. Arguably, then, although they reached a smaller number of people than radio and the press, they provided deeper opportunities for migrants to engage with the homeland. As chapter 9 will show, activities that took place at the clubs, such as Pioneer meetings, allowed migrants to reaffirm their belonging in a social setting and make emotionally powerful memories.

7 Migrants Talk Back: Responses to Surveys

Actors within Yugoslavia, whether at the federal, republican, or local level, tried to cultivate migrants' sense of belonging to the homeland. To that end, they sought to shape the stories that migrants would tell themselves about their own lives, Yugoslavia, and the relationship between the two. Confronted with these narratives, how did Yugoslavs working abroad make sense of their personal experiences as migrants? To what extent did they embrace and reproduce narratives that had been handed to them? As discussed in chapter 4, letters to the radio program *To Our Citizens of the World* provide insights into this question by giving a voice to migrants. Their letters suggest that the program cultivated a loyal audience and created a specific culture of listening that emphasized the ongoing relationship between *listeners* and the homeland articulated around exchanges of greetings and music. They also show that migrants perceived the program as an ally in their struggles to build a life across two states and a mediator in their dealings with Yugoslav authorities. But the culture of listening that the radio program created – at least, what has come down to us, confined to 1964–5 – was limited in scope: it concerned the joys and struggles of the present moment and eschewed politics.

In contrast, an open-ended survey on the conditions that would incite labour migrants to return to Yugoslavia conducted in 1970–1 by the Zagreb-based Institute for Migration and Nationality drew responses covering a much broader range of issues. Asked to reflect on their choices and future plans and express opinions, migrants compared their experiences abroad to their expectations of living and working in Yugoslavia, and commented, often bitterly, on Yugoslav policy and the government and administration. Responses to the survey are extraordinarily rich in their diversity, with some respondents using them to inquire after a job or apartment, others offering well-intentioned suggestions, and yet others treating the survey as an opportunity to vent their frustrations or express their rejection of Yugoslavia and all it stood for.

The timing of the survey is not immaterial: conducted at the height of the nationalist ferment in Croatia, it demonstrates that numerous migrants did indeed hold views that were consistent with those expressed in such newspapers as *VUS* and *Imotska krajina*. Some responses expressed opinions that were more nationalistic than what might be read in the Croatian media, suggesting that hostile émigré organizations were also successful in shaping migrant opinion. However, aside from responses that limited themselves to ideologically charged statements, most responses show that migrants were active participants in constructing the meaning of their life histories and their relationship to the homeland. Certainly labour migrants read Yugoslav newspapers, and these newspapers did shape their attitude toward Yugoslavia, but these narratives were only one reference of several. Many migrants were persuaded that their experiences while living and working abroad provided them with a unique perspective on what was wrong in Yugoslavia and how it might be addressed. And it was inevitable that their sense of self and of their relationship to Yugoslavia would also be shaped by their contacts with and, indeed, embeddedness in their host societies.

The 1970–1971 Survey

As already noted in chapter 2, the Institute for Migration and Nationality carried out a survey in 1970–1 to evaluate the "conditions of return for our workers from temporary work abroad." This project followed an earlier study in 1966 that had collected socio-economic data on labour migrants. It had also collected data on the opinions and habits of migrants, but questions were either in multiple-choice format, or else asked narrowly focused questions, such as "What would you rather read about in the newspaper?" or "What should be improved in the functioning of the Yugoslav consulate?"[1] In contrast, in line with the research question it sought to answer, the 1970 survey was both more concise and open-ended than its predecessor. It featured nine questions, of which the first eight concerned demographic and socio-economic data. The last question asked respondents, "Under what circumstances would you return to the homeland? Pay? A job? An apartment? Interpersonal relations? Other?" Respondents were then given four lines to respond.

The new study employed the same approach as the 1966 study for recruiting participants, promoting the survey through the newspaper

VUS and the radio show *To Our Citizens*. As in the previous study, this strategy ensured that the majority of respondents would be residents of Croatia, although respondents from other republics and of other national backgrounds also wrote in. Surveys were collected between November 1970 and 15 January 1971. Thus the study tuned into migrant opinion at a critical moment, midway between the tenth session of the central committee of the SKH and the twenty-first session of the presidency of the LCY, which effectively bookended the Croatian Spring.[2]

The survey, which collected 1,137 valid responses, exceeded the expectations of its authors. They concluded that the subject of the survey was appealing and close to the workers' hearts, and that they were eager to express their opinions on the problem and its potential solutions: "The letters of up to sixteen pages, letters with philosophical approaches and theoretical solutions to the problem of migration and return, [and] letters with very concrete answers and concrete requests speak to this."[3]

Although they were offered anonymity, respondents often identified themselves and provided return addresses. The authors trusted that the respondents were being honest and open in their replies, whether or not they remained anonymous, which is plausible for most cases. Some respondents used the survey as an opportunity to request a job, accommodation, or other scarce resources – discursively, we should treat those cases as petitions rather than "authentic" opinions, in which the petitioner "performs" loyalty and conformity in the hope of obtaining satisfaction.[4]

The findings were discussed in two reports that remained unpublished for reasons that remain mysterious, in all likelihood related to the sensitivity of the content in the wake of the crackdown on the Croatian national revival and the fall from grace of the institute's director, Komarica, in the purges following the end of the Croatian Spring. According to the authors of one report, the composition of responses did not deviate substantially from the composition of the labour migrant workforce, with the exception of women, who were under-represented. The low response rate for women, representing only 13.4% of responses, but making up a third of the workforce, was attributed to their being over-burdened with work and household duties, "and other problems that are associated with today's emancipated woman who is also a housewife, both at home and abroad."[5] It may also be that, within a traditionally oriented Yugoslav household, the father figure was most likely to speak on behalf of the family, even if the wife was also employed, and even though the survey was addressed to individuals.

Of the 1,137 surveys, 708 were sent from the FRG. Over 68% of respondents were from Croatia, with another 12.4% from Bosnia-Herzegovina, and 8.5% from Serbia. Unsurprisingly, respondents from republics where other languages were dominant were few. Male respondents represented a broad cross-section of age groups: 14.1% were under twenty-five; 22.9% between twenty-six and thirty; 19.9% between thirty-one and thirty-five; and 23.3% between thirty-six and forty-five. In contrast, 44.7% of female respondents were under twenty-five years old, which appears to confirm speculations about the silence of women with families. The educational background of respondents was as follows: trade school, 40.1%; secondary school, 16.4%; eight years of primary school, 10.9%; four years of primary school, 9.4%; and higher education, 7.6%.[6] Respondents varied widely in the duration of their stay abroad, with nearly half clustered between nineteen months and six years.[7]

To analyse the answers to the ninth question about the conditions of return, the researchers coded the responses and grouped them into three categories: problems relating to the country of origin; problems relating to the host country, and problems relating to the phenomenon of migration. As might be expected, the vast majority of statements (6,818) fell into the first category. Within this category, slightly more than half of the statements (3,457) concerned the economic system, while slightly less than half (3,286) concerned the social and political system.[8] Interestingly, the authors of the second internal report on the survey – only fragments of which made it into the archive – commented on the presence of nationalistic opinions in survey responses and tried to make sense of them: "In a self-managed society, the unwinding of social-political, economic, cultural, intellectual, and spiritual life is ever more turbulent, sometimes with different, even conflicting social orientations and intellectual and political currents. This also happened at a moment when the national question was raised as a central political issue, and the nation, rather than working class, was given the central role in social movements."[9]

According to this report, "Our workers are highly interested in the significance of subcategory 1.2.4.6 (nation) in the position of particular groups within our system." This report was remarkably transparent about the respondents' complaints and demands, which they listed as being "changes in national relations within SFRJ, changes in political organization (including the creation of a Croatian state in various forms), changes in the foreign currency and financial regime, but also the elimination of those problems that represent stumbling blocks to 'the declared and necessary brotherhood and unity of our peoples.'" However, they stressed that some respondents were sceptical of nationalist claims: "Not infrequently, they protest the privileging of the national question as a strategic goal, because in their view 'there is no national turmoil between workers,' 'this is the bureaucracy's problem,' and relatedly, 'the main problem, but also the solution, lies in the economic sphere,' 'in economic growth and productive relations, not in the national problem.'"[10] This interpretation was in many ways a nod to the early framing of labour migrants being driven by economic motivations, which had the effect of separating politics and economics. The lack of information on when the report was written makes it difficult to comment on the influence of the political context on the interpretation of the survey results. Either way, the results of the survey were never published – it seems the institute never found a politically acceptable interpretation.

Appropriating the Survey

While the survey leaders were interested in the aggregate results, the individual stories that migrants told about their lives, their opinions, and their hopes tell us a great deal about migrants' expectations of the state and the ways in which their lives at home and abroad were intertwined. The following analysis is based on reading a sample of 400 responses, or slightly more than 35% of all responses.

As the researchers had commented, the survey elicited a surprisingly enthusiastic response, with migrants often sending in pages of reflections. Most commonly, respondents followed the instructions, answering the questions in order and then providing their suggestions and opinions at the very end. Arguably, in choosing such an open-ended format for the last survey question, the designers of the survey were inviting respondents to exercise their agency in speaking about their experiences and expectations, and many accepted this invitation.

A close reading of the replies suggests confusion amongst respondents about the nature of the study. Several respondents who sent in long letters seemed to be under the impression that *Vjesnik u srijedu* was the author of the survey, rather than merely the vehicle used to promote it. Several respondents formatted their responses as letters to either *VUS* or, less commonly, to the Institute for Migration and Nationality. Many of the responses presumed a certain complicity between writer and reader, which was assumed to be an ally. After complaining bitterly about Yugoslavia, the writer would commonly sign off "with comradely greetings." One Croatian migrant based in Linz solicited feedback, "if you think I am on the wrong path."[11] Another, a Croatian with extremist nationalist convictions living in Sweden, speculated that the authors of the survey would not be allowed to print his letter in the Croatian press and recommended that they at least present it to the Croatian government, "and ask them, is it like I've told you, or isn't it?"[12] While the letters displayed a certain naivety about the authors of the study and their intentions and authority, they help us to understand why respondents with such hostility to Yugoslavia, and such little faith in its ability to reform itself, bothered to reply at all. They also show that migrants trusted both *VUS* and Croatian state institutions, a matter of no little consequence during the Croatian Spring.

Occasionally, survey respondents ignored the survey conventions, innovating their own format. Some compressed their answers to the first eight questions into a narrative paragraph, while another inserted extensive comments between individual questions, and others preceded their answers with a long introduction. Yet another reordered the survey by providing his own headings, thereby restructuring the answers according to his own logic. One sent a satirical poem.[13] Some respondents refused to answer the survey outright – most of those who chose this approach used it as an opportunity to express their rejection of the Yugoslav state. Interestingly, most of the respondents who chose to deviate from the prescribed format answered the questions asked of them, suggesting that they did want to "be counted" in the official study.

These responses could be read as disorderly and undisciplined. The assumption underlying the survey as a data collection tool is that the answers should be in the same format in order facilitate comparison and quantification. Indeed, the survey had solicited focused answers to nine questions, and in these cases, the respondents had failed to respect the expectations of the survey format. It would be a mistake, however, to conclude that respondents were simply ignorant or lacked self-discipline. In flouting the conventions of the survey, they were consciously asserting their autonomy by appropriating and subverting the form of the text – in effect, talking back.

Whether or not they conformed to the prescribed format, these respondents appropriated the survey as a vehicle for telling the story that they had in mind. Both those who disregarded the instructions and those who sent in responses that were many pages long posited a different kind of reader than intended by the survey – not a detached researcher mechanically tabulating data, but rather, an interlocutor, who was obliged to listen patiently and perhaps even respond to the writer's own questions.

Migrants did not restrict themselves to expressing their opinions, but also shared their feelings. Whereas surveys strive to project a detached, objective tone, the answers frequently projected a variety of sentiments – most commonly frustration and anger. These emotions could be explicit or discernible in the tone of particular statements and were also captured in progressively larger or messier handwriting, capitalization, underlining, and expressive punctuation.

Migrants also showed scepticism about the purpose and outcome of the survey, expressing derision or even contempt. One thirty-two-year-old seamstress in Sweden began her response by stating that she was "glad to participate in your survey which – I hope – has some kind of purpose."[14] At the end of one particularly bitter response, one forty-seven-year-old carpenter signed off, "Tally up your survey, gentlemen, and stick it under the nose of the managers, at least those in Croatia – allow them to smell and hear the cry of the migrant worker."[15] It is noteworthy that, in spite of their low expectations of the survey, they still took the time to write a full response and mail it in.

From Life Stories to Political Manifestos

In replying to the survey, migrants most commonly narrated their life stories, focusing first on the reasons for their departure, and then on the challenges and successes of their life abroad. This in turn led to a discussion of what they stood to lose in returning home, and on what conditions they would consider doing so. A number of responses by ethnic Croatian migrants, however, were articulated not around life stories, but rather, around a narrative of Croatian oppression within Yugoslavia, or else they blended the two seamlessly. For these migrants, their own stories were merely demonstrations of the larger history of the exploitation of Croatia and Croatians by the Yugoslav state and by other ethnicities, primarily Serbs. Most of these migrants claimed that they would not return until Croatia achieved greater autonomy under the leadership of the reformist communists, while the most extremist demanded complete independence.

Let us take a closer look at these narrative "ideal types," and at some of the variations. Because many of the responses were anonymous, in the interest of the flow of this text, I have assigned pseudonyms to anonymous letters. Pseudonyms are enclosed in quotation marks, whereas true names are not.

Pavle B., for example, articulated his story according to a "then and now" narrative, conflating time and space: then, the disadvantages of life in Yugoslavia, and now, the advantages of Sweden. Born in 1938, he left Umag, Croatia, in 1965 with his wife and three-year-old-son for Växjö, Sweden. He had completed eight years of industrial trade school and had trained as a highly skilled metalworker. His wife had also completed eight years of school and trained as a seamstress. Prior to moving to Sweden, he had worked in his field and taught for two years at the industrial school. According to Pavle, he moved with his family to Sweden because he had been unemployed for eight months, his wife was also unemployed, and they were forced to sublet an apartment, making them "real proletarians."

Pavle described their family's life in Sweden as characterized by hard work rewarded by material success. His family had immediately received an apartment – large by Yugoslav standards, at sixty square metres – and had been granted a residence permit. Both he and his wife worked – he in his field, she part-time as a hospital aide – bringing in a comfortable income and allowing his family to enjoy a middle-class standard of living. "Here, we have a high standard, we have everything from the apartment to the furniture, TV, various appliances. We don't have a car but nor do we intend to get one." Although life in Sweden was expensive, they were able to set aside 200–400 crowns per month. He and his wife were expecting another child in the new year.

Pavle did not explicitly criticize any aspect of life in Sweden, but certain reservations can be read into his narrative that suggest social isolation: Yugoslavs mostly took jobs the Swedes did not want, and he noted that as foreigners, they were quite isolated. Moreover, he expressed distress that his child didn't know Serbo-Croatian well. The main obstacles to the family's return were identical to their reasons for leaving: access to work and an apartment. Pavle was also outraged at Yugoslavia's harsh customs regulations, which would make it impossible for him to return home with his new material wealth. In a sense, Pavle felt trapped abroad, which further increased his aggravation toward the Yugoslav state.

At the end of his response, Pavle sent in a three-page list of recommendations that reflected the challenges that his family had faced in Yugoslavia and continued to face as Yugoslav citizens, and his comparisons between Yugoslavia and Sweden. He recommended providing migrants with more knowledge on how to navigate laws and regulations in foreign states, and suggested changes to customs law to allow migrants to return home earlier without paying customs. He also criticized Yugoslavia for its nonsensical policies and what he perceived as widespread corruption, comparing his homeland negatively to Sweden. For example, he noted that children could get scholarships for school, and workers, jobs, without having to pay bribes, in Sweden. Similarly, he noted that housing distributions favoured managers over workers in Yugoslavia, but not in Sweden.

Pavle's opinions extended beyond the narrow confines of his personal life. He believed that Yugoslav economic policy compared unfavourably to Sweden's. Pointing out that Sweden, "one of the states that gave birth to industry," had only two automobile factories, he asked why Yugoslavia allowed automobile firms to license out their production, "such that it seems that almost every district produces one kind of automobile." He also questioned why incompetent managers were shuffled from one firm to another in Yugoslavia, while in Sweden they would be shown the door.

While Pavle found Yugoslavia sorely lacking in comparison to his new place of residence, he continued to express socialist values. For example, he objected to the increase in salary differentials between workers and management in Yugoslavia, which he felt were creating a class society. He also referred to incompetent directors as "economic criminals," using language that had its roots in Stalinist economic culture. In other words, while Pavle's transnational life allowed him to distance himself from Yugoslavia and identify with certain features of Sweden, he continued to ascribe to Yugoslav political values.[16]

It was common for migrants to focus their narrative on the circumstances that drove them to seek work abroad. Thirty-two-year-old "Ivan," who had completed industrial training as a lathe-operator, explained that his struggles to earn a sufficient salary to meet the cost of living in Zagreb led him to travel to Slovenia to find employment. Having tried his luck in Maribor, Brestanica, and Petrinje, he then requested and was denied an exit visa six times. He finally got permission to leave after completing trade school in 1964 and settled in Germany.

Unlike Pavle B.'s straightforward narrative, Ivan's migration story contained a second, interwoven strand, because he then began to build a house on the outskirts of Zagreb. Indeed, this was a common aspiration for migrants, and numerous responses mention either the current or future construction of a house in Yugoslavia. Pursuing a life in two different states could pose problems for migrants like Ivan. As he explained it, he continued to face hardship, as it was difficult for him as a labour migrant to obtain the necessary documentation to build. Like Pavle, Ivan compared life abroad and life in Yugoslavia, in particular, salaries relative to the cost of living, the ease of obtaining an apartment, and a culture of public cleanliness that he observed in German trains. This last point led Ivan to wonder why Yugoslav children were not taught in school "to value those things that serve us all."[17]

In reflecting on their future within Yugoslavia, migrants like Pavle and Ivan reflected primarily on the difficult choices they felt they had been forced into by lack of opportunity in Yugoslavia. They also compared living conditions, culture, and policies in both states. They felt that their life experiences provided them with the authority to critique ways of doing things in Yugoslavia. This type of narrative, articulated around the life experience of the migrant, was the most common and transcended ethno-national categories.

For these migrants, return hinged on the possibility to translate their standard of living and employment situation into an equivalent in Yugoslavia. Respondents highlighted the difficulty of finding good employment and housing in Yugoslavia. In addition, the difficulty of importing consumer goods into Yugoslavia figured in several responses. One dentist, originally from Belgrade, complained that prohibitive customs regulations made him feel like a second-class citizen. Whereas diplomats could import their household goods and automobile after two years, labour migrants were obliged to wait for ten, which he deemed a "very large injustice."[18] A "group of Yugoslav workers in Germany" who had been working in construction there for four, five, or more years claimed that these rules were delaying their return. They complained that no one buys used items in Germany, so their investment in household goods would be lost if they left.[19] Migrants of peasant origins also requested that customs on tools and equipment be radically reduced. According to Jove L., this would make the difference between poverty and prosperity for Yugoslav peasants.[20]

On the other end of the spectrum were responses, fewer but still numerous, framed around a specific political discourse of the victimization of Croatia and Croats within the Yugoslav federation. The Croatian national revival, which coincided with the survey, clearly had a strong influence on a number of the responses. Numerous respondents showed close familiarity with the actors and political platform of the Croatian Spring, such as a twenty-three-year-old electrician who had studied in Zagreb and now worked in Germany, who placed his hopes in the Communist reformists to correct long-standing injustice and oppression: "I can't stand the unfairness, exploitation, terror, and neglect of Croatia and its people. I and many of our people who left our beloved Croatian land will return when Croatia becomes economically independent. You do not know our bitter feelings when I hear and read in our press what is being made of Croatia and its people. I wish much, much success to the central committee of the League of Communists of Croatia in the work they have begun. May they keep fighting, because otherwise it will be worse for us than it has been."[21]

Similarly, another response, signed collectively by "the embittered" (*ogorčeni*), listed the reformist Croatian communists by name: "I've spoken about this survey to many colleagues, who wish to return home. We would really be happy to return, depending on the composition of your commission. If it is made up of various followers of Bakarić, Žanković,

Puniša Račić, Ranković[22] and others of the same kind, then we won't return. If the commission is made of progressive forces – followers of Savka Dapčević, Miko Tripalo, Ljudevit Jonke, Dragutin Haramija,[23] and others of that kind – we'll return on the first train!"[24]

Respondents frequently borrowed the language and argumentation of the reformist Croatian communists without openly attacking Serbs, focusing instead on how the Yugoslav federation diverted resources that in fact belonged to Croats. Starting from his life story, "Domagoj" then interpreted his misfortune as being a product of Croatia's unequal status within Yugoslavia. A twenty-eight-year-old male lathe operator, his story was that of a young man who left the harsh and economically stagnant mountainous region that ran along the Adriatic, in search of opportunity, only to be disappointed: "As a boy born in the *karst* of Lika, I dreamed to come to the city and become someone. I went to the city, completed my training, and became … a subtenant." Like Ivan, he soon realized that there was no way for him to ever obtain his own apartment in Zagreb, and so he left for the FRG.

Domagoj understood his fate as tied to the lack of economic develop-ment in Croatia, which was no accident, but rather a consequence of Croatia's exploitation. Referring to the vast numbers of labour migrants, he asked, "Why is Croatia biologically and economically impoverished, when it has all the conditions to advance and to strengthen in all areas …: industry, mining, armaments, tourism, etc.?" While he could agree with the principle of redistributing wealth to undeveloped regions to reduce gaps in prosperity, he did not agree that several hundred thousand Croats would work abroad to profit other republics and be left with nothing to support underdeveloped regions inhabited by Croats. In response, he asked a series of questions that implied that the federal cap-ital was appropriating Croatian wealth for its own enrichment. "Why isn't the foreign currency that we send used to build Herzegovinian and Dalmatian districts, instead of being used to build Belgrade?" Doma-goj used terms and arguments similar to those used by the Croatian reformist Communists. He referred to the federation as a "centralist-bureaucratic government" and argued that "when the exploitation of one republic by another ends, each will have the right to the surplus value of his labour."[25]

"Hrvoje," a twenty-six-year-old electrician living in the FRG for four years, expressed similar frustrations about the economic exploi-tation of Croatia. In addition, he wrote about discrimination against the Croatian language, including abroad in consular services. He also complained that Second World War veterans were given preferential access to leadership positions. But for Hrvoje, as for Pavle and Ivan, the most important grievances, which prevented his return, were the low salaries, the difficulty of obtaining an apartment, and the low standard of living in Yugoslavia.[26]

Whether as a result of their location beyond Yugoslavia's borders and contact with political émigrés, or from visiting home and reading the Croatian press abroad, other labour migrants were emboldened to express even stronger nationalist views that were previously taboo. One of the most extreme versions of this response was a letter that devoted all of one sentence to answering the questions in the survey: "I was born in 1932, male sex, finished four years of school, trained as a cook, duration of time abroad ten years." The remainder of the page-long typed letter read like a manifesto against Serbian tyranny in Yugoslavia and for Croatian independence. "Ante" would return when all Serbs who had moved to Croatia after 1945 moved away – those in positions of responsibility, whom he claimed discriminated against Croats, those who worked in the factories, who took jobs meant for Croats; and even sailors and airplane pilots. Summarizing his view, he stated, "Let us keep what is ours, and the Serbs what is theirs; with the Drina separating us, we will live in brotherly love in [separate] Croatian and Serbian states. Oh Croats, we have had enough, let's break ties with Serbs."[27]

Others expressed similar hostility to Serbs and to Yugoslavia, which they portrayed as a tool of Serbian domination. One migrant, who identified himself as "a *Vjesnik* reader in Paris," sent in a two-page anti-Serbian diatribe, without replying to any of the survey questions.[28] "Josip," a twenty-three-year-old man from Vinkovci, who had trained as a machine technician and had been working abroad as a bartender for a year and a half, used the entire survey to express his bitterness toward Yugoslavia. Answering the question of his employment in Yugoslavia prior to his departure, he wrote, "I didn't work, because there is no work for us in that kind of Yugoslavia." While he agreed that a higher salary, employment in his field, and an apartment would enable him to return, he posited an additional condition: "*Independent Croatia, with its own autonomous government, even if it must remain Communist.*" Referring to Prime Minister Nikola Pašić from the interwar Kingdom of Yugoslavia, highly unpopular in Croatia, he added, "Are you blind that you don't see what they are doing, the other Pašićevi – Serbs – those hegemonic Belgrade gossip-mongers?" Josip ended his letter with a threatening postscript in agitated calligraphy, referencing once again the turbulent interwar period: "I'm not some stupid emigrant, but rather an honourable *Croat* who has finally recovered his sight and who will spill his young *blood* tomorrow *only* for *our independent* state and for the ideas of our heroes with Radić at their head."[29]

Other migrant narratives blended autobiographical elements and anti-Serbian statements, which provided an interpretive framework for the migrants' life experiences. A waiter in Hamburg who felt that his Serbian manager had discriminated against him in favour of another Serb, fumed, "We should not expect anything good from those Serbs who are in charge of us in our republic. Some have even said, 'Bre, we had to come from Serbia to raise you Croats up culturally,' and if one of us was to say a single word to the contrary, he would be treated badly and even lose his job. And we figured out that Croatian Serbs are no better."[30]

"Frane," writing from Linz, described how his family had faced discrimination after the Second World War because his father had been a member of the Ustaša Home Guard. As a result, he had not been able to obtain any kind of education and was bullied during his military service. As he narrated it, it was during his military service that he realized that "we are not equal as they claim: of a few dozen officers and NCOs in our battalion there wasn't a single Croat. And on my return home I realized that every single one of the leaders of the place was a Serb." As in the case of Ante, Frane resented that Serbs should be in leadership positions in Croatia. Nonetheless, when he addressed question nine directly, he made no mention of Croatian-Serbian relations. Rather, he claimed he would return when conditions improved for peasants: reclassification of arable land, available credit, and guaranteed prices for agricultural goods. Thus, although Frane had reservations about Serbs in Croatia, they were not an obstacle to his return.[31]

The hostility to Serbs expressed in these letters and the demands for Croatian national independence went far beyond what was advocated by the Croatian communists, who sought to achieve greater autonomy within the Yugoslav federation and steered clear of ethno-nationalism, which they knew to be off-limits. It was closer to the views nurtured by Matica Hrvatska, if less diplomatically expressed. The "Vjesnik reader in Paris" indeed seemed to be following the activities of Matica Hrvatska, as he condemned the banning of the journal *Hrvatski književni list* in 1968, which it published.

Interestingly, a number of responses from Sweden were so similar that they suggest an organized campaign to mobilize Croats to use the survey to make a political statement. These responses used the same kind of language as the reformists and consisted of a paragraph that contained one or more formulaic statements: the respondent would return when the biological and economic impoverishment of Croats was brought to an end; when Croatian firms could decide what to do with their surplus labour; when Croatia – and in particular the regions from which labour migrants hailed – was allowed to keep its workers' remittances.[32]

Migrant Perspectives on Fixing Yugoslavia

While the responses demonstrate migrants' deep continued engagement with Yugoslavia as citizens, and the influence of the Croatian mass media, many also offer striking testimony of the influence of living abroad on the labour migrants' world view. As Pavle's case illustrates, living in a radically different society led migrants to compare their home state to their host state. This reflection, in turn, led migrants to formulate recommendations on how to address Yugoslavia's problems, as well as projects for return. These suggestions indicate that, while some migrants rejected Yugoslavia and saw it as unreformable, many more believed that it could be reformed and that they had useful knowledge that could assist in those efforts. While respondents drew on the dominant discourses of their sending and host societies, they produced innovative ideas that blended both.

Whether respondents identified or not with the Croatian national revival, the majority perceived their predicament as a product of poor economic policy, or structural problems plaguing Yugoslav society. Using language and ideas drawn from mainstream Yugoslav popular discourse, they focused on corruption, generational conflict, and economic mismanagement. Numerous writers expressed their belief that labour migration represented a policy failure by the Yugoslav government, such as the forty-year-old bricklayer who had been living in Germany for four years who wrote, "It is a large-scale national shame that foreign states exploit our workforce, which loves to work and gets excellent recognition. ... I don't know what use this is to our homeland. And we've become foreign slave labour?"[33] A few respondents explicitly noted the irony of the situation, such as the pharmacist from Senj working in a Mercedes factory, who decried the fact that he had "spent the best years of his life building *capitalism*."[34] By bringing out the ideological dimension of their situation, these workers emphasized that dependence on labour migration was deleterious to the legitimacy of a regime whose very raison d'être was to rescue workers from capitalist exploitation. As one migrant put it, "Why is that that the people of the so-called socialist Yugoslavia have to look for their bread in capitalist states and build their economies, and in so doing leave their home and hearth, lose their health, be obliged to found a family in a foreign country, or be unable to found one at all?"[35]

Naturally, many blamed economic reforms for the high unemployment that obliged them to seek work abroad.[36] But many also identified systemic corruption and incompetence in the Yugoslav economy as causes for their forced exile. In particular, they complained about poor management of the economy, the impossibility of getting a job without bribes or connections, and the manifest lack of manager training and talent. Respondents were particularly frustrated that young people who had just completed their studies could not find work in Yugoslavia, because well-connected but unskilled individuals took all the jobs. The ticket to getting a job, they believed, was to be a war veteran or a Communist Party member, or to have an uncle in high places. They also resented the way in which managers received preferential treatment and treated workers with contempt. One migrant worker described the humiliating way he was treated at the Ljubija mine in Prijedor, Bosnia-Herzegovina: "When I asked the head of human resources, he turned away from me and called someone on the phone and they talked about football matches and weekends, and I left." He added that he was not likely to return to Yugoslavia, because he had "no desire whatsoever to experience this again, only someone who has gone through it can know [what I mean]."[37]

For some, the solution to Yugoslavia's economic woes was for the central state to crack down on abuses – a perspective that was deeply anchored in Yugoslav socialism. A twenty-eight-year old skilled worker from Belgrade believed that economic prosperity would return if the League of Communists reasserted its authority. Among his demands, he called for the death penalty for economic criminals, the application of laws passed by the Federal National Assembly without manipulation by the other levels of government, and a reduction of government administration. He also argued that high customs tariffs protected unprofitable enterprises from competition and should be minimized, and that a third nationalization was necessary, "because it's unacceptable that in a socialist system someone can have an apartment, a villa, a car, a yacht, and a weekend home, and that another lives with his children in a basement."[38]

But for the majority of survey respondents, the functioning of the Yugoslav economy was at the heart of the problem, and Yugoslavia would have to undergo fundamental reforms before they would consider returning. Many respondents felt that they had acquired useful insights into sound economic policy, successful management, or a particular branch of business from which Yugoslavia could profit. Their newly acquired knowledge was coloured by the dominant economic discourses of their host societies. A twenty-nine-year-old technical drafter recounted that he had left Yugoslavia because the economy was in such a disorganized state, and he did not expect an improvement. "I have managed quite well in the West," he offered, "and I realized that the secret of their high standard lies in the fact that the state invests carefully and makes all investment according to strict economic criteria."[39] Another, a thirty-year-old electrical engineer working in Germany, had spent time observing his workplace and the functioning of the German economy in general. He had concluded that German workers were not more intelligent than their Yugoslav counterparts; the Yugoslavs just needed greater work discipline. He believed that, in addition to foreign direct investment, a generational turnover in Yugoslavia's industrial management could yield positive results.[40] Several labour migrants noted the dynamic and supportive atmosphere in their workplaces. A cook living in Friederichshafen, who had also worked in Austria, noted that "here people offer you the possibility of perfecting yourself at work, insofar as you desire it and they see that you want to work."[41]

First and foremost, the old generation of management would have to make way for a new, better-trained generation, and jobs would have to be awarded to people with skills and talent. For others, this was not enough; Yugoslavia would have to emulate the booming Western European economies. One thirty-three-year-old electrical engineer saluted the closer economic ties with Western Europe but felt that a massive export of unskilled labour was not the way to go about it. Rather, Yugoslavia should accept foreign investment and introduce the kind of work discipline that prevailed in the German workplace.[42] Another worker, a thirty-eight-year old metal worker from Rijeka, drew up a list of changes he would make to the Yugoslav economy, including reducing the administration, introducing greater work discipline, improving relations between worker and management, reducing the number of meetings, and fixing wages according to skills rather than diplomas. He argued that dealing with such weaknesses in the economy would allow wages to "find their correct levels by themselves."[43] On the basis of his analysis of the strengths of Swedish industry, Pavle B. argued that it was irrational for Yugoslavia to have multiple firms producing the same product, and that decentralization was driving up prices. The entire steel industry, he argued, should be run by one firm.[44] The variety of responses here highlight the fact that living abroad in the 1960s and 1970s might strengthen the migrant workers' faith in free-market capitalism, or conversely, in Western European–style planned economies.

Respondents from an agricultural background appear to have been less prone to focus on high-level policy than migrants from urban backgrounds. They lamented that no matter how hard farmers in Yugoslavia worked, they could not achieve even the minimal standard of living enjoyed by city-dwellers. As a result, they and countless others were forced to earn a living abroad. Their main ambition was to be able to purchase modern farm machinery, and to this end they asked that import tariffs be reduced or that the state provide them with credit. While some of these frustrated agriculturists criticized rural economic policy, their demands remained focused on what could be done, in the immediate moment, to revitalize agriculture and the villages.[45]

Some migrant workers developed entrepreneurial ambitions as a result of their foreign experience. Mario Turković, for example, emerged from his stint working in the port of Hamburg with know-how and a business idea. Having learned about the high profit margin of the leather import-export business, he proposed to reorganize labour in the Rijeka port so that Yugoslavia too could profitably enter this sector.[46] The cook from Friederichshafen proposed to open a kiosk, and a waitress said that she knew what tourists wanted and how to serve it.[47] For many, returning home was contingent on being able to turn their savings into employment, by buying equipment in their host state and importing it into Yugoslavia. Another migrant, who had been trained in Yugoslavia in the production of knit textiles, said he would return if he could import a machine for knitting socks.[48]

On occasion, respondents expressed a preference for the political system of their host country. One migrant worker in Germany, for example, wrote in favour of aspects of the liberal democratic political system, in addition to traditional requests for more modest customs tariffs and a better standard of living for workers and peasants. His wish was "that I can in any environment or situation express what bothers me; democracy like here in West Germany, for example: a multiparty system."[49] He was not hostile to Yugoslavia; although he did not feel that Croatia had found its "place under the sun" in the south Slavic state, he expressed concern for the future of Yugoslavia, emphasizing the importance of brotherhood and unity in these troubled times.

These respondents might still imagine a future in socialist Yugoslavia, however remote. For other workers, however, comparing Yugoslavia to their host country led them to conclusions that undermined the very legitimacy of the Yugoslav regime. Many lamented the fact that they could not earn an honest living in their homeland. In the words of a laboratory scientist in Frankfurt, "When you unite corruption, intrigue, laziness, and meanness, then proclaim demagogy the highest virtue, humiliation and disappointment is the result. Then, with a full heart we work in the foreign world for the research institutions of private compa nies."[50] Several letters emphasized the profound irony that a capitalist, and in the case of Sweden, monarchist state treated them better than their socialist homeland.[51]

Conclusion

Written at the height of the Croatian Spring, the responses to the survey conducted by the Institute for Migration and Nationality testify to the labour migrants' transnational lives and belonging.[52] On the one hand, they highlight the degree to which migrants had continued to be active participants in Yugoslav society. Not only did migrants respond in large numbers, reflecting a desire to share their opinions with surveyors based in Yugoslavia, but their responses reflected a lively engagement with Yugoslav political life. Through their answers, migrants asserted their rights as citizens of Yugoslavia and of their home republics – the right to have their voices heard and counted. Those expressing their rejection of Yugoslavia had not in fact severed ties with the homeland – much to the contrary, they continued to follow events closely and hoped for a serious transformation of Croatia's relationship to the rest of the federation, including, possibly, independence.

While proponents of reform and secession may have been influenced by emigrant organizations hostile to Yugoslavia, as the authorities feared, their opinions also reflect the discourse in Yugoslav newspapers distributed abroad, such as *VUS* and *Imotska krajina*. Yugoslav efforts to keep migrants informed by exporting press publications thus had unintended consequences – they had indeed strengthened the migrants' relationship to the homeland, just not in the way that authorities had perhaps anticipated.

While migrants' opinions were shaped by debates within Yugoslavia, they were equally influenced by their experiences of migration. Just as *Imotska krajina* tried to connect the Croatian Spring to the economic backwardness of the region, the ensuing dependence on labour migration, and its deleterious effects on migrants and their families, migrants from Croatia often sought to make sense of the political claims of the Croatian Spring through their own experiences prior to leaving Yugoslavia, and vice-versa. No matter how persuasive the rhetoric of the Croatian Spring was to them, for most, returning home depended on practical considerations: the ability to find a secure job and an apartment, and to bring home the consumer goods on which they had spent their earnings.

Although migrants repeated the narratives that were suggested by different political actors – whether enduring loyalty to Yugoslavia, or outrage in the face of Croatia's exploitation by Yugoslavia – and enriched them with their own life stories, they had more to say. Their thoughts and ideas emerged from personal experiences and chafed against more simplistic political messaging. Although the personal testimonies of these migrants told of oppression and victimization, they were also stories of personal survival, and even success and accomplishment in the face of adversity. In contrast to representations in film that emphasized the migrants' helplessness, they also testified to migrants' agency – their ability to choose their destiny, and their desire to shape their futures. They were eager to share their perceptions of their host societies, including lessons they had learned that they believed would be of benefit to Yugoslavia. In answer to the question of whether migrants continued to belong to Yugoslavia, or whether they had been lost to new homelands, these testimonies articulated a more complicated practice of belonging, rooted in two or more places, and a life lived across borders.

8 Building a Transnational Education System for the Second Generation

In Želimir Žilnik's film *Druga Generacija* (1984), teenager Pavle Hromiš struggles with his identity. The child of migrant workers in the FRG, he has been sent home to Vojvodina to receive a Yugoslav education. But where is home, exactly? As Pavle laments, "Over there, I'm a foreigner. Here, I'm a foreigner. I have no homeland" – a paradox he is ultimately never able to resolve.

The school is a central stage in this coming-of-age drama – not only is it the place where Pavle painfully acquires education in the ways of Yugoslavia, it is also where he socializes with other people his age and figures out who he is as a person and what he will become. Unfortunately, Pavle's unstable identity prevents him from successfully negotiating any of these challenges. Not only does he chafe at the rote learning of knowledge that makes no sense, but, given his upbringing, he is also constantly confronted with his difference from others – including other children of migrant workers. When he leaves the school, he informs the director that it is because he didn't find a suitable group of friends.

These snippets from *Druga generacija* allude to two key issues that are explored in this chapter: First, the deep anxiety that Yugoslav society felt about the perceived confusion or alienation of the children of migrant workers. Second, the conviction that schooling and extra-curricular activities were the primary vehicle for integrating these children into the Yugoslav nation, and for promoting their mental and spiritual well-being. This chapter focuses not on children like Pavle's classmates – returnees to Yugoslavia – but rather on children living abroad with their parents. It shows that there was substantial pressure both by the Yugoslav state and migrant workers themselves to provide schooling to migrant children. Programming was intended not only to communicate hard skills and knowledge that would be essential upon their presumed return to Yugoslavia, but also to imbue children with Yugoslav values and provide them with a sense of community and belonging to Yugoslavia. Ultimately, as the result of organizational difficulties, limited resources, and unrealistic expectations, Yugoslavs judged supplementary education to be a mitigated success at best.

Genesis of a Transnational Mother Tongue Education System

By 1970 the Yugoslav state gradually began to take an active interest in becoming involved in and expanding educational programming for migrant children. The trigger was a growing awareness that, contrary to earlier trends, where migrants had left their children behind with relatives, they were now taking their children abroad with them. With these children, authorities in Yugoslavia were faced with the task, not of preserving ties with the homeland, but of initiating them. First efforts to address this issue involved instructing consulates to collect data on numbers of children and educational programs, and to examine the experiences of other migration states – Italy, Greece, and Spain – to define an effective approach. A report from February of that year provided partial data showing that there were 6,417 Yugoslav children in the German land of Baden-Württemberg, mostly living in Stuttgart, 839 children in Belgium, primarily in the industrial centre of Liège, and more than a thousand children in Paris, France. It also inventoried established mechanisms for delivering mother-tongue education in states hosting Yugoslav migrant workers. In Seraing, a suburb of Liège, a supplementary school for Yugoslav children was already in operation. In Sweden, the Yugoslav embassy had opened supplementary schools in Malmö and Stockholm, which were paid for by the Swedish state. A school had also been set up in Paris for the 168 children of consular employees and others representing Yugoslavia abroad, which was paid for by parents.[1]

In some states, there were already mechanisms to establish mother tongue-education that Yugoslavia could utilize. Germany, for instance, had a system for bilingual transitional schooling, as well as for supplementary mother-tongue classes offered for five hours per week. In addition to providing classrooms, Germany paid for transitional classes, as well as a portion of the cost of supplementary classes. Switzerland adopted a more hands-off approach. In 1966, it provided classrooms for supplementary education, on the condition that sending states organize and finance the classes. All in all, the report testified that there was both a need and demand for mother-tongue education, and the necessary conditions for offering it.[2]

What was still missing were clear objectives and a comprehensive strategy. Why should Yugoslavia provide education to their school-aged citizens living abroad? What form should this education take, and how should Yugoslavia deliver it? How, in particular, should it deal with the challenge of offering programming outside its state boundaries?

In May of that year, the Federal Committee for Education and Culture (Savezni Savet za obrazovanje i kulturu – SSOK) issued a report on the "social-pedagogical foundation for educational work with the children of our workers employed abroad and recommendations for resolving problems of their schooling," the first comprehensive overview of the topic and the foundation for all further work in this area. Pointing to the increasing numbers of workers abroad – according to the Federal Committee for Labour (Savezni Savet za rad), 55,000 in Austria, 9,000 in Belgium, 4,000 each in Denmark and the Netherlands, 70,000 in France, 300,000 in Germany, and 20,000 each in Switzerland and Sweden – and the long-term nature of this migration, the report made a case for an educational strategy and program for the second generation.[3]

SSOK looked to another country with a similar migration profile – Italy – in its quest for a model for how to build an education program for migrants abroad. A study group visited Italy in December 1969 to examine how Italians approached migrant education, and they were particularly interested in the way in which the educational program was structured, and how responsibilities were shared across ministries. They also admired the emphasis on what they called "functionality" – that is, enabling migrant children to succeed abroad as well as upon their return. In the Italian system, the education of migrant children, focused on providing children with essential knowledge about their homeland, was coordinated with helping them acquire the language of their host country as quickly as possible.[4]

Ultimately, while the Committee could look to Italy for guidance on how to deliver education, the goals of Yugoslav education needed to be firmly rooted in self-managed socialism. The proposed list of principles is striking in its breadth, emphasizing both personal development and the social responsibilities of the individual. Reflecting Marxist values, the first principle was to provide children with a firm foundation in science and the scientific approach to work, and develop a positive and responsible attitude toward work. The second principle was to familiarize children with the social, economic, and political system in Yugoslavia, and rights and responsibilities under self-management. Particular emphasis was put, in this principle, on children playing a progressive role in changing labour relations and in developing their sense of solidarity. The third principle concerned using a scientific approach to understanding the natural world and society, to be familiar with the contemporary achievements of Marxism in the social sciences, and to develop critical thinking – the irony of listing these last two items in succession appears to have been unintentional. Also included in this principle was the encouragement to engage in a life-long struggle for progress, the search for truth, and life-long learning.[5]

The next principle was highlighted in pen by the reader from the Ministry of Foreign Affairs, suggesting that it was seen as the most important one: "Children should be raised in the spirit of belonging to their people or nationality, equality, brotherhood and unity of the peoples of Yugoslavia, loyalty to the socialist homeland, and readiness to defend its independence, in the spirit of respect of other peoples, international solidarity of working people, and peace on earth."[6]

The last few principles were more universal in their orientation. They included developing an appreciation for the ethical, aesthetic, and artistic value of Yugoslavia's cultures as well as world culture; humane and healthy interpersonal relations, including gender relations; and physical and spiritual well-being through physical culture.[7]

The list of principles clarified that the main purpose of this education was to maintain children's ties to Yugoslavia in anticipation of their eventual return. Through the education program, children would continue to participate in Yugoslav society. A subsequent document further elaborated on the rationale for Yugoslavia taking the lead in organizing mother-tongue education for the children of migrant workers: "Today several thousand children of our workers live abroad, of which a part every year reaches [the age of] responsibility for elementary education. Based on the fact that the children of our workers abroad have not ceased to be Yugoslav citizens, the Yugoslav community is responsible for ensuring their education abroad."[8]

The report added that while host states were required by law to attend schooling in the communities in which they resided, their host states were not obligated to offer mother tongue education. This was clearly in Yugoslavia's jurisdiction and national interest. Indeed, ringing an alarmist note, the report argued that it was imperative for Yugoslavia to build a cross-border educational program: "The Yugoslav social-political community, given the opportunity presented to her, cannot allow that her youngest generation develops without acquiring basic knowledge from the national histories, languages, and national geographies, because this could have incalculable consequences."[9]

This would remain the priority of educational programming throughout the period investigated and would take precedence over advocacy on other topics. For example, Yugoslav state officials and pedagogical experts expressed concern that young Yugoslavs were receiving a second-rate education in their home states, restricting their social mobility abroad. This discriminatory treatment was at least in part a result of the youth's lack of command of the host state's language and their social isolation, suggesting that migrant children should focus on acquiring a second language rather than their mother tongue. Indeed, educators and educational authorities in host states often took this position. Yet, while protesting this discrimination, Yugoslavia focused on securing and promoting educational programming the mother tongue. Its priority was not for young people to be well integrated in their host societies, but for them to have the ability to reintegrate into Yugoslav society. In 1978, the Eleventh Congress of the League of Communists of Yugoslavia confirmed this understanding of the role of Yugoslav education programs for migrant workers, as a tool to preserve national identity, combat negative influences, help organize Yugoslav citizens in defence of their interests abroad, and create the conditions for their gradual return.[10]

Because education in Yugoslavia was a republican jurisdiction, building such an educational system was doubly complex. Not only did Yugoslavia need to negotiate with each individual host state, but, afterward it was also obliged to coordinate its own operations with each republic and autonomous province. The complexity of the administrative apparatus reflects this dual challenge, as revealed by the following sketch of the institutions involved and their jurisdictions.

When the Federal Council for Education and Culture, which had first begun providing education to migrant children, was shut down in 1971, its international activities were taken over by the Federal Office for International Scientific, Educational-Cultural, and Technical Collaboration (Savezni zavod za međunarodnu naučnu, prosvetno-kulturnu i tehničku saradnju, also known as YUZAMS). This office took responsibility for seeking bilateral agreements with foreign states and for coordinating with the republics and provinces. YUZAMS had a dedicated staff for "schooling of the children of our citizens abroad" (Odsek za školovanje dece naših građana u inostranstvu), which oversaw day-to-day administration and coordination of instruction, payment of teachers, communication with consulates, and the preparation of materials for bilateral relations.[11]

YUZAMS adopted the position that the cross-border educational program should mirror the structure of Yugoslavia's educational system. Put another way, as Yugoslav citizens, migrant children were entitled to receive an education from their home republics and autonomous provinces. Consequently, the republican and provincial secretariats of education attended a series of meetings starting in November 1972 to establish how they would finance and implement the embryonic educational strategy. In September 1973 the commission adopted basic guidelines for the enactment of a social compact concerning the education of children of migrant workers temporarily employed abroad. The social compact was a type of planning agreement provided for by the 1973 constitution, which established the aims of the educational program as well as the rights and responsibilities of different state organs in providing education, and regulate the relationships between them.[12] In Yugoslavia's decentralized bureaucracy, a social compact was essential to ensure the administrative and financial sustainability of the program. To the dismay of YUZAMS, the republics and provinces struggled to come to an agreement until 1980, causing significant impediments to resolving persistent problems with the educational system.[13]

The meetings of republican and provincial secretariats eventually evolved into a formalized body called the Inter-Republican and -Provincial Commission for Supplementary Education of the Children of Our Workers Temporarily Employed Abroad (Međurepubličko-pokrajinska komisija za dopunsko školovanje dece naših radnika na privremenom radu u inostranstvu – MKDS). In addition to representatives of the secretariats, it included a representative of the Federal Secretariat for Foreign Affairs (Savezni sekretarijat inostrane poslove – SSIP), the Federal Employment Office, the SSJ, and the League of Communist Youth of Yugoslav (Narodna Omladina Jugoslavije – NOJ). The commission's role was to organize operation of the elementary school supplementary education program, to select, train, and send teachers, and to secure textbooks and workbooks and other teaching and extracurricular materials for teachers and students.[14] In a sense, the division of labour can be simplified as follows: YUZAMS preoccupied itself largely with foreign relations, whereas MKDS was focused on domestic aspects of the program.

The administration of educating migrant children relied on a small number of civil servants in Yugoslavia and the diplomatic corps outside it. Four full-time federal employees devoted themselves to educating migrant children in 1977, and Croatia, Serbia, and Slovenia had dedicated workers for this task as well.[15] At the local level abroad, the transmission channels for official policies and resources were the embassies and consulates. By the end of the decade, many consulates had a dedicated educational advisor – four in Germany, two each in Austria, France, and Sweden, and one each in Australia and Switzerland. Consulates liaised directly with MKDS for policy guidance, and with the individual republican educational bodies on matters relating to teachers, textbooks, children's magazines, etc.[16] It should be noted that, prior to the establishment of bilateral relations, and where states refused to collaborate, the consulates were the primary engine for establishing mother-tongue education.[17]

YUZAMS's objective was to secure and shape the educational program in each state where Yugoslav children lived. In particular, it sought to secure financial and logistical commitments from the host state, while maintaining Yugoslavia's control of the teaching staff and curriculum. This was a careful balancing act – as the president of MKDS, Dobrosava Ilić, put it, "The negative side" of this approach was "that states participating in financing strive to include this teaching in their educational system and make it ever more neutral."[18] YUZAMS focused on bilateral negotiations with states that were cooperative and willing to secure conditions for building a network of mother-tongue classes. The Federal Republic of Germany already had a mother-tongue education framework in place, of which Yugoslavia could make use. Collaboration with Sweden was initiated in 1972 and culminated in agreements between YUZAMS and the superior school administration in that state. Denmark reached a similar agreement with Yugoslavia in 1975. Discussions with Austria in 1973–4 led to the establishment of a mixed Austrian/Yugoslav commission, which met at least once a year to deal with problems relating to mother-tongue education. Similar commissions came into existence also with Germany and Sweden. There were working groups in France and, reportedly, the Netherlands as well, and discussions were opened with Belgium and Switzerland in 1977.[19]

By 1977 the European Economic Community bolstered YUZAMS in its efforts by issuing the council directive of 25 July 1977 on the education of migrant workers. Although the directive concerned only migrants from other member states, it pressed member states to recognize, in principle, the children's right to mother-tongue education.[20] For example, YUZAMS estimated that Germany had developed a negative image in European politics as a result of its poor record on second-generation migrants. This had resulted in Germany becoming increasingly active in international organizations dealing with this issue and in improved support for the education of migrant children.[21] It had also led to a change of attitude in Austria and the Netherlands, with the latter introducing supplementary classes for 477 Yugoslav elementary school pupils and plans to introduce such classes at the secondary school level.[22]

Émigré organizations were rivals in the delivery of education and did their best to undermine efforts by the Yugoslav state to develop its supplementary education program. Reports accused the Orthodox and Catholic churches, as well as organizations such as Hrvatska

Kulturna Zajednica of stirring up trouble with school authorities and parents. They were particularly adept at exploiting tensions around Yugoslav language policy. In one case, parent representatives on the school council refused to approve a teacher because they feared that the children would not be taught "clean" language.[23] Diplomats saw such incidents not as instances of parents' legitimate cultural concerns, but as nothing less than an attack on Yugoslavia orchestrated by its enemies: "We need to be aware of the fact that through history the enemies of our reality have always used language to promote strife. This is also true in our time. There are those who today 'cry' over the fate of literary language. But this is not really because of language, but rather because of a hostile sentiment toward everything that is ours, contemporary Yugoslav society, and self-management."[24]

One report catalogued attacks on Yugoslav schools carried out in Switzerland through "intrigue, public letters in the enemy press, anonymous letters." Beyond stirring up disagreements over language, the intrigues included spreading misinformation, such as that the certificates issued by the schools were not recognized in Yugoslavia, as well as rumours that teachers were unqualified. Detractors of the schools claimed they taught Partisan nonsense (*partizanština*) and stirred up the anger of workers by telling them that schools were a waste of their hard-earned foreign currency. While Croatian nationalists claimed the schools were dominated by Serbs, members of the Serbian Orthodox church complained about the refusal of Yugoslav schools to teach catechism. The report admitted that some good-willed persons had been involved in this opposition but assumed that they had been misled by enemies of Yugoslavia.[25] While reports periodically complained about such subversion, they generally expressed confidence that they had the ear of the host state. Thus these interventions were seen more a nuisance than a genuine threat.

The efforts of YUZAMS were focused initially on establishing sustainable elementary school programs, but the scope of its advocacy soon broadened. This shift was tied to a growing anxiety about the alienation of the "second generation," and more specifically, a conviction that children of migrant workers were becoming alienated from Yugoslavia, first and foremost for lack of mastery of a Yugoslav language. Indeed, there were increasing numbers of children born abroad, whose mother tongue was the host state's language.[26] These children were ill prepared to learn in Yugoslav mother-tongue classes, which presumed a basic knowledge of the language in question. Moreover, these children were vulnerable to assimilation, particularly in states like Sweden, which provided opportunities for migrants to take Swedish citizenship. By 1979 they were identified as "the most vulnerable cat-egory of Yugoslav citizens abroad, to whom maximal attention must be paid."[27] There were also less clearly articulated concerns with teenage migrants, including the absence of good job opportunities in their host state or Yugoslavia, the absence of a straightforward path to social and economic reintegration in the homeland, and the general susceptibility to "negative influences."

To address the first issue – children growing up without basic Yugo-slav language skills – YUZAMS began to lobby host states to set up pre-school mother-tongue programming. The inter-republican and inter-provincial commission also set up a group to examine preschool educa-tion more closely in 1976. The German state of Bavaria already had an experimental program in place, which brought together German and Yugoslav children under the supervision of a German-speaking and Serbo-Croatian-speaking teacher.[28] Sweden also incorporated mother-tongue education as part of its own preschooling.[29] While Yugoslavia followed these initiatives with interest, YUZAMS sought to build pro-grams whose main purpose, in the words of educational advisor Hilde Bole, in reference to children in Germany, was to "hinder the integration of children into the German national milieu."[30]

Table 3 shows the development of elementary school mother-tongue education – the best established and most widespread format – between 1973 and 1978. These figures are drawn from the reports of Yugoslav authorities. It should be noted that 1973 figures were highly approxi-mative and in some cases of questionable accuracy. For example, numbers of children for Austria were adjusted in 1975 from 10,000 to 5,200. Nonetheless, they offer a useful snapshot of overall trends in the number of children living abroad and their inclusion in mother-tongue education.[31]

The numbers of children enrolled in preschool education were much more modest, although the numbers of children in preschool were com-parable to and even higher than those of children in elementary school. This was likely due to a combination of factors, including the later start in preschool programming than in elementary school, the reluc-tance of host state authorities to develop such programs, and parental indifference.[32]

Secondary-school programming was even more limited. In Western Europe it was offered only in the Federal Republic of Germany, France, Sweden, the Netherlands, and Great Britain. While precise numbers are unavailable, they appear to have been marginal: 166 students in Great Britain in 1975, and two classes in Austria in 1979, both in Vienna.[33] These low numbers reflect both the low numbers of teenagers living

Table 3. Yugoslav Children Enrolled in Supplementary Education

Host state	In school (1973)	In supplementary classes (1973)	In school (1975)	In supplementary classes (1975)	In school (1976)	In supplementary classes (1976)	In school (1977)	In supplementary classes (1977)	In school (1978)	In supplementary classes (1978)	% in supplementary classes (1978)
Austria	10,000	0	5,200	1,850	5,200	3,000	5,000	2,539	7,440	3,767	50.6
Belgium	ND	70	1,000	140	1,000	200	600	400	600	422	70.0
Denmark			500	300	600	300	530	372	600	400	66.5
France	5,000 (approx.)	450	6,500	1,500	8,500	2,000	8,500	3,000	9,273	4,000	43.1
Netherlands[a]	993	150	350	310	500	350	566	400	650	540	83.0
Luxemburg			100	40	100	50	100	63	96	66	69.0
FRG	2,135	4,544	27,000	14,000	27,000	16,000	28,670	17,231	43,234	22,000	50.9
Switzerland	3,747[b]	ND	2,500	1,200	3,000	1,350	2,500	1,476	2,853	1,769	62.0
Sweden	5,500	1,303	5,400	2,000	6,682	3,462	6,348	2,889	6,193	3,469	56.0
Great Britain			1,000	500	1,000	173	600	261	600	280	46.7
Norway			50	30	50	50	63	15			
Total	43,580 (approx)	6,904	49,600	21,870	53,632	27,292	53,47	28,646	71,639	36,759	51

Sources: These figures are taken from the following documents: for 1973, AJ 142 SSRNJ I-486. Informacija o nekim problemima obezbedjivanja nastave iz nacionalne grup predmeta za decu jugoslovenskih gradjana privremeno zaposlenih u inostranstvu. December 1973, 2; for 1975, AJ 142 SSRNJ A-275. Medurepubličko-pokrajinska komisija za.dopunsko školovanje dece jugoslovenskih gradana na privremenom radu u inostranstvu. Savetovanje o dopunskoj nastavi. 2 June 1976, 2; for 1977 and 1978: AJ 142 SSRNJ A-276. YUZAMS – odsek za školovanje jugoslovenske dece u inostranstvu. Izveštaj rada u 1977. godini, 13.

[a] AJ 142 SSRNJ I-486. Savezni Sekretarijat za inostrane poslove. Uprava za radnike na radu u inostranstvu. Jugoslovenski radnici na privremenom radu u Holandiji. Belgrad, April 1973, 15.
[b] AJ 142 SSRNL I-486. Savezni Sekretarijat za inostrane poslove. Uprava za radnike na radu u inostranstvu. Jugoslavenski radnici na privremenom radu u Švajcarskoj. Belgrad, March 1973, 22.

Table 4. Yugoslav Children Enrolled in Mother-Tongue Preschool Programming in 1978

Host state	Preschool-aged children	Enrolled in preschool program
FRG	61,100	unknown
Sweden	7,000	813
Switzerland	5,696	313
France	4,109	45
Austria	1,500	–
Netherlands	1,000	–
Total	80,405	–

abroad with their parents, and the ambivalence of YUZAMS in defining and addressing the challenges they faced. Yet Yugoslav officials clearly identified this age group as being at risk – one report went so far as to call it the "most vulnerable part of the Yugoslav population abroad, particularly for the reason that most cannot continue their high schooling, and because the possibilities for their education are minimal."[34]

What was less clear was how to address the problem. Were older youth faced with an identity problem, like their younger siblings? Or was it an employment problem? Identity-focused solutions did not seem to produce results. YUZAMS noted the lack of interest of high school youth in Sweden in supplementary education.[35] Some parents expressed interest in sending their children to boarding schools in Yugoslavia, dreading the nefarious influence of the West on their children, but it seems that the numbers involved were too low to really justify such schemes. In fact, one observer commented that parents often chose to return to Yugoslavia once their children were old enough to go to high school.[36] "The situation of youth," a 1978 report countered, "is related to employment." If youth were disaffected and vulnerable to negative influences, it was because of their dismal prospects. The report suggested that adult education might provide a way forward for youth and noted that institutions in Yugoslavia had acknowledged the seriousness of the situation and were seeking a comprehensive solution.[37]

As a side note, YUZAMS also took an interest in the rapid expansion of adult education in the mother tongue, where it adopted a more laissez-faire approach. Given that foreign states had no formal responsibilities in this area, and that Yugoslav adult education enterprises were taking the initiative of setting up wherever there was demand, YUZAMS largely limited its activities to monitoring, although it occasionally expressed a desire to play a coordinating role. Organizations from across Yugoslavia, such as Radnički univerzitet Novi Beograd (based in New Belgrade), Crveni Signal, Automobilski školski centar (Zemun), Radnički univerzitet Radivoj Ćirpanov (Novi Sad), Birotehnika (Zagreb), and Školski Centar (Titograd) opened programs in cities across Germany, Austria, Belgium, France, Great Britain, Switzerland, and Sweden. The majority of programs were technical high school programs, such as skilled metalwork, machine shop training, skilled driver education, transportation technology, automobile mechanics, electrician training, and tourism, although primary and secondary schooling were also offered, and even post-secondary education. A substantial number of workers enrolled in such programs. For example, in Austria, where adult education had begun in 1975, there were 8,899 students enrolled in 1979, of which 4,195 were in primary school and 4,704 in high school programs. Some primary school teachers appear to have supplemented their income by teaching in these programs. There also seem to have been unscrupulous individuals and organizations running unauthorized programs, which YUZAMS tried to put an end to. While the motivation for opening schools abroad may have been the allure of foreign currency, according to Ivanović, the tuition, while onerous to workers, barely covered the cost of the programs – there was not much money to be made in adult education.[38]

Piecing Together the Mosaic

Encompassing nearly 37,000 children across Europe by 1979, the primary school mother-tongue program had by far the greatest impact and absorbed the greatest efforts. Given the decentralized nature of the Yugoslav educational system, the vast dispersion of Yugoslav workers across Western Europe, and the objective limits of Yugoslavia's resources, it was a remarkable achievement.

Reflecting the nature of the bilateral negotiations that produced them, the resulting educational system can best be described as a mosaic. A different version of the educational system emerged in each state, with variations in the commitments of the host state, degree of control exerted by Yugoslavia, and integration into the host state's educational system. While Sweden, Norway, the Netherlands, and some German states covered most expenses, in other states Yugoslavia was responsible for at least part of the costs. In France, Switzerland, Belgium, Luxemburg, Great Britain, and other German states, Yugoslavia covered all costs. In most cases, the Yugoslav republics and provinces were responsible for providing textbooks for the schoolchildren according to the language and the place of residence of the pupil. In Norwegian, Swedish, and German bilingual classes, however, the host state ordered the textbooks, and Sweden also paid for them.[39]

As numbers of migrant children living in Denmark, Great Britain, Norway, the Netherlands, and Luxemburg were marginal, and the documentation on them is scant, the following case-by-case discussion will focus on Austria, Belgium, France, the FRG, Switzerland, and Sweden, where the majority of migrant children were concentrated.

Germany: Migrant Education as Partnership

Mother-tongue education was established most quickly in the FRG, the host state with the largest population of Yugoslav children, given the existence of a framework. By 1976, 187 teachers were providing lessons to Yugoslav children.[40] Mother-tongue schooling in Germany was complicated by the fact that education was a prerogative of the individual states, and each state had its own delivery and funding model. Two basic types of courses dominated: transitional classes, which were full-time programs aimed at immigrant children, combining teaching in the mother tongue and in German; and, more commonly, supplementary classes, which were mother-tongue classes offered once a week, for up to five hours, usually in the afternoon, following the end of German school. With the exception of the state of Hessen, supplementary classes were optional.[41]

In Bavaria, one of the German states with the most migrant workers, 1,583 pupils were registered in bilingual classes in grades one through nine in Munich, Nuremburg, Augsburg, Ingolstadt, and Erlang during the 1977–8 school year. The curriculum in these classes was based on the German curriculum and that of the Republic of Croatia. Yugoslavia was consulted on matters relating to these classes, but its influence was somewhat limited. While Yugoslavia selected the teachers sent to Germany, they were all public employees of the German state and were reportedly forced to swear an oath that they would not spread communist propaganda. Supplementary classes, a different format that was financed entirely by Yugoslavia, were offered in forty-five cities and settlements in Bavaria, encompassing 1,526 pupils in grades one through nine in 1978. They took place once a week for four to five hours. Here, Yugoslav authorities had a great deal more control – local authorities were purportedly not interested in curriculum, limiting their oversight to the length of the class and the number of students enrolled.[42]

Sweden: The Hostile Takeover Approach

Yugoslavs were the second most numerous minority in Sweden after the Finns – they constituted 9.6% of non-citizens. Numbers of workers had been stable since 1971, at roughly 40,000. More than a third of these (14,462) were younger than nineteen years old, and 20% of Yugoslavs living in Sweden were born there.

Sweden adopted the most interventionist approach of all host states, fully treating mother-tongue education as part of the Swedish educational system. As in many other states, education was administered at the local level, with communes responsible for organizing classes if there were more than four pupils. The state paid for a modest 1.1 teaching hours per pupil per week.[43] Unlike Germany, which supported mother-tongue acquisition on the basis that children would eventually return to their homeland, Sweden supported it as a necessary precondition for learning the Swedish language and integrating into Swedish society and culture. For the same reason, it did not allow the teaching of the "national group of subjects" – that is, "my homeland SFRJ" for younger children, and geography and history for older ones. Mother-tongue education had been made a priority in the 1976 school reform, and 36,000 children were enrolled in such classes in fifty different languages in the 1977–8 school year, of which 6,348 were Yugoslav. Sweden covered all expenses, but also retained complete control over education, allowing Yugoslavia to play only a consultative role. YUZAMS was particularly troubled that Yugoslavia could have no influence over the hiring of teachers. Sweden hired its teaching cadre from the ranks of Yugoslavs already living within its borders.[44] Rather than adopting the Yugoslav curriculum and textbooks wholesale, it adopted a modified version in 1975.[45]

YUZAMS tried to push back against Sweden's interventionism through the Yugoslav-Swedish committee for the schooling of Yugoslav children. In particular, it criticized the assimilationist ambitions underlying the Swedish program, which was not in line with Yugoslavia's official policy of temporary migration. YUZAMS hoped that it could use the establishment of a mixed committee as a sort of Trojan horse to erode Swedish convictions that Yugoslavia's role was merely consultative.[46] However, by 1977 the first secretary at the Yugoslav embassy characterized cooperation as one-sided, with Yugoslavs meeting all their obligations, but the Swedes not reciprocating. He recommended a variety of strategies to advance Yugoslav interests in mother-tongue education in Sweden, including using Yugoslav citizens' clubs and associations as advocates for mother-tongue education, organizing trips to Yugoslavia for children, and informing parents of their responsibilities in "preserving all forms of stability for the child."[47]

After its requests that Sweden employ Yugoslav-trained teachers were repeatedly deflected, YUZAMS hoped that Yugoslavia could at least play a role in the training of Swedish hired teachers. When the teachers' college of Malmö, in collaboration with the University of Lund, took the unprecedented step of starting a two-year program for teachers of Serbo-Croatian language in Swedish primary schools and preschools starting in 1977, YUZAMS organized a seven-day field trip to Vojvodina in the fall of 1978, during which student teachers attended lectures and discussions on such themes as educational and preschool reform in Vojvodina, modern children's literature in Serbo-Croatian, the development of preschool education in Serbia and SFRJ, cooperation between preschools and elementary schools, the theory and practice of bilingualism in preschools, spoken language development and bilingualism, and contemporary cultural life in Vojvodina. This trip was judged a success by organizers and participants, who welcomed the opportunity to gain access to relevant pedagogical literature. Consequently, a second, fifteen-day field trip to Yugoslavia was planned for the spring of 1979, which would include stays at Yugoslav schools. The Yugoslav embassy and consulate in Sweden urged that "this collaboration must be given its full importance, as it is the only possibility for us to have a direct influence on the preparation of future teachers of Yugoslav children in Sweden and to create a relationship with them."[48]

Austria, Switzerland, Belgium, and France: From Reluctant Collaboration to Complete Disinterest

Austria had the third-highest number of Yugoslav children in Western Europe. Migrant children faced serious obstacles not only to integration and social mobility, but on a more basic level, to normal development. Unlike Germany or Sweden, Austria had no program for migrant children to acquire the host state language. As a result, Yugoslav children who did not speak German were systematically discriminated against – 10.5% of elementary school students and 14% of high school students were in special education classes. The Yugoslav report attributed these high figures partly to a number of Roma children entering the school system in Austria who had not previously attended school in Yugoslavia – a rare reference to the Roma in the archival documentation on education, and labour migration more broadly. Moreover, 54.7% of children were in the B-stream secondary school, for low-achieving students, while 20.7% were in the A-stream program, for higher-achieving students, and only 6.4% were in gymnasium, which prepared students for university. Nonetheless, the report noted an improvement in the attitude and involvement of Austrian authorities in addressing these issues as a result of the influence of the European Economic Community and UNESCO.[49]

Supplementary classes in Austria followed the standard pattern – once a week for three to five hours, depending on the state. In schools where there were sufficient pupils to form a class – which ranged from seven to thirty-five students – classes were held during school hours, whereas classes made up of students from multiple schools were held in the afternoons. Austria covered most of the expenses: the majority of the teacher's salary, school supplies, and class space. Yugoslavia provided a salary supplement to teachers it sent and covered the cost of textbooks and specialized material, such as maps and films.[50]

With socialist Yugoslavia on its borders, Austria was particularly wary of the threat of communist infiltration. It reserved the right to design the curriculum that would be taught and to approve any textbook that would be used.[51] It also strictly forbade not only extra-curricular activities on school grounds, but even the participation of teachers in activities that could be deemed political, such as Yugoslav national holiday celebrations that included Pioneer activities. Some Austrian states were reportedly overtly hostile to the presence of Yugoslavs, such as Upper Austria and Tirol, but the Ministry of Education could be counted on to intervene on behalf of Yugoslavia in case of conflicts.[52]

In Switzerland the establishment of a network of schools preceded collaboration with the Swiss state. In December 1974 there were 7,210 children in Switzerland under the age of sixteen, of which 2,638 were school-aged. Twenty-one schools teaching 1,182 pupils in forty classes were in operation in 1976, with most students concentrated in the Zurich and Baden areas. Schools were started at the initiative of parents and clubs for Yugoslav workers. There had to be at least sixteen students and the prospect of further growth. The Yugoslav consulates and embassy were actively involved in supporting these schools, which functioned without the assistance of the Swiss state. Yugoslavia contributed one million Swiss francs per year, while parents paid a modest fee of fifty francs to cover school supplies, as well as the cost of leasing the classroom.[53] Like Sweden, Switzerland did not allow Yugoslavia to send teachers, but rather hired Yugoslavs already in the country – primarily wives of Yugoslav labour migrants.[54]

Even in states where Yugoslavia did not have official support in pursuing mother-tongue education, it took root and flourished to a remarkable degree. By 1977, out of 36,209 Yugoslavs living in Switzerland, there were 2,853 children of school age, of which 1,576 were included in primary school mother-tongue education. They were taught by sixty-five teachers, whose honoraria and expenses were paid by YUZAMS. Parents were organized into school boards, which were conceived of as self-managed organizations to engage with Yugoslav migrant workers in their role as parents. Additionally, they could play a role similar to that of the clubs of Yugoslav workers in localities where those did not exist, acting as a focus for Yugoslav community life. The embassy was trying out a new concept for providing access to education to children in remote locations, which involved sending teachers twice a month and organizing home-schooling with parents.[55] By 1979, possibly as a response to the EEC directive, Switzerland had expressed much greater interest in collaborating with YUZAMS to develop pre-school and primary school programming.[56]

As had previously been the case in Switzerland, Yugoslavia was largely obliged to work outside the official school system in Belgium, where there were at least 600 children in 1979. This was in part the result of language laws that mandated that foreign languages not be taught in school until the fifth grade of elementary school. Yugoslavs and other immigrant communities had organized mother-tongue schooling, but they operated without support from the Belgian state. Supplementary classes were organized and run entirely by Yugoslavia and its citizens, with Belgium's only role being that of landlord and provider of chalkboards and chalk. Classes of two to four hours were taught once a week by six instructors (two Serbo-Croatian, one Slovene, two Albanian, and one Macedonian). They were, according to one report, "real oases of Yugoslav spirit," where teachers made optimal use of exceptionally modest resources to achieve positive results. Teachers even resorted to covering expenses out of their own pockets – one had purchased a mimeograph machine, a predecessor of the photocopy machine. While the report might seem overenthusiastic, given the modest proportions of the program, both pupils and teachers showed impressive determination and commitment. Some pupils travelled 30 kilometres to attend classes, and one teacher, Lucija Uzmah, was obliged to travel 700 kilometres weekly to teach all her classes.[57]

The French model was similar to the Belgian one, with supplementary classes operating outside regular school hours, on Saturdays or Sundays. YUZAMS noted in 1979 that France – the state with the highest number of Yugoslav schoolchildren after the Federal Republic of Germany – was the only country of immigration that was completely uninterested in developing bilateral cooperation in the schooling of

Yugoslav migrants. French education officials had even refused invitations to visit Yugoslavia unless their expenses were covered by their hosts. Schooling being entirely financed by Yugoslavia, it had a completely free hand in hiring teachers. The conditions under which schools operated depended on the attitude of local school authorities. While there were cases of positive collaboration, there were also instances of discrimination, including children being forbidden to drink from the school's drinking fountains.[58]

Belgium and France are arguably the states with substantial numbers of Yugoslavs in which the Yugoslavs found the least success in bilateral cooperation. A Yugoslav delegation visited Belgium in 1979 in an attempt to advocate for better conditions for supplementary education. Delegates Anuška Nakić and Abdulj Ramaj reported being treated dismissively. None of their hosts bothered to meet with the Yugoslav visitors, and while the Flemish hosts organized visits with experts and administrators, the French hosts did not organize any meetings. Nakić and Ramaj got the impression that Belgian authorities knew little about supplementary education and felt no responsibility for its success.[59]

The education of Yugoslav migrant children grew rapidly. In 1977 there were 53,470 schoolchildren in Western Europe, of which more than half – 28,646 – were included in mother-tongue classes. A remarkable 627 instructors were employed, of which 259 were in the Federal Republic of Germany alone. Most of these instructors came from Croatia (139) and Serbia (112), but virtually all the languages spoken in Yugoslavia were represented. Beyond the official national languages, there were also Albanian, Hungarian, Romanian, Slovak, and Turkish language teachers.[60] By 1979 the total number of children included in mother-tongue education increased to 37,000, representing 60% of all Yugoslav children living in Europe, and the number of instructors totalled 746, of which a third were sent from Yugoslavia.[61] Its spending on teachers' salaries increased accordingly, from three million dinars in 1972 to eighteen million dinars in 1976.[62] Overall, Yugoslavia spent thirty-two million dinars on the education of migrant children in 1977, or 1.75 million US dollars at the time.[63] By 1984 that amount had increased to twenty-six billion dinars, or an estimated 8–10 million US dollars – a four- to five-fold increase in seven years.[64]

Conclusion

As migrants stayed abroad longer, particularly as work visas became more precarious following the 1973 oil crisis, they brought their families to live with them, and increasing numbers of children were born abroad.

Yugoslav authorities worried that this second generation of migrants, many of whom did not speak their parents' tongue, was losing its ties to the homeland. This anxiety testifies to the continued expectation that migrants and their children would eventually return. The task of wooing children called for a new approach, beyond the newspapers, radio programming, and Yugoslav workers' clubs. In response, they developed a transnational educational system to provide mother-tongue education, which could be adapted to different circumstances in each host state.

As with workers' clubs, the Yugoslav state picked up where grass-roots efforts had already begun the work. In this effort, consular officials continued to play an important role. Additionally, Yugoslavia developed a complex domestic bureaucracy to design and deliver educational programs, which involved federal and republican/provincial collaboration – a topic explored in greater depth in the next chapter. Wherever possible, Yugoslavia sought to collaborate with the host state in the interest of securing foreign funding for the education, while trying to maintain control over the curriculum. While some host states were sympathetic to the project of preparing migrants to return home, others were more interested in assimilating migrants or simply not interested at all.

The resulting system had a lot of moving parts, depending on the collaboration of the different republics and provinces with the federal government, as well as the cooperation of host states. It was remarkably flexible, adapting to varied local contexts. Whereas some localities were characterized by complete disinterest, other partners, like Sweden, aggressively sought to take over and control mother-tongue education, posing very different kinds of challenges. In other places, populations of Yugoslavs were too dispersed to accommodate a traditional educational program. In spite of the difficulties, due to its flexibility and to a significant commitment of resources from Yugoslavia, considering its means, this model for building a transnational educational system was remarkably successful in the number of children it was able to reach. Having examined the development of the educational infrastructure, in the next chapter I will explore how educational programs worked in practice, with a focus on the role of teachers and the content of teaching materials.

9 They Felt the Breath of the Homeland

In order to build an effective transnational educational system on a relatively small budget, Yugoslav authorities wove it into the broader panoply of programs and policies aimed at Yugoslavs living abroad and tapped into educational, youth, and other resources inside Yugoslavia. The first and most critical element of the transnational school system, the linchpin upon which the model was articulated, were the teachers. They were supported by other organizations, with the consulates and the Yugoslav citizens' clubs providing most sustained support. Diplomatic missions intervened on behalf of Yugoslavia and its educators in interactions with the host state, channelled resources from Yugoslavia (funding, textbooks, teaching materials, visiting artistic ensembles), and mediated communication with Yugoslav institutions. They also kept a watchful eye on the activities of educators and hostile political émigré organizations that conspired to undermine Yugoslav education. While their activities were largely supportive, they occasionally led in setting up schools and programming for migrant children. The Yugoslav clubs provided a space for extracurricular activities and for mobilizing the larger community of Yugoslav workers. Other groups also provided assistance in specific areas, ranging from educational and youth organizations and individual teachers in Yugoslavia, to the Yugoslav press targeted at migrant workers and travel firms.

While the archival record does not provide a systematic explanation for the pedagogical principles that informed education, two key principles can be derived from the abundant reports that were collected by SAWPY, the organization that oversaw the education of migrant children. First, as noted in chapter 8, the main purposes of supplementary education were to ensure that children mastered their parents' mother tongue, and that they felt a strong sense of belonging to the homeland. Second, the family unit was the primary space in which a child's national identity was formed, and therefore supplementary education should not only work with the family unit but also strengthen it, particularly if it was disintegrating or absent.

Components of a Yugoslav Education

A 1976 report suggests that, in the process of implementation, the ambitions of educators had adjusted from the expansive and lofty list of aims first drawn up in 1970. Now the objectives were primarily to equip children to read and correctly express themselves orally and in writing. Children should also be introduced to literary language and exposed to the most important works of literature from Yugoslavia, and to the "revolutionary foundations of our peoples and nationalities" as expressed in literature. The aim was to build a foundation for further education in the mother tongue that could be further developed upon the children's return to Yugoslavia, and to instil in children Yugoslav socialist values and morality. As one consular report noted, "It would be utopian to think that in our supplementary school the student will master a higher knowledge of literary language. We need to be realistic about this."[1]

At the elementary school level, these goals were accomplished through language classes, and the subject matter "my homeland SFRJ" (Socijalistička Federativna Republika Jugoslavije – the official name of the state). Children in these classes were to develop a sense of belonging to Yugoslavia by learning about a variety of topics including the beauty and wealth of Yugoslavia, the past of its peoples, the need for mutual cooperation in contemporary society, relations in a self-managed society, significant events through which Yugoslavs realized brotherhood and unity, and the Yugoslav social system. For children in secondary school, this subject was replaced by history and geography lessons. History lessons emphasized the historic ties between Yugoslav peoples and nationalities, geography lessons fostered a sense of love, pride, and protectiveness for Yugoslavia, and a respect for other peoples and nationalities. Students were supposed to simultaneously develop socialist patriotism, humanism, and internationalism.[2]

Organization of the school was expected to be consistent with the official Yugoslav policy of brotherhood and unity and linguistic policy affirming the unity of Serbo-Croatian as a language. Therefore classes in different languages were not to be identified as "national" schools, but as sections in a single Yugoslav supplementary school.[3] Moreover, although classes might be divided along linguistic lines for pragmatic reasons, they were not to be divided along national lines: Croatian, Serbian, and Bosnian children should be in the same class. "There should be no ethnically clean [čist] schools," as one pamphlet explained.[4] Teachers were instructed to explain to children that the language they spoke "is in reality a single language, with two names, which in the Socialist Republic of Croatia is called Croatian, and in the Socialist Republic of Serbia is called Serbian."[5] Teachers were expected to perform remarkable linguistic acrobatics in service of this principle: "The lesson should be conducted in such a way that the literary-linguistic expression of the nation that the child belongs to is respected. This means that the teacher ... must constantly point out differences between this or that expression of the nationalities to which the children belong. In talking to them both in class and outside, the teacher must respect all the specificities of their literary language. They must make corrections such that the specificity of their literary speech is not violated (i.e. 'vlak' vs. 'voz'), no matter how they themselves speak."[6] Vlak and voz were the Croatian and Serbian variants of the word for train.

These policies were regularly challenged by émigré organizations.[7] For instance, in Sweden, the Croatian nationalist Matija Gubec Society petitioned school administrators to have Croatian children set apart from other Yugoslav children in Swedish schools, on the basis that the children should not be subject to communist propaganda. In particular, they were opposed to children learning about the national liberation struggle and the Yugoslav social system. Under pressure from the Yugoslav consulate, school administrators withdrew from discussions with the society, putting an end to this issue.[8]

Let's take a closer look at education at work, examining first the teachers' role, then the ways in which they worked with the Yugoslav citizens' clubs and other organizations to offer enticing extracurricular activities. The teacher's responsibilities were much broader than merely educating children during school hours. Rather, Yugoslav educational policymakers extolled the teacher abroad as a source of knowledge, role model, activist, and leader for the entire community abroad:

> The position of the teacher in a foreign country is exceptionally complex. The teacher here must be educator, political and social worker. He is a figure around which our people gather because he is a tie to the homeland, a source of knowledge, counsel, and help. Entire families arrive at the lesson and, after the events of the week, both parents and children salute the teacher, exchange information, present problems for his consideration. Each child waits for the teacher to say something to him, even the youngest who are accompanying their older brother. The teacher who does his work as he should enjoys such trust and regard that we, looking

at things from the homeland, where the traditional role of the teacher has been divided between different institutions and the media, have trouble imagining.[9]

Another report cautioned teachers to retain a professional distance from parents and children.[10]

Thus, from the outset, it was critical that teachers be not only highly qualified and talented, but also "politically upright" and loyal, as noted in one directive dating from 1970.[11] Teachers were expected to have completed the pedagogical academy, or the faculty of their expertise (such as mother-tongue education or Yugoslav literature).[12] A policy of rotating teachers back to Yugoslavia after five years abroad was also instituted, although in practice it was not always respected, in part because most teachers were not formally Yugoslav employees, but employees of their host states.[13]

Instructors were also expected to engage in regular professional development. Starting in 1972, annual five-day summer seminars were organized in attractive Yugoslav cities such as Poreč (1975) and Belgrade (1976), gathering Yugoslav teachers from across Western Europe, as well as teachers who were about to begin a stint abroad. These seminars included talks by experts on the challenges of teaching migrant children, plenary discussions, workshops, and sightseeing. They were also an opportunity to meet with other teachers and representatives of Yugoslav institutions, including social-political and social organizations at the federal, republican, provincial level, members of the consular offices, the central committee of the League of Communists, and organs for the protection of children. Publishing houses, children's magazines, organizations for leisure and excursions, and representatives of the media also attended these events. The seventh seminar, in Struga, was attended by 137 teachers, of which 95 from Germany and 61 preparing to start their work abroad.[14] In addition to this yearly program, trips abroad by educational experts were organized, in which they gave presentations and visited schools. By the late 1970s, newly hired teachers were expected to undertake a two-day training session before leaving for their posting abroad – sixty-one participated in the 1978 edition in Ohrid.[15]

All of these programs were meant to ensure that teachers were up-to-date in the latest pedagogical scholarship, had an opportunity to socialize with fellow teachers facing the same challenges, and maintained a tight connection to Yugoslavia. Visits by educational professionals were also opportunities to monitor the quality of teaching, and to discipline teachers if necessary. On one such visit, for example, Rodoljub

Ignjatović, representing YUZAMS, chastised instructors of one school in Dusseldorf for not making effective use of national holidays to teach children about patriotic themes.[16]

Teachers were hardly pliant subjects. They challenged authorities about shortcomings of the educational system, unreasonable workload, and inadequate compensation. Their boldness testifies to the relative openness of the Yugoslav bureaucracy to criticism and disagreement from below, but it also suggests that, like their migrant worker co-nationals, teachers were emboldened by their situation beyond Yugoslavia's borders. After all, if they did not feel adequately supported by the Yugoslav state, there were other employment opportunities abroad. Teachers had good cause to complain – for example, in Berlin, they asked to be compensated for the more than 100 kilometres per week that they were required to travel from class to class, demanded the 10% "Berlin supplement" – a top-up offered by Germany to incentivize living in the city during the Cold War – as well as adequate insurance, and asked for more teachers to be sent, to lessen their workload. They also asked whether it was reasonable to expect them to give free lectures in cultural centres, in addition to their already heavy schedules, which included both teaching and extra-curricular activities. This particular argument, however, did not hold sway with Ignjatović, who reminded teachers that this activity was an "integral part of their educational function." Ignatović said that it would be preferable for teaching norms to be lowered than for extra-curricular activities and work with club sections to be neglected, highlighting the emphasis given to promoting a Yugoslav identity in education.[17]

On another occasion, a group of teachers protested about the format of the summer school, which seems to have been ill-suited to their needs. Instead, they asked for a yearly conference to which they could send delegates and requested that seminars take place in each of the republics and provinces during the Easter break, in the place of a single seminar. It is not difficult to imagine that teaching staff wished to spend as much of their summer vacation as possible close to their family and friends back home.[18] Even the prickliest Yugoslav officials, like Ignjatović, seem to have expected and tolerated backtalk. Reflecting on his visit to three German cities, although he cautioned that some teachers had the tendency to be "clannish" and "impatient," he did not see them as insubordinate. To the contrary, he emphasized the teachers' loyalty and praised their hard work and the educational foundation they had built.[19]

There is evidence to support his appraisal of the teachers' loyalty – teachers do seem to have acted as the "eyes and ears" of the Yugoslav authorities. For example, one report describes a "quiet war" between teachers and clerics in Bavaria, a conservative state dominated by Catholicism, who were trying to pressure Yugoslav children into attending their religious education classes. Teachers closely cooperated with Yugoslav authorities to curb this campaign without provoking a backlash:

> They need to be very tactful, to teach the program, develop a scientific out-look on the world, and not come into conflict with the clerics and school authorities. It is out of the question to openly persuade children not to attend religion class. We, along with teachers, insist on signed parental permission for children to attend religion class. Teachers have openly opposed children's attendance in religion class if their parents have not given permission. In one school in Munich, the director warned teach-ers that they would have to provide a written statement noting that they discourage children from attending religious class because one cleric com-plained. On the recommendation of the consulate, the teachers asked for a written statement identifying the initiator of the inquiry, and the com-plaint of the cleric. The school director was not able to provide documen-tation and ceased demanding the statement.[20]

Although the report clearly stated that open confrontation was not an option, neither was compromise. It added, "Given the delicate situation in which teachers find themselves, it is important to only send teachers with strong political commitment and who have a clear position vis-à-vis religion."[21] In a highly polarized context, it was absolutely essential that Yugoslavia be able to count on the staunch loyalty and support of its teachers.

The trouble was that, while Yugoslavia had established a system, however imperfect, for hiring, training, and managing its teaching cadre, it did not have complete control over which teachers were hired. Several states did not allow Yugoslavia any say or oversight in the pro-cess. Sweden recruited its teachers exclusively from within its own bor-ders, posing a special challenge. Yugoslav authorities worried about the "weak moral-political character" of some of its teachers in Sweden, whose political orientation was either hostile or unclear. They judged, understandably, that such teachers were not suitable for teaching the history and social system of Yugoslavia to children. Beyond their poten-tially negative influence, such teachers neglected their duty to engage children in extra-curricular activities.[22]

Teachers were expected to tie their activities into the broader web of Yugoslav programs directed at migrant workers. Thus, in addition to their teaching, they were expected to be leaders at the local Yugoslav clubs, according to their own proclivities.[23] Some of the roles they took on, according to one report, were leadership of the club as a whole or of cultural or artistic sections (such as folklore or choir), participation in sports clubs, and active participation in League of Communists committees or Yugoslav sports leagues.[24] This involvement was in line with their function as role models and communication channels, but it also insured that they would avoid "going native" and remain firmly within the orbit of Yugoslavia.

Vjekoslava Uremović, whose papers have been preserved in an archival fonds dedicated to radio and news media aimed at migrant workers, represented the ideal type of teacher in the scope of her activities and energetic advocacy on behalf of migrants. Among her many other roles, Uremović was the director of the Grigor Vitez supplementary school in Versmold, Bielefeld, as well as head of the local Pioneer group. She worked tirelessly to organize a Yugoslav club, coordinate relations between clubs, and organize activities, such as a bowling section, and courses of interest to migrant women. She was also a correspondent for the newspapers *Vjesnik*, *Front*, and *Vikend* on the challenges facing migrant workers. Uremović's file gives the impression of a loyal activist who worried incessantly about the lack of commitment of parents to their children's success in supplementary classes, the amateurism of the leadership of Yugoslav clubs, and misperceptions about migrants back in Yugoslavia.

For Uremović, promoting attachment to Yugoslavia meant actual and reciprocal contact with Yugoslavia – an approach that permeates all her writings, whether they concern children or adults. In honour of the school's inauguration, she organized a school trip for six Pioneers to two schools in Yugoslavia that shared the same name – Grigor Vitez, who had been a Croatian children's writer – in Žabno and Zagreb, Croatia. She also petitioned for one of her pupils to have the opportunity to meet Tito. In her words, "*Seeing Tito* is the event of one's life." On the occasion of the earthquake in Montenegro in 1979, she wrote to the Federation of Pioneers of Montenegro to express solidarity and sent 100 German marks, which her Pioneer section had raised to support one Pioneer girl and her family.[25]

Uremović's correspondence reveals that she worked doggedly to build a transnational support network not just for migrant children but for adults as well. After receiving no reply to her first letter, she sent a request for collaboration to the SAWPY branch in the Serbian town Požarevac – specifically, she was seeking information about the number of migrants from the town, their profile, and the expectations of support upon returning to Serbia, as well as copies of a local newspaper.

She also shared information on the schooling of migrant children. She encouraged SAWPY to use the local press to inform migrant workers about the problems of education abroad for their children, "that they might obtain from SAWPY booklets and literature on their language, on their region, and their history."[26]

As Uremović's case shows, schools and Yugoslav citizens' clubs were not distinct institutions with separate audiences, but rather interlocking and mutually reinforcing vehicles for creating a Yugoslav community. Conceived as a focus for the social and cultural lives of the entire community of migrant workers, the clubs were a vehicle for nurturing the family unit, which was considered so crucial to a child's national identity. As a result YUZAMS envisioned that they could also play an important role in education:

> This relationship between the parents of the child and the teacher is especially intense where the class takes place in our clubs, such as in Antwerp, because the parents wait for their children for a few hours. While the children work, the parents and other citizens gather in the neighbouring space, and they discuss, read the press, follow the children's singing, and during the break once again they all get together. Parents ask what the children have been doing, what they learned, etc. For these circumstances it's most desirable whenever possible for supplementary schools to be organized in our clubs' space.[27]

In fact, as we have seen, classes tended to be held on the school property of host states rather than at citizens' clubs. Teachers did, however, collaborate closely with clubs in the organization of spectacles for national holidays, of which the Yugoslav calendar was replete: Republic Day (29 November), the Day of the Yugoslav National Army (22 December), New Year's, Women's Day (8 March), Workers' Day (1 May), the day of Youth – Tito's birthday (25 May), and Veterans' Day (4 July). Schoolchildren in their supplementary classes took part in the festivities – sometimes the entire performance consisted of children singing songs, reading poems, and presenting other patriotic material that they had prepared. In other cases, visiting orchestras from Yugoslavia contributed as well.[28] The festivities were educational opportunities for children and key occasions for migrants to affirm their identity as a community. Two pedagogical administrators, reporting on their trip to Belgium, spoke to the power of national holidays to reproduce Yugoslav society and values abroad, uniting people of different backgrounds and generations: "These shows have exceptional value for our people abroad because these are opportunities to gather, find oneself amongst one's own people, and hear one's voice." Indeed, they claimed, there was rarely a dry eye in the house.[29] Preparations for the festivities were as important as the event itself. Describing the creation of a program of music and folklore, they explained,

> Something happened that represents an exceptional experience for every pedagogue, sociologist, and amateur. First, all generations of a family gathered in a common effort. This is exceptionally important because the connectedness of the generations is critical in the preservation of national identity abroad. Second, no one present was an expert in folklore or music, so everyone contributed according to his knowledge and art to the creation of a dance or song. The teacher contributed with his/her organizational skills, basic knowledge of the subject, and clear objectives of group activity, as did a Yugoslav who lives temporarily in Belgium with her spouse and who knew ethnography, and the mothers who remembered some dances from their youth, colleagues from the embassy who knew how to play guitar, and the youth themselves who on their visits in the homeland learned a few dances. In the course of many hours of effort, the contours of the show were created as a collective experience. In reality this joining together of knowledge of all generations and people of different profiles in a common expression is the most valuable educational part of this activity.[30]

This passage shows how, under teachers' leadership, citizens' clubs could become spaces where migrants could reaffirm their ties to Yugoslavia through socializing, the performance of rituals of belonging, and creativity.

Beyond preparing spectacles for the migrant community on national holidays, several other vehicles were used to bind the children to the homeland. Teachers were also expected to lead Pioneer groups. The Pioneer movement, which resembled scouting in other countries, was focused on promoting ideal behaviour, play, and the cultivation of attachment to Yugoslavia. Particularly interesting is the example of the Pioneer club in Stuttgart, which sought to educate children about saving and self-management, by implementing a Pioneer-run savings bank.[31]

Yugoslavia was not the only state to implement scouting to promote loyalty to the homeland amongst children living abroad. In the 1970s, Israel created a scouting organization, Tzofim Tzabar, to strengthen its ties with the children of Israeli emigrants in the United States. In Israel, authorities have tended to perceive emigrants as traitors to the nation, making it particularly urgent to "redeem" their children. Scout organizations carry out their activities in Hebrew and focus on teaching children about Israel. Historically, they have encouraged children to join the Israeli Defence Force after finishing high school, although they have reduced their advocacy in the face of parental opposition. Parents' motivations for enrolling their children in Tzofim Tzabar, as described by Nir Cohen, are instructive. They wanted their children to gain knowledge of Israeli culture and to feel an affinity with Israel, partly as a way to lessen the generational divide that they experienced. However, they did not agree with leaders of the Scout movement that the goal was for children to "return" to Israel. This is worth keeping in mind in the Yugoslav context – parents' motivations for enrolling children in supplementary classes and Pioneer groups were likely somewhat different from those of the Yugoslav state.[32]

Outside of Yugoslavia, it was not usually possible to organize Pioneer activities in the context of schooling, because the Cold War was characterized by deep political polarization. Even in countries with strong bilateral relations, school authorities were suspicious of enabling the spread of Communist propaganda. The Austrians were among the most hostile to the Pioneer movement, which was seen as a kind of Trojan horse. Austrian schools would not allow teachers to gather children after school hours on their premises, on the grounds that schools were not appropriate for political activities of any sort. German and Swiss authorities took a similar position.

Austrian hostility to the Pioneer movement climaxed in an ugly confrontation in Vorarlburg in 1978. Having learned that there would be a swearing-in ceremony for Pioneers at a Day of Youth event, local authorities forbade teachers from collaborating with the clubs in preparing the festivities. Because teachers and children were key to these celebrations, organizers were backed into a corner, and the event was cancelled.[33] Attacks on Pioneer activities in the press were reportedly published in the Austrian, Swiss, and German press in 1978.[34] In spite of the obstacles, Pioneer clubs were formed. In 1977, 600 children were inducted into thirty-six Pioneer troops in Sweden, representing 10% of all schoolchildren. In Austria, Yugoslav citizens' clubs stepped in to provide meeting space, illustrating the interconnectedness of programs aimed at migrant workers.[35]

Children were also invited to imagine their place in Yugoslav society through traveling exhibits, quizzes, and competitions – and sometimes all three at once. While these programs were initiated in Yugoslavia, teachers coordinated the children's participation. One exhibit, "Pioneers in the National Liberation War and the Socialist Homeland," travelled to six German cities in April and May 1979, hosted primarily by citizens' clubs, but also a municipal library and a primary school. In the interest of promoting "an accentuated tone of awakening patriotism," teachers were asked to have their pupils express their experience of the exhibit in prose, poetry, or art. Prizes were awarded for the ten best works, and three best teachers, as well as for the final quiz on the topic of "Tito – Revolution – Victory." According to the report, teachers participated enthusiastically.[36]

The most effective way to nurture a Yugoslav identity in children, not just according to the pedagogical experts who produced the countless reports in the archive, but also migrant organizations themselves, was actual contact with the homeland and with families in Yugoslavia. One widespread mechanism to foster such contact was for teachers to organize pen pal exchanges for their pupils in Yugoslavia.[37] Even better was the opportunity to travel to and experience Yugoslavia firsthand, which was seen as "more significant than every image or written word."[38] One report reveals that these trips were increasingly common by 1978, with children based in the FRG, France, Sweden, and Switzerland taking advantage of opportunities to make classroom trips to Yugoslavia. Because school holidays in Western Europe and in Yugoslavia were on different schedules, they were able to take part in school and extra-curricular activities. This is significant: the objective was not just to see the tourist attractions, but to engage with their peers in Yugoslavia.

The archive contains a particularly rich description of one organized trip to Yugoslavia that took place between 28 March and 7 April 1980 – shortly before Tito's death – under the banner "One Youth – One Homeland." The Association of Yugoslav Citizens' Clubs in Frankfurt initiated the project and realized it with the collaboration of the Organization of Yugoslav Educational Workers and the General Consulate of Yugoslavia in Frankfurt. Of the 2008 children in Frankfurt in grades four through nine who were enrolled in supplementary schooling, an astonishing 700 participated in the trip. Inasmuch as one accepts that migrant workers' associations were authentic popular associations, rather than just puppets of the Titoist regime, this means that "One Youth – One Homeland" was initiated by the grass roots. Certainly the success of the project depended on an enormous investment of time and energy, which suggested that members of the association were truly devoted to the project. The association promoted the project to parents at every available opportunity and committed to subsidizing the cost of the trip for families in need.

At the same time, Yugoslav institutions, firms, and families also made significant contributions. The republican secretariats for culture and education and pedagogical institutes organized the Yugoslav side of the visit. Children were hosted by twenty-three different schools in Zagreb, Split, Ljubljana, Priština, Sarajevo, and Belgrade. The Slovene-based airline Inex Adria, which counted migrant workers amongst its clients to and from Yugoslavia, provided discounts on their flights. And with the exception of Belgrade, where children were accommodated in the Pioneer Village, the visitors were hosted in the families of local school-children. Many host parents purportedly scheduled their vacation time to coincide with the migrant children's visit, to be able to devote to them their full attention.

Two keys to the success of the project, intentionally worked into its design, were lived experience and relationship-building. Lived experience allowed children to gain a full and multifaceted understanding of the homeland, which they could not get from textbooks and countered the anti-Yugoslav propaganda that surrounded them. As the report on the project emphasized, "concrete experience of the homeland" was invaluable, "because, aside from getting to know the school program, natural and historical landmarks, this is how one gets to know the homeland, the brotherhood and unity of our peoples, the economic achievements, as well as the truth about life in the homeland."[39] To this end, aside from schools, the children visited monuments, museums, youth centres, and factories, and they attended various performances, Pioneer and socialist meetings, and sports competitions – a full program indeed for a ten-day visit. The most meaningful aspect of the experience, however, seems to have been the human connection established between children and their hosts, as well as the stimulation of camaraderie with the children from Frankfurt. Tellingly, the report commented that several of the children staying with host families requested that their stay be extended, whereas children at the Pioneer Village spent time on their own instead of with their peers.[40]

Overall, the report triumphantly declared that the children "had felt the breath of their homeland," which, it claimed, would be of great significance when families decided to return. Moreover, it reiterated the necessity to continue to use school programs as a means to "permanently sustain the tightest relationship with the homeland."[41]

Materializing the Homeland: Themes from the Common Textbook

As the scale of mother-tongue education grew, teachers were under increasing strain because of the need to teach children using textbooks from different republics and provinces. Making matters worse, in schools with fewer Yugoslav children, teachers sometimes had to teach multiple grades. By 1976 teachers demanded the creation of a single, common textbook that would simplify their jobs and speak to the experiences of migrant children.[42] YUZAMS took on this task, forming two working groups in 1977 that developed a new curriculum and concept for the textbook that was endorsed by all republics. The process of developing the common textbook dragged on over several years, much to the frustration of YUZAMS and teachers across Europe, who noted that it made Yugoslav authorities look incompetent. The reasons for this delay remain unclear, although the lack of mechanisms to finance and facilitate work on such a project were initially blamed.[43] Even so, Slovenia began work on the final product before the other republics, and the Slovene-language editions of the textbook began to come out in 1979, several years earlier than the Serbo-Croatian editions, the three volumes of which were published in 1983.[44]

In spite of the fact that the common textbooks were published toward the end of the period under study, they provide us with the best glimpse of what children living abroad might have been learning. What makes the textbooks particularly fascinating is the fact that they represent an attempt to negotiate the complicated politics of national belonging in the Yugoslav context, proposing an understanding of homeland and belonging anchored in brotherhood and unity, with all its tensions.

The Serbo-Croatian textbooks, entitled *My Homeland the SFRJ*, were beautifully illustrated full-colour hard-cover books, printed on high-quality paper, each volume corresponding to a range of grades. They were divided into ten loosely thematic sections, focusing on homeland and patriotism, the life of Tito, childhood and play, the people and places of Yugoslavia, labour, mothers, literature and culture, and Yugoslavia's role in promoting peace in the world. While a variety of topics were addressed, the theme of homeland dominated, and indeed, bled into nearly all thematic chapters. The topics of Tito and the Second World War, which were tied to homeland, were also given a privileged place in the textbooks.

Explaining homeland to primary school children was a complicated business in the Yugoslav context – particularly given the fact that many were exposed to rival ideas of homeland through organizations hostile to Yugoslavia. Officially Yugoslavia did not have a corresponding national identity, but rather, was a brotherly socialist federation of nationalities. The idea of homeland was thus anchored in a belonging to a specific nationality, associated with a specific republic, and an attachment to the entire shared Yugoslav federation, a set of ideas encapsulated by the slogan "brotherhood and unity". Yugoslavia was presented as the culmination of the efforts of the different south Slavic people to achieve self-determination. These were subtle, even ambiguous notions for children to grasp. They were communicated to children in a variety of ways, most obviously through the explicit messages of texts and images, as well as the very structure of the textbook, and the choice of authors and alphabets.

Each textbook presented the history and culture of the different republics as both distinctive and belonging to all Yugoslavs. Texts alternated between the Latin and Cyrillic script, and a conscious effort was made to include texts of various periods by significant authors of all nationalities, including some from minority nationalities such as ethnic Albanians and Hungarians. To bring out some of this diversity, I have endeavoured to identify each of the authors I discuss below according to the language in which they did most of their writing, and the republic or province that they were identified with, while fully cognizant of the problems associated with such national categorization. Beyond text, the textbooks were in full colour and presented numerous reproductions of works of art and architectural masterpieces from classical times to the present, as well as photographs of landscapes and scenes from across Yugoslavia. The intention was clearly to allow all Yugoslav children – even those who had never set foot in Yugoslavia – to get a sense of Yugoslavia's rich and diverse heritage and culture.

All three volumes started by conveying an experiential understanding of homeland. For example, in the first volume, aimed at the youngest children, the poem "Our Republic" (*Naša Republika*) by Croatian poet Mladen Bjažić described the homeland through landscapes, but also everyday experiences like weather, rivers of coloured automobiles, stadiums and loud audiences, the army, music, and red Pioneer kerchiefs.[45] Bosnian writer Izet Sarajlić's poem "My Pocket Yugoslavia" (*Moja džepna Jugoslavija*), included in the third volume, described the homeland as a series of spaces and objects that are familiar to the child, starting from the threshold of the house, moving to the birch tree, then the courtyard, the school hallway in which the classmates' coats hang, the table upon which the gramophone sits, and the room full of toys. "This is small, but this too is Yugoslavia." These poems made the abstract concrete, by tying it to lived experience, at a scale that the child is able to understand.[46]

Another piece of writing by Macedonian author Olivera Nikolova, "How the Homeland Grows," rooted the notion of homeland in the expanding horizons and consciousness of the growing child through a powerful metaphor that would have resonated with children living far from home. When you are an infant, it explained, homeland is the nipple on your mother's breast when you are born. It grows with you, becoming your cradle, pillow, then your entire room. As you get older,

Figures 23 and 24. Children were encouraged to learn and be proud of the symbols of Yugoslavia through Pioneer organizations and, in particular, national holidays (*Moja Domovina SFRJ*, vols. 2, 1)

those horizons that define the homeland expand more and more, so that you lose sight of its boundaries and try to chase it, before finally realizing that it is inside of you, beating like your heart – a presence that will always be with you, wherever you are and however many there are of you.[47] In a sense, rather than making the abstract concrete, Nikolova embraced the power of abstraction. Rather than tying the homeland to a far removed place and to specific objects and landscapes, Nikolova turned it into a "spiritual principle," to use Renan's famous words, that was a fundamental part of the child's identity. It also in some sense cautioned children to avoid "chasing belonging" in their host states.

Experiential notions of homeland were of course paired with more traditional fare, poetry and prose associating homeland with specific landscapes and national symbols. Children learned the national anthem "Hej Sloveni," and the Pioneer oath "Druže Tito mi ti se kunemo," as well as the coat of arms of each republic. A number of the poems and texts in the textbooks were odes to the landscapes of Yugoslavia. One representative example, Serbian writer Dobrica Erić's poem "Heart of the Homeland" (Srce Domovine), listed different regions of Yugoslavia (some of them republics, but others not) and the various landscapes, urban and rural, that were associated with them. For example, "Every morning / over Kozara mountain, son / is the heart of Bosnia-Herzegovina. / Along the Vardar / like a grey falcon / with wide wings / is the Macedonian heart." In this way, the poem charted a symbolic geography of Yugoslavia. The poem ended by asserting that "Yugoslavia is made up of six hearts that beat inside the larger heart of Yugoslavia" – a poetic image to illustrate the concept of brotherhood and unity; and more fancifully, that "this heart is like rays of a young star full of young golden seeds that protect us from invasion, illness, or inclement weather."[48]

Children were taught to cultivate an attachment to particular places, defining the national starting from the local. The textbook explained that "we first encounter the homeland through the beauty of our place of birth" (rodni kraj).[49] A nineteenth-century text by Serbian writer Ljubomir Nenadović on the Lovćen mountain in Montenegro illustrated this powerfully. Nenadović describes the majestic mountain and its dramatic climate, and the text is accompanied by a photograph. But, according to Nenadović, Lovćen is more than just an impressive geographical feature – it is the central reference point for Montenegrins, a unique place to which each Montenegrin is bound, no matter how far any wander, by nostalgia and longing. He refers to it as the Montenegrin's "North Star," the first word a Montenegrin infant learns. He adds that it is the last stone that a Montenegrin migrant lays eyes on when leaving for "far, foreign lands": "He lifts his cap and with a heavy sigh, says, 'Farewell, Lovćen, farewell, my home!' And when he can no longer see Lovćen, he looks at the clouds above him with desire. Light ships carry him to all sides of the earth; wherever he passes, he sees gorges and mountains, but never does he see the image of his Lovćen; he, son of the mountain, cannot find in any foreign land such a splendour."[50]

Older children reading texts like "Lovćen" would learn that homeland was first and foremost the landscapes of one's ancestral home, which bound the child to a larger national identity, in this instance, Montenegrin. This focused, emotionally powerful text was arguably more effective in defining homeland for a children's audience than the much denser poems inventorying Yugoslavia's many wonders to children who likely had not experienced most of them.

Kinship was another central trope used to define homeland for children. It could be evoked in the sense of family in the present moment, which was another way to make the notion of homeland concrete and experiential. Croatian writer Ratko Zvrko's poem "Homeland" (domovina) makes this connection explicit in the very last stanza: "Homeland – this is the life of all the lives – this is brother and sister, father and mother."[51] Kinship could also be used in a historical sense, binding children to their ancestors and therefore to the landscapes of Yugoslavia. The poem "Ask Me" (*Pitajte me*), written by Serbian children's author Mira Alečković, ties love of the homeland not just to landscapes, but also to the ancestors who have tilled the land and spilled their blood in defence of it.[52]

While poems like "Lovćen" effectively conveyed an understanding of homeland to older children, Yugoslav identity was more abstract and more difficult to "feel": it was an adherence to certain socialist values, recognition of a shared past among south Slavic peoples, endorsement of a common future, and celebration of the diverse cultures and traditions of the brotherly south Slavic peoples – the six beating hearts that beat inside the larger, protective heart of Yugoslavia. The figure of Tito was instrumental to telling the story of Yugoslavia – providing it with an intelligible narrative – and providing an emotional focal point for children. The centrality of Tito and the national liberation struggle in the textbooks reflected their place in broader Yugoslav society.

In these textbooks, which devoted an entire section to Tito, he was both ordinary and extraordinary, deeply human and mythical, in ways that carry strange echoes of literary representations of Jesus Christ. On the one hand, children could read about Tito's childhood, which was marked by rural poverty, and about his efforts in organizing workers in the Kraljevica shipyards near Rijcka.[53] This Tito was a mischievous,

Figure 25. Tito serves up food to his hungry siblings in "Tito and the Pig's Head" (*Moja Domovina SFRJ*, vol. 1)

well-intentioned child, a somewhat ordinary if committed and principled union activist, and a humble, approachable human being. Upon returning to the shipyard after the war, now president of Yugoslavia, he greets his former co-workers as old friends. The poem "Jožek" on Josip Broz Tito as a child asks whether he was just like every other child: "Did he stuff his fingers in his mouth? Did he run in fear from the dark? ... Did any of the inhabitants of Kumrovec know that he would be a marshal one day?"[54] Phrased in the interrogative form, this poem admitted the possibility that Tito was a human being – and thus, that every child could aspire to become like him.

Tito's transition from human to god (or god-like), at least in these textbooks, took place during the Second World War. Several texts describe encounters with Tito during the war as his Partisans marched through the countryside during the war. Two texts featured Pioneers who would have been the same age as, or just a bit older than, the readers. In "Pinki saw Tito," Boško Palkovljević "Pinki," a young partisan from Srem, manages to reach where Tito and the partisans have arrived to solicit his help. Tito sheds two solitary tears upon hearing of the struggles of the isolated partisans in Srem. In Tito's presence, Pinki feels both very small and endlessly great. He reflects that, if he dies, at least he got to meet Tito – foreshadowing his fate, as Boško Palkovljević was killed in action in 1942.[55]

Other texts emphasized Tito's charisma. Montenegrin poet Mirko Banjević's poem "Tito's Army" (*Titova vojska*) describes how the army following Tito grew larger and larger as he advanced through the mountainous terrain of Bosnia.[56] This magnetic, almost otherworldly greatness was sometimes conveyed through descriptions of his facial expressions. Pinki, for example, is struck by Tito's piercing blue eyes, which seem to see straight through him. For Slovenian artist Josip Vidmar, who made one of the most famous wartime portraits of Tito, "the entire expression of the face is energetic and fascinating; in it is something Napoleonic, and it could be also the face of an artist. His bearing is reserved and peaceful, but his movements are quick and nervous."[57]

The allusion to Napoleon was not coincidental; indeed, Tito was often presented as a world-historical figure. In the same passage, Vidmar reflects that Tito was given his greatness by the national liberation struggle, and that the war now has received its greatness from him.[58] In his poem "Our All-Encompassing Love" (*Naša svekolika ljubav*), Albanian poet Esad Mekuli described Tito as carrying the desires and as-yet unrevealed endeavours of the people. This poem also presented him as the "unquenchable ray of belief of man in life and freedom" and "builder of bridges of brotherhood [and] untiring supporter of the understanding between people and peoples on this big and yet small planet."[59] This sort of hagiography sometimes verged on the caricatural. Albanian poet Rahman Dedaj's fawning poem "Tito," penned shortly after his death, suggested that there was no more need for clocks, as time would be measured by Tito's heart. The same poem described Tito as stepping out of a fairy tale, committing an eternal act, and then returning back to the fairy-tale realm.[60] Here we are far from Tito as a flesh-and-blood person – children were to develop a sense of devotion to Tito that was quasi-religious.

Insofar as historical themes were dealt with in the textbooks – and they were most visible in the third volume, for the oldest children – the Second World War dominated. War stories emphasized the enthusiasm and self-sacrifice of the population in the Partisan struggle, and the cruelty of the enemy, which was only euphemistically identified as the "occupier" and "local fascists." The contributions of children and the elderly were particularly highlighted, for example in the story "One Good Old Lady" (*Jedna dobra starica*) by Rodoljub Čolaković, about an elderly lady who seeks out a Partisan camp in the woods to contribute a modest gift of food to sustain the fighters.[61] Children were not entirely shielded from the violence of war. Just like their counterparts in Yugoslavia, schoolchildren read an excerpt from Ivan Goran Kovačić's graphic and dramatic epic poem "The Hole" (*Jama*), which told the story of a Partisan soldier who is enucleated and thrown into a pit. While the excerpt itself describes a young woman comforting the blinded soldier, it was accompanied by two of the famous illustrations by Zlatko Prica and Edo Murtić, which fully depicted the blood and gore.

The Second World War was portrayed as the culmination of Yugoslav history, the ultimate triumph of a centuries-long struggle for

Figure 26. *Moja Domovina SFRJ* also featured a description of children fighting with the Partisans encountering Tito (*Moja Domovina SFRJ*, vol. 1)

self-determination. Earlier episodes in the histories of the South Slavic peoples were presented as foreshadowing the Partisan struggle, whether implicitly or explicitly. A historical account in the third volume entitled "the struggle of our nationalities and minorities for freedom and independence" provided a neatly linear account that connected the dots between past and present. It connected Croatian and Slovenian struggles to retain their linguistic and cultural autonomy in the Habsburg culture and the armed uprisings of the Serbs, Macedonians, and Montenegrins against the Turks. Subsequently, the Kingdom of Yugoslavia failed to respect the rights of its constituent nationalities and improve conditions for the masses, before it was ultimately defeated by "local and foreign fascists." Finally, the aspirations of the south Slavic peoples were achieved during the national liberation struggle. The grass-roots Partisan movement united the different nationalities rather than dividing them, leading to the foundation of the Socialist Federative Republic of Yugoslavia.[62]

This narrative served as a kind of map for understanding other texts and images in the textbook. Thus, children looking at a painting

MIODRAG ŽIVKOVIĆ SPOMENIK STRELJANIM DACIMA

Figure 27. The textbook encouraged reverence for the Second World War as the culmination of the struggle for national self-determination for the south Slavic peoples. Pictured is the Šumarice Memorial Park in Kragujevac, the site of a mass execution of men and boys by the German occupiers (*Moja Domovina SFRJ*, vol. 2)

depicting the Macedonian nationalist uprising at Mečkin Kamen in 1903, or reading Matija Gubec's speech in August Šenoa's novel *Peasant Uprising (Seljačka buna)*, which explained the 1573 uprising as a struggle for freedom and exhorted the peasants to fight until the death, were led to believe that they were reading about the first stirrings of the struggle to bring Yugoslavia into being.[63]

Beyond these themes – homeland, Tito, and the long arc of Yugoslav history – children were offered glimpses into other sides of Yugoslav culture. They were instructed to respect both agricultural and industrial work through texts like "On the Locomotive" by Tone Seliškar, who, reflecting on his father's labour as a locomotive engineer, commented, "That is when I first understood that workers are heroes."[64] As they got older, they also learned about self-management and Yugoslavia's economy. A number of pieces demonstrating virtuous qualities such as honesty, teamwork, courage, modesty, and kindness were included in all volumes, providing a kind of moral primer for readers. Texts and images promoted world peace and anti-racist messages, and the second and third volume included discussions of Yugoslavia's role as a leader in the non-alignment movement.[65]

The textbooks were made as engaging as possible for migrants' children. One way they did so was by interspersing occasional texts written by other migrant children between literary excerpts and encyclopedia articles. While some of these texts described the author's attachment to the homeland, and others praised Tito, yet others simply described the emotional life of the child and his or her everyday life. One such text by a child in Lyon, France, demonstrated that they had been able to internalize the concept of homeland and relate it to their lives:

> The homeland is far from me, but it is in my heart. It warms me, it helps me, it is like a mother to me. Homeland – this is a big word, it's my white Zadar, it's our blue sea, the bluest in the world. It's my classmates who are now playing in the sun, it's my grandmother who is waiting for us.
>
> My homeland is the most beautiful in the world, and I can't wait to return home. It will be like a new day is starting, sunny and joyful.[66]

These texts were important because they celebrated the children's writings in Serbo-Croatian and validated the children as an integral part of Yugoslavia to their peers.

Almost all the texts, and many of the images, were followed by sections that included lexicons, explanations, grammar exercises, and focused questions, as well as open, interpretive questions, essay topics, and suggested activities. Focused questions tested knowledge and comprehension, ensuring that children absorbed key knowledge, from the very simple – "What is the name of our homeland? What is its capital city?" – to more involved questions about the content of images and texts. Open questions, on the other hand, were used to constantly stimulate children to remember Yugoslavia: could they name a cathedral, monastery, or convent in our country? Could they sing a song or recall a tradition from their region? When they thought of Yugoslavia, what did they think of, what did they remember?[67]

Figure 28. Drawing by a child accompanying the text "Domovina," depicting a port on the Adriatic coast (*Moja Domovina SFRJ*, vol. 1)

Open questions and essays were creative and powerful ways for helping children think through their relationship to the homeland and stimulate their attachment to it. Thus, children were asked, "If you have a relative in Yugoslavia who lives in the village, describe how it would be if you visited. Were there a lot of fruit or vegetables?... What do you enjoy about the village?" They were also prompted to describe their experiences when watching Yugoslavia compete and win in sporting events.[68] Children were invited to engage in activities on the theme of homeland, memorize poems and songs, create scrapbooks, watch films about the Partisan struggle such as *Don't Look Back, My Son* (*Ne okreći se, sine*), attend a folklore performance, and visit memorial sites in Yugoslavia.

Some of the activities focused on the specific experience of living abroad. Younger children were asked to reflect on what it meant to live far from home and to describe their relationship to their host society. Older children were given more complex tasks, such as looking at a map and marking the shortest roads from their current place of residence to Belgrade, or listing in which countries Yugoslav workers reside. They were asked, or rather, told, "No matter where they live and work, Yugoslavs feel a sense of belonging to their homeland, Yugoslavia. Why?"[69]

Questions and activities raised awareness about resources that connected Yugoslavia to its workers: "Who protects the rights of workers in the land where you now live? Who represents Yugoslavia?" Children were encouraged repeatedly to consume Yugoslav media and to seek out publications such as encyclopedias and tourist guides. "Do you listen to programs for our workers temporarily working abroad? What is the name of the program? Which station broadcasts it? How many times a day? What do you like about these programs?" In other activities, children were invited to look in children's magazines for photos, poems, stories, articles, anecdotes, and other items about Tito, or to prepare a report on Yugoslavia's economy by listening to the radio, watching television, and reading the newspapers.[70]

All in all, the textbook materialized the idea of homeland for children, by filling in the concept with content, and by encouraging practices that allowed children to perform belonging and citizenship: remember a shared past, name places of importance, memorize canonical texts, perform rituals, participate in the imagined community by reading newspapers, listening to the radio, and watching television, and tie the idea of homeland to their own feelings and acts of imagination.

Evaluating the Success of Mother-Tongue Education

What impact did the mother-tongue education programs and extracurricular activities have on migrant children? Keeping in mind the fact that roughly half of children did not even attend the classes, what did participants learn and how well did they retain it? To what extent did these programs fulfil the objective of enabling migrant children to feel a sense of belonging to Yugoslavia? Or, to ask a question that is easier to answer, to what extent did the Yugoslav scientific community and authorities perceive that migrant children had developed such a sense of belonging? While scholarly studies were published already in the 1970s, the journal *Migracijske Teme*, first published in 1985 by the Institute for Migration and Nationality in Zagreb, began to pay great attention to this topic. Individual studies focused on different host states and cities and thus dealt with a huge variety of teaching systems and populations, and so it is not possible to generalize from them. However, as a whole, they suggest trends in the way that young people coped with their situation. They also highlight how Yugoslav scholars infallibly approached this topic with a preoccupation with belonging.

Scholars taking stock of the challenges facing migrant children in the early 1980s provided contradictory answers. First, they argued that migrant children were faced with identity crises. Josip Anić and Andrina Pavlinić-Wolf depicted a second generation torn between "two traditions, two languages, two ways of life": the first allowed them to relate to their parents, and the latter, which was dominant, appeared to offer a path to social integration in their host-country. As a result, children "lack a clear national character." Worse, the two cultural and value systems could come into conflict, leading to psychological and behavioural problems. This situation was aggravated by the absence of a path to integration and social mobility in the host society. For Anić and Pavlinić-Wolf, mother-tongue education was critical to counteracting the influence of the dominant culture. While they noted problems associated with existing programs, including the underdevelopment of preschool programs and threats to mother-tongue education, they did not offer an assessment of their effectiveness.[71]

In contrast, Zlata Jukić's research narrowly sought to evaluate the competencies of children in mother-tongue education in Switzerland and Sweden, by testing the language fluency and cultural knowledge of two samples of students. More specifically, she hypothesized that children born in Yugoslavia would perform better than children born abroad, which her study indeed confirmed. According to Jukić, this was explained by the fact that children born in Yugoslavia had acquired a more solid linguistic and cultural foundation, whereas children born abroad demonstrated evidence of "linguistic interference." This study showed that children born abroad faced greater difficulties in acquiring the necessary language skills and cultural knowledge. At the same time, Jukić's discussion of the children's responses still suggested that they had a working knowledge of the language and command of some fairly specific historical, geographical, and cultural knowledge.[72]

While Jukić's study was measured in tone, research by Melita Švob, Zdenko Ivezić, and Zvonimir Kotarac was much more alarmist, reflecting the same anxieties about psychological and social dysfunction found in Anić and Pavlinić-Wolf's study. Inquiring into the behaviour of 232 migrant children in Berlin (8% of the total number) and their attitude toward mother-tongue education, based on the assessment of their teachers, Švob, Ivezić, and Kotarac found that nearly half of pupils (43.1%) displayed behavioural problems such as aggression, neuroticism, and hyperactivity. The majority of children were negatively

disposed toward mother-tongue lessons, with only a quarter expressing satisfaction in this regard. In fact, nearly all of the children had
no friends in their class. Nearly half of students felt more at home in
Germany than in the mother-tongue lessons. This study suggested that
fears of assimilation had been justified and that children were becoming resistant to Yugoslavia's efforts to keep them as loyal citizens. It
might also indicate a profoundly demoralized teaching cadre that felt
overwhelmed by the obstacles placed in their way (such as overly large,
mixed classes and inadequate classrooms). Švob, Ivezić, and Kotarac
were careful to note the specificity of their case study, but it added to
the body of work expressing deep concerns about the effectiveness of
education for the second generation.[73]

Jukić's findings in Berlin were reinforced by the observations of
Branka Vegar, a teacher employed in Vienna, where Yugoslav children
were the most numerous foreign schoolchildren. Even though, in principle, the Austrian authorities supported the importance of allowing
migrant children to learn the language and culture of their homeland,
children who struggled in the Austrian school systems did not see the
value in the mother-tongue classes. She noted that the closed nature of
Austrian society actually strengthened children's resolve to master the
German language and assimilate to Austrian culture. Moreover, many
of these children had learned German before their Yugoslav language,
and the focus on learning grammar was too difficult and tedious for
them, leading many to abandon the optional mother-tongue courses.[74]

Although the stated goals of some of these studies was far more narrow than evaluating migrant children's sense of belonging, the studies
were the product of, and fed into, a broader anxiety about the failings of
mother-tongue education, and national alienation more broadly. But to
what extent was this a fair and objective evaluation? A cautious examination of the methodology employed reveals that the criteria used to mea-
sure belonging were set externally. None of these studies inquired about
children's own sense of belonging to Yugoslavia, which may have been
articulated around different criteria than language fluency and knowledge of history, culture, and geography. This raises an interesting question: to what extent were children aware that their Yugoslav identity was
found wanting, and what impact might this questioning have had on
their own sense of belonging? Like Pavle Hromiš, were they made to feel
like a foreigner both by their host state and in their country of origin?

Jadranka Čačić's characterization of the second generation's dilemma
as pulled between two cultures was very similar to that of the earlier mentioned authors, but her conclusions did not echo their Mani-
chean interpretation. Studying children in the Alsace-Lorraine region

of France, she found that many children did not identify primarily as Yugoslav – in fact, they did not identify primarily by national identity, but rather in reference to gender and personality attributes. However, they identified both cultures positively and expressed a positive self-image. Interestingly, they associated positive qualities more strongly with Yugoslavia than with France. Čačić attributed the persistence of Yugoslav culture to the influence of parents. In sum, these children had maintained their ties to Yugoslavia without feeling as if they were obliged to reject French culture, in contrast to children in other studies. Nonetheless, Čačić ended her article with the following statement by a respondent: "We are strangers here, and we are strangers there." Thus, although her evaluation was more positive, it echoed the previous study in that children did not have a pronounced Yugoslav identity or sense of belonging."[75]

Another study also focusing on migrant children in France, published as part of a French-language collection of scholarly essays by Yugoslav authors, similarly suggested that migrant youth in France had different ways of defining their identities. The essay tellingly used the term "orientation," noting that "among young Yugoslavs from immigrant families, the orientation towards the country of origin is still very present," and this orientation "is an important expression of their cultural identity."[76] Here identity was framed in terms of aspirations rather than knowledge. Sixty-two per cent of Yugoslav students surveyed indicated that they wished to live and work in Yugoslavia, compared to 18% who wished to stay in France, 3% who wished to move elsewhere, and 7% who did not answer. Interestingly, the percentage of students of Yugoslav peasant origin who expressed a desire to return to Yugoslavia was higher than that of Yugoslavs born in France or in an urban Yugoslav milieu with the same aspiration (73% compared to 55% and 56%, respectively).[77] According to the authors, this could be interpreted as a consequence of a greater attachment by villagers to the native land, and also potentially, a less successful adaptation to conditions in urban France. In any case, this study suggests that belonging is a more complex matter than many of the studies in *Migracijske Teme* acknowledged and that, indeed, many Yugoslav migrant youth – at least in France – did feel a profound attachment to the Yugoslav homeland, if a complicated one.

Conclusion

The Yugoslav educational system, with the assistance of the consulates and Yugoslav workers' associations, sought not only to teach migrant children their parents' language, but also to inculcate in them a love for Yugoslavia. Teachers played a critical role in this project and were expected to be active in Yugoslav citizens' associations and act as resources and role models for the entire community. The educational system was integrated into the broader web of governance provided by the associations – every Yugoslav outreach program was intended to support and reinforce the other. Indeed, second-generation education was seen as a way to pull parents more closely into the orbit of the Yugoslav state.

While they were emissaries of the state, teachers had much in common with migrant workers. They dealt with unfamiliar contexts, the hostility of locals and harassment by political émigrés, difficult working conditions and insufficient income, and homesickness. Like migrant workers, their location outside of Yugoslavia's borders also gave them greater latitude to talk back to Yugoslav authorities, although with less impunity, as many were still employees of the Yugoslav state. Indeed, Yugoslavia kept a close eye on teachers and expected them to participate in continuing education programs back home, to ensure they continued to be effective agents.

In the content of education, the central theme in supplementary education, unsurprisingly, was the homeland. Whereas the radio program *To Our Citizens of the World* could leave it up to listeners to imagine the homeland, the same was not possible in educational programs – children needed to be instructed about what was meant by this term. By the 1980s, educators had at their disposal a pan-Yugoslav textbook that attempted to convey to children the complexities of Yugoslav identity through literary texts, images, and exercises. Like *Imotska krajina*, it turned to landscapes, folklore, and the idea of kinship, but it integrated them into the conceptual framework of brotherhood and unity. It also incorporated other ways of understanding the homeland, including heroic narratives that showcased Tito and the national liberation struggle, discussions of socialist values, and ordinary, everyday experiences. This was a rich and complex, if sometimes dogmatic exploration of Yugoslav identity.

In addition to attending supplementary lessons, children were encouraged to join Pioneer organizations, visit exhibitions, take part in contests, write to pen pals, and visit Yugoslavia. These were seen as ways of bringing the abstract notions that were taught in the classroom to life. Direct, unmediated contact with Yugoslavia through school trips and visits to relatives was considered the most powerful vehicle for developing a strong Yugoslav identity.

While social scientists and pedagogues evaluating migrant children's attachment to Yugoslavia came to pessimistic conclusions, it seems that the second generation was always doomed to fall short, belonging "neither here nor there." When scholars abandoned binary notions of belonging and asked different questions – not whether these children met the same standards of knowledge as their peers in Yugoslavia, but whether they felt positively toward Yugoslavia, and whether they aspired to live there – they obtained more encouraging results. Indeed, like their parents, children articulated a more complicated understanding of their place in society than narratives that opposed belonging and alienation could accommodate. Tragically, before most of the research subjects could fully grow up and make choices about their future, Yugoslavia would cease to exist and be torn apart by war. Never entirely real to them, always an "imagined community," the homeland that children would have assiduously read and learned about in *Moja Domovina SFRJ* was destined to become the stuff of fairy tales.

10 Conclusion

Yugoslavia is the only European socialist state to ever adopt a policy that not only allowed its citizens to freely leave the country and seek work abroad in capitalist states, but even encouraged them to do so. It simultaneously sought to foster close ties with those citizens through a variety of cultural, propaganda, and educational programs. While not all Yugoslavs living and working abroad were interested, many responded enthusiastically. This transnational relationship can be described as reciprocal, dynamic, and fraught. A closer look at the programs themselves reveals why.

Yugoslavia's perception of its migrant workers shaped the ways in which it sought to engage with them, and this perception was always reductive. From the outset, Yugoslav authorities saw labour migrants as unskilled workers driven to leave exclusively by economic motivations, and intending to return – these assumptions were embedded into the category "our citizens living abroad." Attempts to collect empirical data on migrants were themselves influenced by these convictions and tended to reaffirm them. Authorities established programs to allow workers to stay in touch with the homeland, primarily radio broadcasts and newspapers. These programs sought to mobilize workers by building their attachment to the homeland.

By the late 1960s, in the face of mounting evidence, authorities worried that these assumptions were incorrect, and in particular, that workers were becoming alienated from Yugoslavia. They responded by intensifying existing and building new outreach programs to strengthen the bond between Yugoslavia and its citizens abroad, including a push to establish citizens' clubs and education for migrants' children. Other actors responded differently to anxieties about labour migration. Politicians, researchers, journalists, and film-makers in Croatia, in particular, sought to use labour migration as a way of critiquing the socialist project, portraying the migrants as victims of Yugoslavia's failed policies, or of its exploitation of Croatia. In many cases, they sought to mobilize migrants themselves behind this counter-narrative.

Just as different actors within Yugoslavia told conflicting stories about the significance of labour migration to advance different political agendas, migrants chose which narratives they endorsed, or else they told their own stories. Because of their position outside of Yugoslavia's borders, they had greater control over what the state knew about them and how they wished to represent themselves. At times they adopted the official narrative, either because it resonated with their life experience or because it helped them to make claims on the state. At other times they pushed back against this narrative by adopting the counter-narrative promoted during the Croatian Spring. Many refused to endorse either narrative, choosing to tell other stories about their lives and aspirations.

Efforts to woo migrants were all articulated around the ideas of homeland and belonging. Conscious of the limited appeal of institutions, authorities played on understandings of Yugoslavia as a place and as an idea to create and strengthen attachments. Radio programs evoked place through the music they played, which came from and celebrated specific places, and the greetings from kin and friends that they broadcast, which connected migrants back to home. Newspapers carried stories of home, past and present, accompanied by images of landscapes; Yugoslav associations organized trips back to Yugoslavia; mother-tongue programs taught children about the geography, cultural heritage, and landscapes of their predecessors.

The idea of Yugoslavia was also promoted through the celebration of key principles of brotherhood and unity and self-managed socialism. These might take the form of slogans and symbols, like oaths and flags in national holiday celebrations and Pioneer induction ceremonies. They could also be communicated through narrative and discussion, such as a retelling of the national liberation struggle in a school textbook, or discussions of constitutional reforms in workers' forums or in the press.

In building an infrastructure for outreach to migrant workers, Yugoslavia consciously opted for a multifaceted strategy depending on a variety of vehicles, including associations, radio broadcasting, print media, schools, and Cultural-Information Centres. These in turn mobilized music, news, literature, art, folklore, sports, and travel in the service of nation-building. These various programs were interwoven with one another, so that each program might leverage another for maximum efficiency. Teachers were also leaders in associations; textbooks encouraged children to read the press; clubs hosted Pioneer groups; the radio promoted tours by performing troops as well as scientific surveys on migration.

Authorities were aware that it wasn't sufficient merely to produce and distribute propaganda, and that they also needed to build a reciprocal relationship with their citizens. In addition, the ideological emphasis on self-management, as well as financial limitations in some instances, led authorities to explicitly put citizen participation at the heart of its approach. Radio and newspapers not only encouraged but depended on citizens writing in with their questions, requests, and suggestions. Associations relied on volunteer labour for their functioning. Schools, which by their nature expected children's active participation, sought to get parents involved.

Thus, these programs were shaped as much by the needs and wants of the citizens that participated in them as by the agenda of the state. Citizens talked back when their expectations were not met: radio listeners sent in annoyed letters; survey respondents laid out their grievances in strong terms. State actors overseeing these programs might try to ignore or redirect unruly participants, such as when they refused to play too many sad songs on the radio, or omitted to publish nationalistic survey responses. But they ultimately did not have any real ability to discipline them. Not all citizens participated with the same degree of commitment – while some were activists, others merely read the newspapers, listened to the radio, or attended social evenings at the club – but flexibility arguably increased the programs' reach.

Affect was central to all the programs discussed in this book, fostering workers' nostalgia for home and patriotism. Radio programming was particularly effective in stimulating powerful emotions, both joyful and sad, as described in listeners' letters. Newspapers like *Imotska krajina* also used pathos to stimulate nostalgia, as well as anger, and school textbooks sought to develop the child's love and longing for the homeland. Both educators and associations understood community as key to attachment to the homeland. They saw social and productive interactions with others – in the sense of working together to achieve a goal – as crucial to creating a feeling of belonging.

While these programs promoted attachment to Yugoslavia as an idea and as a place, the latter concept was more intuitive, and arguably more powerful, than the former. The notion of homeland was a fraught one in Yugoslavia, particularly after the experience of the Second World War, when Yugoslavia had been dismembered, and an Independent State of Croatia under Ustaša control had been created. When Yugoslavs professed their love for the homeland, to which homeland were they referring? The answer to the question depended on both the institutions sponsoring and running a program and their audience. Political decentralization further muddied the waters, by enabling actors at all geographic scales to reach out to their migrants.

Radio programs like *To Our Citizens of the World*, technically a Croatian initiative, avoided this delicate problem by allowing listeners from across Yugoslavia to talk about "the homeland" without having to define it, providing a superficial impression of unity. School textbooks, in contrast, had a different mandate – their role was to help children understand the concept of homeland through brotherhood and unity. Thus, children were encouraged to think of homelands as "nested" – beginning with the family, then growing to encompass locality, republic or autonomous province, and federation. There was no suggestion that any of these loyalties might somehow come into conflict.

Vague, abstract, and complicated ideas about the nature of homeland were subject to contestation. Yugoslavia's federal structure and its reliance on the republican branches to carry out outreach meant that some of these programs were vulnerable to subversion. This is what happened with some Croatian news media, as illustrated by the case of *Imotska krajina*. For a brief time it was clear that the primary, most important homeland was the Croatian one. While some contributors paid lip service to the idea of Yugoslavia as guarantor of self-management, on the whole, the newspaper mobilized its readership in defence of a Croatian homeland against Yugoslavia, until the quashing of the Croatian Spring brought it back into line.

Ultimately, through its programs, Yugoslavia did build a relationship with a significant number of its citizens living abroad. Large numbers of letters to radio programs and newspapers and survey responses, and well-attended education programs and social and sporting events attest to this. Letters and survey responses, in particular, testify to the centrality of the idea of belonging to the homeland, although this idea could be used to bind them more closely to the Yugoslavia and to mobilize them against it. While some migrants found ways to fit their own story into the narratives that were offered to them, others shared stories that were more complicated. Either way, they chose to engage with these outreach efforts, and in so doing, continued to participate in Yugoslav social, cultural, and political life.

As with other initiatives in the history of socialist Yugoslavia, their effectiveness was dampened by decentralization, which acted as a kind of centrifugal force, pulling citizens in different directions. Distinct groups of citizens engaged with specific programs that reflected the interests and agendas of different actors. There was some overlap; a reader of *Imotska krajina* and a member of a Yugoslav club might both listen to Radio Zagreb, but they were unlikely to cross paths elsewhere. Nonetheless, while they might not agree on the name and borders of the homeland, most Yugoslav workers continued to feel an attachment to home and a desire to participate in its affairs. Cultural, informational, and educational outreach had, at the most basic level, succeeded.

Efforts to cultivate migrant loyalties call into question the idea the national identity as an elite project that supplanted local identities. In Eugen Weber's seminal work, in the nineteenth century, state institutions, such as military service and education, as well as national economic integration were responsible for the fact that peasants began to identify as Frenchmen.[1] Benedict Anderson similarly pointed to the importance of a mass print culture in creating national imagined communities.[2] In both instances, local identities did not cease to exist, but national identities replaced them as the primary frame of reference. Scholarship on ethno-nationalism in Yugoslavia has implicitly accepted this framework, focusing exclusively on the "national" scale (meaning Croatian, Serbian, Bosniak, Slovene, and Macedonian). The examples of *Imotska krajina* and textbooks for mother-tongue education show, however, that national identity was often mediated through local identity – the national project did not emerge at the expense of local identities, but rather built on them.

The conclusions drawn from this study suggest interesting avenues of inquiry and comparison for scholars working on other republics within Yugoslavia: What was the nature of the dynamics between the federation and Macedonia, for example, and how did they shape efforts to retain the loyalty of migrant workers? Shifting geographically, what about other outmigration states during the postwar era, including Portugal, Spain, Italy, and Greece (to name only those located in Europe)? To what extent did they cultivate a relationship with their citizens living abroad? How did they perceive migrants, and what programs did they devise and implement? To what extent can differences in their approaches be accounted for by ideological differences – in other words, did a liberal democracy or non-socialist authoritarian state produce approaches and outcomes different from those of a socialist state?

This study ends with the beginning of the 1980s, when Yugoslavia was changing in fundamental ways. With Tito gone, Yugoslavia shifted to a rotating presidency, and, coping with an ever-deepening economic crisis following the second oil shock of 1979, sought to implement major economic reforms. According to Sara Bernard, while the contraction of West European economies forced labour migrants to return home, low-skilled workers from the central and southeastern rural regions of

Yugoslavia were disproportionately affected by the downturn. Unemployment fed into growing disgruntlement in the Serbian countryside upon which Slobodan Milošević would prey. Moreover, returning migrants from Bosnia-Herzegovina and Albania seeking employment in Slovenia were treated as undesirable. Thus the interplay of economic crisis and labour migration contributed to the sorts of ethnicized politics of disenchantment that characterized the downward spiral of the 1980s.[3] Other questions remain: What was the impact of the changing political and economic context on efforts by federal and republican authorities to engage with labour migrants who remained abroad? As for the migrants discussed in this study, how did they respond to the increasing tensions in Yugoslavia in the 1980s and its eventual demise? What happened, in particular, to the Yugoslav citizens' associations?

Other writers have pointed to the importance of emigrant involvement in the breakdown of Yugoslavia and subsequent wars. Indeed, Francesco Ragazzi has described Franjo Tuđman's efforts in the late 1970s and 1980s to engage with Croats living in Western Europe – specifically, with émigré organizations that were hostile to socialist Yugoslavia, although Tuđman ultimately built his support amongst other emigrants, based in North America.[4] The support of Croatian labour migrants in Western Europe for an independent Croatia – both in political support and financing – has not yet attracted scholarly attention, but if the results of the 1970 survey are any indication, it is likely to have been significant. This is a story waiting to be told.

This study also joins other recent scholarship in demonstrating that it is possible, and indeed necessary, to include migrant voices in the history of postwar migration and of state-socialism. Rather than passive subjects or fuzzy shadows that occasionally pop up in a story that is otherwise focused on the development and implementation of policy, migrants were the authors of their own stories. Modern states' desire to know their subjects in order to govern them, in combination with modern mass media's desire to instigate a personal and reciprocal relationship with their listeners, have left us with rich and copious sources that, as radio personality Cino Handl once mused, are waiting to be rediscovered and explored.

Notes

1. Introduction

1 Donna R. Gabaccia, *Italy's Many Diasporas: Elites, Exiles and Workers of the World* (Seattle: University of Washington Press, 2000), 163; Leslie Page Moch, *Moving Europeans: Migration in Western Europe since 1650*. 2nd ed. (Bloomington: Indiana University Press, 2003), 177–86.

2 Ivo Baučić, *Radnici u inozemstvu prema popisu stanovnistva Jugoslavije 1971*. (Zagreb: Institut za geografiju Sveučilišta u Zagrebu, 1973), 38.

3 David Fitzgerald. *A Nation of Emigrants: How Mexico Manages Its Migration* (Berkeley: University of California Press, 2009), 174.

4 Steven Vertovec, *Transnationalism* (London: Routledge, 2009), 2.

5 Steven Vertovec, "Migrant Transnationalism and Modes of Transformation," *International Migration Review* 38, no. 3 (2004): 977–80.

6 Vertovec, "Migrant Transnationalism and Modes of Transformation," 974–5.

7 Vertovec, *Transnationalism*, 85–100.

8 Rogers Brubaker, "The 'Diaspora' Diaspora," *Ethnic and Racial Studies* 28, no. 1 (2005): 1–19.

9 On the constructed nature of diaspora, see Alan Gamlen, "The Emigration State and the Modern Geopolitical Imagination," *Political Geography* 27, no. 8 (2008): 840–56; Jane H. Yamashiro, "Working towards Conceptual Consistency in Discussing 'Diaspora' and 'Diaspora Strategies': Ethnicity and Affinity in the Case of Japan," *Geoforum* 59, (2015): 178–86; Francesco Ragazzi, *Governing Diasporas in International Relations: The Transnational Politics of Croatia and Former Yugoslavia* (New York: Routledge, 2017): 9, 82–110. On the motivations for mobilizing diaspora, see Sara Kalm, "Diaspora Strategies as Technologies of Citizenship," *Global Society* 27, no. 3 (2013): 379–97; Eva Østergaard-Nielsen, *Transnational Politics: Turks and Kurds in Germany*, vol. 8 (London: Routledge, 2003). For an overview

of recent literature on practices of inclusion and exclusion in the framing of diaspora, see Elaine Lynn-Ee Ho, Maureen Hickey, and Brenda S.A. Yeoh, "Special Issue Introduction: New Research Directions and Critical Perspectives on Diaspora Strategies," *Geoforum* 59 (2015): 153–8.

10 See, for example, Nir Cohen, "State, Migrants, and the Negotiation of Second-Generation Citizenship in the Israeli Diaspora," *Diaspora: A Journal of Transnational Studies* 16, no. 2 (2007): 133–58.

11 On the collaboration between the Indian Consulate General in Durban, South Africa, and non-state actors, see Jen Dickinson, "Articulating an Indian Diaspora in South Africa: The Consulate General of India, Diaspora Associations and Practices of Collaboration," *Geoforum* 61 (2015): 79–89. On the potential of assemblage thinking, see Dickinson, "The Political Geographies of Diaspora Strategies: Rethinking the 'Sending State,'" *Geography Compass* 11, no. 2 (2017): 1–12.

12 Ho, Hickey, and Yeoh, "Special Issue Introduction," 154.

13 I explore this in the context of urban planning in Brigitte Le Normand, *Designing Tito's Capital: Urban Planning, Modernism, and Socialism in Belgrade* (Pittsburgh: University of Pittsburgh Press, 2014).

14 For example, Suzy K. Lee, "The Three Worlds of Emigration Policy: Towards a Theory of Sending State Regimes," *Journal of Ethnic and Migration Studies* 43, no. 9 (2017): 1453–71; Francesco Ragazzi, "Governing Diasporas," *International Political Sociology* 3, no. 4 (2009): 378–97; Alexandra Délano and Alan Gamlen, "Comparing and Theorizing State–Diaspora Relations," *Political Geography* 41 (2014): 44.

15 For example, Nir Cohen, "Diaspora Strategies: Actors, Members, and Spaces," *Geography Compass* 11, no. 3 (2017): 2. For a criticism of this fallacy, see A. Wimmer and N. Schiller, "Methodological Nationalism and the Study of Migration," *European Journal of Sociology* 43, no. 2 (2002): 231.

16 Gamlen has argued that the conviction that transborder state–migrant relations are abnormal is a product of the blind spots of the "modern geopolitical imagination," which privileges territorial nation-state units. See Gamlen, "Emigration State."

17 For example, Gary P. Freeman, *Immigrant Labor and Racial Conflict in Industrial Societies: The French and British Experience, 1945–1975* (Princeton, NJ: Princeton University Press, 1979); Ray C. Rist, *Guestworkers in Germany: The Prospects for Pluralism* (New York: Praeger, 1978); Stephen Castles, Heather Booth, and Tina Wallace, *Here for Good* (London: Pluto, 1984); John Berger, *A Seventh Man: Migrant Workers in Europe* (New York: Viking, 1975). Although not a scholar, Jane Kramer's portrait of a Yugoslav migrant worker is also noteworthy. Jane Kramer, *Unsettling Europe* (New York: Random House, 1980).

18 Rita Chin, *The Guest Worker Question in Postwar Germany* (Cambridge: Cambridge University Press, 2007); Jennifer A. Miller, *Turkish Guest Workers in Germany: Hidden Lives and Contested Borders, 1960s to 1980s* (Toronto: University of Toronto Press, 2018); Christopher A. Molnar, "Nation, Migration, and Cold War: Yugoslavs in Germany, 1945–1995" (PhD diss., Indiana University, 2013).

19 English-language publications include Ivo Baučić, *The Effects of Emigration from Yugoslavia and the Problems of Returning Emigrant Workers* (The Hague: Nijhoff, 1972); Baučić, *Social Aspects of External Migration of Workers and the Yugoslav Experience in the Social Protection of Migrants* (Zagreb: Centre for Migration Studies, 1975); Baučić, "Some Economic Consequences of Yugoslav External Migrations," *Collection IDERIC* 6, no. 1 (1976): 87–104. See also Baučić, *Radnici u Inozemstvu Prema Popisu Stanovništva Jugoslavije 1971* (Zagreb: Institut za geografiju Sveučilišta u Zagrebu, 1973); Baučić, "Stanje vanjskih migracija iz jugoslavije krajem sedamdesetih godina," *Rasprave o migracijama* 57 (1979).

20 Othmar Nikola Haberl, *Die Abwanderung Von Arbeitskräften Aus Jugoslawien: Zur Problematik Ihrer Auslandsbeschäftigung u. Rückführung*. 1. Aufl. ed. Vol. 13 (Munich: Oldenbourg, 1978).

21 William Zimmerman, *Open Borders, Nonalignment, and the Political Evolution of Yugoslavia* (Princeton, NJ: Princeton University Press, 1987).

22 Carl-Ulrich Schierup, *Migration, Socialism and the International Division of Labour: The Yugoslav Experience* (Aldershot, UK: Avebury, 1990), 59, 76–97.

23 Schierup, *Migration, Socialism and the International Division of Labour*, 192–3.

24 Ragazzi, *Governing Diasporas in International Relations*; Ulf Brunnbauer, *Globalizing Southeastern Europe: Emigrants, America, and the State since the Late Nineteenth Century* (Lanham, MD: Lexington Books, 2016); Brunnbauer, ed. *Transnational Societies, Transterritorial Politics: Migration in the (Post) Yugoslav Region, 19th–21st Century* (Munich: Oldenbourg, 2009).

25 Kaja Shonick, "Politics, Culture, and Economics: Reassessing the West German Guest Worker Agreement with Yugoslavia," *Journal of Contemporary History* 44, no. 4 (2009): 719–36, https://doi.org/10.1177/0022009409340648; Vladimir Ivanović, "Brantova istočna politika i jugoslovenska ekonomska emigracija u SR Nemačkoj," in *1968 – Četrdeset godina posle*, ed. Institut za noviju istoriju Srbije (Beograd: Institut za noviju istoriju Srbije, 2008), 275–92; Karolina Novinšćak Kölker, "The Recruiting and Sending of Yugoslav 'Gastarbeiter' to Germany: Between Socialist Demands and Economic Needs," in *Transnational Societies, Transterritorial Politics: Migration in the (Post) Yugoslav Region, 19th–21st Century*, ed. Ulf Brunnbauer, 121–44 (Munich: Oldenbourg, 2009); Molnar, "Nation, Migration, and Cold War"; Molnar, *Memory, Politics, and Yugoslav Migrations to Postwar Germany* (Bloomington: Indiana University Press, 2018); Molnar, "On the Move and

Putting Down Roots," in *Migrations in the German Lands, 1500–2000*, ed. Jason Coy, Jared Poley, and Alexander Schunka, 13:191–208 (New York: Berghahn Books, 2016).

26 Слободан Селинић, "Економска Емиграција Из Југославије Шездесетих Година XX Века," *1968–Četrdeset Godina Posle*, 1968, 549–73; Mark Allan Baskin, "Political Innovation and Policy Implementation in Yugoslavia: The Case of Worker Migration Abroad" (PhD diss., University of Michigan, 1986); Ivana Dobrivojević, "U Potrazi za blagostanjem. Odlazak Jugoslovenskih državaljana u zemlje zapadne Evrope 1960–1977," *Istorija 20. veka* 2 (2007): 89–100; Petar Dragišić, "Jugoslovenski ekonomski migranti u Austriji od početka 60-Ih godina do raspada Jugoslavije," *Tokovi istorije* 1–2 (2009): 55–64.

27 Sara Bernard, "Developing the Yugoslav Gastarbeiter Reintegration Policy: Political and Economic Aspects (1969–1974)," Working paper, South East European Studies 5, Centre for Southeast European Studies, University of Graz, 2012; Bernard, *Deutsch Marks in the Head, Shovel in the Hands and Yugoslavia in the Heart: The Gastarbeiter Return to Yugoslavia (1965–1991)* (Wiesbaden: Harrassowitz Verlag, 2019); Jenni Winterhagen, "Die Pioniere von Imotski. Die Verwendung von Remittances am Beispiel des ehemaligen Jugoslawien," in *Gesellschaften in Bewegung. Emigration aus und Immigration nach Südosteuropa in Vergangenheit und Gegenwart. Jahrbuch der Südosteuropa-Gesellschaft* 38 (2009): 61–92; Winterhagen, "Folgen von Abwanderung in Den Heimatorten von Migranten," *Raumplanung* 155 (2011): 94–8. See also Radmila Radić, "Iseljavanje stanovništva sa jugoslovenskog prostora polovinom pedesetih godina," *Istorijski Zapisi* 72, no. 1–2 (1999): 143–73.

28 Carl-Ulrik Schierup, *Houses, Tractors, Golden Ducats: Prestige Game and Migration: A Study of Migrants to Denmark from a Yugoslav Village* (Moesgård: Århus Universitetet, Institut for Etnografi og Socialantropologi, 1973). On the everyday experience of migration, see also Ondřej Daniel, "Gastarbajteri: Rethinking Yugoslav Economic Migrations towards the European North-West through Transnationalism and Popular Culture," in *Imagining Frontiers, Contesting Identities*, ed. Steven G. Ellis and Luďa Klusáková, 277–302 (Pisa: Ed. Plus, Pisa University Press, 2007); Karolina Novinšćak Kölker, "Ein halbes Jahrhundert 'Minhen': Münchens Platz in der Geschichte der Migration aus dem ehemaligen Jugoslawien und seinen Nachfolgerepubliken," in *Migration bewegt die Stadt. Perspektiven wechseln*, ed. Ursula Eymold and Andreas Heusler, 42–54 (Munich: Allitera Verlag, 2018).

29 Petar Dragišić, "Klubovi Jugoslovenskih radnika u zapadnoj Evropi sedamdesetih godina," *Tokovi istorije* 1 (2010): 128–38; Nikola Baković, "Socialist 'Oasis' in a Capitalist 'Desert': Yugoslav State Propaganda

for Economic Emigrants in FR Germany" (PhD diss., Central European University, 2012); Baković, "Tending the 'Oasis of Socialism': Transnational Political Mobilization of Yugoslav Economic Emigrants in the FR Germany in the Late 1960s and 1970s," *Nationalities Papers* 42, no. 4 (2014): 674–90; Baković, "Song of Brotherhood, Dance of Unity: Cultural-Entertainment Activities for Yugoslav Economic Emigrants in the West in the 1960s and 1970s," *Journal of Contemporary History* 50, no. 2 (2015): 354–75; Ivanović, *Geburtstag pišeš normalno*.

30 Lee, "Three Worlds of Emigration Policy"; Elaine Lynn-Ee Ho, "'Claiming' the Diaspora: Elite Mobility, Sending State Strategies and the Spatialities of Citizenship," *Progress in Human Geography* 35, no. 6 (2011): 757–72, https://doi.org/10.1177/0309132511401463; Alexandra Délano, "Immigrant Integration vs. Transnational Ties?: The Role of the Sending State," *Social Research: An International Quarterly* 77, no. 1 (2010): 237–68; David Fitzgerald, *A Nation of Emigrants: How Mexico Manages Its Migration* (Berkeley: University of California Press, 2009); Ahmet Akgündüz, *Labour Migration from Turkey to Western Europe, 1960–1974*, Research in Migration and Ethnic Relations Series (Burlington, VT: Ashgate, 2008).

31 Hilde Katrine Haug, *Creating a Socialist Yugoslavia: Tito, Communist Leadership and the National Question* (London: IB Tauris, 2012), 261. See also Jill Irvine, "The Croatian Spring and the Dissolution of Yugoslavia," in *State Collapse in South-Eastern Europe: New Perspectives on Yugoslavia's Disintegration*, ed. Lenard J. Cohen and Jasna Dragović-Soso, 149–78 (West Lafayette, IN: Purdue University Press, 2008); Dennison Rusinow, *Yugoslavia: Oblique Insights and Observations* (Pittsburgh: University of Pittsburgh Press, 2008).

2. Seeing Migration Like a State

1 James C. Scott, *Seeing like a State: How Certain Schemes to Improve the Human Condition Have Failed* (New Haven, CT: Yale University Press, 1999), 3.

2 Francesco Ragazzi, "The Croatian 'Diaspora Politics' of the 1990s: Nationalism Unbound?," in *Transnational Societies, Transterritorial Politics: Migrations in the (Post-) Yugoslav Region, 19th–21st Century*, ed. U. Brunnbauer (Munich: R. Oldenbourg Verlag, 2009), 155.

3 Baskin, "Political Innovation and Policy Implementation in Yugoslavia," 104, 367.

4 William Zimmerman, *Open Borders, Nonalignment, and the Political Evolution of Yugoslavia* (Princeton, NJ: Princeton University Press, 1987), 75.

5 Archiv Jugoslavije (AJ – Archive of Yugoslavia) 837: Arhiv Predsednika Republike III-A-1-e, SIV, Odbor za ekonomske odnose sa inostranstvom. Zapisnik Odbora SIV a za ekonomske odnose sa inostranstvom održane 12.

novembra 1962. godine; SIV. Odbor za ekonomske odnose sa inostranstvom, Status i mogući devizni priliv od naše radne snage u inostranstvu, Belgrade, 1 November 1962; DSIP, Kabinet državnog sekretara, Str. Pov. 29 January 1963, Jugoslovenskii građani na radu u inostranstvu.

6 Francesca Rolandi, "Heading towards the West: Yugoslav Asylum Seekers in Italy (1955–1968), *Acta Histriae* 23, no. 3 (2015), 559–62; Brigitte Le Normand "Yugoslavia," *in East Central European Migrations during the Cold War*, 368–95 (Berlin: De Gruyter Oldenbourg, 2019); Molnar, "Nation, Migration, and Cold War," 88–9.

7 Brunnbauer, *Globalizing Southeastern Europe*, 270–90.

8 AJ 562: Savezna Komisija za pitanja iseljenika, Kutija "1963 – pov. Arhiva i str. Pov. R-2" Boško Jović, sekretar Matice. Informacija o odlasku naših građana na rad u inostranstvo (sent to Savet za pitanje iseljenika 11. Juni 1963).

9 Hrvatski Državni Arhiv (HDA – Croatian State Archives) 1220: Centralni komitet SKH, D-666-1964, Zapisnik sa sastanka Komisije za društveno-ekonomski razvoj Glavnog odbora SSRN Hrvatske, održanog 13. Travnja 1964. godine, 1.

10 Brunnbauer, *Globalizing Southeastern Europe*, 270–90.

11 Igor Tchoukarine, "Yugoslavia's Open-Door Policy and Global Tourism in the 1950s and 1960s," *East European Politics & Societies and Cultures* 29, no. 1 (2015): 168–88.

12 Tchoukarine, "Yugoslavia's Open-Door Policy," 177.

13 In the original, this law was called "Zakon o prestanku važenja Zakona o oduzimanju državljanstva oficirima i podoficirima bivše jugoslavenske vojske, koji ne će da se vrate u domovinu, te pripadnicima vojnih formacija, koji su služili okupatora i odbjegli u inozemstvo, kao i licima odbjeglim poslije oslobodjenja."

14 AJ 142: Socijalistički savez radnog naroda Jugoslavije, 492, "IO GO SSRNH. Svim Kotarskim i općinskim odborima SSRN Hrvatske. 1.11.1963."

15 For a positive evaluation, see Iva Kraljević. "Matica iseljenika Hrvatske 1964–1968," *Časopis za suvremenu povijest* 41, no. 1 (2009): 75. For a more skeptical view, see Hrvatski Državni Arhiv, 562 Savezna Komisija za pitanja iseljenika, 1965 od br. 201–311. "XI Sjednica savjeta za pitanja iseljenika, održana 14.IX 1966. g. u 9 časova."

16 Zimmerman, *Open Borders*, 76–7; Baskin, "Political Innovation," 67, 72.

17 AJ 142, 495, Socijalistička republika Srbija, Republička skupština, republičko veće, komisija za spoljno-politička i druga pitanja iz odnosa sa inostranstvom, Belgrade, 10 February 1969; Stenografske beleške, 1/5, 13/1-13/3; AJ 142 I-471, Savezni savet za obrazovanje i kulturu, "Društveno-pedagoška osnova obrazovno-vaspitnog rada sa decom naših

radnika privremeno zaposlenih u inostranstvu i predlozi za rešavanje problema njihovog školovanja," Belgrade, 5 May 1970.

18 AJ 837, II 9 K, 1953-1979, Dr. Ljubo Leontić, "Memorandum o iseljeničkoj problematici / sastanku delegata "Matica iseljenika" u Zagrebu 20 februara 1954," 1.

19 AJ 142/2-475, "Otvoreno pismo cjelokupnoj jugoslavenskoj javnosti."

20 HDA 1409: Izvršno vijeće Sabora – Savjet o odnose s inozemstvom, K. 101, SIV, Komitet za pitanja spoljnih migracija, 7 October 1970, correspondence with Republičko izvršno veće SR Hrvatske, 3.

21 AJ 142/2-475, "Nema mjesta za sedmu republiku," Oslobođenje, 18 September 1970; "Šta nije otvoreno u otvorenom pismu," Politika, 17.9.1970.

22 AJ 142-95, SIV, "Pregled poslova koje je do sada vršila Savezna komisija za pitanje iseljenika," 26 June 1968.

23 HDA 1409, 99, Zavod za migracije i narodnosti Zagreb, "Izveštaj o postanku i radu zavod za migracije i narodnosti," Zagreb, February 1968; AJ 142/2-491, "Informacija o dosadašnjoj djelatnosti Matice iseljenika Hrvatske."

24 AJ 142/2, 475, "Podsetnik o nekim aktuelnim političkim pitanjima zapošljavanje naših radnika u inostranstvu." The precise institutions and their names changed over time. A document from a decade earlier lists the following institutions: DSIP, the Federal Secretariat for Legal Administration (državni sekretarijat za pravodnu upravu), the Secretariat for Education (Sekretarijat za prosvetu), the Social Security Service (Služba socijalnog osiguranje), the Committee for Social Protection (Savet za socijanlnu zaštitu). AJ 142. 492. Službe koje se bave iseljeničkim pitanjima i problematika njihove službe.

25 Baković, "Socialist 'Oasis' in a Capitalist 'Desert,'" 44.

26 AJ 562, 1965 F-143, Savezni biro za poslove zapošljavanja, "Predlog o osnivanju stručne službe u inostranstvu koja bi se bavila pitanjima zapošljavanja naših radnika," 16 March 1966, 1.

27 AJ 562, F-1967, SFRJ u Evropskim migracijama rada. Sociološko-ekonomska studija. Zavod za migracije i narodnosti (Zagreb 1967): v–vi (henceforth, SFRJ u Evropskim migracijama rada.)

28 SFRJ u Evropskim migracijama rada, 27–32.

29 HDA, fond 1611: Anketni upitnici zavoda za migracije I narodnosti o radnicima na privremenom radu u inozemstvu, kutija 1, Antun Petak, "Izvještaj o izvršenom anketiranju u Rijeci od 30.VI do 6.VII 1966"; Ivan Čizmić, "Izvještaj o anketiranju naših radnika privremeno zaposlenih u Austriji"; Želimir Katur, "Izvještaj anketara Katura Želimira o izvršenom aketiranju Jugoslavena privremeno zaposlenih u Austriji"; Kruno Kozina, "Izvještaj sa službenog puta u Švedsku."

30 HDA, Fond 1611, kutija 1, "Izvještaj o rezultatima pokušne usmene ankete provedene u SRNj i Nizozemskoj"; Izvještaj o izvršenom anketiranju naših gradjana privremeno zaposlenih u Holandiji."

31 HDA, fond 1611, kutija 1, Ivan Čizmić, "Izvještaj o anketiranju naših
    radnika privremeno zaposlenih u Austriji"; Kruno Kozina, "Izvještaj o
    rezultatima pokušne usmene ankete provedene u SRNj i Nizozemskoj";
    "Izvještaj o izvršenom anketiranju naših gradjana privremeno zaposlenih
    u Holandiji."

32 HDA, fond 1611, kutija 1, "Izvještaj o izvršenom anketiranju naših
    gradjana privremeno zaposlenih u Holandiji."

33 *SFRJ u Evropskim migracijama rada*: 31, 39–40.

34 *SFRJ u Evropskim migracijama rada:* 39.

35 *SFRJ u Evropskim migracijama rada:* 45.

36 *SFRJ u Evropskim migracijama rada:* 38, 41–2.

37 *SFRJ u Evropskim migracijama rada:* 45.

38 *SFRJ u Evropskim migracijama rada:* 46–7, 55.

39 *SFRJ u Evropskim migracijama rada:* 43.

40 *SFRJ u Evropskim migracijama rada:* 47, 49, 50s.

41 *SFRJ u Evropskim migracijama rada:* 58, 61.

42 *SFRJ u Evropskim migracijama rada:* 59.

43 *SFRJ u Evropskim migracijama rada:* 56–7.

44 Respondents could choose up to three answers. *SFRJ u Evropskim
    migracijama rada:* 62.

45 *SFRJ u Evropskim migracijama rada:* 66–7.

46 *SFRJ u Evropskim migracijama rada:* 63.

47 *SFRJ u Evropskim migracijama rada:* 52, 67–8.

48 *SFRJ u Evropskim migracijama rada:* 133.

49 *SFRJ u Evropskim migracijama rada:* 129, 133, 136.

50 *SFRJ u Evropskim migracijama rada:* 132, 135.

51 *SFRJ u Evropskim migracijama rada:* 139.

52 *SFRJ u Evropskim migracijama rada:* 140.

53 See, for example, HDA 1409, k.99, Komisija RIV-a za odnose sa
    inostranstvom, "Problemi jugoslovenske radne snage u inostranstvu,"
    Belgrade, March 1968; HDA 1409, "Prijedlog zaključaka. Odbor za pitanja
    vanjske politike i odnosa s inozemstvom Republičkog vijeća Sabora SR
    Hrvatske zajedno sa Savjetom za odnose s inozemstvom Izvršnog vijeća
    Sabora, na sednici 23. siječnja 1969. godine …"

54 HDA 1409, K.99, Komisija RIV-a za odnose sa inostranstvom, "Problemi
    jugoslovenske radne snage u inostranstvu," Belgrade, March 1968, 28–32
    HDA 1409 K. 100, Ambasada SFRJ Bon. "Položaj naših gradjana u SRN
    u uslovima delatnosti neprijateljske emigracije," January 1970; Molnar,
    Memory, Politics, 61–3.

55 HDA 1409, K.99, Komisija RIV-a za odnose sa inostranstvom, "Problemi
    jugoslovenske radne snage u inostranstvu," Belgrade, March 1968,
    28–32.

56 HDA 1409, K.99, Komisija RIV-a za odnose sa inostranstvom. "Problemi jugoslovenske radne snage u inostranstvu," Belgrade, March 1968, 28–32; HDA 1409, K. 100, Ambasada SFRJ Bon, "Položaj naših gradjana u SRN u uslovima delatnosti neprijateljske emigracije," January 1970.

57 HDA 1409, K.100, Ambasada SFRJ Bon, "Položaj naših gradjana u SRN u uslovima delatnosti neprijateljske emigracije," January 1970.

58 HDA 1409, K.99, Komisija RIV-a za odnose sa inostranstvom, "Problemi jugoslovenske radne snage u inostranstvu," Belgrade, March 1968, 28–32.

59 HDA 1409, 09-331-1968, SSJ, correspondence with Republičko vijeće za Hrvatsku, Zagreb, 9 February 1968.

60 HD 1409, "Prijedlog zaključaka, Odbor za pitanja vanjske politike i odnosa s inozemstvom Republičkog vijeća Sabora SR Hrvatske zajedno sa Savejtom za odnose s inozemstvom Izvršnog vijeća Sabora, na sednici 23. Siječnja 1969. Godine…"

61 A detailed discussion of the events of the Croatian Spring can be found in Rusinow, *Yugoslavia*; Haug, *Creating a Socialist Yugoslavia*.

62 "Naše inozemne migracije danas," *Vjesnik u srijedu*, 30 November 1968, 6 December 1968; Zvonimir Komarica, *Jugoslavija u suvremenim evropskim migracijama*. Vol. 8. Ekonomski institut, 1970.

63 Komarica, *Jugoslavija u suvremenim evropskim migracijama*: 8–9, 16, 26–7, 44, 103–6, 108–9.

64 *Jugoslavija u suvremenim evropskim migracijama*: 12, 42, 44.

65 *Jugoslavija u suvremenim evropskim migracijama*: 46, 70.

66 *Jugoslavija u suvremenim evropskim migracijama*: 110.

67 "Treća konferencija SK Hrvatske: Dr. Savka Dabčević-Kučar: Ono na čemu se mobilizirala radnička klasa Hrvatske ujedno su i životna pitanja Jugoslavije," *Vjesnik* 7 October 1970. As a side note, a cut-out of this article is found in Komarica's personal archival fond at the HDA, many passages emphatically underlined, but not commented. It can be surmised that Komarica agreed with her general line, even though he was guilty of the sorts of inflammatory insinuations she was trying to silence.

68 HDA 1611, Kutija 7, "Anketa 'Uvjeti povratka naših radnika s privremenog rada u inozemstvu,'" 1.

69 HDA 1611, Kutija 7. "Uvjeti povratka naših radnika s privremenog rada u inozemstvu": 7–10.

70 Baučić, *Radnici u inozemstvu prema popisu stanovnistva Jugoslavije 1971*, 17, 18.

71 It seems that, in the absence of clear guidance, most survey-takers in Croatia were inclined to exclude them. Baučić, *Radnici u inozemstvu*, 31–3.

72 Baučić, *Radnici u inozemstvu*, 13–15, 21–2, 26, 36.

73 Baučić, *Radnici u inozemstvu*, 17.

74 Notable contributions to this field include Francine Hirsch, *Empire of Nations: Ethnographic Knowledge and the Making of the Soviet Union*

(Ithaca, NY: Cornell University Press, 2005), 101–44; Florian Bieber, "The Construction of National Identity and Its Challenges in Post-Yugoslav Censuses," *Social Science Quarterly* 96, no. 3 (2015): 873–903; Paul Schor and Lys Ann Weiss, *Counting Americans: How the US Census Classified the Nation* (New York: Oxford University Press, 2017).

75 Nikolai Botev, "Where East Meets West: Ethnic Intermarriage in the Former Yugoslavia, 1962 to 1989," *American Sociological Review* 59, no. 3 (1994): 465.

76 Baučić, *Radnici u inozemstvu:* 36, 94.

77 Baučić, *Radnici u inozemstvu:* 26, 38, 91.

78 Baučić, *Radnici u inozemstvu:* 46–8.

79 Baučić, *Radnici u inozemstvu:* 53, 55, 63, 68.

80 Baučić, *Radnici u inozemstvu:* 44–5.

81 Baučić, *Radnici u inozemstvu:* 37–9, 94.

82 Baučić, *Radnici u inozemstvu:* 42–4.

83 Baučić, *Radnici u inozemstvu:* 68, 81.

84 Montenegrins were treated as a separate ethnic category, but they accounted for only 5260 migrants. Baučić, *Radnici u inozemstvu*, 83–5.

85 Baučić, *Radnici u inozemstvu:* 110.

86 Ivo Baučić, "Stanje vanjskih migracija iz jugoslavije krajem sedamdesetih godina," *Rasprave o migracijama* 57 (1979): 14, table 5.

87 Ljiljana Petković, *Problemi međunarodnih migracija radne snage sa posebnim osvrtom na jugoslaviju* (Beograd: Naučna Knjiga, 1988), 31.

3. Picturing Migrants: The *Gastarbajter* in Yugoslav Film

1 On media portrayals, see David Eugene Goodlett, *Yugoslav Worker Emigration, 1963–1973: Government Policy and Press Coverage* (Lewiston, NY: E. Mellen, 2007); Ivanović, *Geburtstag pišeš normalno*, 297–318; and Sara Bernard, *Deutsch Marks in the Head, Shovel in the Hands and Yugoslavia in the Heart: The Gastarbeiter Return to Yugoslavia (1965–1991)* (Wiesbaden: Harrassowitz Verlag, 2019), 205–12.

2 Nick Miller, *The Nonconformists: Culture, Politics, and Nationalism in a Serbian Intellectual Circle, 1944–1991* (Budapest: Central European University Press, 2007), 160.

3 Miller, *Nonconformists*, 160–8.

4 Radina Vučetić-Mladenović, *Monopol na istinu: partija, kultura i cenzura u Srbiji šezdesetih i sedamdesetih godina XX veka* (Belgrade: Clio, 2016); Aleksandar Petrović, *Novi film* (Belgrade: Institut za film, 1971); Petrović, *Novi film II (1965–1970)* (Belgrade: Naučna Knjiga, 1988).

5 Pavle Levi, *Disintegration in Frames: Aesthetics and Ideology in the Yugoslav and Post-Yugoslav Cinema* (Stanford, CA: Stanford University Press, 2007),

11–56; Daniel J. Goulding, *Liberated Cinema: The Yugoslav Experience, 1945–2001* (Bloomington: Indiana University Press, 2002), 66–83; Ivo Škrabalo, "Croatian Film in the Yugoslav Context in the Second Half of the Twentieth Century," special issue "Croatian Cinema," *Kinokultura* 11 (2011): 35; Petrović, *Novi Film II*, 153. On ways of understanding New Film and its politicization, see Greg DeCuir Jr., "Black Wave Polemics: Rhetoric as Aesthetic," *Studies in Eastern European Cinema* 1, no. 1 (2010): 85; Nebojša Jovanović, "Breaking the Wave: A Commentary on 'Black Wave Polemics: Rhetoric as Aesthetic' by Greg DeCuir, Jr.,'" *Studies in Eastern European Cinema* 2, no. 2 (2011): 161; and Greg DeCuir Jr., "Black Wave Polemics: Rhetoric as Aesthetic," *Studies in Eastern European Cinema* 1, no. 1 (2010): 85–96.

6 "Gastarbajterska balada," *Vjesnik*, 1.11.1977.
7 See also Brigitte Le Normand, "The Gastarbajteri as a Transnational Yugoslav Working Class," in *Social Inequalities and Discontent in Yugoslav Socialism*, ed. Rory Archer, Igor Duda, and Paul Stubbs, 50–69 (Oxford: Routledge, 2016).
8 Bernard, *Deutsch Marks in the Head*, 193.
9 Ines Sabalić, "Inspiracije iz svakodnevnice," *Studio*, 1 December 1984.
10 Ewa Mazierska, "Želimir Žilnik and Eastern European Independent Cinema," *Images: The International Journal of European Film, Performing Arts and Audiovisual Communication* 13, no. 22 (2013): 141.
11 D. Gajer, "Divni Dolasci," *Politika ekspress*, 4 January 1978.
12 Laslo Dorman, "Filizof iz ravnice," *Radio TV revija*, 2 April 1982.
13 Gajer, "Divni Dolasci."
14 Chiara Bonfiglioli, "Women's Political and Social Activism in the Early Cold War Era: The Case of Yugoslavia," *Aspasia* 8, no. 1 (2014): 1–25; Zsófia Lóránd, *The Feminist Challenge to the Socialist State in Yugoslavia* (Cham, UK: Palgrave Macmillan, 2018).
15 Bernard, *Deutsch Marks in the Head*, 183–4.

4. A Listening Ear: Cultivating Citizens through Radio Broadcasting

1 Stephen Lovell, *Russia in the Microphone Age: A History of Soviet Radio, 1919–1970* (Oxford: Oxford University Press, 2015), 43. On the use of radio in the Soviet context during the Second World War, see also James Von Gelderen, "Radio Moscow," in *Culture and Entertainment in Wartime Russia*, ed. Richard Stites, 45–61 (Bloomington: Indiana University Press, 1995). On radio elsewhere in another socialist bloc state, see Christoph Classen, "Between Political Coercion and Popular Expectations: Contemporary History in the Radio of the Early German Democratic Republic," in *Popular Historiographies in the 19th and 20th Century*, ed. Sylvia Paletsche, 89–102

(Oxford: Berghahn, 2011); Linda Risso, *Radio Wars: Broadcasting during the Cold War* (Milton Park, UK: Routledge, 2015).

2 Lovell, *Russia in the Microphone Age*, 51–62.

3 Benedict R. Anderson, *Imagined Communities: Reflections on the Origin and Spread of Nationalism* (New York: Verso, 1991), 35.

4 Franjo Letić and Ivo Baučić, *Informiranje i informiranost vanjskih migranata Iz SR Hrvatske o zbivanjima u domovini* (Zagreb: Centar za istraživanja migracija, 1977), 60.

5 Franz Fanon, "This Is the Voice of Algeria," in *The Sound Studies Reader*, ed. Jonathan Sterne, 329–33 (Milton Park, UK: Routledge, 2012); Nicholas J. Schlosser, *Cold War on the Airwaves: The Radio Propaganda War against East Germany* (Champaign: University of Illinois Press, 2015); A. Ross Johnson and R. Eugene Parta, *Cold War Broadcasting: Impact on the Soviet Union and Eastern Europe: A Collection of Studies and Documents* (Budapest: Central European University Press, 2010); Richard H. Cummings, *Cold War Radio: The Dangerous History of American Broadcasting in Europe, 1950–1989* (Jefferson, NC: McFarland, 2009); Yuliya Komska, "West Germany's Cold War Radio: A Crucible of the Transatlantic Century," *German Politics and Society* 32, no. 1 (2014): 1–14; Michael Nelson, *War of the Black Heavens: The Battles of Western Broadcasting in the Cold War* (Syracuse, NY: Syracuse University Press, 1997); Arch Puddington, *Broadcasting Freedom: The Cold War Triumph of Radio Free Europe and Radio Liberty* (Lexington: University Press of Kentucky, 2000); Linda Risso, *Radio Wars: Broadcasting during the Cold War* (Milton Park, UK: Routledge, 2015).

6 HDA 1409, K.99, Komisija RIV-a za odnose sa inostranstvom, "Problemi jugoslovenske radne snage u inostranstvu," Belgrade, March 1968, 28–32; AJ 142, A-345, "Informacija Dobrosava Ilića o održanom sastanku savetnika za školska pitanja u SR Nemačkoj," 7 September 1976. On foreign-language radio-broadcasting aimed at migrants produced in the Federal Republic of Germany, see Roberto Sala, *Fremde Worte: Medien für Gastarbeiter in der Bundesrepublik im Spannungsfeld von Außen- und Sozialpolitik* (Paderborn: Ferdinand Schöningh, 2011).

7 Sala, *Fremde Worte*, 44.

8 On resistance to popular culture in Soviet radio, see Lovell, *Russia in the Microphone Age*, 199–204.

9 Zlatko Skrbiš, "Transnational Families: Theorising Migration, Emotions and Belonging," *Journal of Intercultural Studies* 29, no. 3 (2008): 231, https://doi.org/10.1080/07256860802169188; Alexandra Dantzer, "Architects of Happiness: Notes on the Mindwork of Migration," *Issues in Ethnology Anthropology* 12, no. 1 (2017): 175–93; Paolo Boccagni and Loretta Baldassar, "Emotions on the Move: Mapping the Emergent Field of Emotion and Migration," *Emotion, Space and Society* 16 (2015): 73–80; Amanda Wise and

Selvaraj Velayutham, "Transnational Affect and Emotion in Migration Research," *International Journal of Sociology* 47, no. 2 (2017): 116–30.

10 Anastasia Christou, "Narrating Lives in (e) Motion: Embodiment, Belongingness and Displacement in Diasporic Spaces of Home and Return," *Emotion, Space and Society* 4, no. 4 (2011): 250.

11 AJ 562, "1966. Bilten saveta za pitanju iseljenika." Broj 11, Belgrade, September 1965; Unnumbered folder, "Zapisnik sa savjetovanja održanog 3.II.1965 u društvenim prostorijama kojega je sazvao Koordinacioni odbor Matice Iseljenika u suradnji sa Savjetom za pitanje iseljenika Socijalističke Federativne Republike Jugoslavije o izdavačkoj djelatnosti i drugim kulturnim aktivnostima namijenjim našim iseljenicima i drugim građanima naše zemlje koji se privremeno nalaze na radu u inozemstvu," 85–6; HR HDA 1409, Kutija 102 – Radnici u inozemstvu 1972–1974, SKJ Centralni Komitet SKH, Opunomoćstvo za djelatnost SKH u vezi s odlaskom i privremenim radom naših radnika u inozemstvu, document to be discussed at meeting on 17 December 1974 entitled "Informativna djelatnost u SR Hrvatskoj prema našim građanima privremeno zaposlenim u inozemstvu," 5; HR HDA 1615, box 9, zapisnici redakcije, 27 August 1964.

12 Letić and Baučić, *Informiranje i informiranost*, 92.

13 Michelle Hilmes, "Radio and the Imagined Community," in *The Sound Studies Reader*, ed. Jonathan Sterne, 351–4 (Milton Park, UK: Routledge, 2012); Jason Loviglio, *Radio's Intimate Public: Network Broadcasting and Mass-Mediated Democracy* (Minneapolis: University of Minnesota Press, 2005), xix.

14 For a brief history of Soviet approaches to radio, see Stephen Lovell, "How Russia Learned to Listen: Radio and the Making of Soviet Culture," *Kritika: Explorations in Russian and Eurasian History* 12, no. 3 (2011): 591–615.

15 HR HDA 1615: Pisma za emisiju "Našim građanima u Svijetu," Radio-Televizije Zagreb, 1964–6, box 9, zapisnici redakcije, 27.8.1964.

16 HR HDA 1615, box 9, zapisnici redakcije, 27.8.1964.

17 HR HDA 1615, box 9, zapisnici redakcije, 5.9.1963 or 1964 (year unmarked); AJ 562, unnumbered folder, "Zapisnik sa savjetovanja održanog 3.II.1965 u društvenim prostorijama kojega je sazvao Koordinacioni odbor Matice Iseljenika ...," 90; "Zvuci domovine," *Vjesnik u srijedu*, 6 January 1965.

18 AJ 562, unnumbered folder, "Zapisnik sa savjetovanja održanog 3.II.1965 u društvenim prostorijama kojega je sazvao Koordinacioni odbor Matice Iseljenika ...," 88–9.

19 HR HDA 1615, box 9, zapisnici redakcije, 17.3.1964.

20 HR HDA 1615, box 9, zapisnici redakcije, 17.3.1964; AJ 562, unnumbered folder, "Zapisnik sa savjetovanja održanog 3.II.1965 u društvenim

prostorijama kojega je sazvao Koordinacioni odbor Matice Iseljenika ...,"
86–8.

21 AJ 562. Beograd; unnumbered folder. Zapisnik sa savjetovanja održanog
3.II.1965 u društvenim prostorijama kojega je sazvao Koordinacioni odbor
Matice Iseljenika ..., 87.

22 HR HDA 1615, box 4, letter from Jelo Jerolimon I Joška Nirić, Vienna, 3
March 64; box 5, Miko Hrsvarić from Illingen, 29 February 1964.

23 HR, HDA 1615, box 9, Josip and Nada Kovačić, Antwerp, 23 February
1964.

24 HR, HDA 1615, box 5, "Jugoslavenski građani u inozemstvu" from Neuss,
19 October 64; "Grupa Slovenaca iz Koblenza," 14 July 1964; box 7, letter
from Stijepan Fuketa, 24 December 1965.

25 A Šeparović, "Zvučni most s domovinom," *Vjesnik u Srijedu* 149, 15
February 1967.

26 HR, HDA 1615, box 9, anonymous letter, Nice, 19 March 1964.

27 HR, HDA 1615, box 4, letter from Živko Lažić from Rattingen, 4 November
1964.

28 HDA 1615, box 5, letter from Anica Huzak, from Riederick, FRG, 3 March
1964; Ana Markota from Munich, 4 March 1965; Franka, from Blumberg,
n.d.; Petar Papp I Ivan Trchek, from Oberkochen-Wurth, n.d.

29 HR, HDA 1615, box 9, Stevo and Nata from Frankfurt, 26 February 1964.

30 HR, HDA 1615, box 9, letter from a woman in Böblingen, 29 October 1964.
See also letter and poem from Franka and Miloš Veža from Wasserburg, 8
March 1964.

31 For example, HR, HDA 1615, box 5, Jovan Djurić to Zemun, n.d., living in
Karlsruhe; Rudolf Cigula, from Niefern/Baden, 1 March 1964; letter from
Branko Vukovic, Wuppertal, October 1964.

32 HR, HDA 1615, box 9, Vlado Huzjak, from Kapellen, 5 October 1964.

33 HR, HDA 1615, box 9, Jaroslav Strnad, from Leopoldshafen, 18 October
1964; Živko Lazić, Dusseldorf, 4 October 1964; Nikola Radošević, Essen,
21 June 1964; Mato Šantić, Stuttgart, 2 June 1964; Andjelko Pleic, from
Salzgitter, 17 October 64; Lucija Kvasina, Augsburg.

34 HR, HDA 1615, box 5, Josip Radenić, Ohringen, 29 September 1964;
Marijana Kovandžić, Zagreb, 4 November 1964. Two anonymous letters
from Willingen, Schwarzwald, 7 April 1964. Letter from Vladimir
Novak, Arleux, France, 27 October 1964; Shtefica Munjko, Zagreb,
26 October 1964; Pero from Oestringen, FRG, 18 October 1964; Ante
Marich, from Obernai, France, 17 August 1964; Anton Štelik, from
Stuttgart, 14 October 1964; Marica Viljevac, from Norrahammer,
Sweden, 3 January 1965, box 9. Lucija Kvasina from Augsburg, n.d.
Worker in Stuttgart to VUS, 30 August 1970. Marijana K., from Zagreb,
4 February 1964.

35 HR HDA 1615, box 5, Marica and Mato Matišić, from Koblenz, Germany, 16 September 1964; Martin Vinko, from Waldorf, 5 October 1964; interview with Juraj Mađarić, nastavnik Saobraćajne škole u Zagrebu, box 9, Ivan Teskera, from Wiesbaden, 26 September 1964.

36 HR HDA 1615, box 5, Nikola Vujatović, from Hamburg, 22 December 1964.

37 "Stan nije sve," *Beogradska nedelja*, 8 April 1965.

38 HR HDA 1615, box 9, Ivan Ivić, from Dortmund, 4 July 1964; Fabjan Topolovec, from Linz, 13 September 1964; Marija and Branko Kos, from Schwenningen am Neckar, 1964; Stjepan Bakšaj, from Hilden, 4 January 1965.

39 HR HDA 1615, box 9. Janez Kadivec in Essen, 31 August 1964.

40 HR HDA 1615, box 5, Franjo Lukšić, from Hanover, 20 October 1964.

41 A. Šeparović, "Zvučni most s domovinom," *Vjesnik u srijedu* 149, 15 February 1967.

42 HR HDA 1615, box 5, Josip Pintarich, from Donzdorf, 5 November 1964.

43 HR HDA 1615, box 9, Štefica Gornik, from Freiburg, 24 August 1964.

44 Cino Handl, "Susreti pisama," *Vjesnik u srijedu*, 1 April 1964.

45 Šeparović, "Zvučni most s domovinom."

46 HR HDA 1615, box 9, Josip Mileta, from Karlsruhe, 29 September 1964.

47 HR HDA 1615, box 9, anonymous letter from Helsingborg, 4 November 1964.

48 HR HDA 1615, box 9, Živko Lazić from Ratingen bei Dusseldorf, 4 October 1964; Živko Lazić from Ratingen bei Dusseldorf, 18 October 1964; Ivan Kolovrat, from Ludwigshafen, 8 March 1964.

49 HR HDA 1615, box 9, Stjepan Gajski, Ludwigshafen, undated.

50 HR HDA 1615, box 9 Većeslav Holjevac; "Flood Inundates Yugoslav City," *New York Times*, 27 October 1964; "Zagreb Lists Ten as Dead in Flood of the Sava River," *New York Times*, 29 October 1964.

51 HR HDA 1615, box 9, Franjo and Slavica Habush, Mannheim, 3 November 1964.

52 HR HDA 1615, box 9, Drago Radić, Luxembourg, 1 November 1964.

53 HR HDA 1615, box 9, Dadić, from Ravensburg, FRG, 27 October 1964.

54 HR HDA 1615, box 9, Tomo Kushen, Ober Roden, 1 November 1964; Nikola Manojlović, 30 October 1964, Neukirchen; Magdalena Poturin, Heddesheim, 5 November 1964.

55 HR HDA 1615, box 9, "Statistics for TO OUR CITIZENS."

56 Letić and Baučić, *Informiranje i informiranost*, 17–18.

5. A Nation Talking to Itself: Yugoslav Newspapers for Migrants

1 HR HDA 1220, CK SKJ, D 4123, Rep Vijeće SSJ za Hrvatsku, Odbor za probleme privremeno zaposlenih radnika u inozemstvu, Međunarodna

aktivnost SSJ sa sindikatima zemalja gdje na radu privremeno borave naši radnici i aktuelni problem, (Materijal za predsjedništvo RV SSJ za Hrv)." Zagreb, January 1970: 27; Baković, "Socialist 'Oasis,'" 38–41.

2 Baković, "Socialist 'Oasis,'" 41–2.

3 HDA 1409, K.99, Soc Rep Hr, Izvrsno Vijece Sabora, Sek za info, Zagreb. "Predmet: informativno-propagandna djelatnost medju našim radnicima u inozemstvu," 17 April 1969; "VUS vam predstavlja svoje inozemno izdanje," *Vjesnik u srijedu*, 1 April 1964.

4 "Doktore odgovorite," *Vjesnik u srijedu*, 6 January 1965, 2 March 1966, 13 November 1968.

5 "Zaštita za sve naše državljane zaposlene u inozemstvu," *Vjesnik u srijedu*, 1 April 1964; "Primjena TEK nakon ratifikacije," *Vjesnik u srijedu*, 13 November 1968; "Nasi ljudi uživaju velik ugled u svim zemljama gdje rade," *Vjesnik u srijedu*, 30 October 1968; "Na radu u tuđini s mislima u domovini," "Domovina gledana iz tuđine," *Vjesnik u srijedu*, 6 January 1965.

6 "Belgija: bez dozvole nema ulazne vize," "Devizni raćun u Jugoslaviji," and "Oženjeni plaćaju manji porez," *Novosti iz Jugoslavije*, 15 October 1966.

7 Baković, "Socialist 'Oasis,'" 39; HDA 1409, kutija 102, Izvršno vijeće Sabora – Savjet o odnose s inozemstvom, Republičko Vijeće SSJ za Hrvatsku, Odbor za probleme privremeno zaposlenih radnika u inozemstvu, "Medjunarodna aktivnost SSJ sa sindikatima zemalja gdje na radu privremeno borave naši radnici i aktuelni problemi," Zagreb, January 1970.

8 Tomislav Jonjić, "Jedno izvješće o prilikama u Splitu i Dalmaciji, u prvim mjesecima nakon uspostave Nezavisne Države Hrvatske," *Časopis za suvremenu povijest* 33, no. 3 (2001): 823, 825.

9 Tomislav Jonjić, "Organised Resistance to the Yugoslav Communist Regime in Croatia in 1945–1953," *Review of Croatian History* 1 (2007): 129.

10 Ivica Lučić, "Hrvatska protukomunistička gerila u Bosni i Hercegovini od 1945. do 1951," *Časopis za suvremenu povijest* 3:631–70. See also Zdenko Radelić, "1945 in Croatia," *Review of Croatian History* 1 (2010): 16.

11 Nedeljko Kujundžić, *Imotska krajina u narodnooslobodilačkoj borbi 1941–1945: pali borci, žrtve fašističkog terora i spomen obilježja* (Imotski: Općinski odbor SUBNOR-a i SIZ za kulturu, fizičku kulturu i njegovanje revolucionarnih tradicija, 1981), 44, 159.

12 On the role of the press in creating imagined communities, see Anderson, *Imagined Communities*.

13 "Uz Prvi Broj," *Imotska krajina*, 1 March 1970.

14 Marcel Cornis-Pope and John Neubauer, eds., *History of the Literary Cultures of East-Central Europe: Junctures and Disjunctures in the 19th and*

20th Centuries. Vol. 3, *The Making and Re-Making of Literary Institutions* (Amsterdam: John Benjamins Publishing, 2007), 42, 270–80.

15 "Omara," *Imotska krajina*, 15 September 1970.

16 "Jamatva," *Imotska krajina*, 1 November 1970.

17 "Jamatva," *Imotska krajina*, 1 November 1970.

18 "Omara," *Imotska krajina*, 15 September 1970.

19 "Vaša Pisma," *Imotska krajina*, 15 September 1970.

20 "Vaša Pisma," *Imotska krajina*, 15 April 1970.

21 "Vaša Pisma," *Imotska krajina*, 15 April 1970.

22 See, for example, "Vaša Pisma," *Imotska krajina*, 1 June 1970.

23 Ante Batović, *The Croatian Spring: Nationalism, Repression and Foreign Policy under Tito* (London: IB Tauris, 2017), 100–1.

24 *Imotska krajina*, "Devize," 1 December 1970.

25 *Imotska krajina*, "Povijesna pouka o hrvatskim selenjima," 1 and 15 February, and 1 March 1971.

26 *Imotska krajina*, "Štetna uloga dijela štampe po jasnoću i razvoj drduštvenih odnosa u Imotskoj Krajini," 15 March 1971, Prilog, 6.

27 "Štetna uloga," 4.

28 "Štetna uloga," 8.

29 *Imotska krajina*, "Hrvatska je jedino mjesto na zemljinoj kugli gdje hrvati mogu stoviri svoju državu," 1 May 1971.

30 *Imotska krajina*, "Vaša Pisma," 1 August 1970.

31 *Imotska krajina*, "Vaša Pisma," 15 January 1971.

32 *Imotska krajina*, "Ponovo s vama," 1 January 1973.

33 *Imotska krajina*, "Problemi pune afirmacije Saveza komunista u nedovoljno razvijenom području," 15 April 1974.

34 *Imotska krajina*, "Radnici ne odlaze zbog niske stope rasta," 1 January 1974.

35 *Imotska krajina*, "Što treba znati?" 15 April 1974.

36 *Imotska krajina*, "Zapošljavanje naših radnika u inozemstvu," 15 February 1973; *Imotska krajina*, "Organizirati povratak naših radnika," 1 March 1973; *Imotska krajina*, "Koliko ćemo ponuditi novih radnih mjesta," 29 November 1973.

37 *Imotska krajina*, "Pionirka – veliki uspjesi i planovi," 1 January 1973; *Imotska krajina*, "Aržano, devizni pogon," 15 January 1973; *Imotska krajina*, "Štednjom osiguravaju radna mjesta u domovini," 1 March 1973; *Imotska krajina*, "Pokus iza leđa gospoda boga," 15 February 1974; *Imotska krajina*, "Mnogo i malo," 1 June 1974.

38 *Imotska krajina*, "U Cisti počela proizvodnja," 1 December 1974. On the lack of success of remittance-based development schemes, see Bernard, *Deutsch Marks in the Head*, 82, 152–7.

39 *Imotska krajina*, "Radnici zaposleni u inozemstvu moraju biti briga ovog društva," 1 May 1973.

6. Weaving a Web of Transnational Governance: Yugoslav Workers' Associations

1 Studies characterizing workers' associations as tools of the Yugoslav state include the following: Nikola Baković, "Tending the 'Oasis of Socialism': Transnational Political Mobilization of Yugoslav Economic Emigrants in the FR Germany in the Late 1960s and 1970s," *Nationalities Papers* 42, no. 4 (2014): 674–90; Petar Dragišić, "Jugoslovenski ekonomski migranti u Austriji od početka 60-ih godina do raspada Jugoslavije," *Tokovi istorije* 1–2 (2009): 55–64; Vladimir Ivanović, *Geburtstag pišeš normalno: Jugoslovenski gastarbajteri u SR Nemačkoj i Austriji, 1965–1973* (Belgrade: Inst. za Savremenu Istoriju, 2012).

2 AJ 562, F-22, Državni sekretarijat za inostrane poslove, Uprava za konzularne poslove, "Teze za savetovanje sa šefovima konzularnih jedinica iz zapadno-evropskih zemalja u kojima je zaposlena naša radna snaga," 25 November 1966, 5.

3 AJ 837, III-A-1-e, Državni sekretarijat za inostrane poslove, Konzularno odeljenje, "Jugoslovenska radna snaga u inostranstvu." Belgrade, November 1962, 32–3.

4 AJ 837, III-A-1-e, Državni sekretarijat za inostrane poslove, Konzularno odeljenje, Jugoslovenska radna snaga u inostranstvu. Belgrade, November 1962, 32–3; AJ 562, F-18, Generalni konzulat socijalističke FRJ. Hamburg, Savetu za iseljenika. "Predmet: Jugoslavenski gradjani u SRN – politički-kulturni rad," 13 December 1965, 3, 6.

5 AJ 837, III-A-1-e, Državni sekretarijat za inostrane poslove, Konzularno odeljenje, Jugoslovenska Radna Snaga u inostranstvu. Belgrade, November 1962, 33.

6 AJ 837, III-A-1-e, Državni sekretarijat za inostrane poslove, Konzularno odeljenje, Jugoslovenska Radna Snaga u inostranstvu. Belgrade, November 1962, 33–4.

7 AJ 562, F-23, ambassador in Copenhagen to Državni sekretarijat za inostrane poslove, 30 June 1967; F-25. Državni sekretarijat za inostrane poslove, regarding spontaneous formation of a folklore club in Ronneby, Sweden; AJ 562, F-31, Jugol. Klub u Zürich. "Godišnji izveštaj o radu između V i VI redovne god. Skupstine (mart 1968 – mart 1969)," February 1969; AJ 562, F-31, Klub Jugoslovenskih građana Zurich, "Izlet u Paris"; AJ 562, F-31, Klub Jugoslovenskih građana, "Dragi jugosloveni u Švajcarskoj!" March 1967.

8 AJ 142, 257, "Informacija o posjeti radnicima zaposlenim na privremenom radu u Zapadnoj Njemačko," September 1966, 4–5.

9 AJ 562, F-18, Generalni konzulat socijalističke FRJ. Hamburg. Savetu za iseljenika, "Predmet: Jugoslavenski gradjani u SRN – politički-kulturni rad," 13 December 1965, 11–12.

10 *SFRJ u evropskim migracijama rada*, 16; HDA 1409, 100, Državni sekretarijat za inostrane poslove, Uprava za radnike na radu u inostranstvu, "Društveno okupljanje Jugoslovenskih radnika u inostranstvu," June 1970, 1.

11 AJ 142, 475, Zajednica kulturno-prosvetnih organizacija Jugoslavije, "Kulturno prosvetne organizacije i klubovi naših radnika u inostranstvu," December 1970, 4.

12 AJ 142, 475, Zajednica kulturno-prosvetnih organizacija Jugoslavije, "Kulturno prosvetne organizacije i klubovi naših radnika u inostranstvu," 8–9; AJ 142, 491, Yugoslav General Consulate in Sweden, "Pregled stanja i aktivnosti u hrvatskoj koloniji na jurizdikcionom području gen. konzulata u Goteborgu"; HDA 1409, 100, Državni sekretarijat za inostrane poslove, Uprava za radnike na radu u inostranstvu, "Društveno okupljanje Jugoslovenskih radnika u inostranstvu," June 1970, 5, 10. See also Molnar, *Memory, Politics*, 39.

13 AJ 142, 491, "Izveštaj sa savetovanja naših diplomatsko-konzularnih predstavnika u Austriji i sa osnivačke skupštine Kluba jugoslovenskih gradjana u Munchen-u."

14 Baković, "Socialist 'Oasis,'" 29–30.

15 HDA 1409, 100, Državni sekretarijat za inostrane poslove, Uprava za radnike na radu u inostranstvu, "Društveno okupljanje Jugoslovenskih radnika u inostranstvu," June 1970, 8–9.

16 HDA 1409, 100, Državni sekretarijat za inostrane poslove, Uprava za radnike na radu u inostranstvu, "Društveno okupljanje Jugoslovenskih radnika u inostranstvu," June 1970, 10–11.

17 Molnar, *Memory, Politics*, 133–8.

18 AJ 507: Opunomoćstvo PKSJ – A. CK SKJ, XXX-K.1, Predlog odluka o obrazovanju Opunomoćstva Predsedništva SKJ za delatnost SK u vezi sa odlaskom i privremenim radom naših radnika u inostranstvu, 12 April 1971; Predlog odluke o delovanju SK u vezi sa odlaskom i privremenim radom naših radnika u inostranstvu 12 April 1971; Podsetnik o problemima i širim zadacima u vezi sa Odlukom Predsedništva SKJ o delovanju SK u vezi sa odlaskom i privremenim radom naših radnika u inostranstvu; K.2, Četvrta sednica Opunomoćstvo, 24 January 1972, p. 12/6.

19 Baković, "Tending the 'Oasis of Socialism,'" 674–90.

20 AJ 507, K.2, Izveštaj opunomoćstvo FSKJ koji su u vremenu od 15. do 28. aprila 1972. godine obišli Švedsku, SR nemačku, Zapadni Berlin, Francusku, Švajcarsku i Holandiju… Belgrade, 18 May 1972, 39; Informacija sa sastanka u Izvršnom birou o problemima naših radnika na privremenom radu u inostranstvu i zadacima SK, 29 May 1972, 3–4.

21 AJ 507, K.2, Teze u samoorganizovanju.

22 Baković, "Socialist 'Oasis,'" 33–4.

23 Ana Margheritis, "Transnational Associational Life and Political Mobilization of Ecuadorians and Argentines in Spain and Italy: What Role for Sending State Policies?," *Diaspora: A Journal of Transnational Studies* 19, no. 2 (2017): 254. See also David Fitzgerald, *A Nation of Emigrants: How Mexico Manages Its Migration* (Berkeley: University of California Press, 2008); Mohammad Morad and Francesco Della Puppa, "Bangladeshi Migrant Associations in Italy: Transnational Engagement, Community Formation and Regional Unity," *Ethnic and Racial Studies* 42, no. 10 (2018): 1–20; Ernest Pineteh, "Memories of Home and Exile: Narratives of Cameroonian Asylum Seekers in Johannesburg," *Journal of Intercultural Studies* 26, no. 4 (2005): 379–99; João Sardinha, *Immigrant Associations, Integration and Identity: Angolan, Brazilian and Eastern European Communities in Portugal* (Amsterdam: Amsterdam University Press, 2009); Zeynep Sezgin, "Turkish Migrants' Organizations in Germany and Their Role in the Flow of Remittances to Turkey," *Journal of International Migration and Integration* 12, no. 3 (2011): 231, https://doi.org/10.1007/s12134-010-0157-1; Sezgin, "Turkish Migrants' Organizations: Promoting Tolerance toward the Diversity of Turkish Migrants in Germany," *International Journal of Sociology* 38, no. 2 (2008): 78, https://doi.org/10.2753/IJS0020-7659380206; Dirk Halm and Zeynep Sezgin, *Migration and Organized Civil Society*, Routledge/ECPR Studies in European Political Science (London: Routledge, 2013).

24 Charles Tilly and Lesley J. Wood, *Social Movements 1768–2012* (London: Routledge, 2015).

25 Kristen Ghodsee, "Pressuring the Politburo: The Committee of the Bulgarian Women's Movement and State Socialist Feminism," *Slavic Review* 73, no. 3 (2014): 538–62, https://doi.org/10.5612/slavicreview.73.3.538; Mary Fulbrook, *Anatomy of a Dictatorship: Inside the GDR, 1949–89* (Oxford: Oxford University Press, 1995); Igor Duda, *Danas kada postajem pionir. Djetinjstvo i ideologija jugoslavenskoga socijalizma* (Zagreb; Pula: Srednja Europa; Sveučilište Jurja Dobrile, 2015); Ildiko Erdei, "'The Happy Child' as an Icon of Socialist Transformation: Yugoslavia's Pioneer Organization," in *Ideologies and National Identities: The Case of Twentieth-Century Southeastern Europe*, ed. John R. Lampe and Mark Mazower (Budapest: Central European University Press, 2004).

26 Christian Gürtler, *Vereine und Nationale Bewegung in Breslau 1830–1871* (Frankfurt am Main: Lang, 2003); Jürgen Kocka, *Civil Society and Dictatorship in Modern German History* (Hanover, NH: University Press of New England, 2010); Robert D. Putnam, Robert Leonardi, and Raffaella Y.

Nanetti, *Making Democracy Work: Civic Traditions in Modern Italy* (Princeton, NJ: Princeton University Press, 1994).

27 Amy Milne-Smith, "A Flight to Domesticity? Making a Home in the Gentlemen's Clubs of London, 1880–1914," *Journal of British Studies* 45, no. 4 (2006): 798.

28 Novosti iz Jugoslavije, no. 210, 19 December 1974, 15, cited in Baković, "Tending the 'Oasis of Socialism,'" 363.

29 Baković, "Song of Brotherhood, Dance of Unity," 354–75.

30 AJ 142, 487, Izveštaj o gostovanju ekipe programa "večeras zajedno" radio Beograda u Švedskoj. 10 December 1973.

31 Baković, "Song of Brotherhood, Dance of Unity."

32 AJ 142, 487, "Informacija," Belgrade, 8 October 1973; "Informacija o razgovorima o ustavnim promjenama sa jugoslovenskim građanima na privremenom radu u Švajcarskoj," 28 September 1973; "Izveštaj o boravku u Francuskoj od 25.IV do 1.V. 1974 god."; Kurtesh Saliu, "Informacija o boravku u Zap. Nemačkoj i razgovorima sa radnicima u vezi ustavnih promena u Jugoslaviji," 22 September 1973; Ivica Lovrić. "Zabelješka o boravku u Frankfurt od 27.VI do 3.VII 1973. Godine"; Ivica Lovrić, "U vezi boravka u Londonu od 12. do 15. oktobra – Izveštaj"; "Informacija. U vremenu od 30.IX do 7.10 1973."

33 AJ 142, 475, Zajednica kulturno-prosvetnih organizacija Jugoslavije. Kulturno prosvetne organizacije i klubovi naših radnika u inostranstvu, 6–7; AJ 142, 487, Sekretarijat za inostrane poslove. Uprava za radnike na radu u inostranstvu. "Jugoslavenski radnici na privremenom radu u Švajcarskoj," Belgrade, March 1973.

34 AJ. 142, 491, consulate general in Zurich to Savezna Konferencija SSRNJ, "Predmet: Izveštaj o reorganizaciji Jugoslovenskog kluba u Zurichu," 22 March 1973; "Izveštaj o radu Jugoslovenskog Kluba Zurich u 1972 god."

35 HDA 1409, 103, Savezni sekretarijat za inostrane poslove, Uprava za radnike na radu u inostranstvu, "Jugoslovenski radnici na priviremenom radu u Švajcarskoj. / Problematika zapošljavanja, rada i boravka u 1974," / Belgrade, Maja 1975, 18; AJ 142, 487, Sekretarijat za inostrane poslove, Uprava za radnike na radu u inostranstvu, "Jugoslavenski radnici na privremenom radu u Švajcarskoj," Belgrade, March 1973.

36 AJ. 1409, 103, SRH IVS Komisija za vanjske migracije, "Informacija o nekim formama društvenog okupljanja i samoorganiziranja naših radnika u inozemstvu i problemima u vezi s tim," Zagreb, December 1975; AJ 142, 491, "Izveštaj o jednogodišnjem sprovođenju zaključaka SKJ, SFRJ i SKSSRNJ o politici zapošljavanja i položaju naših građana na privremenom radu u inostranstvu"; HDA 1409, 103, Savjet za međunarodne odnose i suradnju, Odbor za iseljeništvo i probleme naših radnika privremeno zaposlenih u inozemstvu, Ivan Iveković, "Informacija

o nekim problemima organiziranja radnika iz SR Hrvatske na teritoriju Švedske – prijedlozi i sugestije," Zagreb, 11 April 1975.

37 AJ 142, 491, "Izveštaj sa skupštine kluba u Štutgartu," Belgrade, 22 May 1973.

38 AJ 142, 491, "Izveštaj sa skupštine kluba u Štutgartu," Belgrade, 22 May 1973; Informativni centar SFRJ Stuttgart, "Klubovi jugoslovena u pokrajini Baden-W," 31 March 1973; Informativni centar SFRJ Stuttgart to SK SSRNJ, addressed to Franc Šebjanić, "Spisak društvenih i nogometnih, odnosno sportskih društava u pokrajini B-W," 4 March 1973.

39 AJ 562, F-32, "Klub Jugoslovena E.V.," 27 June 1969; AJ 142, I-487, Ibrahim Šator, "Izveštaj sa puta u SR Njemačku /Minhen, Nirnberg, Štutgart/ na putu bio 19.-23. novembra o.g.," 7 December 1973.

40 AJ 142, 487, Ibrahim Šator, "Izveštaj sa puta u SR Njemačku /Minhen, Nirnberg, Štutgart/ na putu bio 19.-23. novembra o.g.," 7 December 1973; AJ 142, 491, "Sastanak proširenog upravnog odbora kluba jugoslavena e.v. u München, koji je održan dana 14.I.1973 a trajao je od 11 sati prije podne do 21.30 sati na veće"; Uroš Andreevski, "Izveštaj sa obilaska nekih naših institucija na području SR Nemačke, Austrije i Luksemburga," 7 December 1973; HDA 1615, Kutija 9, "Skupština zajednice klubova Bielefeld," 28 January 1979.

41 AJ 142, 487, Savezni sekretarijat za inostrane poslove, Uprava za radnike na radu u inostranstvu, "Jugoslovenski radnici na privremenom radu u Austriji," Belgrade, March 1973; "Informacija," Belgrade, 8 October 1973, 4; HDA 1409, 103, Savezni sekretarijat za inostrane poslove, Uprava za radnike na radu u inostranstvu. "Jugoslovenski radnici na priviremenom radu u Austriji. / Osvrt na problematiku zapošljavanja, rada i boravka naših radnika u Austriji u 1974. Godini," Belgrade, March 1975.

42 HDA 1409, 103, Savjet za međunarodne odnose i suradnju, Odbor za iseljeništvo i probleme naših radnika privremeno zaposlenih u inozemstvu, Ivan Iveković, "Informacija o nekim problemima organiziranja radnika iz SR Hrvatske na teritoriju Švedske – prijedlozi i sugestije," Zagreb, 11 April 1975.

43 HDA 1409, K100, Državni sekretarijat za inostrane poslove, Uprava za radnike na radu u inostranstvu, "Društveno okupljanje jugoslovenskih radnika u inostranstvu," June 1970.

44 HDA 1409, K102, "Izveštaj o poseti jugoslovenske medjurepubličke poslaničke delegacije radnicima iz Jugoslavije koji su privremeno zaposleni u Francuskoj," Belgrade, May 1972; AJ 142, 487, "Rezime izveštaja Tome Nikolovskog, presednika GSV Skoplja, koji je juna 1973. boravio u francuskom CGT, u vezi sa jugoslovenskim radnicima privremeno zaposlenim u Francuskoj"; "Izveštaj o diskusiji o ustavnim promenama među našim radnicima u Francuskoj"; "Izveštaj o boravku

u Francuskoj od 25.IV do 1.V. 1974 god."; Nedjo Borković, Boško Lukić, "Izveštaj o boravku u Francuskoj od 25.IV do 1.V. 1974 god."

45 AJ 142, 487, Savezni sekretarijat za inostrane poslove, Uprava za radnike na radu u inostranstvu, "Jugoslovenski radnici na privremenom radu u Holandiji," Belgrade, April 1973.

46 AJ 142, 487, Ivica Lovrić, "U vezi boravka u Londonu od 12. do 15. Oktobra – Izveštaj."

47 AJ 142, 487, "nezadovolnji radnici s područja grada Stockholma."

48 HDA 1615, Kutija 5, "Izvještaj o radu kluba "jedinstvo" Versmold"; AJ 142, 491, member of club in Vienna to SSRNJ.

49 AJ 507, K1, "Informacija sa sastanka u Izvršnom birou o problemima naših radnika na privremenom radu u inostranstvu i zadacima SK," 3.

50 AJ 142, 487, "Informacija o jugoslovenskim informativnim centrima u Zapadnoj Evropi"; Sekretarija SIV-a za informacije, "Zaključci i stavovi." See also Baković, "Socialist 'Oasis,'" 35–7.

51 AJ 142, A-278, Kulturno-informativni centar SFR Jugoslavije Štutgart, "Realizacija programa za period od 1. aprila do 30. Juna 1980," 12–17, 19–22; AJ 142, 487, Informativni centar SFRJ Štutgart, "Godišnji izveštaj o radu u 1972," 7.

52 AJ 142, A-278, Kulturno-informativni centar SFR Jugoslavije Štutgart, "Realizacija programa za period od 1. aprila do 30. Juna 1980," 17–19, 25–32.

53 AJ 142, A-278, Kulturno-informativni centar SFR Jugoslavije Štutgart, "Realizacija programa za period od 1. aprila do 30. Juna 1980," 1–8.

54 AJ 142, A-278, Kulturno-informativni centar SFR Jugoslavije Štutgart, "Realizacija programa za period od 1. aprila do 30. Juna 1980," 6–7.

55 AJ 142, A-278, Kulturno-informativni centar SFR Jugoslavije Štutgart, "Realizacija programa za period od 1. aprila do 30. Juna 1980," 9–12; KIC SFRJ Stuttgart, "Dan Mladosti – dokumentacija," July 1980.

56 AJ 142, A-278, KIC SFRJ Stuttgart, "Dan Mladosti – dokumentacija," July 1980. The "Borba" article is drawn from this collection.

7. Migrants Talk Back: Responses to Surveys

1 HDA 1046: Zvonimir Komarica, K.6, "Anketa o radu u inozemstvu."

2 HDA 1611, kutija 7, "Anketa 'Uvjeti povratka naših radnika s privremenog rada u inozemstvu,'" 2 (henceforth "Uvjeti povratka").

3 "Uvjeti povratka," 2–4.

4 See "Chapter 5: Speaking Bolshevik," in Stephen Kotkin, *Magnetic Mountain: Stalinism as a Civilization* (Berkeley: University of California Press, 1997), 198–237.

5 "Uvjeti povratka," 5.

6 These categories are approximations of the Yugoslav educational system – original terms are, in order, škole drugog stupnja radničkog tipa, srednjom "činovnikom," 8 razreda osnovne škole, 4 razreda osnovne škole, visoka i viša stručna sprema. "Uvjeti povratka," 9–10.

7 "Uvjeti povratka," tables 1, 2, 3, 6.

8 "Uvjeti povratka," 13–14.

9 HDA 1611, kutija 7, fragment of report on 1970 survey, 20.

10 HDA 1611, kutija 7, fragment of report on 1970 survey, 21.

11 HDA 1611, registrator 18, response from a thirty-eight-year-old man living in Linz, dated 29 October 1970.

12 HDA 1611, registrator 18, response from a man born in 1923 living in Sweden, dated 27 October 1970.

13 HDA 1611, registrator 18, letter from migrant in Triberg, dated 28 October 1970.

14 HDA 1611, registrator 16, response from thirty-two-year-old woman from Zagreb trained as typist.

15 HDA 1611, kutija 7, response from forty-seven-year-old man from Zagreb with high school certificate in construction trade.

16 HDA 1611, registrator 16, response from Pavle B. from Vaxjo, Sweden, 29 September 1970.

17 HDA 1611, registrator 18, anonymous response from thirty-two-year-old man who completed eight-year primary and industrial school, lathe-operator by trade.

18 HDA 1611, registrator 18, fifty-four-year-old male dentist previously employed in Novi Beograd.

19 HDA 1611, registrar 18, letter from "a group of Yugoslav workers in Germany."

20 HDA 1611, registrator 18, response from cabinetmaker previously employed in Travnik; response from Jove L., thirty-eight, from Ugljevik – Bosnia Herzegovina.

21 HDA, fond 1611, kutija 7, anonymous letter from twenty-three-year-old male in Germany.

22 Vladimir Bakarić, a moderately liberal Croatian communist; Puniša Račić, assassin of Stjepan Radić and other members of the Croatian Peasant Party in 1928, Alexandar Ranković, unitarist Communist of Serbian ethnicity.

23 Savka Dapčević-Kučar and Mika Tripalo, leaders in the Croatian Spring; Ljudevit Jonke, Croatian linguist.

24 HDA 1611, registrator 18, response signed "Ogorčeni." See also HDA, fond 1611, Kutija 7, response from twenty-three-year old male from Šibenik employed as elevator electrician in Germany.

25 HDA 1611, registrator 18, Response by twenty-eight-year-old male lathe operator, dated 28 October 1970.

26 HDA 1611, registrator 18, Response by twenty-six-year-old male from Šibenik, working as electrician in FRG.
27 HDA 1611, registrator 18, response by male born in 1923, living in Sweden, sent 27 October 1970.
28 HDA 1611, registrator 18, reponse from a man writing from Paris, dated 28 October 1970.
29 HDA 1611, kutija 7, response from twenty-three-year-old man from Vinkovci.
30 HDA 1611, registrator 15, response no. 369.
31 HDA 1611, registrator 18, response from a thirty-eight-year-old man with driver training from Orahovica, sent from Linz, dated 29 October 1970.
32 See, for example, HDA 1611, Registrator 16, anonymous response from thirty-year-old man; registrator 18, anonymous response from thirty-one-year-old male.
33 HDA 1611, Kutija 7, response from forty-year-old male in Germany.
34 HDA 1611, registrator 18, response from Juraj Lončarić.
35 HDA 1611, registrator 18, response 331.
36 For example, HDA, fond 1611, registrator 18, response from Juraj Lončarić; anonymous response from thirty-year-old male in Dormagen.
37 HDA 1611, registrator 16, anonymous response from male from Čirkićima working in France.
38 HDA 1611, registrator 16, response from Ljubomir Miličić.
39 HDA 1611, registrator 18, anonymous response from twenty-nine-year-old male.
40 HDA 1611, registrator 18, anonymous response from thirty-year-old male in Dormagen, 33.
41 HDA 1611, registrator 15, response no. 390.
42 HDA 1611, registrator 18, anonymous response from thirty-year-old male in Dormagen.
43 HDA 1611, registrator 18, anonymous response from thirty-eight-year-old male.
44 HDA 1611, registrator 16, response by Pavle B.
45 See, for example, HDA 1611, kutija 7, response from thirty-five-year-old male; registrator 18, response from Jove Lukić; response from forty-year-old peasant; registrator 15, responses no. 337, 371, 391, 398.
46 HDA 1611, registrator 18, response from Mario Turković.
47 HDA 1611, registrator 15, response no. 390.
48 HDA 1611, registrator 18, response by J. in Sweden, born 4 January 1929.
49 HDA 1611, registrator 15, response no. 354.
50 HDA 1611, registrator 18, anonymous response from forty-two-year-old male in Frankfurt.
51 See, for example, HDA 1611, registrator 15, response no. 331; registrator 16, response from thirty-two-year-old woman.

52 Nina Glick Schiller and Peggy Levitt, "Conceptualizing Simultaneity: A Transnational Social Field Perspective on Society," *International Migration Review* 38, no. 3 (2004): 1002–39; Morad and Della Puppa, "Bangladeshi Migrant Associations," 3.

8. Building a Transnational Education System for the Second Generation

1 AJ 142/2, I-471. DSIP Uprava za radnike na radu u inostranstvu, Saveznom savetz za obr. I kulturu, "Predmet: dopunsko školovanje dece jugoslovenskih gradjana zaposlenih u zemljama Zapadne Evrope," 16 February 1970.
2 AJ 142/2, I-471. DSIP Uprava za radnike na radu u inostranstvu, Saveznom savetz za obr. I kulturu, "Predmet: dopunsko školovanje dece jugoslovenskih gradjana zaposlenih u zemljama Zapadne Evrope," 16 February 1970.
3 AJ 142/2, I-471, Savezni savet za obrazovanje i kulturu, "Društveno-pedagoška osnova obrazovno-vaspitnog rada sa decom naših radnika privremeno zaposlenih u inostranstvu i predlozi za rešavanje problema njihovog školovanje," Belgrade, 5. May 1970, 3–6.
4 AJ 142/2, I-471, Savezni savet za obrazovanje i kulturu, "Društveno-pedagoška osnova ...," 7–10.
5 AJ 142/2, I-471, Savezni savet za obrazovanje i kulturu, "Društveno-pedagoška osnova ...," 11.
6 AJ 142/2, I-471, Savezni savet za obrazovanje i kulturu, "Društveno-pedagoška osnova ...," 12.
7 AJ 142/2, I-471, Savezni savet za obrazovanje i kulturu, "Društveno-pedagoška osnova ...," 11–12.
8 AJ SSRNJ I-471, DSIP, Uprava za radnike na radu u inostranstvu, "Dopunsko školovanje dece naših radnika na radu u inostranstvu. Predlozi za moguća rešenja." Belgrade, 3 June 1970, 2.
9 AJ SSRNJ I-471, DSIP, Uprava za radnike na radu u inostranstvu, "Dopunsko školovanje dece ..."
10 AJ 142, A-350, YUZAMS, "Predmet: Nacrt društvenog dogovora o vaspitanju i obrazovanju građana SFRJ na privremenom radu i boravku u inostranstvu," 20 March 1979.
11 AJ 142, A-345, Speech by Dobrosava Ilić, 29 June 1976. Included in materials from a meeting held in Novi Sad on the topic of supplementary education, to be discussed at meeting held on 31 July and 1 August 1976 at YUZAMS; Letter from YUZAMS, 19 July 1976.
12 AJ 142, I-486, Predlog društvenog dogovora o školovanju dece jugoslovenskih radnika privremeno zaposlenih u inostranstvu," November 1973.

13 AJ 142, A-350, YUZAMS, "Predmet: Nacrt društvenog dogovora o vaspitanju i obrazovanju građana SFRJ na privremenom radu i boravku u inostranstvu. Obrazloženje," 20 March 1979, 3.

14 AJ 142, A-345, Dobrosava Ilić, speech 29 June 1976, 2–3.

15 AJ 142, A-276, YUZAMS – odsek za školovanje jugoslovenske dece u inostranstvu, "Izveštaj rada u 1977. Godini"; AJ 142, SSRNJ I-486, "Informacija o nekim problemima obezbeđivanja nastave iz nacionalne grupe predmeta za decu jugoslovenskih građana privremeno zaposlenih u inostranstvu," 16–17 December 1973, 4.

16 AJ 142, A-276, Antun Mijatović, "Ambassada SFRJ u Švedskoj. Godišnji izveštaj za 1977. godinu o školovanju jugoslovenske dece u Švedskoj," 8.

17 AJ 142, A-350, "Vaspitno-obrazovni rad s jugoslovenskom decom u inostranstvu," 2.

18 AJ 142, A-345, Speech by Dobrosava Ilić, 29 June 1976, 7.

19 AJ 142, A-276, YUZAMS – odsek za školovanje jugoslovenske dece u inostranstvu, "Izveštaj rada u 1977. godini"; AJ 142, SSRNJ I-486, "Informacija o nekim problemima obezbeđivanja nastave iz nacionalne grupe predmeta za decu jugoslovenskih građana privremeno zaposlenih u inostranstvu," 16–17 December 1973, 5; AJ 142 SSRNJ A-275, YUZAMS, "Predmet: dopunsko školovanje jugoslovenske dece u Austriji," 15 March 1976.

20 Council of the European Communities, Council Directive 77/486/EEC. 25 July 1977. https://eur-lex.europa.eu/legal-content/EN/TXT/PDF/?uri=CELEX:31977L0486&from=EN. Accessed 11 December 2020.

21 AJ 142, A-350, YUZAMS, "Izveštaj o 6. sastanku mešovite jugo-nemačke komisije za školovanju jugoslovenske dece u SR Nemačkoj, koji je održan u Splitu od 6. do 8. juna 1979," 1. Concerning pressure on Belgium, see AJ 142, SSRNJ A-350, "Izveštaj o poseti Anuške Nakić i Abdulj Ramaja u Belgiji," 24 July 1978, 9.

22 AJ 142, A-353, "Izveštaj o vaspitno-obrazovnom radu na maternjem jeziku s decom jugoslovenskih građana na privremenom radu u Austriji u toku 1979. godine," 12; AJ 142 SSRNJ, A-350. YUZAMS. "Izveštaj o 4. sastanku Jugoslovenske-holandske radne grupe za školovanje jugoslovenske dece u Holandiji, održanom u Hagu 14. i 15. maja 1979." Belgrade, May 1979.

23 AJ 142, A-275, YUZAMS. "Predmet: dopunsko školovanje jugoslovenske dece u Švedskoj." Belgrade, 21–2.4.1976, 3.

24 AJ 142, A-275, YUZAMS. "Informacija ambasade SFRJ u Bernu," 7.

25 AJ 142, A-275, YUZAMS. "Informacija ambasade SFRJ u Bernu," 10–11.

26 AJ 142 SSRNJ, A-276, YUZAMS – odsek za školovanje jugoslovenske dece u inostranstvu. "Izveštaj rada u 1977. godini," 9–10.

27 AJ 142, A-350, "Vaspitno-obrazovni rad s jugoslovenskom decom u inostranstvu," 11.
28 AJ 142, A-345, Dobrosava Ilić, 29 June 1976, 5.
29 AJ 142, A-275, YUZAMS, "Predmet: 8 sastanak Jugoslovenskog-švedskog komiteta za školovanje jugoslovenske dece u Švedskoj," 10 May 1976, 3–4.
30 AJ 142, A-275, YUZAMS, "Izveštaj Hilde Bole sa puta u SR Nemačkoj," 19 January 1976, 12.
31 The data in table 3 come from the following sources: AJ 142 SSRNJ, I-486, "Informacija o nekim problemima obezbedjivanja nastave iz nacionalne grup predmeta za decu jugoslovenskih gradjana privremeno zaposlenih u inostranstvu," December 1973, 2; AJ 142 SSRNJ, A-275, Međurepubličko-pokrajinska komisija za dopunsko školovanje dece jugoslovenskih građana na privremenom radu u inostranstvu, "Savetovanje o dopunskoj nastavi," 2 June 1976, 2; AJ 142 SSRNJ, A-350, "Vaspitno-obrazovni rad s jugoslovenskom decom u inostranstvu," 1.
32 The data in table 4 are drawn from AJ 142 SSRNJ, A-350, "Vaspitno-obrazovni rad s jugoslovenskom decom u inostranstvu," 7.
33 AJ 142, A-275, YUZAMS, "Statističke podatke o učenicima i nastavnicima dopunske škole u Londonu"; AJ 142 SSRNJ, A-353, "Izveštaj o vaspitno-obrazovnom radu na maternjem jeziku s decom jugoslovenskih građana na privremenom radu u Austriji u toku 1979. godine."
34 AJ 142, A-350, YUZAMS, "Predmet: Nacrt društvenog dogovora o vaspitanju i obrazovanju građana SFRJ na privremenom radu i boravku u inostranstvu. Obrazloženje," 20 March 1979, 2.
35 AJ 142, A-276, Antun Mijatović, Ambassada SFRJ u Švedskoj. "Godišnji izveštaj za 1977. godinu o školovanju jugoslovenske dece u Švedskoj," 11.
36 AJ 142, A-276, YUZAMS, "Predmet: izveštaj Dr. Ljubice Prodanović o boravku u Švedskoj," 25 April 1978; AJ 142 SSRNJ, A-275, "Izvod iz godišnjeg izveštaja GK Cirih za 1975. godinu."
37 AJ 142, A-350, "Vaspitno-obrazovni rad s jugoslovenskom decom u inostranstvu," 10–11.
38 AJ 142, A-276, YUZAMS – odsek za školovanje jugoslovenske dece u inostranstvu, "Izveštaj rada u 1977. Godini"; "Godišnji izveštaj o dopunskoj nastavi na maternjem jeziku za decu naših gradjana privremeno zaposlenih u Švajcarskoj za 1977. Godinu"; YUZAMS – odsek za školovanje jugoslovenske dece u inostranstvu, "Izveštaj rada u 1977. godini"; "Školovanje jugoslovenske dece u Bavarskoj, godišnji izveštaj za 1977"; AJ 142 SSRNJ, A-353, "Izveštaj o obrazovanju naših građana u Austriji u 1979. godini"; Ivanović, *Geburtstag pišeš normalno*, 207.
39 AJ 142, A-350, "Informacija o načinu upućivaja udžbenika za potrebe dopunske nastave"; "Vaspitno-obrazovni rad s jugoslovenskom decom u inostranstvu."

40 AJ 142, A-275, YUZAMS, "Informacija o trenutnoj situaciji u oblasti školovanja dece jugoslovenskih građana na privremenon radu u SR Nemačkoj," March 1976.

41 AJ 142, A-350, YUZAMS, "Izveštaj o 6. sastanku mešovite jugo-nemačke komisije za školovanju jugoslovenske dece u SR Nemačkoj, koji je održan u Splitu od 6. do 8. juna 1979," 13. For a comparison of migrant education systems in Bavaria and Berlin, see Ray C. Rist, "On the Education of Guest-Worker Children in Germany: A Comparative Study of Policies and Programs in Bavaria and Berlin," *School Review* 87, no. 3 (1979): 242–68.

42 AJ 142, A-350, SR Nemačka. Generalni konzulat SFRJ, Minhen, "Godišnji izveštaj o dopunskoj nastavi na maternjem jeziku za decu naših građana privremeno zaposlenih u Bavarskoj za 1978. Godinu," January 1979.

43 AJ 142, A-276, Antun Mijatović, Ambassada SFRJ u Švedskoj, "Godišnji izveštaj za 1977. godinu o školovanju jugoslovenske dece u Švedskoj," 9.

44 AJ 142, A-275, YUZAMS, "Predmet: 8 sastanak Jugoslovenskog-švedskog komiteta za školovanje jugoslovenske dece u Švedskoj," 10 May 1976.

45 AJ 142, A-276, YUZAMS – odsek za školovanje jugoslovenske dece u inostranstvu, "Izveštaj rada u 1977. godini."

46 AJ 142, A-275, YUZAMS, "Predmet: 8 sastanak Jugoslovenskog-švedskog komiteta za školovanje jugoslovenske dece u Švedskoj," 10 May 1976.

47 AJ 142, A-276, Antun Mijatović, Ambassada SFRJ u Švedskoj. "Godišnji izveštaj za 1977. godinu o školovanju jugoslovenske dece u Švedskoj," 12, 19–20.

48 AJ 142, A-350, "Informacija o saradnji sa Visokom školom za nastavnike u Malmeu"; "Izveštaj o boravku studenata Pedagoške akademije iz Malmea u SAP Vojvodini."

49 AJ 142, A-353, "Izveštaj o vaspitno-obrazovnom radu na maternjem jeziku s decom jugoslovenskih građana na privremenom radu u Austriji u toku 1979. godine," 3–4, 11–12.

50 AJ 142, A-353, "Izveštaj o vaspitno-obrazovnom radu na maternjem jeziku s decom jugoslovenskih građana na privremenom radu u Austriji u toku 1979. godine," 12–13.

51 AJ 142, A-275, YUZAMS, "Predmet: dopunsko školovanje jugoslovenske dece u Austriji," 15.3.1976.

52 AJ 142, A-353, "Izveštaj o vaspitno-obrazovnom radu na maternjem jeziku s decom jugoslovenskih građana na privremenom radu u Austriji u toku 1979. godine," 11, 24.

53 AJ 142, A-275, YUZAMS, "Izvod iz godišnjeg izveštaja GK Cirih za 1975. Godinu"; YUZAMS, "Informacija ambasade SFRJ u Bernu (stanje 15.04.1976)."

54 AJ 142, A-345, Speech by Dobrosava Ilić, 29 June 1976.

55 AJ 142, A-276, "Godišnji izveštaj o dopunskoj nastavi na maternjem jeziku za decu naših gradjana privremeno zaposlenih u Švajcarskoj za 1977. godinu" (prepared by Služba za školstvo.)

56 AJ 142, A-350, YUZAMS, "Izveštaj o razgovorima, koji su vođeni od 17. do 18. aprila 1979. u Bernu između jugoslovenske i švajcarske delegacije o školovanju u Švajcarskoj." Belgrade, May 1979.

57 AJ 142, A-350, "Izveštaj o poseti Anuške Nakić i Abdulj Ramaja u Belgiji," 24 July 1978, 5–14.

58 AJ 142, A-350, YUZAMS, "Predmet: Izveštaj s nastavnicima dopunske nastave u Strazburu i Parizu."

59 AJ 142, A-350, "Izveštaj o poseti Anuške Nakić i Abdulj Ramaja u Belgiji," 24 July 1978, 5–14, 1–4.

60 AJ 142, A-276, YUZAMS – odsek za školovanje jugoslovenske dece u inostranstvu, "Izveštaj rada u 1977. godini," 13–16.

61 AJ 142, A-350, YUZAMS, "Predmet: Nacrt društvenog dogovora o vaspitanju i obrazovanju građana SFRJ na privremenom radu i boravku u inostranstvu. Obrazloženje," 20 March 1979, 1.

62 AJ 142, A-345, Speech by Dobrosava Ilića, 29 June 1976, 1–2.

63 AJ 142, A-276, YUZAMS – odsek za školovanje jugoslovenske dece u inostranstvu, "Izveštaj rada u 1977. godini," 3. Exchange rate is based on Biljana Stojanović, "Exchange Rate Regimes of the Dinar 1945–1990: An Assessment of Appropriateness and Efficiency," in *The Experience of Exchange Rate Regimes in South-Eastern Europe in a Historical and Comparative Perspective,* ed. Peter Mooslechner (Vienna: Österreichische Nationalbank, 2007), 220.

64 Josip Anić and Andrina Pavlinić-Wolf, "Socijalni i individualni problemi djece migranata," *Migracijske i etničke teme* 2, no. 1 (1986): 57. The exchange rate used in this article is quite different from the previous one, but corresponds to a period of rampant inflation.

9. They Felt the Breath of the Homeland

1 AJ 142, A-275, YUZAMS, "Informacija ambasade SFRJ u Bernu," 5–7.

2 AJ 142, A-275, YUZAMS, "Informacija ambasade SFRJ u Bernu," 5.

3 AJ 142, A-275, YUZAMS, "Informacija ambasade SFRJ u Bernu," 7.

4 AJ 142, A-276, YUZAMS, "Predmet: informacija o jezičnoj praksi u Jugoslaviji," Belgrade, 21 September 1978.

5 AJ 142, A-275, YUZAMS, "Informacija ambasade SFRJ u Bernu," 7.

6 AJ 142, A-276, YUZAMS, "Predmet: informacija o jezičnoj praksi u Jugoslaviji," Belgrade, 21 September 1978.

7 AJ 142, A-275, YUZAMS, "Izveštaj o seminaru za jugoslovenske nastavnike održanom u Bernu 8. i 9.05.1976. god."

8 AJ 142, A-273, Savezni Sekretarijat za inostrane poslove, "Naši radnici na radu u Švedskoj. Problematika zapošljavanja, rada i boravka u 1974," April 1975, 22–3.

9 AJ 142, A-350, "Izveštaj o poseti Anuške Nakić i Abdulj Ramaja u Belgiji," 24 July 1978, 17.

10 AJ 142, A-275, YUZAMS. "Informacija ambasade SFRJ u Bernu," 7.

11 AJ 142, I-471, DSIP, Uprava za radnike na radu u inostranstvu, "Dopunsko školovanje dece naših radnika na radu u inostranstvu, Predlozi za moguća rešenja." Belgrade, 3 June 1970, 4–5.

12 AJ 142, A-276, YUZAMS, "Predmet: informacija o jezičnoj praksi u Jugoslaviji," Belgrade, 21 September 1978.

13 AJ 142 SSRNJ, A-350, "Vaspitno-obrazovni rad s jugoslovenskom decom u inostranstvu," 8–10.

14 AJ 142, A-275, Medjurepubličko-pokrajinska komisija za dopunsko školovanje dece jugoslovenskih građana u inostranstvu, "V. Seminar za jugoslovenske nastavnike u inostranstvu." Belgrade, 2.-6 August 1976; AJ 142, A-276, YUZAMS, "Predmet: 7. seminar za jugoslovenske nastavnike."

15 AJ 142, A-350, Vaspitno-obrazovni rad s jugoslovenskom decom u inostranstvu, 6.

16 AJ 142, A-275, YUZAMS, "Predmet: Seminar za nastavnike u inostranstvu," 25 June 1976, 5.

17 AJ 142, A-275, YUZAMS, "Predmet: Seminar za nastavnike u inostranstvu," 25 June 1976, 3.

18 AJ 142, A-350, YUZAMS. "Predmet: Izveštaj s nastavnicima dopunske nastave u Strazburu i Parizu," 6.

19 AJ 142, A-275, YUZAMS, "Predmet: Seminar za nastavnike u inostranstvu," 25 June 1976, 3, 7.

20 AJ 142, A-350, SR Nemačka, Generalni konzulat SFRJ, Minhen, "Godišnji izveštaj o dopunskoj nastavi …" January 1979, 16–17.

21 AJ 142, A-350, SR Nemačka, Generalni konzulat SFRJ, Minhen. "Godišnji izveštaj o dopunskoj nastavi …" January 1979, 16–17.

22 AJ 142, A-273, "Naši radnici na radu u Švedskoj. Problematika zapošljavanja, rada i boravka …," April 1975.

23 AJ 142, A-350, SR Nemačka, Generalni konzulat SFRJ, Minhen, "Godišnji izveštaj o dopunskoj nastavi …," January 1979, 2.

24 AJ 142, A-353, "Izveštaj o vaspitno-obrazovnom radu na maternjem jeziku s decom jugoslovenskih građana na privremenom radu u Austriji u toku 1979. godine," 21.

25 HDA 1615, Letter to "Grigor Vitez" school in Žabno dated 30 September 1978; letter from Pionirski Kutić "Grigor Vitez" to Savez pionira Crne Gore, dated 24 April 1979; letter to RTZ requesting that a schoolgirl be given the opportunity to meet Tito.

26 HDA 1615, Undated letter from Pionirski kutić "Grigor Vitez" "Općinskoj konfereciji soc. Saveza rad. Naroda Požarevac."
27 AJ 142, A-350, "Izveštaj o poseti Anuške Nakić i Abdulj Ramaja u Belgiji," 24 July 1978, 17.
28 AJ 142, A-350, SR Nemačka, Generalni konzulat SFRJ, Minhen. "Godišnji izveštaj o dopunskoj nastavi ..." January 1979, 2.
29 AJ 142, A-350, "Izveštaj o poseti Anuške Nakić i Abdulj Ramaja u Belgiji," 24 July 1978, 20–1.
30 AJ 142, A-350, "Izveštaj o poseti Anuške Nakić i Abdulj Ramaja u Belgiji," 24 July 1978, 20–1.
31 Ivanović, *Geburtstag pišeš normalno*, 216.
32 Cohen, "State, Migrants, and the Negotiation of Second-Generation Citizenship in the Israeli Diaspora," 133–58.
33 AJ 142, A-353, "Izveštaj o vaspitno-obrazovnom radu na maternjem jeziku s decom jugoslovenskih građana na privremenom radu u Austriji u toku 1979. godine," 24; AJ 142, A-276, YUZAMS, "Godišnji izveštaj za 1977. godinu o školovanju jugoslovenske dece u Austriji." 1.3.1978.
34 AJ 142, A-350, "Vaspitno-obrazovni rad s jugoslovenskom decom u inostranstvu," 3.
35 AJ 142, A-276, "Godišnji izveštaj za 1977. godinu o školovanju jugoslovenske dece u Švedskoj."
36 AJ 142, A-350, Generalkonzulat der SFRJ, "Izložba 'Pioniri u Narodnooslobodilačkoj borbi i socijalističkoj domovini' na području GK SFRJ u Frankfurtu/M – 24.IV.–23.V 1979," 27 June 1979.
37 AJ 142, A-350, SR Nemačka, Generalni konzulat SFRJ, Minhen. "Godišnji izveštaj o dopunskoj nastavi ...," January 1979, 3.
38 AJ 142, A-350, "Boravak u Jugoslaviji 700 naših učenika dopunske nastave sa područja Frankfurta," 5.
39 AJ 142, A-350, "Boravak u Jugoslaviji 700 naših učenika dopunske nastave sa područja Frankfurta," 3.
40 AJ 142, A-350, "Boravak u Jugoslaviji 700 naših učenika dopunske nastave sa područja Frankfurta."
41 AJ 142, A-350, "Boravak u Jugoslaviji 700 naših učenika dopunske nastave sa područja Frankfurta, 5."
42 AJ 142, A-275, YUZAMS, "Izveštaj o seminaru za jugoslovenske nastavnike održanom u Bernu 8. i 9.05.1976. god," 3.
43 AJ 142, A-275, YUZAMS – odsek za školovanje jugoslovenske dece u inostranstvu, "Izveštaj rada u 1977. godini," 4, 8; AJ 142 SSRNJ, A-276, "Godišnji izveštaj o dopunskoj nastavi na maternjem jeziku za decu naših gradjana privremeno zaposlenih u Švajcarskoj za 1977. godinu," 16.
44 AJ 142, A-350, "Vaspitno-obrazovni rad s jugoslovenskom decom u inostranstvu," 5.

45 *Moja domovina SFRJ 1*: 20.
46 *Moja domovina SFRJ 3*: 12.
47 *Moja domovina SFRJ 2*: 10–11.
48 *Moja domovina SFRJ 2*: 134.
49 *Moja domovina SFRJ 2*: 60.
50 *Moja Domovina SFRJ 2*: 21–2.
51 *Moja Domovina SFRJ 1*: 60.
52 *Moja Domovina SFRJ 1*: 7.
53 Josip Broz Tito, "Moje djetinstvo," *Moja Domovina SFRJ 1*: 66; France Bevk, "Titovi Drugovi," *Moja Domovina SFRJ 2*: 45–6.
54 Slobodan Lazić, *Moja Domovina SFRJ 1*: 65.
55 Jovan Popović, *Moja Domovina SFRJ*, vol. 2, "Pinki je video Tita," 49–50.
56 *Moja Domovina SFRJ 2*: 48.
57 Josip Vidmar, "Lik maršala Tita," *Moja Domovina SFRJ 3*: 37.
58 Josip Vidmar, "Lik maršala Tita," *Moja Domovina SFRJ 3*: 38.
59 *Moja Domovina SFRJ 3*: 41.
60 *Moja Domovina SFRJ 2*: 41.
61 *Moja Domovina SFRJ 3*: 56.
62 "Borba naših naroda i narodnosti za slobodu i nezavisnost," *Moja Domovina SFRJ 3*: 46.
63 *Moja Domovina SFRJ 3*: 146, 157.
64 Tone Seliškar, "Na lokomotivi," *Moja Domovina SFRJ 1*: 116.
65 "Pokret nesvrstavanje," *Moja Domovina SFRJ 3*: 73.
66 "Homeland," *Moja Domovina SFRJ 1*: 179.
67 *Moja Domovina SFRJ 1*: 16, 2: 56, 149, 3: 175.
68 *Moja Domovina SFRJ 1*: 43, 3: 84–5.
69 *Moja Domovina SFRJ 3*: 10, 14.
70 *Moja Domovina SFRJ 1*: 35, 45–6, 79–81.
71 Anić and Pavlinić-Wolf, "Socijalni i Individualni Problemi Djece Migranata," 43–59.
72 Zlata Jukić, "Pokušaj ispitivanja učenika u Jugoslavenskoj dopunskoj nastavi o poznavanju elemenata kulture naroda koji govore srpskohrvatskim, odnosno hrvatskosrpskim jezikom," *Migracijske i etničke teme* 2, no. 2 (1986): 15–35.
73 Melita Švob, Zvonimir Kotarac, and Zdenko Ivezić, "Ponašanje i odnos djece prema dopunskoj školi u Berlinu," *Migracijske i etničke teme* 5, no. 1 (1989): 21–6.
74 Branka Vegar, "Jugoslavenska djeca u Bečkim školama," *Migracijske i etničke teme* 2, no. 1 (1986): 75–9.
75 Jadranka Čačić, "Francuzi, Jugoslaveni ili nešto treće?," *Migracijske i etničke teme* 4, no. 3 (1988): 249–64.
76 Mirjana Morokvasić and Dejan Kuzmanović, "Les jeunes issus de l'immigration yougoslave en France," in *L'identité culturelle des jeunes*

migrants yougoslaves en France: Recueil de textes, ed. Dušan Davidović and Dejan Kuzmanović, 133–56 (Paris: Agence pour le développement des relations interculturelles, Savez socijalistiecke omladine Jugoslavije, 1986).
77 Morokvasić and Kuzmanović, "Les jeunes issus de l'immigration yougoslave en France," 141.

10. Conclusion

1 Eugen Weber, *Peasants into Frenchmen: The Modernization of Rural France, 1870–1914* (Chicago: Stanford University Press, 1976).
2 Anderson, *Imagined Communities*.
3 Bernard, *Deutsch Marks in the Head*, 108–24.
4 Ragazzi, "Governing Diasporas in International Relations," 82–110.

Bibliography

Periodicals

Imotska krajina
Novosti iz jugoslavije
Politika ekspress
Radio TV revija
Studio
Vjesnik
Vjesnik u srijedu

Literature

Akgündüz, Ahmet. *Labour Migration from Turkey to Western Europe, 1960–1974*. Research in Migration and Ethnic Relations Series. Burlington, VT: Ashgate, 2008.

Anderson, Benedict R. *Imagined Communities: Reflections on the Origin and Spread of Nationalism*. New York: Verso, 1991.

Anić, Josip, and Andrina Pavlinić-Wolf. "Socijalni i Individualni problemi djece migranata." *Migracijske i etničke teme* 2, no. 1 (1986): 43–59.

Baković, Nikola. "Socialist 'Oasis' in a Capitalist 'Desert': Yugoslav State Propaganda for Economic Emigrants in Germany." PhD thesis, Central European University, 2012.

– "Song of Brotherhood, Dance of Unity: Cultural-Entertainment Activities for Yugoslav Economic Emigrants in the West in the 1960s and 1970s." *Journal of Contemporary History* 50, no. 2 (2015): 354–75.

– "Tending the 'Oasis of Socialism': Transnational Political Mobilization of Yugoslav Economic Emigrants in the FR Germany in the Late 1960s and 1970s." *Nationalities Papers* 42, no. 4 (2014): 674–90.

Baskin, Mark Allan. "Political Innovation and Policy Implementation in Yugoslavia: The Case of Worker Migration Abroad." PhD diss., University of Michigan, 1986. ProQuest (AAT 8621251).

Batović, Ante. *The Croatian Spring: Nationalism, Repression and Foreign Policy under Tito.* London: IB Tauris, 2017.

Baučić, Ivo. *The Effects of Emigration from Yugoslavia and the Problems of Returning Emigrant Workers.* The Hague: Nijhoff, 1972.

– *Radnici u inozemstvu prema popisu stanovništva Jugoslavije 1971.* Zagreb. Institut za geografiju Sveučilišta u Zagrebu, 1973.

– *Social Aspects of External Migration of Workers and the Yugoslav Experience in the Social Protection of Migrants.* Zagreb: Centre for Migration Studies, 1975.

– "Some Economic Consequences of Yugoslav External Migrations." *Collection IDERIC* 6, no. 1 (1976): 87–104.

– "Stanje vanjskih migracija iz jugoslavije krajem sedamdesetih godina." *Rasprave o migracijama* 57 (1979).

Berger, John. *A Seventh Man: Migrant Workers in Europe.* New York: Viking, 1975.

Bernard, Sara. *Deutsch Marks in the Head, Shovel in the Hands and Yugoslavia in the Heart: The Gastarbeiter Return to Yugoslavia (1965–1991).* Wiesbaden: Harrassowitz Verlag, 2019.

– "Developing the Yugoslav Gastarbeiter Reintegration Policy: Political and Economic Aspects (1969–1974)." Working paper, South East European Studies 5, Centre for Southeast European Studies, University of Graz (2012).

Bieber, Florian. "The Construction of National Identity and Its Challenges in Post-Yugoslav Censuses." *Social Science Quarterly* 96, no. 3 (2015): 873–903.

Boccagni, Paolo, and Loretta Baldassar. "Emotions on the Move: Mapping the Emergent Field of Emotion and Migration." *Emotion, Space and Society* 16 (2015): 73–80.

Bonfiglioli, Chiara. "Women's Political and Social Activism in the Early Cold War Era: The Case of Yugoslavia." *Aspasia* 8, no. 1 (2014): 1–25.

Botev, Nikolai. "Where East Meets West: Ethnic Intermarriage in the Former Yugoslavia, 1962 to 1989." *American Sociological Review* 59, no. 3 (1994): 461–80.

Brubaker, Rogers. "The 'Diaspora' Diaspora." *Ethnic and Racial Studies* 28, no. 1 (2005): 1–19.

Brunnbauer, Ulf. *Globalizing Southeastern Europe: Emigrants, America, and the State since the Late Nineteenth Century.* Lanham, MD: Lexington Books, 2016.

– ed. *Transnational Societies, Transterritorial Politics: Migration in the (Post) Yugoslav Region, 19th–21st Century.* Munich: Oldenbourg, 2009.

Čačić, Jadranka. "Francuzi, Jugoslaveni ili nešto treće?" *Migracijske i Etničke Teme* 4, no. 3 (1988): 249–64.

Castles, Stephen, Heather Booth, and Tina Wallace. *Here for Good: Western Europe's New Ethnic Minorities.* London: Pluto, 1984.

Chin, Rita. *The Guest Worker Question in Postwar Germany.* Cambridge: Cambridge University Press, 2007.

Christou, Anastasia. "Narrating Lives in (e) Motion: Embodiment, Belongingness and Displacement in Diasporic Spaces of Home and Return." *Emotion, Space and Society* 4, no. 4 (2011): 249–57.

Classen, Christoph. "Between Political Coercion and Popular Expectations: Contemporary History in the Radio of the Early German Democratic Republic." *Popular Historiographies in the 19th and 20th Century*, edited by Sylvia Paletschek, 89–102. Oxford: Berghahn, 2011.

Cohen, Nir. "Diaspora Strategies: Actors, Members, and Spaces." *Geography Compass* 11, no. 3 (2017): 1–13.

– "State, Migrants, and the Negotiation of Second-Generation Citizenship in the Israeli Diaspora." *Diaspora: A Journal of Transnational Studies* 16, no. 2 (2007): 133–58.

Cornis-Pope, Marcel, and John Neubauer, eds. *History of the Literary Cultures of East-Central Europe: Junctures and Disjunctures in the 19th and 20th Centuries*. Vol. 3, *The Making and Re-Making of Literary Institutions*. Amsterdam: John Benjamins Publishing, 2007.

Cummings, Richard H. *Cold War Radio: The Dangerous History of American Broadcasting in Europe, 1950–1989*. Jefferson, IA: McFarland, 2009.

Daniel, Ondřej. "Gastarbajteri: Rethinking Yugoslav Economic Migrations towards the European North-West through Transnationalism and Popular Culture." In *Imagining Frontiers, Contesting Identities*, edited by Steven G. Ellis and Luďa Klusáková, 277–302. Pisa: Ed. Plus, Pisa University Press, 2007.

Dantzer, Alexandra. "Architects of Happiness: Notes on the Mindwork of Migration." *Issues in Ethnology Anthropology* 12, no. 1 (2017): 175–93.

DeCuir, Greg, Jr. "Black Wave Polemics: Rhetoric as Aesthetic." *Studies in Eastern European Cinema* 1, no. 1 (2010): 85–96.

– "'Once You Go Black …': A Counter-Response to Nebojša Jovanović's 'Breaking the Wave." *Studies in Eastern European Cinema* 3, no. 1 (2012): 81–7.

Délano, Alexandra. "Immigrant Integration vs. Transnational Ties?: The Role of the Sending State." *Social Research: An International Quarterly* 77, no. 1 (2010): 237–68.

Délano, Alexandra, and Alan Gamlen. "Comparing and Theorizing State–Diaspora Relations." *Political Geography* 41 (2014): 43–53.

Dickinson, Jen. "Articulating an Indian Diaspora in South Africa: The Consulate General of India, Diaspora Associations and Practices of Collaboration." *Geoforum* 61 (2015): 79–89.

– "The Political Geographies of Diaspora Strategies: Rethinking the 'Sending State.'" *Geography Compass* 11, no. 2 (2017): 1–12.

Dobrivojević, Ivana. "U Potrazi za blagostanjem. Odlazak Jugoslovenskih državaljana u zemlje zapadne Evrope 1960–1977." *Istorija 20 veka* 2 (2007): 89–100.

Dorman, Laslo. "Filizof iz ravnice." *Radio TV revija*, 2 April 1982.

Dragišić, Petar. "Jugoslovenski ekonomski migranti u Austriji od početka 60-Ih godina do raspada Jugoslavije." *Tokovi istorije* 1–2 (2009): 55–64.

"Klubovi jugoslovenskih radnika u zapadnoj Evropi sedamdesetih godina." *Tokovi istorije* 1 (2010): 128–38.

Duda, Igor. *Danas kada postajem pionir. Djetinjstvo i ideologija jugoslavenskoga socijalizma*. Zagreb; Pula: Srednja Europa; Sveučilište Jurja Dobrile, 2015.

Erdei, Ildiko. "'The Happy Child' as an Icon of Socialist Transformation: Yugoslavia's Pioneer Organization." In *Ideologies and National Identities: The Case of Twentieth-Century Southeastern Europe*, edited by John R. Lampe and Mark Mazower. Budapest: Central European University Press, 2004.

Fanon, Franz. "This Is the Voice of Algeria." In *The Sound Studies Reader*, edited by Jonathan Sterne, 329–33. Milton Park, UK: Routledge, 2012.

Fitzgerald, David. *A Nation of Emigrants: How Mexico Manages Its Migration*. Berkeley: University of California Press, 2009.

Freeman, Gary P. *Immigrant Labor and Racial Conflict in Industrial Societies: The French and British Experience, 1945–1975*. Princeton, NJ: Princeton University Press, 1979.

Fulbrook, Mary. *Anatomy of a Dictatorship: Inside the GDR, 1949–89*. Oxford: Oxford University Press, 1995.

Gabaccia, Donna R. *Italy's Many Diasporas: Elites, Exiles and Workers of the World*. Seattle: University of Washington Press, 2000.

Gajer, D. "Divni Dolasci." *Politika Ekspress*, 4 January 1978.

Gamlen, Alan. "The Emigration State and the Modern Geopolitical Imagination." *Political Geography* 27, no. 8 (2008): 840–56.

Ghodsee, Kristen. "Pressuring the Politburo: The Committee of the Bulgarian Women's Movement and State Socialist Feminism." *Slavic Review* 73, no. 3 (2014): 538–62. https://doi.org/10.5612/slavicreview.73.3.538.

Goodlett, David Eugene. *Yugoslav Worker Emigration, 1963–1973: Government Policy and Press Coverage*. Lewiston, NY: E. Mellen, 2007.

Goulding, Daniel J. *Liberated Cinema: The Yugoslav Experience, 1945–2001*. Bloomington: Indiana University Press, 2002.

Gürtler, Christian. *Vereine und Nationale Bewegung in Breslau 1830–1871*. Frankfurt am Main: Lang, 2003.

Haberl, Othmar Nikola. *Die Abwanderung Von Arbeitskräften Aus Jugoslawien: Zur Problematik Ihrer Auslandsbeschäftigung u. Rückführung*. 1. Aufl. ed. Vol. 13. Munich: Oldenbourg, 1978.

Halm, Dirk, and Zeynep Sezgin. *Migration and Organized Civil Society*. Routledge/ECPR Studies in European Political Science. London: Routledge, 2013.

Haug, Hilde Katrine. *Creating a Socialist Yugoslavia: Tito, Communist Leadership and the National Question*. London: IB Tauris, 2012.

Hilmes, Michelle. "Radio and the Imagined Community." In *The Sound Studies Reader*, edited by Jonathan Sterne, 351–4. Milton Park, UK: Routledge, 2012.

Hirsch, Francine. *Empire of Nations: Ethnographic Knowledge and the Making of the Soviet Union*. Ithaca, NY: Cornell University Press, 2005.

Ho, Elaine Lynn-Ee. "'Claiming' the Diaspora." *Progress in Human Geography* 35, no. 6 (2011): 757–72. https://doi.org/10.1177/0309132511401463.

Ho, Elaine Lynn-Ee, Maureen Hickey, and Brenda S.A. Yeoh. "Special Issue Introduction: New Research Directions and Critical Perspectives on Diaspora Strategies." *Geoforum* 59 (2015): 153–8.

Irvine, Jill. "The Croatian Spring and the Dissolution of Yugoslavia." In *State Collapse in South-Eastern Europe: New Perspectives on Yugoslavia's Disintegration*, edited by Lenard J. Cohen and Jasna Dragović-Soso, 149–78. West Lafayette, IN: Purdue University Press, 2008.

Ivanović, Vladimir. "Brantova istočna politika i jugoslovenska ekonomska emigracija u SR Nemačkoj." In *1968 – Četrdeset godina posle*, edited by Institut za noviju istoriju Srbije, 275–92. Beograd: Institut za noviju istoriju Srbije, 2008.

– *Geburtstag pišeš normalno: Jugoslovenski Gastarbajteri u SR Nemačkoj i Austriji, 1965–1973*. Belgrade: Inst. za Savremenu Istoriju, 2012.

Johnson, A. Ross, and R. Eugene Parta. *Cold War Broadcasting: Impact on the Soviet Union and Eastern Europe : A Collection of Studies and Documents*. Budapest: Central European University Press, 2010.

Jonjić, Tomislav. "Jedno izvješće o prilikama u Splitu i Dalmaciji, u prvim mjesecima nakon uspostave Nezavisne Države Hrvatske." *Časopis za suvremenu povijest* 33, no. 3 (2001): 819–36.

– "Organised Resistance to the Yugoslav Communist Regime in Croatia in 1945–1953." *Review of Croatian History* 3, no. 1 (2007): 109–45.

Jovanović, Nebojša. "Breaking the Wave: A Commentary on 'Black Wave Polemics: Rhetoric as Aesthetic' by Greg DeCuir, Jr." *Studies in Eastern European Cinema* 2, no. 2 (2011): 161–71.

Jukić, Zlata. "Pokušaj ispitivanja učenika u Jugoslavenskoj dopunskoj nastavi o poznavanju elemenata kulture naroda koji govore srpskohrvatskim, odnosno hrvatskosrpskim jezikom." *Migracijske i etničke teme* 2, no. 2 (1986): 15–35.

Kalm, Sara. "Diaspora Strategies as Technologies of Citizenship." *Global Society* 27, no. 3 (2013): 379–97.

Kocka, Jürgen. *Civil Society and Dictatorship in Modern German History*. Hanover, NH: University Press of New England, 2010.

Komarica, Zvonimir. *Jugoslavija u suvremenim evropskim migracijama*. Vol. 8. Zagreb: Ekonomski institut, 1970.

Komska, Yuliya. "West Germany's Cold War Radio: A Crucible of the Transatlantic Century." *German Politics and Society* 32, no. 1 (2014): 1–14.

Kotkin, Stephen. *Magnetic Mountain: Stalinism as a Civilization*. Berkeley: University of California Press, 1997.

Kramer, Jane. *Unsettling Europe*. New York: Random House, 1980.

Kraljević, Iva. "Matica iseljenika Hrvatske 1964–1968." *Časopis za suvremenu povijest* 41, no. 1 (2009): 71–92.

Kujundžić, Nedeljko. *Imotska krajina u narodnooslobodilačkoj borbi 1941–1945: pali borci, žrtve fašističkog terora i spomen obilježja*. Imotski: Općinski odbor SUBNOR-a i SIZ za kulturu, fizičku kulturu i njegovanje revolucionarnih tradicija, 1981.

Lee, Suzy K. "The Three Worlds of Emigration Policy: Towards a Theory of Sending State Regimes." *Journal of Ethnic and Migration Studies* 43, no. 9 (2017): 1453–71. https://doi.org/10.1080/1369183X.2016.1237284.

Le Normand, Brigitte. *Designing Tito's Capital: Urban Planning, Modernism, and Socialism in Belgrade*. Pittsburgh: University of Pittsburgh Press, 2014.

– "The Gastarbajteri as a Transnational Yugoslav Working Class." In *Social Inequalities and Discontent in Yugoslav Socialism*, edited by Rory Archer, Igor Duda, and Paul Stubbs, 50–69. Oxford: Routledge, 2016.

– "Yugoslavia." In *East Central European Migrations during the Cold War*, 368–95. Berlin: Berlin: De Gruyter Oldenbourg, 2019.

Letić, Franjo, and Ivo Baučić. *Informiranje i informiranost vanjskih migranata Iz SR Hrvatske o zbivanjima u domovini*. Zagreb: Centar za istraživanja migracija, 1977.

Levi, Pavle. *Disintegration in Frames: Aesthetics and Ideology in the Yugoslav and Post-Yugoslav Cinema*. Stanford, CA: Stanford University Press, 2007.

Levitt, Peggy, and Nina Glick Schiller. "Conceptualizing Simultaneity: A Transnational Social Field Perspective on Society." *International Migration Review* 38, no. 3 (2004): 1002–39.

Lóránd, Zsófia. *The Feminist Challenge to the Socialist State in Yugoslavia*. Cham, UK: Palgrave Macmillan, 2018.

Lovell, Stephen. "How Russia Learned to Listen: Radio and the Making of Soviet Culture." *Kritika: Explorations in Russian and Eurasian History* 12, no. 3 (2011): 591–615.

– *Russia in the Microphone Age: A History of Soviet Radio, 1919–1970*. Oxford: Oxford University Press, 2015.

Loviglio, Jason. *Radio's Intimate Public: Network Broadcasting and Mass-Mediated Democracy*. Minneapolis: University of Minnesota Press, 2005.

Lučić, Ivica. "Hrvatska protukomunistička gerila u Bosni i Hercegovini od 1945. do 1951." *Časopis za suvremenu povijest* 42, no. 3 (2010): 631–70.

Margheritis, Ana. "Transnational Associational Life and Political Mobilization of Ecuadorians and Argentines in Spain and Italy: What Role for Sending State Policies?" *Diaspora: A Journal of Transnational Studies* 19, no. 2 (2017): 254–79.

Mazierska, Ewa. "Želimir Žilnik and Eastern European Independent Cinema." *Images: The International Journal of European Film, Performing Arts and Audiovisual Communication* 13, no. 22 (2013): 133–49.

Miller, Jennifer A. *Turkish Guest Workers in Germany: Hidden Lives and Contested Borders, 1960s to 1980s.* Toronto: University of Toronto Press, 2018.

Miller, Nick. *The Nonconformists: Culture, Politics, and Nationalism in a Serbian Intellectual Circle, 1944–1991.* Budapest: Central European University Press, 2007.

Milne-Smith, Amy. "A Flight to Domesticity? Making a Home in the Gentlemen's Clubs of London, 1880–1914." *Journal of British Studies* 45, no. 4 (2006): 796–818.

Moch, Leslie Page. *Moving Europeans: Migration in Western Europe since 1650.* 2nd ed. Bloomington: Indiana University Press, 2003.

Molnar, Christopher A. *Memory, Politics, and Yugoslav Migrations to Postwar Germany.* Bloomington: Indiana University Press, 2018.

– "Nation, Migration, and Cold War: Yugoslavs in Germany, 1945–1995." PhD diss., Indiana University, 2013.

– "On the Move and Putting Down Roots." In *Migrations in the German Lands, 1500–2000,* edited by Jason Coy, Jared Poley, and Alexander Schunka, 13:191–208. New York: Berghahn Books, 2016.

Morad, Mohammad, and Francesco Della Puppa. "Bangladeshi Migrant Associations in Italy: Transnational Engagement, Community Formation and Regional Unity." *Ethnic and Racial Studies* 42, no. 10 (2018): 1–20.

Morokvasić, Mirjana, and Dejan Kuzmanović. "Les jeunes issus de l'immigration yougoslave en France." In *L'identité culturelle des jeunes migrants yougoslaves en France: Recueil de textes,* edited by Dušan Davidović and Dejan Kuzmanović, 133–56. Paris: Agence pour le développement des relations interculturelles, Savez socijalistiecke omladine Jugoslavije, 1986.

Nelson, Michael. *War of the Black Heavens: The Battles of Western Broadcasting in the Cold War.* Syracuse, NY: Syracuse University Press, 1997.

Novinšćak Kölker, Karolina. "Ein halbes Jahrhundert 'Minhen': Münchens Platz in der Geschichte der Migration aus dem ehemaligen Jugoslawien und seinen Nachfolgerepubliken." In *Migration bewegt die Stadt. Perspektiven wechseln,* edited by Ursula Eymold and Andreas Heusler, 42–54. Munich: Allitera Verlag, 2018.

– "The Recruiting and Sending of Yugoslav 'Gastarbeiter' to Germany: Between Socialist Demands and Economic Needs." In *Transnational Societies, Transterritorial Politics: Migration in the (Post) Yugoslav Region, 19th–21st Century,* edited by Ulf Brunnbauer, 121–44. Munich: Oldenbourg, 2009.

Organisation for Economic Co-operation and Development. *Migration for Employment: Bilateral Agreements at a Crossroads.* Paris: Organization for Economic Cooperation and Development, 2004.

Østergaard-Nielsen, Eva. *Transnational Politics: Turks and Kurds in Germany.* Vol. 8. London: Routledge, 2003.

Petković, Ljiljana. *Problemi međunarodnih migracija radne snage sa posebnim osvrtom na jugoslaviju.* Beograd: Naučna knjiga, 1988.

Petrović, Aleksandar. *Novi film.* Beograd: Institut za film, 1971.

– *Novi Film II (1965–1970).* Beograd: Naučna knjiga, 1988.

Pineteh, Ernest. "Memories of Home and Exile: Narratives of Cameroonian Asylum Seekers in Johannesburg." *Journal of Intercultural Studies* 26, no. 4 (2005): 379–99.

Puddington, Arch. *Broadcasting Freedom: The Cold War Triumph of Radio Free Europe and Radio Liberty.* Lexington: University Press of Kentucky, 2000.

Putnam, Robert D., Robert Leonardi, and Raffaella Y. Nanetti. *Making Democracy Work: Civic Traditions in Modern Italy.* Princeton, NJ: Princeton University Press, 1994.

Radelić, Zdenko. "1945 in Croatia." *Review of Croatian History* 1 (2016): 9–66.

Radić, Radmila. "Iseljavanje stanovništva sa jugoslovenskog prostora polovinom pedesetih godina." *Istorijski Zapisi* 72, no. 1–2 (1999): 143–73.

Ragazzi, Francesco. "The Croatian 'Diaspora Politics' of the 1990s: Nationalism Unbound?" In *Transnational Societies, Transterritorial Politics: Migrations in the (Post-) Yugoslav Region, 19th–21st Century*, edited by U. Brunnbauer, 145–67. Munich: R. Oldenbourg Verlag, 2009.

– "Governing Diasporas." *International Political Sociology* 3, no. 4 (2009): 378–97.

– *Governing Diasporas in International Relations: The Transnational Politics of Croatia and Former Yugoslavia.* Routledge Studies in Liberty and Security. New York: Routledge, 2017.

Risso, Linda. *Radio Wars: Broadcasting during the Cold War.* Milton Park, UK: Routledge, 2015.

Rist, Ray C. *Guestworkers in Germany: The Prospects for Pluralism.* New York: Praeger, 1978.

– "On the Education of Guest-Worker Children in Germany: A Comparative Study of Policies and Programs in Bavaria and Berlin." *School Review* 87, no. 3 (1979): 242–68.

Rolandi, Francesca. "Heading towards the West: Yugoslav Asylum Seekers in Italy (1955–1968)." *Acta Histriae* 23, no. 3 (2015): 555–74.

Rusinow, Dennison I. *Yugoslavia: Oblique Insights and Observations.* Pittsburgh: University of Pittsburgh Press, 2008.

Sabalić, Ines. "Inspiracije iz svakodnevnice." *Studio*, 1 December 1984.

Sala, Roberto. *Fremde Worte: Medien für Gastarbeiter in der Bundesrepublik im Spannungsfeld von Außen- und Sozialpolitik.* Paderborn: Ferdinand Schöningh, 2011.

Sardinha, João. *Immigrant Associations, Integration and Identity: Angolan, Brazilian and Eastern European Communities in Portugal.* Amsterdam: Amsterdam University Press, 2009.

Schierup, Carl-Ulrik. *Houses, Tractors, Golden Ducats: Prestige Game and Migration: A Study of Migrants to Denmark from a Yugoslav Village.* Moesgård: Århus Universitetet, Institut for Etnografi og Socialantropologi, 1973.

– *Migration, Socialism, and the International Division of Labour: The Yugoslavian Experience.* Aldershot, UK: Avebury, 1990.

Schlosser, Nicholas J. *Cold War on the Airwaves: The Radio Propaganda War against East Germany.* Champaign: University of Illinois Press, 2015.

Schor, Paul. *Counting Americans: How the US Census Classified the Nation.* Oxford: Oxford University Press, 2017.

Scott, James C. *Seeing like a State: How Certain Schemes to Improve the Human Condition Have Failed.* New Haven, CT: Yale University Press, 1999.

Sezgin, Zeynep. "Turkish Migrants' Organizations: Promoting Tolerance toward the Diversity of Turkish Migrants in Germany." *International Journal of Sociology* 38, no. 2 (2008): 78–95. https://doi.org/10.2753/IJS0020 -7659380206.

– "Turkish Migrants' Organizations in Germany and Their Role in the Flow of Remittances to Turkey." *Journal of International Migration and Integration* 12, no. 3 (2011): 231–51. https://doi.org/10.1007/s12134-010-0157-1.

Shonick, Kaja. "Politics, Culture, and Economics: Reassessing the West German Guest Worker Agreement with Yugoslavia." *Journal of Contemporary History* 44, no. 4 (2009): 719–36. https://doi.org/10.1177/0022009409340648.

Škrabalo, Ivo. "Croatian Film in the Yugoslav Context in the Second Half of the Twentieth Century." Special issue, "Croatian Cinema," *Kinokultura* 11 (2011). http://www.kinokultura.com/specials/11/croatian.shtml.

Skrbiš, Zlatko. "Transnational Families: Theorising Migration, Emotions and Belonging." *Journal of Intercultural Studies* 29, no. 3 (2008): 231–46. https:// doi.org/10.1080/07256860802169188.

Sterne, Jonathan. *The Sound Studies Reader.* Milton Park, UK: Routledge, 2012.

Stites, Richard. *Culture and Entertainment in Wartime Russia.* Bloomington: Indiana University Press, 1995.

Stojanović, Biljana. "Exchange Rate Regimes of the Dinar 1945–1990: An Assessment of Appropriateness and Efficiency." In *The Experience of Exchange Rate Regimes in South-Eastern Europe in a Historical and Comparative Perspective*, edited by Peter Mooslechner, 198–243. Vienna: Österreichische Nationalbank, 2007.

Švob, Melita, Zvonimir Kotarac, and Zdenko Ivezić. "Ponašanje i odnos djece prema dopunskoj školi u Berlinu." *Migracijske i etničke teme* 5, no. 1 (1989): 21–6.

Tchoukarine, Igor. "Yugoslavia's Open-Door Policy and Global Tourism in the 1950s and 1960s." *East European Politics and Societies* 29, no. 1 (2015): 168–88.

Tilly, Charles, and Lesley J. Wood. *Social Movements 1768–2012*. London: Routledge, 2015.

Trumbetaš, Dragutin, *Gastarbeiter Gedichte 1969–1980*. Velika Gorice: Turopolja, 1995.

Vegar, Branka. "Jugoslavenska djeca u Bečkim školama." *Migracijske i etničke teme* 2, no. 1 (1986): 75–9.

Vertovec, Steven. "Migrant Transnationalism and Modes of Transformation." *International Migration Review* 38, no. 3 (2004): 970–1001.

– *Transnationalism*. London: Routledge, 2009.

Von Geldern, James. "Radio Moscow." In *Culture and Entertainment in Wartime Russia*, edited by Richard Stites, 44–61. Bloomington: Indiana University Press, 1995.

Vučetić-Mladenović, Radina. *Monopol Na Istinu: Partija, Kultura i Cenzura u Srbiji Šezdesetih i Sedamdesetih Godina XX Veka*. Beograd: Clio, 2016.

Weber, Eugen. *Peasants into Frenchmen: The Modernization of Rural France, 1870–1914*. Chicago: Stanford University Press, 1976.

Wimmer, A., and N. Schiller. "Methodological Nationalism and the Study of Migration." *European Journal of Sociology* 43, no. 2 (2002): 217–40.

Winterhagen, Jenni. "Die Pioniere von Imotski. Die Verwendung von Remittances am Beispiel des ehemaligen Jugoslawien." In *Gesellschaften in Bewegung. Emigration aus und Immigration nach Südosteuropa in Vergangenheit und Gegenwart. Jahrbuch der Südosteuropa-Gesellschaft* 38 (2009): 61–92.

– "Folgen von Abwanderung in den Heimatorten von Migranten." *Raumplanung* 155 (2011): 94–8.

Wise, Amanda, and Selvaraj Velayutham. "Transnational Affect and Emotion in Migration Research." *International Journal of Sociology* 47, no. 2 (2017): 116–30.

Yamashiro, Jane H. "Working towards Conceptual Consistency in Discussing 'Diaspora' and 'Diaspora Strategies': Ethnicity and Affinity in the Case of Japan." *Geoforum* 59 (2015): 178–86.

Zimmerman, William. *Open Borders, Nonalignment, and the Political Evolution of Yugoslavia*. Princeton, NJ: Princeton University Press, 1987.

Селинић, Слободан. "Економска Емиграција Из Југославије Шездесетих Година XX Века." *1968–Četrdeset Godina Posle*, 1968, 549–73.

Index